# Heinle Development English

## New for 2000

### Writing

Rogers/Rogers, *Patterns and Themes: A Basic English Reader,* 4th Ed.
Robinson/Tucker, *Texts and Contexts: A Contemporary Approach to College Writing,* 4th Ed.
McDonald/Salomone, *The Writer's Response: A Reading-Based Approach to College Writing,* 2nd Ed
McDonald/Salomone, *In Brief: A Handbook for Writers*

### Reading

Maker/Lenier, *College Reading with Active Critical Thinking Method, Book 1,* 5th Ed.
Maker/Lenier, *College Reading with Active Critical Thinking Method, Book 2,* 6th Ed.
Sotiriou/Phillips, *Steps to Reading Proficiency,* 5th Ed.

### Study Skills

Van Blerkom, *College Study Skills: Becoming a Strategic Learner,* 3rd Ed.

## Other Developmental English Titles

### Writing

Richard-Amato, *World Views: Multicultural Literature for Critical Writers, Readers, and Thinkers* (1998)
Salomone/McDonald, *Inside Writing: A Writer's Workbook, Form A.* 4th Ed. (1999)
Wingersky/Boerner/Holguin-Balough, *Writing Paragraphs and Essays: Integrating Reading, Writing, and Grammar Skills,* 3rd Ed. (1999)

### Reading

Atkinson/Longman, *Reading Enhancement and Development,* 6th Ed. (1999)
Maker/Lenier, *Academic Reading with Active Critical Thinking* (1996)

### Study Skills

Longman/Atkinson, *College Learning and Study Skills,* 5th Ed. (1999)
Longman/Atkinson, *Study Methods and Reading Techniques,* 2nd Ed. (1999)
Sotiriou, *Integrating College Study Skills: Reasoning in Reading, Listening, and Writing,* 5th Ed. (1999)
Smith/Knudsvig/Walter, *Critical Thinking: Building the Basics* (1998)

FIFTH EDITION

# Steps to Reading Proficiency

PETER ELIAS SOTIRIOU
Los Angeles City College

ANNE G. PHILLIPS
(Formerly) Santa Monica College

THOMSON
™
HEINLE

Australia  Canada  Mexico  Singapore  Spain  United Kingdom  United States

**Steps to Reading Proficiency**
**Fifth Edition**
*Peter Elias Sotiriou and Anne G. Phillips*

**Executive Manager:** *Elana Dolberg*
**Senior Development Editor:** *Kimberly Johnson*
**Project Editor:** *Christal Niederer*
**Print Buyer:** *Mary Noel*
**Permissions Editor:** *Joohee Lee*
**Production:** *Melanie Field/Strawberry Field Publishing*
**Copyeditor:** *Molly Roth*
**Cover Design:** *John Odam*
**Cover Image:** *Robert Schezen/Esto*
**Compositor:** *G&S Typesetters, Inc*
**Printer:** *Webcom Limited*

Printed in Canada
2 3 4 5 6 7 8 9 10   06 05 04 03 02

For more information contact Heinle, 25 Thomson Place, Boston, MA 02210 USA,
or you can visit our Internet site at http://www.heinle.com

**ISBN: 0-1550-6273-5**

Library of Congress Catalog Card Number: 99-37226

# CONTENTS

• • • • • • • • • • • • • • • • • •

## CHAPTER FIVE: STUDY READING      193

### INTRODUCTION TO STUDY READING      194

### PRACTICES: STUDY READING      208

### SELECTIONS: STUDY READING      214

• • • • • • • • • • • • • • • • • •

## CHAPTER SIX: CRITICAL READING      255

### INTRODUCTION TO CRITICAL READING      256

### PRACTICES: CRITICAL READING      270

### TIMED SELECTIONS: CRITICAL READING      287

• • • • • • • • • • • • • • • • • • • • • •

• • • • • • • • • • • • • • • • • • • • • •

## *APPENDICES*

# TO THE INSTRUCTOR

Good teachers listen—to their colleagues, to their students, to their own experience and good sense. They are flexible enough to change their course materials over the years. We have tried to be conscientious, too, as we produce each edition of *Steps to Reading Proficiency*. We think this new fifth edition will move college reading instruction ahead, into the twenty-first century.

## The Same . . .

Of course, some things we are not flexible about. (1) We continue to aim our discourse and materials at college and university students and their knowledgeable instructors. As such, the book does not include perception drills, vocabulary study, or other remedial materials. (2) We have kept the same basic structure since the first edition, which published more than seventeen years ago, because instructors and students alike find it effective. The chapters are still organized from lower-level, essential reading skills to higher-level college materials and purposes. En route, there is some speeded or time-pressured reading of moderate, general materials. (3) Our primary goal is still to teach reading techniques that students can apply with flexibility, depending on their materials and purposes. (4) We have kept the same organization within most chapters: a checklist of symptoms to arouse student interest, an expository introduction to the skill, a summary, then several short practices and four to ten longer selections. (5) We have retained the underlying concepts that set our book apart from similar advanced-reading texts: the conviction that print is two-way communication, reading is the flip side of writing, and good readers can train themselves to "follow the writer's path" when they read. The corollary is that students must read well and widely before they can write well.

## And Also Different . . .

We have incorporated several suggestions from our reviewers of the fourth edition. First, Chapter 1, "Essential Reading Skills," has been streamlined considerably. We include fewer exercises and have shortened some of the original ones. We believe these changes will enhance students' learning of essential skills. Further, teachers can now move much more quickly through this review chapter. In Chapter 5, "Study Reading," we have included more learning theory concepts and more-recent mapping practices such as the semantic web. The last step, "Review," now includes "reflection" as part of the process. In Chapter 6, "Critical Reading," we have added discussions on drawing conclusions from evidence, recognizing propaganda and bias, and determining mood and tone in literary works. These additions have broadened this introduction, making it a more challenging critical-reading discussion.

Almost half of the reading selections have been replaced with more-recent material, again with the themes of family, work, the environment, and breaking the law—topics that our reviewers have still found to be thought provoking. Where helpful, the practices have also been revised to rely on more recent reading material. Finally, in Chapters 3 and 4, some practices have been deleted in order to move the students into the reading selections sooner.

Most importantly, we have included an Internet activity at the end of each chapter to encourage students to make the Internet an integral part of their college studies. Wadsworth has Internet resources that students can use to supplement what they have learned. At the end of each chapter, students are given specific questions to answer from these Internet sources; in the thematic chapters (3, 4, 5, and 6), students are asked to explore further the given topic through Wadsworth's research source called InfoTrac® College Edition. We encourage students to complete these assignments collaboratively. We also include follow-up questions in each chapter.

## The Research Basis

*Steps* has always followed pedagogical truisms: Skills build from easy to more difficult and are practiced repeatedly; techniques are described more than once; the content of the readings is relevant to today's student. Also, we encourage readers to self-evaluate occasionally, and to monitor their progress via easy-to-use graphs.

Beyond these traditional rules, however, many of the book's features are solidly grounded in current learning theory:

1. We take the "thematic approach." Recent research in cognitive psychology has confirmed that the more contexts learners can establish during reading, the richer and more lasting their reading experience. Such readers can also better predict the content of new materials on the same subject. So, as students work through a series of selections about, say, the family, they can incorporate the previous information toward understanding the new selection. Thus, their reading becomes progressively more purposeful and successful.

2. We continue to end each selection with a few questions "For Discussion and Writing." Instructors may feel they have no time for these. However, recent research in language theory has bolstered our personal convictions that reading and writing are interconnected. When students write about what they have read, they not only understand the material more thoroughly, but also develop their own writing styles in the process.

3. Often, these discussion questions ask students to explore their reactions to the selection or compare it with their own experiences. "Application" is a significant topic among contemporary theorists, who are asking questions like "What does this experience mean to the individual?" "How is understanding really self-understanding?" As it pertains to our students, "application" implies that reading becomes meaningful, becomes more than just a successful mechanical strategy, only when readers place the printed material they have read into the rich context of their own lives.

4. Recent research has shown that collaborative learning benefits students as they work through particularly difficult concepts. We have included collaborative activities in many chapters so that students can learn more from each other about the reading skill they have completed and about the thematic material they have read and written about. We also encourage discussion of Internet activities so that students can see how their peers accessed material on the Internet and learn to "surf the net" more efficiently.

# SUPPLEMENTS

## Print Supplements

**Instructor's Manual** (0-534-57313-4). This manual contains answers for all of *Steps'* practices and selections. It also includes tests, sample rapid-reading drills and answer keys, a sample time-block rate chart, extra copies of a progress chart, and other suggestions for teaching.

## Electronic and Online Supplements

- **Web Site.** You can visit Wadsworth's Developmental English web site at **http://devenglish.wadsworth.com.**
- **Wadsworth/Internet Developmental English at a glance Trifold** (0-534-54744-3). This guide shows your students where to find online reading and writing resources. You can obtain this trifold card with any Wadsworth Developmental English text. Please contact your local Wadsworth representative for more information.
- **InfoTrac® College Edition.** This fully searchable online database, with access to full-text articles from over 600 periodicals, provides a helpful resource for additional readings on the topics presented in *Steps*. InfoTrac College Edition offers authoritative sources that are updated daily and go back as far as four years. Both you and your students can receive unlimited online use for one academic term. (Please contact your Thomson Learning representative for policy, pricing, and availability; international and school distribution is restricted.)
- **Custom Publishing.** You can combine your choice of chapters from specific Wadsworth titles with your own materials in a custom-bound book. To place your order, call the Thomson Learning Custom Order Center at 1-800-355-9983.
- **Videos.** Wadsworth has many videos available to qualifying adopters on topics such as improving your grades, note-taking practice, and diversity. Contact your local Wadsworth representative for more information.
- **AT&T World Net.** You can help your students gain access to the Internet through this Internet access service provider.

• • • • • • • • • • • • • • • • •

## *ACKNOWLEDGMENTS*

We would like to thank everyone who helped produce this fifth edition. As before, reviews by users of our previous edition were indispensable. Reviewers included:

>    Linda Allen, Hill College
>    Nancy Anter, Wayne State University
>    Ruth Becker, Pensacola Junior College
>    Lyn Becktold, Saddleback College
>    Betty Brace, Mt. Hood Community College
>    Jessica Carroll, Miami-Dade Community College, Wolfson Campus
>    Melanie Haeri, Irvine Valley College
>    Karen Weaver-Coleman, Reading Area Community College
>    Sylvia Wolff, Reading Area Community College

Reviewers of previous editions included:

>    Cheryl Altman, Saddleback College
>    Barbara Bayerkohler, Blinn College
>    Lyn Becktold, Saddleback College
>    Betty L. Brace, Mt. Hood Community College
>    Ann Depry, University of Wisconsin, Green Bay
>    Mala R. Farmer Bailey, Texas A&M University
>    Gwendolyn Gray, Eastern Kentucky University
>    Stephen Moro, University of Maine at Augusta
>    Eleanor C. Pronath, Edison Community College
>    Barbara Tuntland, Illinois Valley Community College

All members of the production team at Wadsworth and Melanie Field at Strawberry Field Publishing have been most professional and accessible as they guided us through the book's development, a process that has taken almost two years. We are especially grateful to the following individuals: Karen Allanson, Wadsworth's publisher, who made sure that *Steps* was one of the company's titles available for the year 2000; Kim Johnson, the senior development editor who faithfully saw to it that our questions were answered promptly and helpfully; Joohee Lee, the permissions editor who efficiently tracked down a few difficult-to-locate permissions responses; and copyeditor par excellence, Molly Roth.

Finally, we are lucky to have Vasi Sotiriou and Bob Phillips for our spouses. They give us sympathy when our electronic gear doesn't work, and, amazingly, they know how to fix it. Peter Sotiriou would again like to thank his sons, Elias and Dimitri, who knew when to let their father work on yet another textbook project.

•  •  •  •  •  •  •  •  •  •  •  •  •  •  •  •  •  •  •

# *ABOUT THE AUTHORS*

Together, the authors have over 40 years of experience teaching English, reading, study skills, composition, and literature in various community colleges and universities. Peter Elias Sotiriou holds an M.A. in English and American literature from UCLA. In 1991, he earned a Ph.D. in English from the University of Southern California, with a specialization in Rhetoric, Linguistics, and Literature. He is fluent in Greek and French as well as English. Anne G. Phillips holds an M.A. in English and American literature from the University of Chicago and has done work toward the Ph.D. at UCLA.

Both authors have had training in the teaching of reading. They have taught all levels of adult reading, including many years of the advanced reading from which *Steps* originally developed.

At this stage of their careers, both authors are professional writers. Phillips was one of the original authors of the series *Reading Faster and Understanding More* (Little, Brown), and is now a freelance writer and editor. Her fiction, nonfiction, and poetry have been published in various newspapers and periodicals. Sotiriou has written articles for the academic press on the teaching of reading and writing. He has published three other textbooks for Wadsworth: *Integrating College Study Skills* (5th edition), *Composing Through Reading* (2nd edition), and *Critical Thinking and Popular Culture*. The authors' own writing activities have proved to them the soundness of the *Steps* theme that reading and writing are inseparable.

## Speaking Personally . . .

Besides the degrees and the teaching, however, we derive much of our approach from our own personal reading experiences. As lifelong students ourselves, as well as avid recreational readers from our preschool days to the present, we know how many kinds of reading materials and purposes there are. This is why our goal when we teach college reading continues to be flexibility. Proficient readers vary their mindset and reading techniques according to what they are reading and why they are reading it.

Finally, we both know the satisfaction of learning through reading. In many ways the print medium is still the best. It is still necessary. And—it is still the most fun! We hope *Steps* proves our point.

# TO THE STUDENT

## Underlying Premises

*Steps* begins with several assumptions: (1) Reading and writing are two sides of the same coin. Learning about one helps us learn about the other. (2) Writing and print, and therefore reading, are here to stay, at least in the foreseeable future. (3) The volume of printed material that we must read or want to read continues to increase. (4) The kinds of printed material vary tremendously, as do our reasons for reading. (5) Efficient and proficient readers will therefore vary their mindsets and reading techniques accordingly. (6) Everyone can learn to be aware, alert, and flexible in his or her reading; it is a matter of changing a few habits. (7) Timing ourselves and answering comprehension questions helps us pay attention.

## Organization of the Book

*Steps to Reading Proficiency* divides college reading proficiency for the advanced reader into seven areas: essential reading skills (a review), preview skimming, rapid reading, overview skimming for main ideas, study reading, critical reading, and scanning. Each chapter builds on the previous skills, so we recommend that you proceed in the given order. However, some instructors may prefer to vary the sequence.

Except for Chapter 1, all chapters have a similar internal organization. They open with a checklist of symptoms, which can help pinpoint your strengths and weaknesses in a given area. Next comes an introduction, with a thorough exposition of the skill to be learned and practical ways to perfect it. In Chapters 1 and 2, you will find practices at the end to reinforce your understanding and exercise of the skill. In Chapters 3 through 6, practices will help you reinforce various skills. A series of selections follow these practices. The selections allow you to build proficiency in that skill through the sustained reading of actual college-level material. Chapter 7 shows you how to improve your scanning ability by using the material from the previous chapters in various timed practices.

Answers to the odd-numbered practices in Chapters 1 and 7 and to all odd-numbered selections will be found in Appendix C. For answers to all other practices and to all even-numbered selections, please check with your instructor.

Try to keep good records on the progress charts that end Chapters 3, 4, and 6. They can really motivate you toward better comprehension and efficiency.

Although this is not a vocabulary-building text, all reading tends to expand our vocabularies. Most students will benefit from bringing paperback dictionaries to every class. Your instructor may supply word-study material as well.

## Practices

Practices illustrate the skill being described and prepare you for success in the selections. Some are timed, some are untimed. Follow directions exactly. Practices may be done as in-class warmups or homework, as your instructor directs. In any case, always do them in the sequence established in the introductions. They have been carefully designed to reinforce each skill, step-by-step. Recall that answers to the odd-numbered practices in Chapters 1 and 7 are in Appendix C; your instructor can supply you the rest of the practice answers.

## Timed Selections

1.  Please do not—*ever*—read ahead in these. (Not an easy rule for avid readers to follow!) To be effective at all, any timed material must be done in class under pressure and monitored by your instructor. For the same reason, do not preread quiz questions or scan back for answers unless the directions tell you to do so.
2.  Follow all directions *exactly*. This includes accurate timing in minutes and seconds (usually to the nearest 15 seconds). Your instructor may time the group, or you may time yourself.
3.  Check your quiz scores against the target percentages, marked by an arrow ▶. Objective quizzes are not the best measures of comprehension, but ours will give you some quick feedback on your performance.
4.  Keep good progress charts!

 ## For Discussion and Writing

These sections are not timed. They give you a chance to reread a selection more carefully, analyze its style and organization, think over the content and your personal reactions to it, prepare to discuss it, and perhaps write a response. You may do these in class, in small groups, or as homework assignments.

## Conclusion

While you are working through this text and class, remember also to use these skills in your outside reading—pleasure reading, course work, reading lists, magazines, and newspapers. Your habits should show a gradual but permanent change. If the authors could change the way they read in mid-life—and they did—you can, too.

When you have finished the seven chapters and polished up your charts, you should be well on your way to reading proficiency and flexibility. You will know how to preview most materials through force of habit, read easy material rapidly with good comprehension, skim anything for main ideas at high speed, comprehend and retain textbook information, find deeper levels of meaning in complex materials, and scan through pages of print for exact answers.

Enjoy!

# *Steps to Reading Proficiency*

# CHAPTER 1

# Essential Reading Skills

*T*his opening chapter reviews many of the basic reading skills required to comprehend the literal, surface meaning of English prose. You will look for topic, main idea, and supporting details. Literal comprehension also includes recognizing writing patterns and summarizing the content. In all this, you will see how reader and writer cooperate in the transfer of meaning through the written word. Though you probably know much of this material already, it will help prepare you for the chapters that follow.

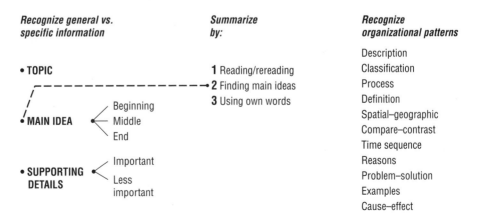

**Recognize general vs. specific information**

- **TOPIC**
- **MAIN IDEA** — Beginning / Middle / End
- **SUPPORTING DETAILS** — Important / Less important

**Summarize by:**

1 Reading/rereading
2 Finding main ideas
3 Using own words

**Recognize organizational patterns**

Description
Classification
Process
Definition
Spatial–geographic
Compare–contrast
Time sequence
Reasons
Problem–solution
Examples
Cause–effect

# *I*NTRODUCTION TO
# *ESSENTIAL READING SKILLS*

To *comprehend* written material means to understand its meaning. To understand this meaning, the reader must retrace the writer's path. Luckily, trained writers of exposition—informational prose—present their ideas in a structured way. Being aware of this structure helps you unlock the work's meaning. You can then more easily grasp the literal content: who, what, when, where, how, and why. You will also be able to discover the topic, the main idea about the topic, the support for the main idea, and how the support is arranged or organized. With a little more effort, you can uncover the *inferences*—unstated meanings that lie just under the surface of the literal content.

Let's review basic comprehension—how people comprehend the literal content of a written work.

• • • • • • • • • • • • • • • • • • •

## *THE TOPIC*

First, the writer chooses or is assigned a *topic*, or what the writer has chosen to write about. Other names for the topic are *subject*, *subject matter*, or *subject area*. When good communication takes place, both writer and reader can express this topic in a word or short phrase. To find the topic, you simply ask, "What is this poem/story/article/editorial/screenplay/chapter/report/letter about?"

**Examples of topics (subjects)**
1. Olympics, the Winter Olympics, sports technology, ski jumping, new technology in ski jumping, a silver medal winner
2. crime, violent crime, recent trends in violent crime, juvenile crime rates, public perceptions of crime
3. U.S. history, immigration into the United States, current immigration, opposing views about current immigration, my personal view of current immigration
4. dogs, working breeds of dogs, golden retrievers, our retriever Amy, Amy's sense of humor

As you try to discover the writer's topic, avoid expressing it so specifically that you include the writer's comment on the topic. If you do this, you have really discovered what we call the main idea of the passage. (See the next section.) In almost all cases, the topic does not include the writer's comment or point of view on the topic.

**Example of a *topic* alone**

new technology in Olympic ski-jumping events

**Example of a *topic plus comment*, i.e., a statement of the *main idea***

Athletes who competed in the Olympic ski-jumping events benefited from new technology in various ways.

Note how the topic addresses new technology and Olympic ski jumping, whereas the main idea states that Olympic ski jumping has benefited from this new technology. The main idea thus expresses a specific point of view. Turn to Practice 1.1 on page 19. As in all chapters, target scores are marked with an arrow ▶.

Now you are ready to grasp quickly the topic of a short expository paragraph—"what it's about." If this seems too easy, remember that a well-crafted paragraph follows the same rules of clarity and structure as does a good essay, editorial, feature story, or any nonfiction piece. So, if you master the basic reading skills when reading a paragraph, you can use them on longer works.

See if you can determine the topic in the following paragraph. Remember, a topic is what the writer has chosen to write about, not his or her attitude toward this topic:

> For centuries people raised children in order for them to help on the family farm. The young girls usually tended to the domestic work, and the boys learned the farming skills of the father. In the 1800s in Europe, children, some as young as eight, worked in factories. It is for these reasons that historians have considered children as the family's property.

Did you determine that the writer has chosen to write about the uses parents have found for their children over the centuries? This is the topic, whereas the main idea is best expressed in the last sentence: Children have traditionally been considered property of the family. Unlike the topic, this main idea expresses a particular point of view regarding children and their parents.

Turn to Practice 1.2 on page 19.

. . . . . . . . . . . . . . . . . . .

## THE MAIN IDEA

Skilled writers may discuss a topic and include many examples, details, pros and cons, and so forth—even at book length! In every case, they must make a main point about the topic—a *main idea, controlling idea, theme, thesis*—or else the work will have no unity or focus. The skilled reader, in turn, must try to grasp this main idea. Some readers try to express it in a phrase, but a phrase is incomplete both grammatically and intellectually. "How" or "why" phrases are more complete than most, but they state only one-half of a writer's main idea.

Study this set of main-idea statements. Are they vague or clear?

### Examples of main ideas, Set A

- preparation and the tornado
- the search for a cure for HIV
- the connection between alcohol and family violence
- why airbags should be required on all new cars
- improved economies as a result of base closings

Did you notice how vague these sound, especially the first one? Even so, many students begin writing a term paper or other composition with little more in mind than this kind of simple pairing. Then they rewrite, and rewrite, hoping an argument will develop. Even the "why" topic leaves us with a question, but no answer.

If there is real unity and focus, both the writer and the reader should be able to express the main idea in one clear, grammatically complete statement. If nothing else, it is good discipline for both. If you have trouble constructing such a sentence about what you have read, either you or the writer is probably guilty of fuzzy thinking.

Consider the main-idea statements in Set B. Are these clear or vague?

### Examples of main ideas, Set B

- Good preparation helped the town survive on the day the tornado struck.
- The HIV virus is capable of almost infinite variations, making the search for a cure extremely problematic.
- A recent study reveals the major role alcohol plays in incidents of family violence.
- Senators presented three important reasons why airbags should be required on all new cars.
- While most communities have suffered economically because of base closings, a few have actually experienced a new prosperity.

Notice that each sentence could be a summary of an entire article or chapter because it explains in a *general* way what the paragraph or paragraphs are about. These are clear main-idea statements. If the main-idea statement sums up a paragraph, it is called the *topic sentence*. If it sums up the main idea of a longer work—article, essay, term paper, editorial—it is called the *main idea statement* or *thesis statement*. Look again at the two sets, making sure you understand why Set B clearly expresses main idea statements and Set A does not.

You will now be asked to recognize sentences in which the writers state their main ideas for you. Then you will be asked to compose your own statement from an implied main idea. In the second case, you will need to be not only an intelligent reader, but also a proficient writer.

. . . . . . . . . . . . . . . . . . .

## *THE MAIN IDEA—STATED*

If the writer has clearly stated his or her main idea in so many words, all you have to do is find it, and the other parts of the work fall into position. You can do this easily in a passage only one or two paragraphs long. The main idea statement is harder to recognize in a longer work—editorial, speech, and so on. But if you analyze how you did it in one paragraph, you can apply the same methods to longer works.

How do you know the main idea of a passage when you see it? Here are three brief tips.

**TIP 1**    *Recognize an umbrella idea; discriminate it from specific ideas.* An umbrella idea includes the lesser ideas that fit under it. Look again at the paragraph on children and family to see how children as property is suggested in each of the details presented:

> For centuries people raised children in order for them to help on the family farm. The young girls usually tended to the domestic work, and the boys learned the farming skills of the father. In the 1800s in Europe, children, some as young as eight, worked in factories. It is for these reasons that historians have considered children as the family's property.

Do you see how the details—helping on the farm, domestic work, and working in the factories—show how children provided a service to their family? This way, when you get to the last sentence, you are prepared for it because you see how all the details you have read fall under its umbrella statement: children as property.

Finding umbrellas may be difficult for you at first, but as you continue to practice seeing how details fall under a pattern, identifying the umbrella will become easier.

**TIP 2**   *Know where a professional writer is likely to state the main idea.* Direct your eyes to such places. In a paragraph, the main idea usually appears in the first sentence or two. In longer works, a professional writer of expository prose usually states the main idea in the title, the subtitle if any, the lead (a short, separate introduction), and the first paragraph. Sometimes the writer withholds it until the last sentence or the conclusion. However, the main point will hardly ever be buried in the middle. Thus, the best places for you to look are (1) the beginning and (2) the ending. Remember this tip when you learn how to preview skim (Chapter 2), rapid read (Chapter 3), and overview skim (Chapter 4). Remember, when you read any long, well-developed paragraph, you should focus on its beginning and ending.

**TIP 3**   *Notice any repetition of the umbrella idea.* You will see this in longer works, where the writer repeats the theme or thesis for emphasis. Notice any repetition of the general idea, in the same or similar words. Notice how repetition has been used in the following paragraph excerpts:

> (1) nobody becomes a skilled musician overnight. . . . takes hard work and patience. . . . people think it's easier than it really is. . . . most arts take both talent and hard work. . . . playing an instrument is no exception. . . .

> (2) program shows enormous variety of world's music. . . . every imaginable area and ethnic group represented. . . . exciting, unusual types of music. . . . opens your ears to possibilities. . . . wide range of sounds that humans call "music." . . .

> (3) students angered over level of campus violence. . . . are critical of administration, propose changes. . . . cite past problems and also demand solutions. . . . rally indicates level of dissatisfaction. . . .

Your eyes should go to these sorts of words and phrases as you search for the umbrella, or main idea, of written materials.

Turn to Practice 1.3 on page 21.

• • • • • • • • • • • • • • • • •

# THE MAIN IDEA—IMPLIED

As we have said, comprehending a work is much harder when main ideas are not stated directly, but only hinted at. In this case, you cannot follow the three tips and point at general, umbrella statements. You can only read all the evidence, try to follow the writer's train of thought, and reach for—*infer*—what it adds up to.

Though not common in informational prose, this style often appears in writing of a more literary nature. For example, you will often have to infer the main ideas in fiction, advertising, arguments, and persuasive pieces. Such works do have main ideas, but the writers may choose to convey their messages indirectly. Or perhaps their goal is to create suspense, a mood, a character, or a historical period. When you read such works, you must search for their deeper meaning. You may have to discuss, debate, or even disagree about the main ideas. This is particularly the sort of reading and discussion you will experience in Chapter 6, on critical reading.

For now, see if you can infer the main idea in the following sample paragraph:

> Scientific studies show that the Pacific tree frog is in decline, as is the Western toad. Two species of toads in England are decreasing in number. Frogs and toads in Mexico and Central America, some of them famous for their jewel colors, can be found less often than in the past years. Many Asian and African amphibians that were common a few years ago are becoming rare.

When you located the umbrella sentence from details, you asked the question, "What do all the sentences, together, suggest?" You ask the same question when you determine an unstated main idea. In the sample paragraph, each sentence identifies a type of amphibian in decline. An acceptable main idea for this paragraph would thus be "Certain amphibians are currently decreasing in number throughout the world."

Turn to Practice 1.4 on page 23.

• • • • • • • • • • • • • • • • •

# SUPPORTING DETAILS

So far, you have learned that writers may either state their main ideas clearly or only imply them. If main ideas are stated, you know where they will likely be located: at the beginnings and sometimes in the endings of paragraphs and longer works.

Of course, no writer can inform or convince a reader merely by stating and restating a main idea or thesis. Starting with Aristotle, writers of traditional expository prose have written with (1) a beginning, (2) a middle, and (3) an end. (Or, as many composition instructors call them, an introduction, a body, and a conclusion.) Professional writing—most of what college students read for class—follows this structure. Given that the first and last parts usually contain the general, umbrella ideas, you can guess that the middle (body) of a work contains the development of the thesis—that is, the supporting details.

You can also guess that the two general parts of a work tend to be fairly short. The middle, where the writer tries to convince the reader by piling on explanations and details, will tend to be the longest part.

Students commonly mistake an interesting detail for a main idea. Here are some tests for supporting details: (1) A detail differs from a main idea. It does not simply restate it. (2) A detail falls *within* the main idea, or *under* the umbrella idea. (3) Compared with the main-idea statement, a supporting-detail statement is more specific and less general, more concrete and less abstract, and often more factual. (4) A detail may be an example, a descriptive fact, a cause, an effect, an explanation, or an illustration—supporting or filling in the writer's main point about her or his topic.

To help readers follow their arguments or descriptions more easily, writers often verbally point at separate sections or details. That is, they announce the development of their argument with useful words and phrases called *signals* or *transitions*.

You should always notice signals words such as *first, second, finally*, and *therefore*. Do the same with signal phrases such as *in the first place, the next step, to sum up*, and *as a result*. The longer and more complex a work, the longer its transitions. A shift in content may require a complete sentence or even an entire paragraph. Here is an example of a complete sentence transition that might link sections of a long report or news feature:

> However, the administration did not accept all the students' demands, but countered with proposals of their own.

Note how the signals *however* and *but* introduce a new direction to this discussion of administrators and students.

Study the following paragraph to see how supporting details are used and effectively introduced by transitions.

> In our multicultural city, the different ethnic groups have tended to settle in certain areas. For example, a large Latino population has settled in the city's south side, many of them new arrivals from Central America. Just east of this area is "Little Seoul," a Korean enclave that is rapidly sprouting new bank and shopping plazas. North of Little Seoul lies the original business core of the city. Here we see the Anglo names on the older businesses, interspersed with Asian and European newcomers. Finally, the western edge of the city toward the river has been a melting pot of Mediterranean immigrants for decades.

Note how transitions like *for example* and *finally* introduce some of the many details about the Latino(a) and Mediterranean populations. Other details include information about Korean, other Asian, Central American, and European residents. Each of these details supports the main idea—that this city is multicultural.

Turn to Practice 1.5 on page 25.

# LESS IMPORTANT SUPPORTING DETAILS

In the short passages you read in Practice 1.5, most details were important to the main idea; they truly supported it. The same economy prevails in certain academic fields, such as mathematics, engineering, law, medicine, and most sciences. There are very few "interesting but unimportant details" in any kind of technical material. Readers who skip over details in an installment contract, directions for a chemistry experiment, or an eviction notice do so at their peril.

However, prose styles in the social sciences and humanities are usually less concise. (Exceptions include poetry and short fiction, where every word counts.) Writing styles in the popular reading we do outside of class—bestsellers, magazines, much of the newspaper beyond straight news—will often be even more discursive: Commercial writers will often "discourse" or converse, rather than present only facts and important ideas. The abundance of details may be interesting or fun, but they do not equally contribute to a grasp of the main argument.

Say you are reading quantities of print for background, for review, or for only the main ideas. Your time is limited. You want to follow the thread of the presentation, concentrating on key sections. This means you must skim lightly over less important details or even skip them entirely. (Later chapters in rapid reading and overview skimming will have you do the same thing in complete texts, under time pressure.)

Consider the following statement from a television review and the four details that follow. Which are the most relevant to the review?

*Statement:* The new TV series about a police detective is worth watching.

*Details:* (1) realistic situations, (2) reruns of *NYPD Blue*, (3) up-to-date problems, and (4) solid acting, not just famous faces.

Do you see how (1), (3), and (4) describe the key criteria that make this show effective—problems that are realistic and current as well as strong acting performances. The discussion of *NYPD Blue* is not central to the review of this particular program, though it may be discussed incidentally.

Turn to Practice 1.6 on page 26.

# ORGANIZATIONAL PATTERNS

You have now retraced the expository writer's path quite a distance toward the final, finished product: the chapter, article, essay, feature story, opinion piece, argument, report, and so on. You know that the writer begins with a topic, then establishes a main idea about the topic, then develops support for the idea through details. You know that the writer often "points" at the major details or sections with signals or transitions.

There is one more aspect to the structure of informational prose that a skilled reader finds useful: organizational or writing patterns. Writers do not just throw all their supporting details at you. They usually develop their main point according to one or more recognizable patterns.

Say, for example, a writer has been assigned an article explaining what the loss of funding for the SSC (superconducting super collider) means to the scientific community. The writer decides to focus on the effect this event has caused on physics majors and the hundreds of professionals already working on the project. He or she decides to interview the top scientists already engaged in the project. Most of them agree about the effects, but a few disagree, so a subpattern emerges of comparison and contrast among those interviewed. The writer may have to provide a little background for the average reader: a (very) simple description of particle physics and the SSC, plus a short history of the project told in time sequence or chronologically. But in this actual article, the dominant overall pattern remains cause and effect—the effects caused by scrapping the SSC. (See Andrew Campbell, "Ghost of the Machine," *University of Chicago Magazine,* February 1994, 31–34.)

The concept of organizational patterns is really no more complicated than that. Often, the thesis is set up so clearly in the introduction that it indicates which pattern or two will govern the supporting details.

Naturally, the longer the work, the more patterns will appear. Several subpatterns can operate at once, as you saw in the analysis of the SSC article. When you read, however, look for only the dominant patterns, and only to the extent that this helps you comprehend better and more quickly.

Here are eleven common writing patterns. For each, we give a description, a one-paragraph demonstration, and words or phrases that frequently signal the pattern. Be aware that other experts in composition and rhetoric may teach more, or fewer, than eleven; they may use slightly different names, like "thesis-examples" for "example/illustration."

1.  **Examples pattern.** The writer lists two or more specific examples of his or her main idea or thesis. Examples are often facts or figures—actual persons, places, dates, events, things, numbers, and so on.

    If the thesis is supported by only one well-developed example, the pattern may be called a *thesis-illustration pattern.* (The illustration may consist of an anecdote, an episode, or an example discussed at length.)

    Examples may be typical or specific. A *typical* example will not name specific individuals, dates, places, and so on but will support the idea with a general case. A *specific* example, on the other hand, does name one particular individual, date, place, and so on. You will learn to recognize both kinds of examples in the practices.

    - **Example (typical):**
      The kind of breakfast I most enjoy is one with the most calories and variety of foods. For example, an outstanding breakfast must have eggs, meat, pastries, pancakes, fruits, and coffee. Anything less is simply a business breakfast.

- **Example (specific):**
  Our family enjoys getting together once a month for Sunday breakfast. For example, last Sunday we all met at 9 A.M. at Farmer Joe's, a family-style restaurant on the west side of town. We sat, all ten of us, around a big, round table and shared bacon and eggs, pancakes, and good conversation.
- **Signals:**
  *for example, to illustrate, to give just one example of, for instance, specifically, in particular, especially, one example is, as in the case of, proof is found in*

2. **Time-sequence (sequence of events, chronological) pattern.** In this organizational pattern, the writer develops his or her thesis in time order, in a series, or step-by-step. It is probably the oldest and simplest of the patterns, going back to storytelling. Time sequence is the dominant pattern in any narrative, anecdote, story, movie, play, biography, or autobiography. In nonfiction prose, time sequence is also used in directions (*how-to*), process, the development or evolution of something, archaeology, history, and so on.

   - **Example:**
     The first sign any of the hikers had of the impending storm was a tall white cloud looming in an otherwise bright blue Sierra sky, far to the north. Late that day, the cloud had grown larger and had moved closer. By sundown, the sky had turned uniformly gray; the temperature dropped ten degrees. They made camp hurriedly, ate a cold meal, and set up camp as snugly as possible.
   - **Signals:**
     *first, second, third,* and so on; *now, later, next, soon, then, finally, afterward, before, after.* Times and dates are also common.

3. **Cause-and-effect pattern.** Here the writer tries to show a causal connection between two or more events (outcomes, situations, and so on). *A* is believed to lead to *B*, or *B* is the result of *A*. Since a cause can hardly occur simultaneously with an effect, this pattern often includes a strong chronological component as well. The writer must assemble proof, evidence, logical reasons, or data, or must appeal to shared experience, to convince the reader that *A* did indeed bring about *B*. This pattern is commonly used in the social sciences, the physical sciences, medicine, laboratory research, biography, and autobiography.

   - **Example:**
     Some popular experts say that a large vocabulary is closely correlated with a large income. It is no doubt true that high-salaried people in business and the professions have fair-sized vocabularies, because they nearly always possess college and university degrees. Also, they must learn the specialized jargon of their fields. But how much more civilized to show a relationship between knowledge of one's language and the ability to think. After all, words are thoughts. Without words, we could not have an abstract idea; we could only react and feel. Our high-

salaried sample may simply be people who could learn and listen, could think and express themselves. Their big vocabularies did not lead directly to dollars but to an effective, civilized person—who might or might not choose to make a lot of money.

- **Signals:**
  *cause, effect, because, leads to, result, results in, brings about, ends in, traced back to, correlation, correlated with, link between, causal relationship, contributes to, proceeds toward, brings about, thereby, hence, since, if this . . . then that*

4. **Reasons (reasons why) pattern.** The writer gives one or more reasons why the thesis is sound or valid. This pattern is common in opinion, persuasion, and argumentation. Fields that commonly use the reasons pattern are medicine, history, the social sciences, and the natural sciences. The writer begins with an assumption that some belief or condition exists and then tries to show why it exists. Or the writer presents a conclusion (an outcome) and supports it with logical reasons. The reasons pattern is sometimes hard to distinguish from a cause-and-effect pattern. "Why did this happen?" is not very different from "What caused this to happen?"

  - **Example:**
    The hikers had no reason to expect anything but beautiful late-summer weather. Storms seldom moved in before the end of September. And this weekend of September 5, the rangers assured them, would be three days of fair weather. So they were totally unprepared for the sudden blizzard that swept down on them Saturday night.
  - **Signals:**
    *so, reasons, why, because, hence, therefore, as a result.* (And of course the ubiquitous *first, second, third.*)

5. **Process pattern.** The writer tells how something works or functions, or how something came about. (If the writer tells *you* how to do or make something, the process is informally called a *how-to.*) We often see this pattern in history, the physical and social sciences, and vocational courses. As we mentioned before, writing patterns often overlap or coexist. A process, a procedure, or a development by its nature occurs chronologically; it probably also involves some cause-and-effect pattern.

  - **Example:**
    How does a person grow up to be an Easy Reader? Usually the process starts soon after birth. The first necessity is parents who read to the child from earliest days on, holding him or her warmly and sharing a delight in the big picture books. Then the child notices that the home has books and magazines scattered about (good for playing with), and sometimes Mother and Father are sitting reading with evident enjoyment. The family sometimes give the child not just toys and money for presents, but wonderful books; they are the child's, to cherish as he or she cherishes games and other toys. The people in this thoughtful home

read things to each other—sharing fun, facts, ideas. To this child, the whole world reads—so he or she reads—not well at first, but as naturally as learning to ride a bicycle. By the time the child is a teenager, he or she likes many activities, many ideas. Of course one of them is reading.

- **Signals:**
  *process, procedure; first, second, third; next, then, later, finally; happen; when, as, during; after, afterward, following; step(s);* dates and times; *interactions; leads to*

6. **Problem-solution pattern.** In a sense, this pattern is a special type of cause-and-effect pattern because the problem causes the solution to be necessary.

   The writer's main idea or thesis is that a problem exists, and there are one or more possible solutions to the problem. The exposition usually falls into two parts: a description of the problem in detail followed by a presentation of the possible solution(s). A signal word, phrase, sentence, or paragraph (in long works) announces the second part.

   This pattern often occurs in business and government writing because individuals in both areas must do so much problem solving: balancing budgets, designing better products, complying with environmental and consumer regulations, and so forth. If the problem is complex or not commonly recognized as a problem, the first part will be longer than the second. We often see this lopsided organization in "Letters to the Editor," where the writer presents a gripe in great detail followed by a brief solution: "Throw them out of office!" Here is a more evenly balanced use of the pattern.

- **Example:**
  Major depressive disorder—often referred to as depression—is a common illness that can affect anyone. About 1 in 20 Americans—over 11 million people—get depressed every year. Too often, people do not get help for their depression, because they don't recognize the symptoms, have trouble asking for help, blame themselves, or don't know that treatments are available. But help is available and effective. If you have symptoms of depression, you can start by going to your family practitioner, clinic, or HMO. These health-care providers will find out if there is a physical cause for the depression, they can treat the depression, and they can refer you to a mental-health specialist if necessary. If you do not have a regular health-care provider, contact your local health department, community mental-health clinic, or hospital. University medical centers also provide treatment for depression.*

- **Signals:**
  words such as *problem* and *solution, issue, if . . . then, the way things are now, the current crisis, the present situation* (and varying degrees of alarm); *but,*

---

*Adapted from U.S. Department of Health and Human Services booklet, *Depression Is a Treatable Illness—A Patient's Guide,* April 1993.

*if, solve, resolve, compromise, answers, a way out, propose, handle, suggest, demand, urge* (and varying degrees of certainty); questions such as *"How can we solve . . . ?," "What can be done . . . ?"*

*Note:* The writer did not need to spend much time on proving that there is a "problem"—depression is a common condition. After the one-word transition, which we hope you saw immediately, she launched into the "solutions."

7.  **Compare-contrast pattern.** The writer discusses two or more subjects and points out differences (contrast), similarities (comparison), or both differences and similarities (comparison), which are usually points, features, or aspects of the two subjects. The passage may describe the features of one subject, then the features of the other subject(s), in separate sections. Or the writer may proceed one by one through the features, alternating among two or more subjects. This pattern is useful in all writing—fiction, nonfiction, light reading, or serious reading. We often learn what something is by noting how it is like or unlike something else.

    *   **Example:**
        The demonstration in our city was similar to several others around the country that day, in numbers and makeup. However, the outcome was very different. Unlike the mass arrests in Boston and Atlanta, no one was arrested, and in fact the demonstration did not even make the television news.
    *   **Signals (comparison):**
        *also, like, compared with, similarly, in the same way, as, just as, likewise, similar to, resemble*
    *   **Signals (contrast):**
        *however, unlike, in contrast, whereas, but, on the contrary, opposite, opposing, on the other hand, unlike, differing from, contrary to, dissimilar, unique, unusual*

8.  **Spatial-geographic pattern.** The writer organizes the details according to physical placement and spatial relationships. The details are often largely visual, structural, and quantitative; you read about amounts, distances, sizes, or outlines. This pattern asks you to visualize, imagine, or see relationships. Graphics such as photographs, sketches, diagrams, and maps may also be added to the text to help you "see" the writer's ideas.

    Like the other patterns, this pattern is found in all reading and in every field, but it is especially common in the natural and life sciences, medicine, mathematics, engineering, architecture, art, urban and ethnic studies, anthropology, history, population studies, and so on. These are fields in which parts, movement, proximities, and physical interrelations are paramount.

    *   **Example:**
        The new mall is planned to be user-friendly. The ground floor will contain food shops, fountains, benches, and tables where people can stroll, eat, and chat. The second and third floors will contain the thirty or so

shops—the business heart of the mall. The top floor will be open to the sun and sky, with small gardens and fine restaurants, and a 180-degree view of the bay.

- **Signals:**
  *left, right, up, down, in the rear, behind, in front; upper, lower, outward, inward; external, internal, dorsal, ventral, anterior, posterior; east, west, north, south; bordering, adjacent, next to*

9. **Definition pattern.** The writer tries to explain or define a concept or object by delineating its qualities or aspects. Of course, a dictionary contains definitions of words—their *denotations.* Usually, the entry begins by assigning the general class of the word. Then it gives the particular features of the word that distinguish it from others in its class. (For example, "A horse is a large, four-legged, hoofed mammal that has been domesticated for riding and for carrying loads.") In our other reading, terms may be defined just as briefly, with one or two sentences, or the writer may expand on a word for a paragraph, a chapter, or even a book.

   Whether brief or lengthy, correct definitions of terms and concepts are essential if one is to learn anything in any field. In mathematics and the sciences, most terms lend themselves to clear and universally accepted definitions. In the social sciences, terms may not be so easy to define or may vary somewhat with the writer or with the context: aggression, adaptability, free elections, and so on. In the arts and in our daily lives, definition is even more difficult. What do you—or I—mean by a healthy mind? A romantic idea? Natural foods? Beauty? Success?

   A pure definition is usually fairly brief. If the writer goes on at length about the term, the pattern may verge on general description rather than being simple definition. This is especially true when *connotations* (the associations a word calls up) or specific examples and anecdotes are used to help explain the term.

   - **Example (denotation):**
     *Depression* is a mental condition of gloom or sadness; dejection.
   - **Example (personal definition, connotations):**
     *Depression* is the conviction that nothing matters, nothing will work out. Depression is also the physical feeling of being twenty pounds heavier, twenty years older, than usual. You can hardly take a deep breath or move your large ungainly body. You can feel the sad droop of your eyes, each weighted down by puffiness.
   - **Signals:**
     *define, definition, describe accurately, explain exactly, mean, meaning, aspects of, discuss, analyze, is*

10. **Classification pattern.** The writer discusses a subject by breaking it down into parts, which are then organized on the basis of traits, interrelationships, hierarchies, or some other system. Groups, classes, categories, types, flowcharts, family trees, chains of command in companies, job analyses—all

these subjects lend themselves to the classification pattern. It is often the dominant pattern in these fields—botany, biology, and linguistics (language families)—as well as in popular articles about types of cars, travelers, students, colleges, fashions, and so on.

- **Example:**

  We can all recognize the three dominant types of students at this college. First, we have the overachievers—they do everything twice as well as necessary, worry themselves sick over grades and exams, and usually get A's. Then there are the remittance kids—their parents are paying to keep them in college and out of trouble. They do the minimum, ignore exams and grades, and try to get D's just for showing up in class. The third type is the . . .

- **Signals:**

  *classify*, *group*, *type*, *sort out*, *analyze*, *order*, *arrange*. This pattern often includes diagrams, flowcharts, "trees," and other graphics to show groupings.

11. **Description pattern.** The writer recreates a subject for you—a person, place, event, experience, mood, object, time, and so on—through many specific details. These details may be highly personal and imaginative, as in essays and stories, or they may be factual, as in a scientific or a police report. The details are often sensory; that is, they involve the senses of sight, sound, smell, taste, and touch. Writers add description anywhere. They insert it within other dominant patterns to enliven the content and make it vivid. Descriptive details can make a vague or abstract discussion more concrete. They help the reader see or experience the topic. As in all organizational patterns, a description may include a stated main idea or thesis. But sometimes the main idea—the focus of all those details—will be implied, left for the reader to infer.

    Descriptive passages are so common, and the pattern is so vague, that you may easily be tempted to label much of what you read *description*. However, outside of fiction, few long works are descriptions alone. Most description functions within some other dominant pattern. For example, a detailed description of a boat will form part of a chronological account of a prehistoric dig.

    The description pattern itself is sometimes broken down into kinds of description, or subpatterns: facts and statistics, spatial-geographic, and so on.

- **Example:**

  This self-portrait by the Mexican painter Frida Kahlo is striking, even when reproduced in a textbook in black and white. She has set herself before a backdrop of lush tropical greenery; a small pet monkey peers enigmatically from behind her right shoulder. Like the monkey, she stares straight out of the canvas—unsmiling, serious, self-aware, proud but not defiant. Her head and neck take up most of the frame; she has given herself an extremely long, straight, strong neck, almost a pillar. Her face . . .

- **Signals:**
  *describe, description, the appearance, the look, in detail.* (The writer may use no signals. He or she may simply begin to describe, filling in the broad statements with many specific details.)

Turn to Practice 1.7 on page 28.

## SUMMARIZING

Say that you have read an entire passage. You are fairly competent in the essential reading skills: You know immediately what the topic is, you can discover the main idea, you can spot the supporting details, and you can recognize how they are organized. All these skills are necessary before you can advance to the next skill: summarizing what you have read.

*Summarizing* means condensing, "squeezing down," the content of a passage into a shorter form. A formal summary of a long expository work is often called a *precis.* You do not necessarily have to follow the original order of ideas. You must, however, take care to (1) state fairly the umbrella or main idea, (2) include the most significant or striking supporting details, plus the pattern of organization, and (3) do all this in a short space, without serious omission or distortion of the writer's message.

Note that a summary is more complete than a restatement of the writer's main idea or theme. For example, the main idea of the movie *Schindler's List* follows: Through the six years of horror that was the Holocaust, a shady German businessman develops from a cynical exploiter of slave labor to a compassionate man who saves many Jews from death. (Dominant pattern is time sequence, because the story is told chronologically.)

The summary of the plot could be any length, but definitely longer than the statement of the theme. It would include some important details, as follows:

> Based on a fictionalized true story by Thomas Kenneally, *Schindler's List* recreates in deeply moving black and white the nightmarish efficiency of the Nazi genocide of European Jews. At the same time, we follow the personal histories of several fascinating characters, especially the con-man industrialist, Oskar Schindler. At first, Schindler builds a fortune on the forced labor of Jewish prisoners. As time goes by, he gradually realizes the extent of the horror and ultimately spends his fortune devising ways to save hundreds of lives. We see the power that one individual possesses to change for the better, and in the process, save the lives of others.

Note that the summary tries to be objective, fair, and complete. It does not include the summarizer's personal opinions or any critique of the writing, acting, and so on. Those responses are more akin to critical thinking and reading, covered in Chapter 6.

Some expository styles are so concise that a reader can find little to eliminate in a summary. As we have said, this may occur in mathematics, the sciences, legal and medical materials, straight news, operating manuals, a very pared-down fiction style, poetry, and so on. But much of what we read, even in textbooks, is wordier than it needs to be. In these cases, main ideas and important supporting details should stand out, making a condensation possible.

One question often arises: When you summarize, are you allowed to copy the writer's own words? Ask your instructor for an opinion on this. In our view, as long as you use quotation marks or other attribution(s), you should not be guilty of plagiarism. Usually, however, your summary will be more satisfying if you paraphrase (use synonyms for the original wording). Even better, you should condense the content into your own words, without referring back to the original. Imagine that you are telling a friend the gist of what you have read. This will help the summary flow naturally rather than sound like an patchwork of odd phrasings.

Summarizing is not easy to learn. Remember that you must first comprehend the material completely—not just the surface facts, but also the relationship of major to minor ideas, plus any important inferences the writer intends you to make. Also note that a summary does not have to present the details in exactly the same order as the original. Finally, you must use your best judgment about what matters and what does not.

Here is a sample paragraph, followed by two sample summaries. First, read the paragraph several times. (Do not read the summaries.) You will see that it is not a science experiment or a rental contract; the style is casual and rather wordy. Second, locate and underline the topic sentence(s). Third, without looking back at the paragraph, write a summary in your own words. Two or three sentences should suffice. Finally, compare your summary with the two we wrote.

## Sample paragraph:

Lucy H. Hedrick makes a valuable point in her book, *365 Ways to Save Time* (New York: Hearst Books, 1992). As we might expect, she explains how to organize our time in order to accomplish various tasks. But this noted efficiency expert also argues that there's a positive value in something we all do but feel guilty about: wasting time. According to Hedrick, even the most pressured individual needs to schedule some free time, away from those tasks. This time is not really wasted, as the American work ethic has conditioned us to believe. Rather, it is a necessary "reward" for setting goals and reaching them. To use our working time most efficiently, she says, we must be able to look forward to an occasional time to relax and do nothing at all.*

## Sample summaries:

1. In a book about the efficient use of time, Lucy H. Hedrick stresses that even the most efficient people need to schedule some free time. This isn't wasted time; it's a reward they can look forward to.

_____

*Adapted from a review by Donald Munro, *SLO Telegram-Tribune*, November 20, 1992.

2.  Author Lucy Hedrick says in her recent book that even the most efficient people should not try to work constantly. They need to reward themselves with occasional free or "wasted" time—which isn't wasted, because it makes them work better.

Neither of our versions quoted sentences 3 and 4 of the original, which contain the main idea. Both versions used only two sentences, compared with the original seven, and only about one-third as many total words. We saved the main idea, of course, but we shortened it and eliminated the writer's unnecessary repetition. How did your summary compare?

Turn to Practice 1.8 on page 30 and Practice 1.9 on page 32.

. . . . . . . . . . . . . . . . . . .

# SUMMARY

This first chapter has provided a review of familiar, essential skills because they are essential to the more advanced skills in later chapters. You cannot preview, skim, study college texts, read critically, or scan without learning the first step— basic literal comprehension. You must understand the topic, the main ideas, the supporting details, and how they all are organized. Further, you need to see reading and writing as two sides of the same process: the giving and receiving of information through print. A professional writer takes a certain path, always with the reader in mind. In expository writing expecially, the topic, thesis or main idea, and organizational patterns are located and developed in fairly predictable ways. By giving you ways to see this, reading instruction can help you become proficient more rapidly than if you were to work alone.

If you have done well so far, you can add the sensible step of previewing (Chapter 2), and then you will be ready to do some time-pressured reading in Chapters 3 and 4.

Note that the following chapters will have a new format. Each introduction will open with a checklist of symptoms, followed by a description of the skill, a summary of the introduction, and some practices. Some chapters include a series of timed selections. Finally, each chapter presents activities asking you to explore further the material you have studied.

# PRACTICES:
## ESSENTIAL READING SKILLS

Answers to the odd-numbered practices are provided in Appendix C. Ask your instructor for answers to the even-numbered practices.

1.1 DISTINGUISHING BETWEEN TOPIC AND MAIN-IDEA STATEMENT
1.2 IDENTIFYING THE TOPIC OF A PARAGRAPH
1.3 UNDERSTANDING THE MAIN IDEA WHEN STATED
1.4 DISCOVERING THE IMPLIED MAIN IDEA
1.5 FINDING SUPPORTING DETAILS
1.6 DISCRIMINATING BETWEEN IMPORTANT AND LESS IMPORTANT DETAILS
1.7 RECOGNIZING ORGANIZATIONAL PATTERNS
1.8 SUMMARIZING PARAGRAPHS
1.9 SUMMARIZING A LONGER PASSAGE

## 1.1   DISTINGUISHING BETWEEN TOPIC AND MAIN-IDEA STATEMENT

Which of the following are topics only? Which are really topics plus comments, and therefore could be statements of the main idea of a paragraph or longer work? Place a *T* next to each topic and an *MI* next to each main idea.

_____ 1. "working breeds" of dogs
_____ 2. golden retrievers
_____ 3. golden retrievers are a good example of a working breed
_____ 4. a golden retriever is happiest when it has a job to do
_____ 5. our dog Amy
_____ 6. our dog Amy had an almost human sense of humor
_____ 7. a book entitled *The Hidden Life of Dogs*
_____ 8. *The Hidden Life of Dogs* is well-written and provocative
_____ 9. the book's conclusions are flawed
_____ 10. the author's research methods

Score = number correct × 10.

Score _____ %

▶ 80%

Check answers on p. 350.

## 1.2   IDENTIFYING THE TOPIC OF A PARAGRAPH

Read each of the following paragraphs quickly, identify the topic, and write it in the blank. Remember to use a word or phrase only, not a complete sentence. Avoid including any comment on the topic.

**Paragraph 1**

Learning to play a musical instrument—keyboard, piano, flute, guitar—is a long-term project. You should get a good teacher, one whom you respect and like. You should plan to practice every day for at least a year before you see any real progress, and several years before you play well. You should be patient; like everything else that's worthwhile, success will not come easy. If you do all this and you still sound terrible, well, maybe you just weren't born with a musical gene!

Topic (word or phrase): _____

**Paragraph 2**

The radio program, "Music of the World's Peoples," opens a window for the listener onto the enormous variety of musical expression created by humans today. The commentator presents recordings of all kinds: singing groups, instrumentals, combinations, soloists. And these are drawn from every continent, nation, and ethnic group imaginable, demonstrating every possible instrument and vocal style. For the average American, used to mostly European musical styles with some African and Latin influences, the program sometimes sounds puzzling or harsh. But it is never dull.

Topic (word or phrase): _____

**Paragraph 3**

Everybody likes music. Jazz, classical, film and stage music, bluegrass, country western, ethnic, pop, opera, R & B, rock—we all enjoy listening to our radios, tapes, and CDs; we all go to concerts from time to time. But many of us never experience what is even more satisfying: making music as opposed to hearing others make it. People who play instruments or sing are doing something active and creative even if they never sound great. Also, by making their own music, they learn to appreciate the enormous skill that professional musicians have. Anyone who only listens passively to others is missing out on some of the greatest pleasures music can give.

Topic (word or phrase): _____

**Paragraph 4**

University students held a rally last week to protest what they see as the administration's indifference to the crime problem on campus. Handmade signs and dozens of speakers voiced their specific grievances and their demands for solutions. They accused the administration of covering up recent instances of robbery, rape, and theft, as well as not budgeting enough money for adequate security measures. To solve the crisis, students made several demands. They insisted that (1) crime statistics be kept and publicized, (2) a task force be set up that would include students, and (3) funds be earmarked for increased security patrols and better lighting.

Topic (word or phrase): _____

**Paragraph 5**

We Americans have certainly changed our attitudes toward recycling in the last thirty years. In the 1960s and 1970s, few people besides Boy Scouts on their annual newspaper drive recycled anything at all. Cans, bottles, and paper were for discarding—the good guys tossed them into the trash can, the bad guys tossed them all over the landscape. It seemed that resources were endless, landfill space was infinite, and burning waste or dumping it in the ocean got rid of it for good. In the 1990s, the situation is not perfect, but it certainly is different. The word *recyclables* has become a common noun. Machines cough up money for our cans and bottles. In many cities, trash collectors will pick up recyclables at the curb. Nearly everywhere today, a person seen tossing an aluminum can gets disapproving stares—and deserves them.

Topic (word or phrase): _____

Score = number correct × 20.

Score _____ %

▶ 80%

Check answers with your instructor.

## 1.3    UNDERLINING THE MAIN IDEA WHEN STATED

In each of the following five paragraphs, one sentence best expresses the paragraph's main idea. Read each paragraph, then reread it to locate the main-idea sentence. Place the number of this sentence in the space provided.

**Paragraph 1**

[1] Success in the engineering field depends partly on certain personality traits. (This may explain why some people can spot an engineer a block away!)    [2] First, the student should like mathematics.    [3] Electrical engineering probably requires the most math, but all specialties demand some background in it.    [4] Secondly, the student should enjoy working with mechanical and physical objects. [5] The primary goal of all engineering is to "build a better mousetrap"—to make a new object or system that is more efficient and more economical. Another important trait is that of being methodical and precise.    [6] Professional engineers spend much of their career running tests and collecting data.    [7] While this may sound dull, engineering majors can expect an exciting career, because they will always be looking to design something new and better.

Main-idea sentence: _____

**Paragraph 2**

[1] *Engineering* is a broad term for a major that encompasses many subtypes. [2] Civil engineering is probably the best known to the public: These men and women work to improve buildings, roads, bridges.    [3] Mechanical engineering involves any kind of working object or engine.    [4] Metallurgical and chemical

engineering involve just what their names imply and require the least mathematics of any type.    [5]Electrical engineering majors decide whether to enter the power field or—a big specialty today—the electronics field.    [6]Not all engineers work in design: Some specialize in the legal or business aspects of engineering.    [7]One can even combine an interest in technology (not necessarily a degree) with writing ability and work as a technical writer.

Main-idea sentence: _____

### Paragraph 3

[1]For better or worse, money is a major element in our modern lives.    [2]How can adults teach their children good habits regarding the use and saving of money?    [3]Child psychologists say the best way is to be good role models.    [4]If we show how we ourselves work for money, shop carefully, and build savings, children will remember this example better than any lectures.    [5]It is easier, but also important, to guide our children as they handle their own money.    [6]We should start them on the habit of saving part of their earnings, say 10 percent, perhaps sweetening the pill by pointing out that they get to spend 90 percent.    [7]Children are surprised by how this modest plan can build a savings account, a lesson they will need as adults.    [8]Lastly, in many families children can earn money for chores and good grades.    [9]However, experts say we must take care not to overpay and not to imply that every civilized action in life leads to money.

Main-idea sentence: _____

### Paragraph 4

[1]How can we define "good writing"?    [2]Does it have to be "literary"? "Imaginative"? "Arousing"?    [3]Actually, all good writing shares more or less the same characteristics.    [4]Whether short story, essay, project report, legal brief, novel, or business letter, the reader expects the writer to deliver the "message" according to accepted criteria.    [5]One is conciseness: When you compose, you should use only as many words as needed for your intended message or effect.    [6]Another criterion is unity: Focus on your theme, making sure your reader will get the main point.    [7]No one enjoys being terminally confused, whether the writer intended it or was simply inept.    [8]Still another is the matter of style.    [9]Style, or form, should be adapted to your reading audience; you should choose the vocabulary, sentence/paragraph length, and amount of detail that will most effectively convey your thoughts.

Main-idea sentence: 4 _____

### Paragraph 5

[1]Global warming of Earth through trapped human-made gases is so far only a hypothesis.    [2]But if the process has begun, then certain small countries will be the first to feel its effects.    [3]These are the 34 nations comprising the Alliance of Small Island States (ASIS).    [4]Scientists agree that any global increase in heat will cause the polar ice caps to melt.    [5]This would in turn cause ocean levels to rise and flood low-lying lands around the world.    [6]Many populated islands are

fairly low; for example, 45,000 people live in the Marshall Islands, where the average elevation is only 25 feet above sea level.   [7]As a result, alarmed representatives from ASIS are pressuring the developed countries, who mainly cause the problem, to move faster in studying and combating the climate change.*

Main-idea sentence: _____

Score = number correct × 20.
Score _____ %
▶ 80%
Check answers on p. 350.

## 1.4   DISCOVERING THE IMPLIED MAIN IDEA

In each of the following excerpts, the author does not directly state the main idea. Underneath each paragraph, write a complete sentence accurately stating the implied main idea of each.

### Paragraph 1

[1]Studies have shown that a steep decline in amphibian populations has taken place largely in the last 25 years.   [2]In this same period, more ultraviolet radiation has reached the earth, especially UV-B, because the ozone layer has been steadily thinning.   [3]Scientists decided to test the hypothesis that there is a connection between UV-B and the amphibian decline.   [4]They have hatched amphibian eggs in the wild, with protection from UV-B, and also hatched control groups with no protection.   [5]The hatch rate of the protected eggs rose dramatically, while the hatch rate of the unprotected control groups dropped severely.[†]

Implied main idea (complete sentence): _____

### Paragraph 2

[1]Students who start or return to college after age twenty-five often take a reading/study course to brush up on their efficiency.   [2]These reentry students have had experience in the world of work and family, they bring this knowledge to their course work, and they know exactly what they want from college.   [3]They use their time well because their busy lives force them to; family, exercise, study, jobs must be carefully balanced if they are to succeed.   [4]Students who are middle-aged and older often study harder and get better grades, for personal satisfaction but also, perhaps, because of a sense of competition with their younger classmates.

Implied main idea (complete sentence): _____

---

*Adapted from "Fear of Rising Seas—Island Nations Worry Global Warming May Submerge Them," *San Luis Obispo County Telegram-Tribune*, September 15, 1992.

†Adapted from "Ozone Layer Loss Is Croaking Amphibian Eggs," *San Luis Obispo County Telegram-Tribune News Services*, March 3, 1994.

### Paragraph 3

[1] The armed policeman forcefully opened the downtown hotel room door.    [2] He noticed that the window facing the highway was open, and cigarette smoke was trailing out the window.    [3] Looking more carefully, the young officer found a cigarette butt burned almost to the filter resting in an ashtray on the bedstand. [4] The light through the bathroom slipped through a tightly shut door, and the officer could hear the trickling of water droplets as they fell slowly into the wash-basin drain.

Implied main idea (complete sentence): _____

### Paragraph 4

[1] Some individuals become homeless because, for various reasons, they have no network of friends and relatives.    [2] If they also have no financial cushion, they "drop through the cracks" and end up on the streets.    [3] Some have mental ill-nesses severe enough to prevent them from keeping a job; in the past, they might well have been institutionalized.    [4] Others are mentally capable but have physi-cal conditions that prevent them from working.    [5] Without medical coverage, their health continues to worsen.    [6] Some homeless individuals abuse alcohol or drugs and would require long-term treatment to overcome their addictions. [7] Some, especially women, have been abused and lack the self-esteem necessary to reverse their situation.    [8] Finally, a growing proportion—one-third of all the homeless individuals in 1994—are families with small children.    [9] Parents have lost jobs and housing and find themselves on the streets for the first time in their lives.

Implied main idea (complete sentence): _____

### Paragraph 5

[1] Overnight visits by family members to men in prison are still permitted in this state.    [2] Some legislators want to pass a bill outlawing the practice.    [3] They cite the number of crimes committed by prisoners during these visits, point out that these relations are not constitutionally guaranteed, and quote victims of crime who feel prisoners do not deserve this amenity, especially in cases of sex crimes. [4] Opponents of the bill state that the goal of imprisonment is not only to punish but to rehabilitate.    [5] They cite statistics showing that violence increases among inmates who are denied conjugal visits, thus creating greater danger for the guards.    [6] There is also some evidence that such visits help maintain the stabil-ity of their families, a plus for society during the prison term and later when in-mates are released.

Implied main idea (complete sentence): _____

Score = number correct × 20.

Score _____%

▶80%

Check answers with your instructor.

## 1.5    FINDING SUPPORTING DETAILS

Read each paragraph carefully for supporting details and transitions. Then write down the numbers of the sentences introducing supporting details. Finally, list the transitional phrases that introduce the supporting details.

### Paragraph 1

[1]Advanced technology helped break some records at the Winter Olympics. [2]For example, practicing in an aerospace-type wind tunnel showed ski jumpers exactly what angle their skis should be held in. [3]The luge athletes trained on special tracks with built-in sensors. [4]Bobsleds were made to specifications derived from auto design. [5]The boots of some speed skaters were developed through new plastics procedures.

Supporting-detail sentences: _____

Transitions: _____

### Paragraph 2

[1]*The Hidden Life of Dogs* by Elizabeth Marshall Thomas (Boston: Houghton Mifflin, 1993) is a short but intriguing nonfiction book about our household pets. [2]The author is a professional anthropologist who used typical "field methods" to try to understand the minds of dogs, especially her own eleven dogs. [3]First, she observed and recorded their behaviors day by day for many years. [4]Then she wrote of her experiences and conclusions in a vivid and accessible style. [5]We ultimately learn a great deal about Bingo, Maria, Misha, Koki, and the others, and therefore about all dogs and the author herself.

Supporting-detail sentences: _____

Transitions: _____

### Paragraph 3

[1]In her book *The Hidden Life of Dogs*, author Elizabeth Marshall Thomas reaches some surprising conclusions. [2]For one, she decides that what matters most to a dog is—not food, not humans—but other dogs. (So much for our common assumption that we owners are the most important things in a dog's life!) [3]A dog spends its entire life trying to establish a secure, clear social relationship with the other dogs in its environment. [4]Secondly, a dog's happiest moments come when everything is quiet, peaceful, and stable. [5]What we primates see as emptiness and boredom, a dog sees as the perfect achievement. [6]Finally, Thomas says, dogs when left to themselves will revert to the behaviors of their ancestors, the wolves.

Supporting-detail sentences: _____

Transitions: _____

### Paragraph 4

[1]U.S. men and women have differing opinions about many issues. [2]For example, a poll conducted in the early 1980s showed they differed in their political

views: Women tended to vote more liberally and men more conservatively. [3] One-third of all women voters call themselves liberals, while only one-fourth of the men do so.   [4] This split is increasing in the 1990s.   [5] Another example of gender difference is seen in men's and women's views of job equity.   [6] Over 70 percent of the men thought they had been fairly paid for their work, but only 55 percent of the women thought so.   [7] A third instance of gender difference occurred in Congress in 1993, when that body considered an amendment to ban funds for medicaid abortions.   [8] Nearly all the women who make up 10 percent of Congress voted against the ban, while nearly all the male representatives voted for it.

Supporting-detail sentences: _____

Transitions: _____

## Paragraph 5

[1] When researchers compare U.S. men and women on the basis of how they stand on various issues, wide differences in the sexes have been obvious for at least fifteen years.   [2] Men are more likely than women to consider themselves conservative and to vote Republican.   [3] They tend to think the economy is getting better.   [4] And only one-fourth of U.S. men are dissatisfied with their incomes. [5] In contrast to men, U.S. women are more likely to consider themselves liberal and to vote Democratic.   [6] They tend to think the economy is getting worse, perhaps because their average annual income is much lower than that of men. [7] And about half the women polled think they have not received adequate pay throughout their working years.

Supporting-detail sentences: _____

Transitions: _____

Score = number correct × 20.

Score _____ %

▶ 80%

Check answers on p. 350.

## 1.6   DISCRIMINATING BETWEEN IMPORTANT AND LESS IMPORTANT DETAILS

Each of the following is a main idea for an article, followed by various details that might be found within the article. For each group, read the main idea carefully and retain it mentally. Then read through the list of details. Place a check mark next to each detail that directly supports the topic. The others may be interesting but do not directly pertain to the main idea. Work through each main idea and supporting details quickly.

1.   Young new stand-up comedian Bob Smith will be a hit.
    a.  _____ little big-time experience so far
    b.  _____ clever material, smoothly presented

    c. \_\_\_\_\_ easy to identify with his characters, situations

    d. \_\_\_\_\_ upbeat humor; not mean, hostile, vicious

2. The earthquake caused major physical damage.

    a. \_\_\_\_\_ collapses on three freeways

    b. \_\_\_\_\_ homes on cliffs hard hit

    c. \_\_\_\_\_ new structures destroyed as well as old

    d. \_\_\_\_\_ residents' nerves jangled by 500 aftershocks

3. The earthquake caused long-lasting psychological damage.

    a. \_\_\_\_\_ people driving more erratically in traffic

    b. \_\_\_\_\_ children sleep poorly at night

    c. \_\_\_\_\_ adults jump at loud noises

    d. \_\_\_\_\_ many stores and schools must be repaired before use

    e. \_\_\_\_\_ big rise in psychosomatic illnesses

4. Treatments for obesity should be covered by health insurance.

    a. \_\_\_\_\_ originally intended by Nature as survival mechanism

    b. \_\_\_\_\_ in one-third of all U.S. citizens, obesity possibly causing other serious medical problems

    c. \_\_\_\_\_ obesity caused by genes, not lack of willpower

    d. \_\_\_\_\_ often leads to heart attacks, high blood pressure, diabetes

5. This expert recommends ways we can teach children about money.

    a. \_\_\_\_\_ examples: adults who never learned value of money

    b. \_\_\_\_\_ examples: kids who are sensible about money

    c. \_\_\_\_\_ be role models in our own attitudes and use of money

    d. \_\_\_\_\_ pay them realistically

    e. \_\_\_\_\_ start them on "savings habit"

6. Compulsive gambling is an addiction much like drug, alcohol, and nicotine dependencies.

    a. \_\_\_\_\_ examples: people who lost fortunes, died in misery

    b. \_\_\_\_\_ Old West romantic stereotype of gambler

    c. \_\_\_\_\_ definitions of terms: compulsion, addiction

    d. \_\_\_\_\_ victims want to stop, find they cannot

    e. \_\_\_\_\_ winning gives gambler a "high"

    f. \_\_\_\_\_ possible but difficult to change these gamblers

7. Congress's refusal to continue funding the SSC (superconducting super collider) may have a big negative impact on basic scientific research.*

    a. \_\_\_\_\_ $2 billion already spent toward building, $1 billion required to shut it down

    b. \_\_\_\_\_ would have been largest in world

    c. \_\_\_\_\_ description of one interviewee's office

    d. \_\_\_\_\_ would have answered ultimate questions about matter, universe

    e. \_\_\_\_\_ best students/faculty in physical sciences may go elsewhere

    f. \_\_\_\_\_ bad precedent—will hurt funding for similar projects

---

*Adapted from Andrew Campbell, "Ghost of the Machine," *University of Chicago Magazine,* February 1994, 31–34.

8. Are "diversity courses" good additions to college curriculums?
   a. _____ examples—where offered, what kind of content
   b. _____ comments from students, administrators
   c. _____ cost of college education continues to rise
   d. _____ con: not education, just "politically correct"
   e. _____ con: may increase separateness, work against unity
   f. _____ pro: help students prepare for living/working in pluralistic world
9. How can the older, reentry student succeed in college?
   a. _____ talk to other older students—support group
   b. _____ huge campus, many young faces
   c. _____ take advantage of materials, workshops on efficient studying
   d. _____ establish rapport with professors—office hours, etc.
   e. _____ on average, takes one year to relearn how to be a full-time student
   f. _____ remember pluses: mature, focused, serious student
10. Let's admit it: Writing on a computer is not 100 percent better than using the old-fashioned typewriter!
   a. _____ commonly causes strain in back/neck/wrist
   b. _____ encourages wordiness
   c. _____ new programs/computers constantly make your expensive setup obsolete
   d. _____ neater—no more cut-and-paste, no piles of waste paper
   e. _____ can lose hours/days of hard work in a moment
   f. _____ deleting/inserting/moving can produce many small errors in printed text

Score = number correct × 10.

Score _____%

▶ 80%

Check answers with your instructor.

## 1.7   RECOGNIZING ORGANIZATIONAL PATTERNS

Here you will find five paragraphs on various subjects. Read each one carefully for its organization. Then determine which of the eleven patterns it best follows. Write this pattern under each paragraph. Remember the eleven patterns: examples, time sequence, cause-and-effect, reasons, process, problem-solution, compare-contrast, spatial-geographic, definition, classification, and description.

### Paragraph 1

Linguists, those scientists of language, tell us that human languages are living entities that constantly change over time. Their histories can be traced almost as if they were persons. English, like all the others, has its long history of change and influences. It belongs to the large family called Indo-European, which researchers think originated somewhere in what is now eastern Europe and northern Iran 5,000 to 6,000 years ago. Using advanced techniques, they have reconstructed some of this parent language, Proto-Indo-European. Tribes migrated, lost contact with each other. Over hundreds and thousands of years, languages developed into dialects and then separate tongues. One branch of Indo-European, the Germanic, split into North, East, and West subgroups. West Germanic moved into England with the Anglo-Saxons around A.D. 500–600. Even the Norman (French) invasion of 1066 did not shake loose this dominant language of the British Isles. Fifteen hundred years later, the basic grammar and over 90 percent of our common, daily words are still "native"—that is, a modern version of the Anglo-Saxon spoken by those Germanic tribes.

Organizational pattern: _____

## Paragraph 2

Social scientists do not agree on whether blue- and white-collar workers have become increasingly alike in their values and attitudes in recent decades, but they may continue to look at life differently even at similar income levels. Regarding marriage, for example, working-class couples tend to emphasize values associated with parenthood and job stability, whereas white-collar partners are more inclined to value companionship, self-expression, and communication. Middle-class parents value self-direction and initiative in children, whereas parents in working-class families stress obedience and conformity.*

Organizational pattern: _____

## Paragraph 3

The amateur sport of triathlon seems to be growing in popularity in the United States and the rest of the world. Perhaps this is because triathlons vary widely, from short and fairly easy to extremely grueling—for example, the "Iron Man" annual triathlon in Hawaii. Somewhere, every weekend of the year, there is a triathlon for every level of athletic ability except Confirmed Couch Potato. One local event is designed for novices. Another one, a rigorous regional championship event, announces that it is open to "the professional, the elite age-group triathlete, and the first-time long-course competitor." For yuppie types, the sport provides a goal, a reason to keep in shape. For many other young men and women, it's simply the thing to do; a triathlon is a social event. For serious athletes, triathlons are a way of life or almost an obsession: They may train six hours a day, six days a week to compete for lucrative endorsements. It seems the only thing triathlons have in common is the "tri" events: swimming, bicycling, and running.

Organizational pattern: _____

## Paragraph 4

The United Nations Food and Agriculture Organization announces [1994] that 600 breeds of domestic animals are now extinct worldwide. These include chickens, pigs, cattle, goats, sheep, horses, and donkeys. Four hundred other breeds

---

*Mary Ann Lamanna and Agnes Riedmann, *Marriages and Families,* 4th ed. (Belmont, CA: Wadsworth, 1991), 35.

are listed as endangered. Of the 4,000 breeds existing in the world today, one-fourth are not being valued and preserved as they should, and so they may be headed for extinction. For example, only 1,000 Rubia De El Molar sheep exist today, and only 30 Andalusian spotted pigs. Yet both were developed over many centuries for their value to humans and—more importantly—their ability to flourish in harsh conditions. Animal geneticists are alarmed. They warn that unless genetic stocks of valuable farm animals are preserved, the loss to humans will rival the loss of genetic variety that we already see in the destruction of the world's rain forests.*

Organizational pattern: _____

**Paragraph 5**

What is major depressive disorder, or depression? It is not just "feeling blue" or feeling "down in the dumps." It is more than being sad or feeling grief after a loss. In fact, one major form of depression—bipolar or manic-depressive disorder—includes periods of euphoria, or "highs." Depression is a medical disorder—just as diabetes, high blood pressure, or heart disease are medical disorders—that day after day affects one's thoughts, feelings, physical health, and behaviors. It can be caused by genetics, other general medical illnesses, certain medicines, drugs or alcohol, and by other psychiatric conditions. Depression is not a weakness or "your fault." It is a medical illness, and thus it is treatable.[†]

Organizational pattern: _____

Score = number correct × 20.

Score _____%

▶ 80%

Check answers on page 350.

### 1.8   SUMMARIZING PARAGRAPHS

Read the following five paragraphs carefully. Then, in one or two sentences, summarize it. As you summarize, ask yourself if you have considered the topic of the paragraph, the main idea, and one important detail. When you first identify these parts of each paragraph, your one- or two-sentence summary should prove accurate.

**Paragraph 1**

The complexity of the meaning of love is illustrated by the fact that the language of classical Greece differentiated three aspects of love within a couple: *philos*, which referred to an attraction characterized by deep, enduring friendship; *eros*,

---

*Adapted from William D. Montalbano, "Dangers of Narrowing the Field," *Los Angeles Times*, December 23, 1993, 1.

†Adapted from U.S. Department of Health and Human Services booklet, *Depression Is a Treatable Illness—A Patient's Guide*, April 1993.

which referred to a passionate sexual attraction; and *agape*, which referred to the self-sacrificing, nondemanding spiritual satisfaction a person feels when providing for the other. There was no single word for love in classical Greece.*

Summary in your own words (1–2 sentences): _____

_____

## Paragraph 2

One obvious component of loving is liking. However, loving is not simply an extreme manifestation of liking. One of the first scientific studies of love found that both liking and loving are characterized by respect, attraction, affection, need, care, trust, and tolerance. However, liking emphasizes respect, attraction, and affection, whereas loving emphasizes need, care, trust, and tolerance.[†]

Summary in your own words (1–2 sentences): _____

_____

## Paragraph 3

The Smoke Mountain Triathlon is an exciting event through our county's late-spring wildflowers. It consists of a .25-mile swim in Williams Lake, which will be warm this time of year, an 8-mile bike ride along a construction road on the mountain, and a 1.5-mile run down the other side, mostly in shade and by a stream. The Smoke Mountain is designed for people who are new to triathlon, and it offers a wide range of categories for boys, girls, men, and women. Age groups begin at ten years and continue to seventy-plus. Local businesses will be offering a variety of merchandise for prizes: T-shirts, shoes, food, and wines. If you have never tried a triathlon, this may be the best introduction to the sport. See you there in May!

Summary in your own words (2–3 sentences): _____

_____

## Paragraph 4

A middle-aged woman, with an MBA from the University of Chicago, owns and operates an unusual business in Los Angeles. It's a school designed to teach clients how to save their lives when confronted by hardened street criminals. Through a harrowing experience of her own, plus several years in a volunteer street patrol, the woman decided that surrendering to attackers does not guarantee one's safety. In fact, police records show that compliant victims are as likely to be killed as resistant ones. So, the school shows adults and children how to counterattack viciously enough to escape. But first, clients must learn acting skills. They must seem to surrender while actually waiting for the chance to disable their attackers. The techniques are so violent that the actors who train with

---

*Lloyd Saxton, *The Individual, Marriage, and the Family*, 8th ed. (Belmont, CA:Wadsworth), 53.
[†]Saxton, p. 53.

clients must wear heavy protective clothing. The fit, attractive owner has apparently identified a need and is meeting it; her classes are filled long in advance.*

Summary in your own words (2–3 sentences): _____

_____

### Paragraph 5

Every modern government offers some form of subsidies to its food producers. Farmers and ranchers the world over rely on these programs. But international studies are turning up dismaying evidence that subsidies often do more harm than good to a nation's soil and its food consumers. For example, cheap electricity causes excessive pumping of water, which lowers the water table. Low-priced water and pasture fees encourage growers to plant the wrong crops for an area, ranchers to overgraze their cattle on public lands. These two "savings" lead to depletion of natural water supplies, excess pesticide use, desertification of large areas, and long-term erosion of vast tracts of land. Food-growing practices that are not naturally sustainable end up costing all of us heavily, in damage to our environment and to our health.†

Summary in your own words (2–3 sentences): _____

_____

Score = number correct × 20.

Score _____ %

▶ 80%

Check answers with your instructor.

## 1.9  Summarizing a Longer Passage

In this multiparagraph passage, you will be putting many of the skills you learned in this chapter together. Look for the topic and the main-idea statement of the entire passage, transitions, main supporting details, and dominant writing pattern. The main idea should be stated in one sentence (by you or the author). Your summary will include a few major details, but it should not run more than one long sentence, or possibly two to three shorter sentences.

---

*Adapted from C. A. M., "Street Smarts," *University of Chicago Magazine*, February 1994, 39.

†Adapted from *San Luis Obispo County Telegram-Tribune*, October 11, 1993.

# WHY DO WOMEN LIVE LONGER?

1    There are six million more women than men in the United States.* [2] Women outlive men not only in the United States but in all industrialized nations. [3] Despite different cultures, different ways of life, different diets, and different causes of death, there is one overriding constant: Women outlive men by about seven years throughout the industrialized world (Dolnick 1991).

4    Differential survival rates begin at conception, and at all life stages thereafter mortality rates are higher for males than for females. [5] Male infants die in larger numbers than do female infants. [6] Throughout childhood and adolescence, males continue to have higher death rates. [7] As adults, every one of the leading causes of death—heart disease, lung cancer, homicide, cirrhosis of the liver, and pneumonia—kills men at a rate about twice that of women.† [8] More male disorders are inherited, predisposing men to have lower life expectancies (Renzetti and Curran 1989; Sorensen et al. 1985).

9    Part of the damage that leads to men's higher death rates is self-inflicted. [10] About a third of the longevity gap can be traced to the ways men act. [11] Men smoke more than women, drink more, and take more life-threatening chances. [12] Men are murdered (usually by other men) three times as often as women are, and men commit suicide two or three times as often as women do.** [13] Male drivers are more likely to drive through a red light, more likely to drive after drinking, and less likely to signal a turn.

[14] Men have twice as many fatal accidents per mile driven as women do (Dolnick 1991).

15    But behavior doesn't explain all of the longevity gap. [16] Even among nonsmokers, for example, death rates from heart disease, lung cancer, and emphysema are two to four times higher for men than they are for women.*

17    During the 1950s stress was commonly blamed for men's higher mortality rates. [18] It was hypothesized that men were subject to significantly more stress in the workplace than women experienced at home. [19] However, from the 1950s to the 1990s the proportion of women employed outside the home more than doubled. [20] Women who work away from home were found to be just as healthy as women who work at home (Dolnick 1991).

21    Researchers have suggested that one reason for females' lower mortality rate from infancy on may be a result of the production of immunogenic agents in the genes of the X chromosome. [22] Researchers have also hypothesized that females have a higher ability than males to fight infections because of the action of female hormones (estrogen and progesterone) on certain blood cells (Lips 1988).

23    It should be noted, however, that despite their lower mortality rate, women have higher levels of stress than men and higher rates of exhaustion, headaches, dermatology problems, mental illness, and chronic illnesses (Berkow et al. 1987; Sheldrake, Cromack, and McGuire 1976).

Lloyd Saxton, *The Individual, Marriage, and the Family*, 8th ed. (Belmont, CA: Wadsworth), 30–31.

*U.S. Bureau of the Census, "Total Population, by Sex, Race, and Age: 1989" (1991).

†U.S. National Center for Health Statistics, "Death Rates by Selected Causes and Selected Characteristics: 1978 to 1989" (1991).

**U.S. National Center for Health Statistics, "Death Rates . . . 1978 to 1989."

*"Death Rates . . . 1978 to 1989."

Topic of entire passage: _____

Main idea—a sentence in your own words: _____

Dominant pattern: _____

Summary in your own words (1–3 sentences): _____

_____

_____

Score = number correct × 25.

Score _____%

▶75%

Check answers on p. 350.

## Follow-Up

Now that you have completed these nine practices in essential reading skills, you may want to consider how your skills have improved. Individually, in small groups, or in large groups, you may want to consider the following questions.

1.  Which one of the reading skills you have practiced now seems easiest for you?
2.  Which skill(s) do you need to practice further?
3.  How would you evaluate your summary skills now?
4.  Which organizational patterns are still difficult for you to identify as you read? Why do you believe this is so?

## Internet Activity

Use the Internet to find out more information about essential reading skills. Break up into groups of four or five to answer the following questions. Go to the online Writing Center at Marist College and find information on study-skills habits. Then return to your group with your information.

1.  What new information on essential reading skills did you find?
2.  How does this information differ from what you learned about essential reading skills in this chapter?
3.  Describe how you located this information.

**C H A P T E R   2**

# Preview Skimming

*T*his chapter presents the first of several "special" skills in the book, one that takes little time but offers large rewards. Preview skimming is a crucial first step in all efficient reading.

Previewing gives you a unified view of reading material, a sense of the whole, well before you plunge into its details, difficult vocabulary words, and so on. With previewing, you will see the forest before the individual trees.

| *Why?* | *How to (book, article):* |
|---|---|

**Why?**

- Arouse interest
- Prove what you know
- Increase comprehension
- Double reading rate

**How to (book, article):**

- **FIND:**

| **1** Title, source | **2** Subheads | **3** Graphics |
|---|---|---|
| **4** Difficulty | **5** Structure | **6** Ask or find questions |

# INTRODUCTION TO PREVIEW SKIMMING

. . . . . . . . . . . . . . . . . . .

## CHECKLIST OF SYMPTOMS

Do you often

_____ 1. miss the last items in a test because you never turned the page over?

_____ 2. start studying a textbook chapter at midnight without realizing it is seventy-five pages long?

_____ 3. think your paperback dictionary is incomplete because you never noticed the separate lists at the end?

_____ 4. ignore completely the table of contents and other front matter of your textbooks?

_____ 5. mistake a novel for nonfiction because you never read the back cover?

If you checked one or more of these symptoms, you have a lot of company. This chapter is the first in a series that will, we hope, change you from a passive and incurious reader to an active, efficient one. Ideally, you will learn to check everything out *before* starting to read or study.

To back up a little: In Chapter 1, you reviewed the basic skills essential for good reading comprehension. You also practiced the next level or step: how to make sound inferences, recognize common organizational patterns, and summarize the writer's ideas in your own words. If you have been reading for years, none of this should have struck you as "new."

On the other hand, preview skimming, while instinctive for some students, may well be new to you. Like the essential skills presented in Chapter 1, you will use previewing from here on in the chapter introductions and reading selections. Unlike the essential skills, previewing is the first step toward increasing not only your reading comprehension but your *rate* or *speed* as well. Many students find that previewing allows them to read average informational prose twice as fast as usual, with no loss of comprehension. In fact, their comprehension usually improves.

. . . . . . . . . . . . . . . . . . .

## WHAT IS PREVIEW SKIMMING?

As you may know, to *skim* means to pass lightly and quickly over something. We distinguish between *two kinds of skimming: preview* and *overview*. Neither kind is true reading, as will be explained in Chapter 3. Some experts call skimming techniques "selective reading," "semi-reading," or "skip-reading."

In this chapter, we concentrate on preview skimming only. Since "pre-" means "before," a preview skim is your first view of the article, chapter, or book, before you actually read the entire work. Other experts may call it "pre-reading" or "reading prep." An especially thorough form of previewing is advised when you study-read; you will learn to "survey" in Chapter 6. However, a briefer preview will do for lighter materials in which we can read everything rapidly (Chapter 3), or that we are overview skimming for main ideas only (Chapter 4). For these materials, you will be asked to spend only a few seconds to a minute on your preview. As such, you will be reading at rates over 800 words per minute (wpm) when you preview skim.

Whatever the expository style of a piece or the amount of time you spend on it, preview skimming will probably be your single most effective tool for increasing your reading proficiency. Reading a work doggedly from the opening word is like driving around in a strange city without a map. If you have unlimited time for driving (reading), and if you like being surprised and confused, then you should not look at a map first (you should not preview your reading first).

Students often object that they have no time to preview. But consider that if you start with a preview, you will be able to go back and read a text in half the time you would have, and with better comprehension.

They also object that previewing ruins a good story or novel. Of course, no one wants to come in at the climax of an adventure movie or read a detective novel backward. But we are assuming you took this course not to find out how to entertain yourself better, but rather, how to do your necessary reading better—the piles of textbooks, required reading, and background reading that make you an educated and informed person. And, if you are like most students, you are under time pressure.

Also, if you were to study an assigned film or novel prior to writing a critical analysis of it, you would gain a great deal by preview skimming all the way to the end, because you could then interpret details in their larger context as you watch or read them for the first time.

Specifically, what do you gain from preview skimming before reading? A good preview should

1. arouse your interest in the content; raise questions in your mind that you expect to be answered in your reading.
2. show you what you already know about the subject so you can see where you are starting from. Learning can occur only on top of prior learning or contexts; that is, we cannot learn about a subject if we know absolutely nothing to start with. In reading, what we bring *to* the page lets us draw *from* the page.
3. tell you the length and difficulty of the piece, as well as the mental attitude you need to learn the content; prepare you for the time you will need for reading; point out the main ideas and organization.
4. as a bonus, double your reading rate with no loss of comprehension when you return to the text and read it carefully.

. . . . . . . . . . . . . . . . . . . . . .

## HOW TO PREVIEW SKIM—IN GENERAL

First, time yourself. If you do not, you will find yourself reading every word slowly and carefully, just as you have always done. Second, consciously direct your eyes to key areas only. This will be hard to do at first, but remember that you preview in order to comprehend better when you return and read. Previewing is not reading. Tell yourself to look only at the following:

1. title; subtitle (if any); photos or graphics (if any)
2. lead, if any (short summary in italics or large print at beginning); introduction or beginning
3. author, plus his or her credentials; date and source (when and where published)

An intelligent preview covers the highlights of a selection. Do not worry about missing any content—remind yourself that you will return in a moment to read carefully for every detail. Also, if you preview skim first, then read, you will be reading the most important parts twice, an excellent technique for comprehension and learning. You will aim for 100 percent comprehension of what you actually preview skim.

How much time should you spend on preview skimming? Here are some suggestions:

| *Selection Length* | *Preview Skim for* |
| --- | --- |
| up to one page | 10–20 seconds |
| several pages; one chapter | $\frac{1}{2}$–2 minutes |
| entire book | 15–20 minutes |

A few seconds or minutes is not much time to invest for more thorough and efficient comprehension.

As with all the techniques in this book, practice during the school year will teach you to preview skim with more control and purpose and to gain more content from previewing.

. . . . . . . . . . . . . . . . . . . . .

## HOW TO PREVIEW A BOOK

Actually, you have already previewed a book if you have ever flipped through a paperback before buying it. It can be done in as few as five minutes, or even two. But we will show you how to preview more alertly and systematically in books required for course work.

- *Assigned novel:* A novel has a plot, and plots are time-sequenced, or chronological, events. Be sure to preview skim in only one direction, from beginning to end. Read the first chapter carefully. Then read with care the beginnings and the endings of the following chapters. Finally, read carefully the last chapter.

This takes self-discipline—previewing is not browsing. Also, do not expect a quick preview to make everything clear to you. What it will do, beyond the usual benefit of unity, coherence, and wholeness, is (1) show you length, writing style, and degree of difficulty; (2) introduce you to setting, time period, elapsed time of plot, major characters; and (3) reveal the culmination, or climax.

After you preview, start again and read the entire novel carefully. You will find that the book flows well and that your concentration and memory have improved. You will also save time.

- *Course textbook:* It is absolutely *essential* that you preview skim any textbook before studying it. Otherwise, you may end up like the student who spent several weeks wrestling with homework problems in a text before discovering that half the answers had been in the appendix all along. No student need fall into that trap.

  *Note:* If you have not previewed this fifth edition of *Steps,* either on your own or in class, it is not too late, because Chapter 1 was mostly a review.

Turn to Practice 2.1 on page 41.

## HOW TO PREVIEW AN ARTICLE OR OTHER SHORT WORK

Previewing an article is less strenuous, of course, than examining the framework of an entire book. However, the approach is the same: Focus on the beginning, graphics, major divisions (marked by transitions), and the ending. In the next practice, see what you can glean from these key extracts of published articles and note the questions you would expect to answer if you went back to read carefully.

Turn to Practice 2.2 on page 41.

## SUMMARY

Preview skimming is a logical first step for reading all printed material, unless you are reading for pure enjoyment. Whether it is a one-page test or an entire textbook, whether you spend a few seconds or a few minutes, you should PIF—"preview it first." Previewing introduces you to the length, content, and structure of a work before you settle down to read it for comprehension. It lets you see "the big picture" before you slog through the details, so that the careful reading that follows will be deeper and more efficient.

Like summarizing, the skill of previewing informational prose is considered somewhat advanced, because it requires proficiency in basic skills. (Refer to Chapter 1 for any needed review.)

When used on study materials such as textbooks, the preview technique has to be systematic and thorough. One study system calls it a "survey." In materials that are less dense but still expository, many skilled previewers find they can nearly double their reading speed without any loss of—and often with a gain in—total comprehension.

Continuing from Chapter 3, you will be asked to preview skim or survey every selection in the book. However, you will not truly benefit from this tool until you no longer pick up a textbook chapter, article, or business report and begin by reading it word by word. Having acquired the PIF habit, you will preview it first.

## SUMMARY BOX: PREVIEW SKIMMING

| What? | Why? | Acceptable Comprehension | Acceptable Rate |
|---|---|---|---|
| A preview introducing you to a work's length, content, and structure | To prepare for a more thorough reading | 100% of what your eyes see | Over 800 wpm |

# PRACTICES:
## PREVIEW SKIMMING

Answers for these two practices are not provided in Appendix C. Sample answers are available from your instructor.

2.1 PREVIEWING A TEXTBOOK—TWO-MINUTE STANDING SKIM
2.2 PREVIEW SKIMMING ARTICLES

## 2.1 PREVIEWING A TEXTBOOK—TWO-MINUTE STANDING SKIM

Stand (do not sit), hold *Steps*, note your beginning time or wait for your instructor's signal, then start learning all you can about this textbook in two minutes. Look for title, subtitle (if any), authors, date published, number of pages, apparent audience for the book, major divisions, number and titles of chapters, graphics (if any), front matter (prefaces, table of contents), back matter (footnotes, glossary, indexes), typical style and layout, any print on the front and back covers, any answer keys in back, any unusual material. After two minutes, sit down and close the book.

Now, *without looking back at the book*, "recite" what you know about the book on a separate piece of paper. You may instead "tell a friend"—pair off with another student and take turns recalling what you both learned.

Because you already know a lot about reading, much of the book's contents make sense. Do not worry if you cannot recall everything. You will get better as you practice. For instance, you probably noticed which section of a text provides answers for most of the items on our list. In any case, our main point is that you have familiarized yourself with the book and can more easily gain what you want from it.

**Warning:** Did you notice the many sections of *Steps* that are *timed?* Please *do not read ahead, now or later, in any timed practices or selections.* They are not tests. We have carefully set them up according to number of words and minutes/seconds allotted for reading. If you read or even preview any timed materials before your instructor schedules them, you will completely invalidate your speed or comprehension scores. Worse, you will not benefit from the step by step guidance provided by your class and instructor.

Score: Answers will vary.

## 2.2 PREVIEW SKIMMING ARTICLES

Imagine you plan to read each of the following informative articles. First, you skim through quickly, noting the key parts presented here. Time yourself, allowing only 30–40 seconds to read each set. Then answer the informal questions that follow.

### Example

Article found in "Investigations" (current research) section of university magazine. Title: "Talking Hands." One page, about 12 paragraphs. Three photos of a man obviously talking and waving his hands around. Familiar—something everybody does.

Short lead: "More than just outlets for nervous energy, hand gestures reveal the inner workings of the mind."

Beginning: "linguistics professor and psychology chair McNeill". . . . Book, *Hand and Mind: What Gestures Reveal About Thought.* . . . "some surprising discoveries about the nature of gestures. . . ." "relationship between gesture and speech. . . ."

Middle: "'The key . . . is that we have to watch to hear. . . .'" "There's more to gestures than. . . ." "From careful study of these videotapes. . . ." "also studied whole categories of hand movements with other functions. . . ." "Another category is. . . ." "A third category. . . ." "Another narrative gesture. . . ."

Ending: "Now that he understands just how unified speech and gesture are . . . he can use that knowledge to understand a new subject. . . ."*

Did you finish in 40 seconds? If not, reread the quoted excerpts again, making sure to stay within the time limit.

Your preview skim would tell you that this is a book review, the target audience is university educated, and the book is scholarly (based on research). The subject—gesturing with our hands when we talk—is familiar, so the review and the book will not be completely incomprehensible to you. In any case, the preview prepared you to be an alert reader of this rather difficult article and perhaps aroused your interest in the book itself.

Now preview Article 1 in the same manner. Give yourself only 30 seconds, then try to answer the questions without looking back.

### Article 1

Found in travel magazine. Five pages. Heavenly photos. Title: "One Week in Paradise—the Island of Kauai, Hawaii."

Beginning: Spring Week. . . . College credit. . . . Go with group of 25 students, save money.

Middle: Friendly couple as leaders. . . . Stay in public campgrounds. . . . See the island as other tourists never do. . . . Learn plants, geology, ancient customs by day. . . . Evenings: you're free to do as you wish. . . . Happy campers—snapshots, reports, testimonials. . . . "You don't want to miss this!"

Ending: Cost (very small print): only $1,800, includes airfare from East coast, paid in advance, many restrictions.

Were you able to preview in 30 seconds or less? If not, try again.

---

*D. L., "Talking Hands," *University of Chicago Magazine*, June 19, 1994, 13. Review of David McNeill, *Hands and Mind* (Chicago: University of Chicago Press, 1992).

1. What was the target audience for this article? Are you part of it?
2. Would you want to go back and read the article carefully? What part would be most crucial?

Now, give yourself 40 seconds to preview Article 2.

## Article 2

Found on science-news page in daily paper. Title: "Ice Core May Hold Key to the Future." Two columns, over twenty short paragraphs.

Lead: "Scientists read the layers to learn where we've been, where we're headed." No subheads spaced through article. Many facts, numbers.

Beginning: "Frozen in prehistoric layers of ice, buried deep in the surface of the world's largest island, is a time machine. Led by a professor from the University of New Hampshire, teams of scientists are analyzing sections of an ice core extracted through five years of drilling in Greenland."

Middle: "one day tell us what the future holds . . . now, what they tell us about our past. . . ." "Like the rings in a cross section of tree trunk . . ." "'Ice is like a book. . . .'" "250,000 years old. . . ." "climate records. . . ." "'We have to understand the future. . . .'" "That can be determined by correlating the core with ones drilled in other parts of the world. . . ." "Some scientists hope to take prehistoric bacteria from the ice. . . ."

Ending: "But . . . it would take 15 years to get those kinds of records; interpreting them will take still longer."*

Were you able to preview within 40 seconds? If not, try again.

1. What kind of readers are targeted in this news item? How can you tell?
2. What do you already know about the subject matter, making it possible for you to learn when you reread the item?
3. What questions would you expect to answer when you read for details?

A personal question: Did the preview arouse your curiosity?
Now, give yourself 40 seconds to preview Article 3.

## Article 3

Found in a Catholic news journal. Title: "Humanizing the Debate: The Dialogue Experience in Wisconsin." Two pages, well-developed paragraphs.

Lead: "Group Forms to Exchange Views on Abortion." No graphics or subheads.

Beginning: "Wisconsin . . . the 'Dialogue Experience'. . . ." "Begun by small group of family therapists. . . ."

Middle: Two sides, pro-choice and pro-life, don't usually get chance to talk to each other . . . no progress . . . tragic. Therapists are trying to get dialogue going. . . . They set up meetings, invited opponents, discussed abortion.

---

*San Luis Obispo County Telegram*, September 11, 1993, 1.

Rule: nobody allowed to try to change views of others. . . . The two groups found out they have more in common than they thought. . . . The discussions changed their perceptions of each other. . . . Conversations will continue. . . .

Ending: no miracle, but . . . may be model for future dialogue?*

Were you able to preview in 40 seconds or less? If not, try again.

1.  Is the date (Autumn 1992) important to the issue under discussion? Why or why not?
2.  What questions did your preview raise about the project that you would expect to answer when you read the entire article?
3.  Did the preview arouse your curiosity? Can you explain why or why not?

Now give yourself 40 seconds to preview Article 4.

### Article 4
Found in monthly newsletter of local Sierra Club chapter. Title: "North American Population, Consumption, and Pollution Policies." One-half page, wide column, four paragraphs. No graphics or lead.

Beginning: "Due to overpopulation, overconsumption (most profligate society in history), and excessive pollution, the U.S. now exceeds its carrying capacity. This means that its 'capital' of natural resources is being irreversibly used up at the expense of future generations."

Middle: one-time bonanza of aquifers created during the ice ages is being depleted. . . . 35 of 50 states are overdrafting water supplies. . . . U.S., more than 250 million people, growing faster than ever before. . . . is world's third largest nation and fastest growing developed country, except Ireland. . . . solar energy could sustain less than 100 million Americans. . . . Immigrants currently contribute one-half of net growth. . . . U.S. accepts about half of world's immigrants, more than all other nations combined. . . . If native reproduction dropped low enough, immigration could continue yet not increase overall numbers. . . .

Ending: For the long-term survival of the species and planet Earth, essential that *Homo sapiens* attain a sustainable balance of people, consumption, pollution, and resources as soon as feasible.†

Were you able to preview these in 40 seconds? If not, try again.

1.  Does the "article" sound interesting, or too factual and scholarly?
2.  Of the few facts repeated here, were any new to you?

Score: Answers will vary.

Ask your instructor for sample answers.

---

*Adapted from Maggi Cage, "Humanizing the Debate," *Conscience*, Autumn 1992, 10–11.
†Adapted from an article by Dominic Perello, *Santa Lucian*, October 1993.

## Follow-Up

Now that you have completed these two practices in preview skimming, you may want to consider how your preview-skimming skills have improved. Individually, in small groups, or in large groups, you may want to consider the following questions.

1. What value do you now find in preview skimming a textbook?
2. What value is there in preview skimming an article?
3. Has it become easier for you to skip over large chunks of reading material? If not, why do you think it is still difficult?
4. What areas of preview skimming do you still need to work on?

## Internet Activity

Use the Internet to find out more information about preview skimming. Break up into groups of four or five to answer the following questions. Go to the web site entitled "Virginia Polytechnical Institute Study Skills Self-Help Information" and look for material on study-skills habits. Then return to your group with your information.

1. What new information on previewing textbook material did you find?
2. How does this information complement what you learned about textbook previewing in this chapter?
3. Describe how you located this information.

**CHAPTER 3**

# *Rapid Reading*

*C*hapter 3 continues to build on the reading skills you studied in Chapters 1 and 2. It is the first of two chapters that will teach speeded (time-pressured) reading. In both this chapter and Chapter 4, nearly all the practices and the longer selections are timed exactly, following the general introduction. It is essential that you do not read ahead in any timed sections! In these chapters, you will learn the rationale behind speeded reading, some cautions about it, and a variety of methods to try out. Some of these methods you will eventually adopt as your own.

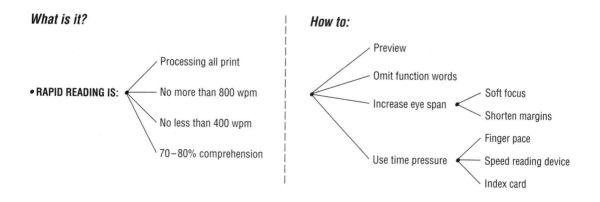

**What is it?**

• RAPID READING IS:
- Processing all print
- No more than 800 wpm
- No less than 400 wpm
- 70–80% comprehension

**How to:**
- Preview
- Omit function words
- Increase eye span
  - Soft focus
  - Shorten margins
- Use time pressure
  - Finger pace
  - Speed reading device
  - Index card

# INTRODUCTION TO RAPID READING

· · · · · · · · · · · · · · · · · ·

## CHECKLIST OF SYMPTOMS

Do you often

_____  1. "hear" every word clearly in your head, even when you read silently?

_____  2. read everything in the same way, at the same speed (that is, slowly and carefully) whether you need to or not?

_____  3. read an article so slowly that by the time you reach the end, you can't remember the beginning?

_____  4. avoid courses in literature or any subject that requires much outside reading?

_____  5. own several good books you have "never had time to finish"?

If you checked one or more of these symptoms, you need to learn how to read more rapidly. By now, you have probably learned the essential reading skills (topic, main idea, support, patterns, and summarizing) presented in Chapter 1. You also know the benefits of PIF—previewing it first—presented in Chapter 2. You may be an A student, enjoy reading widely, or have a successful career.

You are also, apparently, the typical compulsive reader—still reading everything slowly, correctly, "orally" just as you did in grade school. But these days you supposedly read silently, not orally. Also, as an adult, your reading tasks vary tremendously according to your reading material and your purpose for reading it. So it is inappropriate, to say nothing of inefficient, for you to use one single reading style and rate for everything you read. In fact, the one main lesson we hope you carry from this book is that the proficient reader is not plodding and rigid, but alert and flexible.

From now on, the summary box at the end of each introduction will feature this theme of flexibility. You will deliberately be choosing your reading rate and technique according to what you are reading and why you are reading it—the What and the Why.

The old word-by-word method is especially inefficient for the mass of general reading that you do, or should do—newspapers, magazines, and light books. These fairly easy materials do not require study reading. You do not have to memorize today's newspaper or take a test on this week's *Time* magazine.

So why do most of us tend to read light material so slowly? First, when we first learned how to read, we did it slowly. Second, it has become a comfortable habit. Third, we're afraid we'll "miss something" or "lose comprehension" if we skip a few words.

These old habits can slow us down unnecessarily. The paradoxical truth is that *when reading matter is fairly easy, our comprehension actually drops if we read it too slowly.* For one thing, we can miss the flow of the writer's story line or argument. For another, our minds wander if we don't feed them information at optimum speed—that is, we lose concentration. Many studies have shown that average readers can often *double* their rate in general reading with no loss of basic comprehension. Many even *increase* their comprehension because they concentrate better at the higher speeds.

A note of caution: Do not push your speed if you have serious vision or perceptual problems. Further, you should not push to increase your rates if you do not have good basic skills, as reviewed in Chapter 1, at least an average vocabulary or better, and a ninth-grade level of comprehension. Finally, if at your own slow rate, you have scored less than 70 percent on the practices given so far, you are not ready for time-pressured reading. You will find it frustrating, and you may make even more errors in comprehension than before.

Now for the good news. If you have none of these problems, you are ready to venture into rapid reading. Just remember these two things:

1. Make sure your material (the What) is fairly easy for you. You should know something about the subject matter and have no major problems with the vocabulary, style, or ideas. Don't expect to read *Scientific American* or Spinoza's philosophy rapidly and with full comprehension the first time through, unless you are a scientist or philosopher.
2. Make sure your purpose for reading (the Why) is appropriate for rapid reading. Do you need to memorize the contents of the material? Discuss it in detail? Do you want to savor the style? Are you aiming at 100 percent understanding of new, difficult principles, as when you study read a textbook? If so, do not expect a single, fast reading to suffice. Your purpose should not be study, as in Chapter 5, or analysis, as in Chapter 6. Although a single rapid reading prior to study or analysis is often very useful, your purpose when you decide to read rapidly should be general information and enjoyment.

• • • • • • • • • • • • • • • • • •

## *WHAT IS RAPID READING?*

Take the word *reading.* In this book we use it to mean seeing and processing all, or nearly all, the words on the printed page. Tests prove that human eyes can do this only at rates up to *800 wpm (words per minute).* Above this rate, the eyes must skip some words or sentences. So, rates over 800 wpm indicate you are "skip-reading"—skimming—not reading in the strictest sense.

You have already practiced one kind of skip-reading: preview skimming, in Chapter 2. There you learned to read selectively: You focused on the key parts of a work such as graphics, title, introduction, subheads, and ending, and you skipped over nearly everything else. When you read rapidly, however, you will read most of the words on every page and grasp most of the content.

The "rapid" in rapid reading simply means a reading rate faster than normal for the average reader—in other words, speeded or time-pressured reading. The average high-school graduate who is not trained in efficient reading reads general material—newspapers, magazines, easy paperbacks—at 200–300 wpm. To qualify as a rapid reader in this chapter, you should aim for at least *400 wpm*.

The target rates in this chapter, then, range from *400–800 wpm*. One side benefit of reading above 400 wpm is that at these speeds, hearing the words, or subvocalizing, tends to drop out. We simply cannot mentally talk that fast.

If reading rapidly makes you a little anxious, remember the Why of general reading—no tests, no analysis. In fact, you should never aim for 100 percent comprehension of the literal or surface content. Rather, your goal should be only *70–80 percent*. Why so low? First, if you aim for 100 percent comprehension in all your light reading, you will never relax enough to read any faster than you do now. Second, the selections in this chapter, like most of your daily reading, do not matter enough for you to comprehend and retain 100 percent. After all, it is better to read a great deal and be widely informed than to be so letter-perfect that you seldom read or finish anything.

Most of our daily materials are one-dimensional. Because they require a single reading for surface content only, you should read them as rapidly as possible. A single, slow rate prevents you from dipping into all the great material that is out there awaiting your pleasure.

· · · · · · · · · · · · · · · · · · · · ·

## HOW TO READ MORE RAPIDLY

For best results, do not start right in by forcing yourself to read at 800 wpm, especially if you are a habitually slow reader. Instead, read the following six tips and do the practices in order. (Some of the practices require an easy paperback book, so please have one handy before you start.)

As you learn to read easy materials rapidly, you will find that Tips 1, 2, and 3 will become part of your new reading habits. At that point, you can concentrate on increasing your rate with no loss of basic literal comprehension.

**TIP 1**   Approach rapid reading with a relaxed, confident mind-set. First, forget any 100 percent compulsion you may have built up over the years. Remind yourself that in the future, no one is going to test you on your leisure reading. Once you leave this book or course, you will be free to use your rapid reading techniques without fear of test scores. Second, leave the slow rates—100–300 wpm—to talking or reading aloud. Your eyes can see all the words on a page at speeds of up to 800 wpm, and your brain can operate at thousands of words per minute. So, feed yourself printed words at a more challenging pace—400–800 wpm.

**TIP 2**   Trust your sense of closure, or the mind's ability to complete what is incomplete, to "fill in the blanks." All adult readers know enough about English words, sentence patterns and common logic to understand most of the contents of a page even if they do not clearly see every word. Function words—those not essential to literal comprehension—may easily be omitted. Key words—subject and verbs—are important to comprehension. Depending on how concise a writer's style is, we can omit 10–50 percent of the words in ordinary prose without losing any basic literal comprehension.

Turn to Practice 3.1 on page 54, and try reading passages consisting of only key words.

**TIP 3**   Use your eyes efficiently. A slow reader tends to fixate, or focus, on every single word across the line. Yet the average eye span on the printed page is about $1\frac{1}{2}$ inches. By fixating on one point, you can identify many words above, below, and to the sides of that point. This is called using your *peripheral vision*. Fixating less often on a printed line causes less eyestrain. It also guides us toward the prime goal of faster reading, reading the ideas on a page instead of the individual words. To test your own eye span, mark a small $x$ in the middle of this paragraph, and draw a circle around it about $1\frac{1}{2}$ inches in diameter. Can you identify most of the words within the circle without moving your eyes off the $x$?

To increase your eye span, ask your instructor for phrase-reading drills or other materials.

Two popular speed reading techniques will help you increase your visual efficiency:

a.   Soft focus as you read. Do not peer tensely at the words. Relax your eye and face muscles. Let your peripheral vision do more of the work. Look slightly above the line of print, and let your eyes float down the page. Try to read phrases, not each word.

b.   Use shortened margins. Do not fixate on the first and last word of each line. Rather, fixate about a half inch from each margin, letting your peripheral vision pick up the words to the side. Like soft focusing, doing this efficiently takes practice.

Remember, though, that the best eye span and soft focus technique will not by themselves make a proficient rapid reader. Reading takes place in the mind, not in the eyes. As you concentrate on the ideas on a page rather than on each word, and as you increase your rate on easy materials, your mind will become more alert, and you will soon forget what your eyes are doing.

Turn to Practice 3.2 on page 55.

**TIP 4**   Use all the essential reading skills, as presented in Chapter 1. You will need to pay attention to important transitions and other signals and to notice organizational patterns—all signposts on the writer's path. Even when you read rapidly, your goal is to grasp the writer's message as accurately as possible.

Also, PIF—preview it first—for length and structure, as you learned in Chapter 2. Previewing helps with all our reading, but it is crucial in rapid reading. You will never increase your speed if you do not begin with a "map of the territory."

**TIP 5**   Use time pressure. This is an outgrowth of Tip 1. Be confident that your mind can handle print faster than you can talk or read aloud. To read rapidly, you should be physically relaxed but mentally active. Most people find that some tension helps them concentrate on their reading. In fact, skilled rapid readers are not passive and comfortable. In rapid reading, you must be conscious of time passing. So, time yourself, have someone else time you, or work up a little competition with peers.

One tried-and-true way to apply time pressure is to chart your reading rate. As usual, choose a fairly easy book and make sure your purpose is enjoyment. Keeping an accurate list, chart, or graph is essential, since we seldom know just how fast we are reading.

Whether handmade or commercial, rate charts operate the same way. Graphic records of your ups and downs will spur you to faster and more consistent speeds. Even a simple time-bloc record is helpful. With this, you read for a fixed time, then stop, count the pages read, and list or graph the number. Your instructor can provide you with a sample from the teacher's manual. For another chart, see the one at the end of this chapter.

Another easy way to keep your rate over 400 wpm is to time your reading of a paperback book page by page. Because the average paperback page contains 350–450 words, your speed will fall into the lower range of rapid reading if you can read at least one page per minute.

Turn to Practice 3.3 on page 56 for directions on how to time and pace your reading of light paperback books.

**TIP 6**   Use a crutch until you can read rapidly without one. If you try the first five tips and still continue to read easy materials at a word-by-word rate, the following may help you concentrate and speed up:

a.   Use your finger as a pacing device. You can move your index finger rapidly from left to right under each line, down the center of the page, or in a left-to-right spiral motion down the page. These techniques will encourage you to skip unimportant words.

b.   Use a speed reading device set at 400 wpm or higher. You may need to watch filmstrips or a computer screen. The imposed pacing will force you to keep going, no matter how uncomfortable your pace. As such, you will eventually keep up with the machine, comprehending more and more of the content. As soon as the rate feels comfortable, increase it.

c.   Use an index card as your own portable shutter. Place the card at the top of each page and move it down quickly. Like commercial gadgets, the card prevents you from regressing to previous lines of print. Also, by using your arm and hand to move the card down the page, you are more physically engaged in the reading. Unlike other gadgets, an index card is cheap, is easy to carry with you, and can double as a bookmark. Do not forget to use the soft focus and shortened-margin techniques as you move your card down the page.

Turn to Practice 3.4 on page 57 for more directions on using an index-card pacer.

All these crutches—finger, machine, card—help keep your attention on the page and pressure you to read faster. Some readers continue to use their favorite crutch for years, especially when they feel distracted. Eventually, though, it is best if you can really change your old habits of unnecessary slow reading, throw away your crutch, and read general materials at 400–800 wpm simply by using your eyes and mind. Here is a good slogan to keep in mind: "Read the ideas on the page, not the words."

Test your skill by turning to Practice 3.5 on page 57, a mini-selection that will help prepare you for the timed selections to follow.

• • • • • • • • • • • • • • • • • • • • •

## SUMMARY

All of us began reading in the primary grades, with a slow, word-by-word, mainly oral method of reading. This old habit dies hard. However, reading this way does not serve the adult whose reading tasks vary tremendously from easy, light materials to difficult, serious materials. For the former kind of reading—newspapers, magazines, light paperbacks, or so-called general reading—we should develop a faster reading rate. We can physically see and read words up to 800 wpm (above that, we skip or skim). In rapid reading, we aim to read all the material at rates of 400–800 wpm. Also, since the materials are not for study or analysis, we aim for 70–80 percent comprehension, not 100 percent.

In rapid reading, besides changing an old habit, we must build confidence in our ability to read light materials at a faster-than-average rate. With practice, most of us discover that we can double our reading rate with no loss of comprehension. In fact, comprehension often improves because we are reading fast enough to see the material as a whole and to focus on the content. Reading under some time pressure actually helps keep our minds active and interested, rather than become passive and bored.

Here are the six tips for reading light materials more quickly:

1. Have a confident mind-set—forget any 100 percent compulsion and leave the slow rates to talkers and oral readers.
2. Trust your sense of closure.
3. Use your eyes efficiently by soft focusing and shortening your margins.
4. Use all the essential reading skills.
5. Use time pressure.
6. Use a crutch at the beginning.

## SUMMARY BOX: RAPID READING

| What? | Why? | Acceptable Comprehension | Acceptable Rates |
|---|---|---|---|
| light or general reading—newspapers, magazines, most popular paperbacks | enjoyment, keeping up with popular reading, some background reading | 70–80% | 400–800 wpm |

# PRACTICES:
# RAPID READING

Answers for these exercises are available from your instructor, not in the appendix.

3.1 PRACTICE FOR TIP 2, "TRUST YOUR SENSE OF CLOSURE"
3.2 PRACTICE FOR TIP 3, "USE YOUR EYES EFFICIENTLY"
3.3 PRACTICE FOR TIP 5, "USE TIME PRESSURE"
3.4 PRACTICE FOR TIP 6, "USE A CRUTCH"
3.5 PRACTICE IN RAPID READING—MINI-SELECTION

## 3.1 PRACTICE FOR TIP 2, "TRUST YOUR SENSE OF CLOSURE"—KEY-WORD READING, WITH FUNCTION WORDS DELETED

Read through this excerpt quickly. Can you comprehend it?

> Take reading. We use reading mean seeing, processing all words on page. Eyes do this to 800 wpm. Above, eyes skip some words, sentences. Over 800 imply skip reading, not reading.
>
> You practiced skip reading: preview skimming. Learned read selectively, key parts. Skipped nearly everything else. But when rapid read, read most words on every page, grasp most content.

The original passage was written in fairly concise textbook style. Yet even here, by retaining only the key words, we were able to delete almost half the total words (56 of the original 133) and still convey the meaning to a reader.

Next, do some key-word reading in an article you have never seen before:

> Vinegar as food 5,000 years, Babylonians, from date palms. In war—Hannibal, clear boulders in elephants' path; heated rocks, vinegar split them. Vinegar gourmets hold tastings like wine—"clarity, aroma."*

This news item was even more tightly written. But (with difficulty!) we were able to cut the original 80 words down to 30. Again, you could probably understand the content of the original paragraphs.

Now, on your own, try marking the key words of a passage.

1. Start reading the first paragraph of this chapter summary (starting "All of us began . . .") as rapidly as you can, underlining only the key words (p. 53). Do not worry about being precise; this is not a grammar test. Be relaxed and confident that your sense of closure is as good as that of any other English-speaking reader.

---

*Adapted from 80 words of a long article by Caleb Solomon, "Have a Problem? Chances Are Vinegar Can Help Solve It," *Wall Street Journal*, September 30, 1992.

2.  Continue for several paragraphs, picking up speed if you can.
3.  Pause, go back, and silently read only the marked words.
4.  If you are working with a group, read your version to the others to check against serious omissions or distortions.

If you managed to delete most of the inessential words, and you or your listener could comprehend the writer's ideas from your key-word version, you have done the exercise correctly.

## 3.2  PRACTICE FOR TIP 3, "USE YOUR EYES EFFICIENTLY": SOFT FOCUS AND SHORTENED MARGINS

For this practice, you should have an easy-to-moderate paperback book. (You may also substitute earlier pages in this chapter, but please do not use any materials still ahead in the book.)

When you try to soft focus, relax your facial and eye muscles as you read a page of print. Imagine that your eyes are tired or that you're on vacation at the beach—you simply can't peer closely at every word. Yet you're curious about the story, viewpoint, or information before you. Some people find it helpful to look slightly above the line of print (soft focusing on the space above, or "space-reading"). Try letting your eyes drift down a page of this book or a paperback book. Keep in mind that it's okay to miss some words or details.

When you use shortened margins, you are also trying to avoid eyestrain by letting your peripheral vision do some of the work.

1.  Bring out your paperback again—or use an earlier page in this book. With a pencil and ruler (or steady hand), draw a vertical line down both sides of the page, a half inch or less in from the margin.
2.  Begin to read from the top of the page. Consciously relax your facial and eye muscles. Try to soft focus as you read down the page. Try not to fixate (look carefully) outside your two vertical lines. (If you do, simply pull back and read the line again, fixating as often as needed but only between the two lines.) Do try to let your eyes float or drift down the page. Let your mind see the action, get the thoughts. Don't worry about comprehension at this point. It will pick up later, as you become accustomed to reading more rapidly.
3.  Read the page several times this way; try to increase your speed, from 1 minute down to half a minute.
4.  Move onto the next page—you may have memorized the first one already! Mark the shortened-margin lines, remind yourself to soft focus, and practice again.

Spend at least 5 to 10 minutes in each session. You will find that these new eye-use techniques become more comfortable each time you do them. Soon you will no longer need to draw margin lines; your eyes will handle each line efficiently without conscious direction.

Some readers with good peripheral vision eventually fixate an inch or more inside the margins; they read a page in a relaxed meander or zig-zag down the page at 600–800 wpm; and they can still recite nearly all the content of the page! Others are happy if they learn to read at 400 wpm without headaches.

### 3.3   PRACTICE FOR TIP 5, "USE TIME PRESSURE": PAGE-BY-PAGE TIMING

1. Bring out a paperback book again, making sure it is fairly easy fiction or nonfiction. Sit near a watch or clock that has a second hand.
2. Prepare your mind for the "reading mode." If the book is new, read one or two pages carefully without timing. If you are currently reading the book, turn back to a page you have already read.
3. When the second hand is on the minute, start reading from the top of the page. When the minute is up, stop reading.

Did you finish the entire page? If not, start at the top again; read the same page, this time within 1 minute. If you still cannot finish the page, try again, this time reminding yourself to soft focus and shorten the margins. Depending on the density of the print, a one-minute pace should yield from 350 to 450 wpm, a reasonable goal for beginning rapid readers.

4. Move to the top of the next page. Repeat the 1-minute timing down the page. Start at the top of a new page whenever the signal is given. **Important:** If you have not finished the page, do not continue reading to the end after the minute is up. Always skip to the top of the new page. Soon you will be so determined not to miss the ending of a page that you will pressure yourself to reach it in time. Eventually the pace will seem almost normal, and you will comprehend most of what was on the page. In other words, your brain will speed up to grasp the content; you will become an alert and active reader!

Remember that readers are individuals. Success arrives fairly soon for some readers, but for others only after many sessions, discouragements, and encouragements.

Any speed demons who finish before time has sounded must wait for the signal to begin a new page. If this happy state continues, they can switch to half-minute timing—thus doubling their rate to 700–900 wpm. Such a rate in light, general reading should be gratifying to anyone.

Suppose, though, that you still have trouble reading one page per minute or keeping your mind on the book.

5. Optional. Try using your finger as a pacing device. When the clock's second hand is on the minute, draw your finger smoothly down the middle of the page. Read the print one or two lines above your finger. To make sure you do not fixate on margins, use very little side motion (a slight wiggle is permissible). Allow your finger to draw your (soft-focused) eyes down from line to line. Continue reading down the page even if you feel your comprehension lagging. Only by repeatedly forcing yourself to read at this pace will you reach the 1-minute-per-page rate.

Always remember that in any pacing or charting program, you must not allow yourself extra time. Without a sense of time pressure, you will simply revert to your slow, careful, passive habits.

In their rapid-reading practice, some students use several methods at once. They first draw shortened-margin lines down several pages, then go back and time their reading of each page, all the while using a finger to pace steadily down the center. Others preview skim ahead for five to ten pages for general structure, then go back and time each page. Is that cheating? Absolutely not. Whatever works to increase your rate is legal.

One last note: If you want to know your typical words-per-minute rate in your current book, count the number of words printed on three separate, average-looking pages, and then take the average of the counts.

## 3.4    PRACTICE FOR TIP 6, "USE A CRUTCH": INDEX CARD

Choose any plain card, preferably no larger than the print portion of your book page. Rest your hand comfortably on it. Starting at the top of a page, draw the card down over your reading and read below the card. Do not hold the card *beneath* your reading, because you could then easily regress.

You are allowed to pause for a moment to let your thoughts catch up, but never move the card and peek to see what you have missed. In fact, you may have to take The Pledge: "I will not lift the card. Anything I have missed is lost forever." The psychological gimmick here is that if you know you must read below your card, you will move it down at a realistic and steady pace and will keep your mind on your reading.

As usual, remember to use soft focus (but an alert, aggressive mind) and shortened margins. Some students draw short lines up from the bottom edge on their cards to correspond with the shortened-margin areas of the page. These lines continuously remind them not to fixate on the empty margins. Other students prefer to draw the usual lines directly on each page, at least at the beginning. Eventually, you may be among those who do their best and fastest light reading using only their eyes and brains.

Now, try the index-card technique on your paperback book. After a few pages, begin to add one-minute timing per page.

Here are some general points drawn from years of reader experience about methods designed to increase rate:

1.  Don't give up easily. It took years for you to develop your present reading methods, and it will take more than a few days to change them.
2.  When you practice a new technique, continue the session for at least a half hour to an hour.
3.  Practice your new methods frequently—once a day if possible.

## 3.5    PRACTICE IN RAPID READING—MINI-SELECTION

Think about all the tips you have just read. Then try reading the following short selection at a rapid reading rate (400 wpm or faster). Time yourself very precisely. Even though this selection is short, PIF—preview it first, in the recommended time. (Later, for the timed selections, we'll ask you to do formal previews with separate quizzes.)

As stated in the introduction to this chapter, rapid reading will yield about 80 percent of the content. This little reading quiz covers the main ideas, not every little detail. Check answers with your instructor.

As you can imagine, it's no fair reading the questions beforehand, or looking back for answers! (Maybe cover them with a card.) You should get 100 percent correct with little trouble.

Preview skim in 30 seconds. Rapid read in 1 minute (= 580 wpm) or 1 minute, 15 seconds (1:15) (= 465 wpm).

## CREATING A LIVING LEGACY

*by Leslie Ansley (580 words)*

1   The nine children of David and Dovetta Wilson gave birth to a tradition that honors their past and nods toward the future—a scholarship fund set up in their parents' name.

2   All recently gathered with their mother at the Staten Island, N.Y., home of Bernard Wilson, 38, chaplain for Naval Station New York. Six still live within 30 miles of their childhood home in Harlem. The others are sprinkled around the country.

3   But distance is no barrier to communication. The brothers and sisters meet by conference call monthly to discuss the David & Dovetta Scholarship Fund, established last year. They grant nine scholarships, representing each of the siblings, to students educated at public schools who demonstrate qualities their parents instilled in them: a sense of dignity, concern for community, faith, and a desire for excellence in education.

4   They started by contributing $1,000 each, and last May gave away about $3,000 in scholarships, ranging from $125 to $1,000.

5   "Dad had always stressed doing something in the community," says David Jr., 48, who owns five Hallmark stores in New York and Baltimore.

6   David Sr. died at age 70 in 1985. He had been a trackman for the New York City Transit Authority and had finished through the eighth grade in South Carolina. Dovetta Wilson, 68, a cafeteria aide, went as far as the fifth grade in Alabama. Yet among their children, seven have four-year college degrees, five have postgraduate degrees and two are graduates of business institutes.

7   The path the Wilson brothers and sisters chose led from a small three-bedroom apartment in a Harlem housing project. David and Dovetta Wilson ran a strict household. The children's outdoor playing hours were restricted; TV was limited to an hour a night. And their mother kept them busy cleaning house, says Carolyn Blair, 28, an actress. "On Saturdays, we would wash walls and clean closets. We had the cleanest walls in the projects. We would rather go to school than stay home, because Mom would make us wash something."

8   A strong influence was the Revival Temple Church of God in Christ in Harlem, which they attended every night and all day on Sundays. "We would go to church on Friday night," says Amelia Mullen, a 45-year-old teacher in Brooklyn, "and stay on our knees until Sunday."

9   Education was equally stressed. "Each kid had to give our parents a high school diploma," says Ruby Waluyn, 34, a senior trainer at New York Life. "That was like payment for growing up in a house and having good food and good shelter."

10   Bernard sometimes speaks of his father as if in awe. "My father had a city job, but he managed to feed all of us. There were 11 people in that house, but we were never left wanting. And when someone else would come along, he'd just say, 'Add more water to the soup.'"

11   The Wilsons are motivated by a desire to help others, but the fund also makes financial sense, says Stan Chadsey, president of Capital Planning Associates in New York City. "It's fully sheltered," he says. "There is also the income tax deduction, and no gift tax because there's an un-limited charitable deduction for gifts."

12   Next year, the Wilsons hope to award nine $1,000 scholarships to students around the country. "It does seem awfully altruistic, but we are giving back," says Charles, 33.

13   Dovetta Wilson, 68, sits through all this, nodding silently and smiling, clearly proud of her children. "You can search all over the world, and you cannot find any children like these. I hope one day they'll be able to sit back and look at what I'm looking at."

14   A final question: Do they all still go to church? Yes, Bernard says, "but not as long."

Leslie Ansley, "Creating a Living Legacy," *USA Weekend*, November 22–24, 1991, 8. © 1991 USA Weekend, Reprinted with permission.

• • • • • • • • • • • • • • • • • • • • • • • • • • • • • •

Write in or circle the correct answers:

1.  The __9__ adult children of the Wilsons give away __nine__ scholarships, one for each of them.

2.  In raising their children, the parents stressed two major elements:
    a. church
    b. education
    c. martial arts

Check answers with your instructor.

# TIMED SELECTIONS: RAPID READING

The ten full-length timed selections in this chapter, as well as those in Chapter 4, may be done with an instructor or on your own. Here are the What and Why of this activity:

1. *What* are these materials? Most of these selections are fairly light and therefore suitable for rapid reading. We hope you find them enjoyable as well. If any content greatly interests you, do not slow down; tell yourself you can always reread it later.

2. *Why* are you reading them? You are learning to (1) change your reading habits for greater efficiency and flexibility, (2) read light, general materials more rapidly. Be assured that the comprehension quizzes that follow will also be fairly general—no fine details or analysis.

To help you focus more easily on the content from one selection to the next, all selections have the same general topic as that of the Mini-Selection—"the family."

For maximum usefulness, please follow the step-by-step instructions carefully. Do not skip any step or change its order.

First, do not preread any selection. This is a hard rule to follow, especially for people who love to read anything and everything. However, to help you change your reading habits, we must set up a rigorous pattern for you to follow.

Second, time yourself precisely, to the nearest 15 seconds. We indicate the times required to reach preview skimming or rapid reading rates, and you should try to stay within them. If, on a first try, your time is less or more than ours, find your wpm rate in the rate table at the back of the book.

Finally, do not preread the quizzes or refer back to the selections while you answer the questions. Our questions will not be tricky or require more knowledge than can be expected of an average preview or rapid reading. You are welcome to reread any material afterward. Place the answers to each quiz in the box that follows it.

As you know, the target scores for comprehension quizzes are marked with an arrow ▶. The preview questions are so reasonable that we expect you to get 100 percent on them. For the reading quizzes, a score of 70–80 percent is the accepted sign of success.

The answers to the odd-numbered quizzes are given on pages 350–351. Please ask your instructor for the answers to the even-numbered quizzes.

Record your rapid-reading comprehension scores and your rates on the progress chart on page 117.

Before you begin these selections, you may want to consider the following general questions on the family. Answering these questions will help uncover the beliefs that you and your peers already have concerning the family. You may want to respond to these questions individually or discuss them in small or large groups in class:

1. How would you define *family?*
2. What are parents' responsibilities to grown children?
3. When is the best time to get married?
4. Have families had the same structure throughout history?
5. What are some of the problems facing families today?

TIMED SELECTIONS: RAPID READING

1. "Thanks Giving," p. 61
2. "The Pain of Men," p. 64
3. "Back to the Nest," p. 68
4. "Together Again," p. 73
5. "Giving Their Best—Again," p. 78
6. "Life Is Precious—Even at the End," p. 83
7. "Marriage: When and Why," p. 88
8. "Life in the Traditional European Family," p. 94
9. "Modernization and Romance, Kinship, and Divorce," p. 101
10. "Everyplace, Enemies of the Family," p. 107

## SELECTION 1

Your first timed selection is a well-written short essay by a social worker. Because it deserves more than a rapid reading, you may want to reread it after the exercise is over. Use some or all of the tips you have seen in this chapter.

Follow these steps:

A. Preview skim the essay. Then answer the three-item preview quiz.
B. Read the essay rapidly. Then answer the four-item reading quiz.

## A. Preview Skimming

Preview the essay in 45 seconds (= 907 wpm). Focus on its title, length, and source; glance at the beginning and end to get a sense of the essay's content. Then take the preview quiz without looking back at the essay.

. . . . . . . . . . . . . . . . . . . .

███████████    *THANKS GIVING*

. . . . . . . . . . . . . . . . . . . .

███████████    *by Anji Citron (680 words)*

1      We have a tradition in our family for Thanksgiving. It's called the "I'm Thankful" basket. It started several years ago when the turkey was in the oven—that is, when everyone got a bit giddy from hunger and had cabin fever as the wind howled outside. . . .

2      The basket sits on a table in the living room, and many small pieces of paper and pens sit next to it. Throughout the day, anyone who wishes may write (or dictate if too young to write) something for which he or she feels thankful. Later, between the turkey and the pecan pie (still giddy but moving much more slowly now) we pass the basket around the table and each person reads a few offerings. Some are somber, others are about the pie, and many are very very silly.

3      An "I'm Thankful" basket is one of many ways parents can bring the concept of thankfulness and reverence into their home. But it would be a shame to limit this expression to only once a year. There should be daily opportunities for us to reflect on where we are, what we have, and how we feel about our lives.

4      Many families say some sort of blessing before meals. Families thank God, or some the earth. Others simply sit together in silence for a moment before they eat. Reflecting on how the food has come to us is an important beginning to a meal. How did that food come to be on our table? This is a question that, if we really focus on its enormity, should fill us all with reverence and awe for the world of nature and the endeavors of human beings.

5      A ritual before eating can be a wonderful way to sustain a feeling of family togetherness. If you would like to start one in your family, try one of the following. Hold hands and "pass a squeeze" around the table. Memorize a short poem that you say before the meal; quite soon everyone will learn it and say it along with you. Learn one of many songs about thankfulness. Have everyone say "thank you" for one thing on the table. Or simply close your eyes and breathe for a moment, all together, before digging in.

6      Another opportunity for ritual thankfulness is before bedtime. Children can talk about their favorite part of the day. Both parents and children can say a blessing before sleep. Doing this ritual by candlelight makes for a lovely, restful ceremony.

7      Everytime we go outside there are occasions for incorporating thankfulness and reverence. The earth is literally "awe-some"; so often, we pass right by without seeing. But our children notice, and if we allow them to slow us down we can find constant opportunities to feel wonder. Find a spot away from "civilization" to sit with your child. How many colors do you see from that one place? How many moving, tiny creatures? How many shapes and textures? Smells and sounds? Kids are naturally in touch with this "non-civilized" part of the world, but instruments of modern technology (television and computers in particular) have taken away the simple wonders for all too many kids and adults. Spiders building webs, ants carrying huge loads on their backs, cloud formations floating by, light reflecting on the water, sunrises and sunsets . . . there is no video that compares with the real thing.

8      Our lives are often so fast-paced that we miss many chances to breathe together and think about all the riches we have. The earth is wonder-filled. Having respect and devotion for the natural world can be a value we bring to our families at mealtimes, bedtime, and many other times throughout the day and year. Let your

children find some special "nature items" to decorate the table each night; create a place in a shared room to display seasonal objects like colored leaves and pinecones. Spend time outside with your children, without a watch on! Take walks and really look around you. Learn songs that speak of the wonders of the world. Breathe and give thanks, this month and throughout the year. Blessings on all of your families.

Anji Citron, MSW, CSW, "Thanks Giving." *Northwest Family*, November 1996. Used by permission of the author.

• • • • • • • • • • • • • • • • • • • • • • • • • • • •

1. The essay's date of publication is 1996.
   a. true
   b. false
2. There are several subheads within the piece to help the reader.
   a. true
   b. false
3. The writer is talking about the ways families can give thanks for this beautiful world.
   a. true
   b. false

---

**Sel. 1**   P-Skim                     1. ____

**Time**   :45 = 907 wpm          2. ____

**Score**   ____%                      3. ____

▶ 100%                      **Check answers on p. 350.**

**Score** = number correct × 33.

---

## B. Rapid Reading

Write your starting time in the next answer box, or wait for the signal to begin reading. Try to finish reading in 1 minute and 30 seconds (453 wpm). If your reading time differs from this suggested rate, record it to the nearest 15 seconds. Then look up your wpm rate in the rate table on page 343.

1. The main idea of this essay is that
   a. Thanksgiving is a misunderstood holiday
   b. families do not know how to give thanks to each other
   c. families need to provide ways to give thanks regularly
2. Which way of giving thanks is *not* mentioned in the essay?
   a. the "I'm Thankful" basket
   b. taking your children shopping
   c. taking your children outside to give thanks to the beauty of nature

3. According to the writer, who seems to notice the beauty of nature most easily?
   a. parents
   b. children
   c. grandparents
4. The author suggests
   a. we live in a hectic world
   b. Thanksgiving should be celebrated every day
   c. both a and b

---

| Sel. 1   R-Read | 1. _____ |
| --- | --- |
| **Finish** ___:___ | **2.** _____ |
| **Start**    ___:___ | **3.** _____ |
| **Time**    ___:___ | **4.** _____ |
|      min    sec | Check answers on p. 350. |
| **Rate**___wpm | **Record rate and score on p. 117.** |
| **Find rate on p. 343.** | |
| **Score** ___% | |
| ▶ 75% | |
| **Score** = number correct × 25. | |

---

 C. For Discussion and Writing

The timed selections throughout this textbook will be followed by questions that are neither timed nor based on immediate recall of details from the selection. To answer these questions, you may reread the selection and refer back to it as needed.

1. What is the dominant writing pattern of this essay? Provide two or three examples to support your choice.
2. What is your response to Citron's suggestions? Do you think they are realistic? Impractical? Explain.

• • • • • • • • • • • • • • • • • • •

## SELECTION 2

Your second timed selection for rapid reading is a well-written essay by an expert in gender relations. Reprinted in other publications, it deserves more than a rapid reading; remember, you can always return and reread after the timing is over. For the present, PIF and then read for 70–80 percent—not 100 percent—of the ideas it contains.

Follow these steps in reading the selection:

A. Preview skim the essay, then answer the three-item preview quiz.
B. Read the essay rapidly, then answer the four-item reading quiz.

## A. Preview Skimming

Preview the essay in 45 seconds (= 1,200 wpm). All you have to do is get a "map of the territory"—focus on the title, subtitle, length, source, subheads within the body of the work, and possibly the ending. Then take the preview quiz, without looking back at the essay.

## THE PAIN OF MEN: AS SEEN THROUGH THE EYES OF A WOMAN THERAPIST

*by Maryhelen Snyder (900 words)*

1 A decade or so ago, I was at a workshop where women were encouraged to tell men what it was like to grow up female in our society. It was a moving experience to have the caring attention of our "brothers" as we allowed ourselves to feel and describe the oppression of women as we had personally experienced it.

2 Many years later, at a workshop under the same auspices, men were invited to share what it was like to grow up male. It had taken that long to ask men the same question because *there was an assumption, shared by both* men and women, that the women had been far more hurt than the men—and further, that to ask men what growing up had been like for them, was equivalent to asking Whites to talk about their painful experiences in the same setting where Blacks had just talked about the pain in their lives.

3 Telling what it was like to grow up in our culture seemed more difficult for men than for women. They spoke more stoically, less emotionally—as though it didn't matter all that much that many of them had been physically hurt or physically scared at school or in the streets, that they'd grown up knowing they might well go to war to kill or be killed, that they'd felt ashamed of crying, that they'd often watched their fathers weighted down with responsibility, that they frequently perceived work as duty rather than delight, that they hadn't known much about how to get close to men or women, and that there seemed to be lots of taboos against both.

## SOCIETY SAYS: DON'T ACKNOWLEDGE PAIN

4 Lately, in my practice, I've been noticing that the deepest pain for men seems to lie in the fact that it hasn't been okay to notice the pain. As Alice Miller points out in her book, Thou Shalt Not Be Aware, the most destructive parental and societal message is one that says not to notice, or remember, that one has been hurt. A human being can cope with pain if s/he is allowed to feel it, express it, confront it, process it. But when the person is told, as children and men and women

have been told for centuries, that there is nothing to complain about, that all is as it should be, then the pain is suppressed—and becomes far more destructive.

5      Many women have been focusing during the last decades on what they feel and what they want. Perhaps because men have only started doing this more recently, the men I see in therapy (more than most women) feel "split" into a "good" responsible self and a "bad" impulsive self. And neither the "good" nor the "bad" feels to them like it's who they really are. Men report feeling "dead" or "empty" with greater frequency than women.

## A LONGING TO ESCAPE

6      They also report a great longing to escape from both the pressures and the emptiness, a longing to be "left alone" by the world, and specifically by the primary women in their lives. As women pursue them for "more relationship," men often retreat into addictive practices that either permit relief from the need to perform or give them the confidence that makes them believe they can perform.

7      I find that as I deal more fully with my own issues as a woman, I can hear more fully what men are feeling. I am more interested and less judgmental. And I can see more clearly the obvious truth, a truth I have always known about my own sons, that men are good. This is an important truth to acknowledge because sensitive men, as members of the sex that has historically been dominant and oppressive, tend to feel guilty. Women, in expressing their pain to men, have—even without intending to—implied that men are bad.

8      As a therapist, I help couples really talk with each other, really listen to each other. When they do, each of them discovers in themselves, and in one another, an almost bottomless grief. Both sexes have been painfully dehumanized by cultural practices we are always trying to understand and change. But the dehumanization of each sex has taken a different form. I appreciate all that women have been learning about themselves and teaching men. And I am glad that *men are now taking more and more time to learn about men and teach women.*

9      Toward the close of Mark Medoff's play, *Children of a Lesser God*, when the intensity of difference and lack of communication has reached its agonizing climax, the woman approaches the man with proud and humble words that heal and move us forward in the world: "I will teach you," she says, "if you will teach me."

Maryhelen Snyder, "The Pain of Men," *Journal of Men's Wellness*, June 1988. Reprinted by permission of the author. [Italics ours.]

• • • • • • • • • • • • • • • • • • • • • • • • •

1.  The date of the essay's first publication, as seen here, was 1988.
    a. true
    b. false
2.  There are no subheads within the piece.
    a. true
    b. false
3.  A male therapist is talking about men's problems in a men's journal.
    a. true
    b. false

```
Sel. 2   P-Skim                    1. _____
Time    :45 = 1,200 wpm           2. _____
Score   _____ %                   3. _____
        ▶ 100%                     Check answers with your instructor.
Score = number correct × 33.
```

## B. Rapid Reading

Write your starting time in the next answer box, or wait for the signal to begin reading. Try to finish reading in 2 minutes (= 450 wpm), and certainly no longer than 2:15 (= 400 wpm). If your reading time differs from those, record it to the nearest 15 seconds and look up your wpm rate in the rate table on page 343.

1.  The main idea of this essay seems to be that, in our culture,
    a. women have been far more hurt than men
    b. men have been far more hurt than women
    c. men and women have been hurt equally and can help each other
2.  The worst damage for men, Snyder says, occurs because
    a. the women's movement has made men feel insecure
    b. our society tells us not to acknowledge any pain
3.  Ironically, as women feel freer to ask for more "relationship," the men in their lives often
    a. turn violent
    b. long to escape
4.  The author suggests that
    a. in 1988 at least, women were ahead of men in discussing their experiences in society
    b. the two sexes can do much to help each other overcome their "grief" at social roles and expectations
    c. both a and b

```
Sel. 2   R-Read                   1. _____
Finish  _____ : _____           2. _____
Start   _____ : _____           3. _____
Time    _____ : _____           4. _____
           min    sec             Check answers with your instructor.
Rate _____ wpm                   Record rate and score on p. 117.
```

> **Find rate on p. 343.**
>
> **Score** _____%
>
> ▶ 75%
>
> **Score** = number correct × 25.

 C. For Discussion and Writing

1. The dominant writing pattern is probably description—that is, of male clients the author sees in her practice. However, notice the many time-sequence signals she uses in the first five paragraphs. Summarize the content of this first chronological half of the essay.

2. If you are a woman, does this short but moving piece tell you anything new about men? Does any of it apply to the men—whether old, young, or "middling"—in your life?

3. If you are a man, what key points about the modern American man do you agree with? Disagree with?

• • • • • • • • • • • • • • • • • • • • • •

## *SELECTION 3*

"Back to the Nest" will not be easy to preview or rapid read, because it has the typically short, undeveloped paragraphs of a daily newspaper. Even so, you should build some skill at this. Speeded reading is especially handy for reading selected parts of the daily newspaper.

Follow these steps in reading this article:

A. Preview skim the article and answer the three-item quiz.
B. Read the article rapidly, and answer the five-item reading quiz.

## A. Preview Skimming

Preview the article in 1 minute (= 1,400 wpm).

## BACK TO THE NEST

*by Sherry Joe (1,400 words)*

**Just as parents kick back and relax, their adult children return. How do families make the best of the new circumstances?**

1    Short of bolting the door or moving without a forwarding address, how do parents get rid of children they thought were fully grown and gone?

2    David Heath, 45, just had to wait it out. His daughters waited until they were 20 and 23 to trade the four-bedroom home they shared with Heath and their grandparents for their own quarters in Oxnard.

3    "They felt it was time for a little bit more independence," says Heath, a counselor and advocate for the physically disabled at the Independent Living Resource Center in Oxnard. "I'm glad they're out, but I miss having them around."

4    "Boomerang children"—adults largely in their 20s and 30s who either return home temporarily or postpone leaving because of economic pressures, emotional upheavals and their parents' longer life expectancy—are finding it takes longer and longer to duplicate Mom's and Dad's standard of living.

5    The number of boomerang children totals about 5 million and increases each year by 1%, according to the U.S. Census Bureau. In 1983, 54% of adults ages 18 to 24 lived at home. Now, 57% live with their parents, experts say.

6    As a result, a growing number of middle-aged parents who expected an empty nest are confronting parenthood again—or still.

7    Robert Sheehan, 54, of McLean, Va., whose 25-year-old daughter and 24-year-old son returned home this year, says he misses the peace he and his wife enjoyed.

8    "We have the space for them, but we both lose the privacy we gained when they were both at school," Sheehan says.

9    And Sandi Carstensen, 49, of Oakland, says she's looking forward to the day when her two sons, ages 19 and 22, move out so she and her husband can retire.

10    "I would probably like a smaller house with a half-acre of land—something flat, so I could have a garden," Carstensen says.

11    Parents can help boomerang kids move out quickly by setting a time limit, charging them rent or drawing up a contract, says Phyllis Jackson Stegall, co-author of the 1987 book "Boomerang Kids: How to Live With Adult Children Who Return Home."

12    "Parents ask me, 'How do we set a time limit?' The child is becoming all too comfortable [at home]," says Stegall, a Seattle psychotherapist.

13    For parents facing the return of a grown child, Stegall and others offer these tips:

- Establish ground rules before allowing your child to come home. "Parents should expect that the child become a fully functional family member, that the child come here and pull his own weight," she says.

- Parents should duplicate conditions in the real world as much as possible at home. If the "boomeranger" has no money, demand household chores in lieu of rent.

14    At various times, David Heath says, he charged his daughters rent. "When there were problems with money, I let them slide," he recalls. "It was more principle than the money. I had just decided, when you're 18 years old and not going to school, you have to pay your own way."

- Parents and children should draw up an agreement or contract that stipulates how the family will function together—for example,

"'I agree to mow the lawn twice or three times a week.' 'You are expected to have a job in two months,'" Stegall says. Contracts help prevent many conflicts between parents and children.

- Once your children have jobs, they should be expected to pay rent on a gradually increasing scale. If they are flipping hamburgers, rent could be $25 a week until a more lucrative job is found.

15    Karl Carstensen, 22, didn't begin paying rent until he had a full-time job as a police services technician in Oakland. Now he pays his parents $325 a month.

- Shared housing remains the best alternative to living at home, says Sheehan, a consulting economist with the National Apartment Assn. "Rent a house and double up with roommates," Sheehan advises young adults. "Be willing to accept something less than they're used to. For generations, that's the way you became a homeowner."

16    Many young adults say they are reluctant to share housing because it doesn't reflect true independence. "They had a room of their own. When you have shared housing, that's not true," Stegall says. "You have a shelf in the refrigerator, a curfew on TV."

17    Karl Carstensen agrees.

18    "You know it's not yours," he says. "There's no sense that you belong to an apartment."

- Just as important as allowing children to return home is being able to lock them out, Stegall says. Refuse to admit "boomerangers" who are addicted to drugs or alcohol or who abuse family members.
- Do not permit your child to live at home when there is not enough money or space.
- Say no to children who repeatedly ask to come home. Instead, offer advice over the telephone. "You're really doing something loving for them," Stegall says.

19    According to Stegall, many young adults are reluctant to sacrifice material comfort for financial independence because they were spoiled as children.

20    "Because they were raised with so much, they feel they were entitled to have whatever they wanted without any real effort," she says.

21    But some stay-at-homes have a different opinion.

22    Connie, a 23-year-old USC graduate who declined to give her last name, supported herself for six months before returning to her parents' Northridge home to save money.

23    "I felt I was wasting money," says Connie, who was spending more than $1,000 a month on rent, bills and dining out at trendy eateries.

24    Now that she's at home, Connie plans to save about $500 a month—from the money she spent on rent—for a down payment on a townhouse.

25    Even more important, she says, living conditions have improved. "My house happens to be much nicer than my apartment," says Connie, who shared a duplex with three roommates. "It's always clean. Even if you have the best roommates in the world, you have to worry about who's going to do the dishes."

26    Jeffrey Kim, 24, also chose to live at home until he graduates from Cal State Los Angeles next year. In the meantime, he provides a valuable service for his parents, Korean immigrants who do not speak English fluently.

27    "I do a lot of paperwork for them," Kim says. "I talk to lawyers, the phone company. . . ."

28    Others didn't have a choice.

29    According to Korean tradition, 23-year-old Ann Choi is expected to stay at home until she marries—or can afford a down payment on a house.

30    "It's 50–50," Choi says of the chances of realizing either option. "It could go either way."

31    The former USC sociology major earns about $21,000 annually as a customer service representative for a thread manufacturer. Choi saves about $200 a month but doesn't know when she will move out.

<sup>32</sup> Right now, she says, she enjoys spending time with her close-knit family.

<sup>33</sup> "Even if I wanted to [move], I'm used to my parents," Choi says. "As far as major decisions, I made them on my own, but I'm so used to a big family, I knew I would get homesick."

<sup>34</sup> But tension blossoms in even the best of families.

<sup>35</sup> "I like to drink more than [my sisters] do and stay out late and go in pubs and cafes," says Choi, who says her parents "trust me 100%."

<sup>36</sup> That doesn't stop Joon Choi, 53, from worrying about her daughter.

<sup>37</sup> "I get heart palpitations," Choi says. "You know L.A.—there's too many crazy drivers. I worry about them until they come home."

<sup>38</sup> Rules about the shower and kitchen are the most common conflict in the Carstensen household.

<sup>39</sup> "Karl doesn't stay with the family chores," Sandi Carstensen says. "Even if he is paying rent, we shouldn't have to tell him, 'You're supposed to clean the shower.'"

<sup>40</sup> Some parents actually may have difficulty in letting their children leave.

<sup>41</sup> For example, divorced parents who raised their children on a family battleground may feel guilty and want to atone by inviting them back home during hard times, says Stegall, who advises parents to concentrate on the future.

<sup>42</sup> "You can't say *mea culpa, mea culpa* forever," she says.

<sup>43</sup> Some parents also are reluctant to abandon the care-giver role that has become their source of identity, she adds.

<sup>44</sup> "This was my identity. I was a parent, a mom," Stegall says of those who refuse to cut the cord. "When this opportunity presents itself, I'm all for it."

<sup>45</sup> Whatever the reason for delayed independence, the phenomenon has caught many parents off guard.

<sup>46</sup> David Heath, whose daughters recently moved to a two-bedroom beachfront apartment, remembers when financial independence was synonymous with high school graduation.

<sup>47</sup> "When I was 17, 18, 19 years old, a couple of guys could rent a real decent apartment on Seal Beach for $150 a month," Heath says. "Now, even if you spend one-quarter of your income [on housing], you still live in a depressed neighborhood."

<sup>48</sup> As a result, parents and children alike may need to alter their expectations of independence, Stegall says.

<sup>49</sup> "Everything is geared toward leaving home," she says. "In our culture, we raise children to be independent. [Parents and children] need to reorder their expectations."

<sup>50</sup> But changing times have not dissuaded Sandi Carstensen from her principles.

<sup>51</sup> "I don't believe in letting them freeload," she declares. "That's not teaching them to be responsible."

Sherry Joe, "Back to the Nest," *Los Angeles Times,* October 28, 1991. © 1991, Los Angeles Times. Reprinted by permission.

•  •  •  •  •  •  •  •  •  •  •  •  •  •  •  •  •  •  •  •  •  •  •  •  •  •  •  •  •  •  •  •  •

1. This writer presents
   a. a useful question within the lead
   b. a list of items set off by markers
   c. both a and b
2. The author develops her thesis mainly with
   a. real-life individuals
   b. results of national surveys

3.  The source is a
    a.  magazine
    b.  newspaper

---

**Sel. 3**   P-Skim                     1. _____

**Time**   1:00 = 1,400 wpm            2. _____

**Score** _____ %                       3. _____

▶ 100%                                  **Check answers on p. 350.**

**Score** = number correct × 33.

---

## B.  Rapid Reading

Write your starting time in the next answer box, or wait for the signal to begin. When you are done, write your finishing time, or ask for your total time to the nearest 15 seconds. Try to read the entire article in 3 minutes (= 466 wpm) or less, and certainly no more than 3:30 ($3\frac{1}{2}$) minutes (= 400 wpm).

1.  Starting with her lead, what overall, dominant pattern does the writer use?
    a.  question-answer (i.e., how-to or problem-solution), with individual examples
    b.  classification (kinds of parents and adult children)
    c.  extended definition (of "boomerang" children)
2.  In 1991, when this was published, roughly how many of adult children aged 18–24 were living with their parents still—or again?
    a.  about 10 percent of them
    b.  about one-fourth
    c.  over half
3.  The author advises that families head off potential trouble by
    a.  drawing up a contract or rules
    b.  expecting some payment, chores, and other responsibilities
    c.  refusing to allow destructive behavior
    d.  understanding housing costs have increased hugely in the last decades
    e.  all of these
4.  One recommended alternative to living in your parents' home is
    a.  living in a camper or mobile home
    b.  sharing housing with a roommate
    c.  converting a garage into living quarters

| | |
|---|---|
| **Sel. 3**   R-Read | 1. _____ |
| **Finish** _____:_____ | 2. _____ |
| **Start** _____:_____ | 3. _____ |
| **Time** _____:_____ | 4. _____ |
|       min    sec | **Check answers on p. 350.** |
| **Rate**_____**wpm** | **Record rate and score on p. 117.** |
| **Find rate on p. 343.** | |
| **Score** _____% | |
|       ▶ 75% | |
| **Score** = number correct × 25. | |

 ## C.  For Discussion and Writing

1.  Professional writers and journalists have certain readers in mind—their "au-dience"—when they write. In your opinion, was this article aimed at parents of adult children or at the adult children themselves? Is it biased toward either group? Use evidence from the article to support your view.
2.  Which parents or adult children do you personally identify with? Describe and explain.
3.  In paragraph 48, the psychotherapist Stegall says that today's economy forces U.S. citizens to "alter their expectations of independence." This is a tall social order. Do you think this "reordering" can occur? Is it already occurring?

• • • • • • • • • • • • • • • • • • •

# *SELECTION 4*

To continue with readings about the family, here is an article about identical twins, a subject that most people find interesting. It addresses the old question of nature versus nurture—genes versus environment.

Follow these steps:

A.  Preview skim the article. Then answer the three-item quiz.
B.  Rapid read the article. Then answer the five-item quiz.

## A.  Preview Skimming

Take 1 minute (= 1,800 wpm) to preview for the usual features.

. . . . . . . . . . . . . . .
████████████     *TOGETHER AGAIN*
. . . . . . . . . . . . . . .
████████████     *by Alice Vollmar (1,800 words)*

### Twins raised apart offer new insights into heredity and environment

1    Standing on the sidelines cheering for her son's baseball team, Dianne Cunningham looks like any enthusiastic mother, balancing her pink-bonneted 6-month-old in a back carrier. Only she can't clap, because in her arms she holds a second pink-bonneted 6-month-old.

2    "Twins?" asks another parent. "May I hold one for you?" Gratefully, Cunningham rests her tired arms. A group gathers around the babies and their mother. "It gets easier," one woman reassures. "Just hang in there. See No. 13 up at bat now? He's one of my twins."

3    "Twins. What a miracle," murmurs another onlooker. "Yes, well, I'm glad the miracle happened to her and not to me," replies her companion.

4    Twins draw attention wherever they go. And recently twins have been the center of a different kind of attention: Scientists at the University of Minnesota are studying twins raised apart—and coming up with new insights into what makes human beings tick.

5    "Everyone is very surprised," says Dr. Nancy Segal, one of about 15 researchers associated with The Minnesota Study of Twins Reared Apart, begun in 1979 by Dr. Thomas J. Bouchard Jr., University of Minnesota psychologist.

6    Long interested in environment's role in shaping human beings, Bouchard read a newspaper story about the reunion of a set of adult twins and saw a rare chance to draw a line between the effects of heredity and environment. What if he could study those 39-year-old twins from Ohio? Since identical twins have the same set of genes, differences between those two individuals reared apart could then be attributed to environment.

7    The enthusiastic university professor located funding, put together a team of scientists and did indeed bring the Ohio twins, Jim Lewis and Jim Springer, to the University of Minnesota. In March 1979, within the modern, red brick walls of Elliott Hall, they began one week of intense testing. Since then, 38 identical and 16 fraternal sets of reared-apart twins have followed in their footsteps, undergoing extensive physical, psychological and intelligence tests, and answering thousands of questions.

8    Bouchard has found long lists of similarities, suggesting that genes and heredity play a far more powerful role in who we are and how we got that way than previously suspected.

9    Lewis and Springer, the first twins studied, turned out to have more in common than just their first names and birthdate:

- Voices and mannerisms were alike.
- Both divorced women named Linda and married second wives named Betty.
- They named their sons James Allan and James Alan, and at one time each owned a dog named Toy.
- Both suffer similar tension-migraine headaches, prefer the same brand of beer and cigarettes, chew their fingernails, drive Chevrolets, vacation on the same beach in Florida, and like woodworking.
- Each built a white bench around a tree in his yard.
- Both liked math and disliked spelling in school.
- They have identical blood pressures, pulse rates and sleep patterns, and show similar psychological inventory profiles.

10    Another set of twins shares claustrophobia, timidity about ocean bathing, mistrust of escalators and a habit of compulsive counting.

11    Gregarious British twins Daphne Goodship and Barbara Herbert both have:

- Crooked little fingers.
- The same highly distinctive giggle.
- A penchant for avoiding controversy.
- A taste for coffee cold and black.
- A love of chocolate and liqueurs.
- A habit of pushing up their noses, which each calls "squidging."

12    While scientists may be excited about their findings, the feelings of most identical twins reunited after years of separation can be even stronger. Many are euphoric about finding their "other selves."

13    "It was like two friends meeting, as though we had always known each other," one twin said. Another twin, separated from her sister for 53 years, noted that "you wouldn't normally pick up the phone and speak to someone you'd never seen before for half an hour, non-stop."

14    "We are complete now," said another. In overwhelming numbers, whether they have been reared apart or together, twins are glad to be twins. "We always warn our friends that they will never be 'first.' We are—and always will be—each other's best friend," say Lora Stewart and Linda Longerbone, reared-together identical twins, now co-presidents of the Minnesota Twin Cities Twin Club.

15    Researchers find that twins who have been reared apart are sometimes more similar than those raised together. It seems to be a matter of establishing identity: Twins raised separately have no chance to interact or be compared with one another. Twins growing up together often work to create identities distinct from one another. To cut down on comparisons, they may choose different activities, friends or clothing.

16    A twin admits it can be hard to know who you are when there's another person who is so much like you. Also, most of the world looks at twins and sees a pair—rather than two distinct individuals—and expects them to act and dress alike.

17    "When we were young," recalls Lora Stewart, now 39, "it was easier just to dress alike, because so many people would make comments when we didn't."

18    Thus, twins reunited as adults may have avoided some hassles that go with growing up in the shadow of a twin, and emerge with their natural inclinations more intact.

19    To scientists, the wide-ranging similarities in twins' inclinations—from choices in clothing, food and names to medical, behavioral and intelligence patterns—mean that many of our traits may have more of a genetic tie-in than suspected. The research adds an even subtler insight: Our genes may combine in unique and individual ways to make each of us even less alike than we could have guessed.

20    "Much of what we think of as human individuality—temperament and pace and all the idiosyncrasies that make you different from your friends—may relate a lot more to your particular genetic individuality than we thought," observes research team member Dr. David Lykken, University of Minnesota professor of psychiatry.

21    "A lot of the things that I've assumed to be true about the influence of early experiences are now in doubt," Lykken says. For example, the capacity for happiness seems to be "more strongly [genetically] wired in than I had thought." Lykken works in an office in which all manner of twins peer out of pictures on the walls. Several composite pictures consist solely of sets of twins' eyes and ears—highly hereditary features—creating an unusual and fascinating environment for his work.

22    Lykken's explanation means, for instance, that little Mary's sunny disposition may be part of her genetic makeup, enhanced by—but not the result of—her adoring parents' care. Which, in a way, can be welcome news to parents. Some of those hard days, when smiling is next to impossible, may have little long-term effect on the children.

23    Parents of twins know about "hard days." There are times when sanity comes hard: when both babies are crabby from teething, a mountain of soggy baby laundry looms and there's not been a minute alone to brush your teeth or comb your hair.

24    "I just cry a lot," says Dianne Cunningham, who brought fraternal twins Anna and Rebekah home to four brothers aged 3 through 9. "My recuperation was so much longer because I had one baby naturally and one by Caesarean. When I'd start to do something I'd done in the past with ease, I just couldn't handle it. My older kids probably wonder if a day will come when I won't cry while I'm fixing dinner."

25    What the final result will be of The Minnesota Study of Twins Reared Apart is unknown. Funded by a variety of private and government foundations in addition to the University graduate school's support, the study will test 100 identical and 50 to 70 fraternal twins. No date for completing the study is projected; it will not end until the desired number of sets of twins can be found who will participate.

26    Although it's not always the case in most serious scientific studies, publicity is welcomed, and necessary: Publicity is how new twins are recruited for the study. Twins who've found one another hear about the study and contact Bouchard—or someone will come to him with a possible lead on a twin.

27    How do separated twins find one another? Researcher Segal says it often starts with mistaken identity. Someone says, "Hey, I saw you in Cambridge on Saturday." Only you weren't in Cambridge on that day. Such cases of identity confusion can lead to a search for the lookalike—and to the discovery there is an identical twin.

28    Being able to connect with such reunited pairs is critical to Bouchard's study. But along with publicity comes controversy. Some people doubt the motives behind the study, or the techniques that are involved in the testing.

29    In a January 1981 article in *Psychology Today*, Dr. Susan Farber wondered if the study was asking the right questions. Peter Watson, in his book, *Twins: An Uncanny Relationship?*, questioned a "methodological flaw" in Bouchard's approach. Repeatedly, Bouchard and associates attest to the open-ended, exploratory nature of

their project, and Lykken says the debate over causal forces that shape human beings has "gone on for many years . . . as to which is more important for which characteristics." Inevitably, shaking the old heredity/environment tree brings down both sweet and sour apples.

30    However, information coming out of the study of those rare, reared-apart twins may have a big impact on how we live with one another—in our families and in society.

31    "We may need to rethink policies for modifying behavior, prescribing treatment for certain kinds of diseases, identifying persons at risk for certain problems or boosting IQ," Segal speculates. "For instance, Head Start programs [designed to give preschoolers from less-advantaged homes an equal chance in school] have attempted to boost children's IQ, and have done so. But the long-term gains are somewhat in question. It may be we have to reshape those kinds of environmental programs."

32    Lykken emphatically warns lay people not to jump to improper conclusions: "Of course, you can't become something that your genetic potential will not allow, but you don't know what that is until you try. . . . Most of us do not come close to exploiting our genetic potential in our lifetimes.

33    "I think we can do a better job of parenting and educating if we realize everybody is starting out with a different deck . . . rather than treating kids as if they all start with the same cards," says Lykken. "We need to adapt our efforts to fit what each kid has to start with."

34    We have probably all heard parents comment, "Our children are so different; you'd hardly guess they came from the same family." In the light of present findings from Bouchard's study, those parents appear astutely wise.

35    We may all be more different, one from the other, than any of us ever dreamed.

1. The year of publication is 1994.
   a. true
   b. false
2. Write the lead from memory as accurately as you can.

   _____

   _____

3. Besides the lead, there are lists marked with bullets (dots), and at the end there are two sections with subheads.
   a. true
   b. false

---

**Sel. 4**   P-Skim            1. _____

**Time**   1:00 = 1,800 wpm    2. _____

**Score**   _____%            3. _____

   ▶ 100%                    **Check answers with your instructor.**

**Score** = number correct × 33.

---

## B. Rapid Reading

Write your starting time in the box, or wait for the signal. Now go back to the article and read rapidly, in 3 to 4 minutes (= 600 wpm to 450 wpm). As usual, for other reading times, look up your wpm rate in the table on page 343. Then answer the quiz without looking back.

1. The Minnesota study indicates that identical twins who have always been reared apart, ignorant of each other's existence, have turned into adults who are
   a. amazingly similar—genetics are all-important
   b. reasonably different because they grew up in different environments
2. This selection suggests that many of our personality traits are genetically programmed, not the result of "nurture."
   a. true
   b. false
3. The Minnesota study is so well constructed, that so far it has had no criticism from within the profession.
   a. true
   b. false
4. At the time of publication, the findings of this famous research project were
   a. completed and well accepted
   b. still incomplete and ongoing
   c. suggestive, but treated with caution
   d. both b and c

5.  The article ends with
    a.  tips on how to raise twins
    b.  a commentary on how different each human being is

---

**Sel. 4   R-Read**                1. _____

**Finish** _____:_____             2. _____

**Start**   _____:_____            3. _____

**Time**    _____:_____            4. _____

        min   sec     Check answers with your instructor.

**Rate**_____wpm                   Record rate and score on p. 117.

**Find rate on p. 343.**

**Score** _____%

    ▶80%

**Score** = number correct × 20.

---

 C. For Discussion and Writing

1.  Reread paragraph 19, where the thesis is presented clearly. Summarize the thesis of this article.
2.  In light of this article and the Minnesota study, and after you reread the article thoughtfully, can you explain what the last paragraph (35) means?
3.  In your opinion and from your experience, evaluate the evidence given for the dominance of heredity over environment—"nature" over "nurture." Does it convince you? Do you see possible dangers in the belief that we are born the way we are and will be? See especially paragraphs 31–35.

• • • • • • • • • • • • • • • • • • •

# SELECTION 5

This next piece describes the conflicts that commonly arise between grown children and their parents. (These are not necessarily the same children that were coming "back to the nest" in Selection 3.) Several high-profile therapists and authors are quoted, and the issues are painful. Nevertheless, remember to preview systematically, and read rapidly!

Follow these steps when you rapid read this selection:

A.  Preview skim the article, then answer the three-item preview quiz.
B.  Read the article rapidly, then answer the four-item reading quiz.

## A.  Preview Skimming

As usual, begin with PIF—previewing it first. Check for title, lead, length, source, and date in 30 seconds (= 2,500 wpm).

### GIVING THEIR BEST—AGAIN

*by Leslie Dreyfous (1,250 words)*

**Today, baby boomers bridge rifts by revealing and healing.**

1   They gave their baby boom children shelter, clean clothes, food to eat, bikes to ride, family vacations. They went to Little League games and summer potlucks, bandaged skinned knees and attended school plays. They weren't perfect, but they tried.

2   So why, these parents now wonder, are we being broadsided? Why are so many grown children coming home these days primed for confrontation?

3   When physical, psychological, or sexual abuse are involved, the reasons are obvious. But in recent years, a whole range of subtler, less easily defined family issues have worked their way into the mainstream psyche.

4   More and more, "adult children" have re-examined their pasts and found shadows: parents who were emotionally distant or overly critical; who disciplined a little too harshly, or spent more time at the office than at home; who, wittingly or not, discouraged big dreams or eroded self-esteem.

5   Aging parents have a common response to these reproaches: "I did the best I could." Most adult children agree.

6   But still, many want to push beyond, to discuss and understand their disappointments. Confronting the past is integral to a lot of today's therapeutic, self-help, and recovery programs.

7   "These parents have to understand: Their kids are the most therapized generation in history," said Victoria Secunda, 52, author of "When You and Your Mother Can't Be Friends" and "Women and their Fathers."

8   "Young adults are doing what their parents couldn't—expressing emotions and dealing with losses. Raising these issues is incredibly important," she said. "But, like in any negotiation, it's important to approach it right."

9   If only it were simple. Though often eager to help, many older parents find the landscape foreign or outright rocky. Their child-rearing decisions were made long ago, influenced by the times and particular circumstances.

10   For generations raised during the Depression and World War II, making do was doing pretty well. Most reached adulthood without ever hearing the cry of their "wounded child within" or the siren song of self-help.

11   Bernice Bratter, director of Senior Health and Peer Counseling in Santa Monica, has watched parents in their 50s, 60s, and even 70s struggle to understand the issues broached, sometimes angrily, by their grown children. Many feel guilty, at pains to right whatever is wrong.

12   But many others ask: What's the point here?

13   Bratter readily admits she is among those who subscribe to a "get over it" philosophy. "We're talking about different generations," she said, "different kinds of mindsets."

14   "It's natural for young people to explore and healthy to look at what's gone on in the family," said Bratter, 55.

15    "Where it crosses into difficulty is when people use that to keep themselves from moving on with their lives, where they say 'I'm not successful because Mommy didn't tell me I was wonderful.'"

16    All the parenting manuals weren't out there 30 years ago, and self-esteem was barely in the lexicon. Even a decade ago, talk shows and 12-step programs, therapy and support groups weren't nearly so widespread.

17    But it's all available now. And given the new awareness, many young adults are committed to breaking what they regard as destructive family patterns, behavior they believe ultimately hurts both parent and child.

18    That's fine, said psychologist Renana Brooks. "But it's not enough just to air your grievances," she said. "Once you do that, you've got to figure out what you're going to do with those feelings."

19    While she recognizes the liberation many have found in re-examining their childhood hurts, Brooks has problems with some of the recovery rhetoric.

20    "The movement makes certain assumptions, some of which have to do with believing that damage is irreversible, that all character flaws relate to early childhood wounds, and that it all reflects parental misconduct," she said from Washington, D.C.

21    "It's polarizing," said Brooks, who conducts blame-busting workshops. "The more the children demand that their parents take blame, the more the parents say, 'Grow up and forget about the past.'"

22    These cross-purposes are painful, and often hurtful. But with good groundwork, therapists say, half the battle is won. It's helpful for adult children to go gently, with empathy, into tender areas.

23    When Marvin Allen's son spoke up, the circumstances weren't exactly ideal: the exchange took place on stage during "The Oprah Winfrey Show."

24    The 48-year-old therapist and author of "In the Company of Men" was discussing models of fatherly supportiveness and sensitivity when suddenly his grown son "absolutely confronted me."

25    "He didn't say I cussed him out or beat him, like my dad did me. But I neglected him terribly. My wife and I got divorced. I was chasing women and money," said Allen, who lives in New Braunfels, Texas. "My sins hurt my son. I had to accept that."

26    It was a painful dose of honesty. But, perhaps because of his background in therapy, Allen was able to digest his son's comments fairly quickly. This is something many bewildered parents find difficult to do.

27    "To say my mom has been torn apart would be an understatement. She's totally caught in the middle," said Jennifer Bestor of Menlo Park, whose sister has withdrawn from the family.

28    "At some point, she said she was going into therapy and before we knew it, we were getting phone calls with incredibly harsh and nasty allegations. She claims she's a victim, that either directly or indirectly we're responsible for everything that's wrong in her life," said Bestor, 37. "To try to have a rational conversation around this is impossible."

29    Susan Forward, author of "Toxic Parents" and other popular self-help books, said she has helped thousands of adult children through the recovery process—a process she believes is both essential and, ultimately, healing.

30    "Every adult child I've ever worked with has lain awake at night just fantasizing how it would sound to hear a parent say 'I'm sorry. I didn't realize I hurt you that much,'" she said from Bel Air.

31    "I see confrontation as a chance for several things: one, to break through the denial and half-truths and secrecy and two, to determine what kind of real relationship you can have with your toxic parents."

32    Agreeing with "wounded child" guru John Bradshaw's estimate that the vast majority of American families are dysfunctional, Forward sees an enormous pool of people in need of reconciliation.

33    Many, however, believe such presumptions are tenuous, if not outright dangerous. Sto-

ries of therapists coaxing their clients into false memories of childhood incest and other forms of abuse further undermine credibility.

34    Such doubts are especially hurtful to the legions of men and women coping with often long-repressed, very genuine histories of abuse. They also undermine those who want neither to overblow nor to diminish childhood pain.

35    The point is to promote understanding, and frank discussion about whatever is on a family member's mind. The trick is to do it constructively.

36    Unfortunately, Elizabeth Van Wormer, a clinical social worker in Portland, Ore., finds herself doing a lot of painful cleanup work.

37    "I have had experience with people who have gone to a one- or two-day workshop that provokes feelings, which can be very, very good," she said. "The downside is that getting in touch with your feelings is only the first step. You're left with simply an event, and who's out there to blame it on?"

38    "Sometimes I wish I could say, 'Get a life. Go someplace else and take your garbage with you,'" said Shirley Ernst Jefferson, 55. "You do feel defensive. . . . But Amber gave me comfort and a tone of understanding."

39    Her daughter, Amber Rose Brown, did not come to that tone easily. She had to get past a lot of anger. "I blamed my dad: If he hadn't left, I wouldn't have been poor or a welfare child. I blamed my mother for not holding me," Brown, 30, said from Alexandria, Va.

40    Brown grew into womanhood feeling isolated by a depression she could neither understand nor lift on her own. With the help of therapy, she has come to see the strains and constraints faced by her mother, who raised seven children alone. "She had a tough life and a tough love attitude," Brown said. "She didn't believe in warmth and tenderness and affection."

41    Says her mother, who lives in Cincinnati: "Amber had some valid points, which I could see. But the thing is: I dealt the best I could with what was going on at the time."

42    They are two women, raised in different times and offered different opportunities. Jefferson wasn't raised to ponder; she was raised to cope. Brown wasn't satisfied with coping; she wanted to understand.

43    But ultimately, through a willingness to give on each side, mother and daughter found each other. The ground isn't always smooth, but it's solid.

44    "She came and talked. She brought things out and gave me room for rebuttal," Jefferson said.

45    "The bottom line is love. The trick is love, and trying again. Always try again," Brown said. "It's painful and hard, but it's so worth it when you finally start to hear, and start to learn from each other."

Leslie Dreyfous, "Giving Their Best—Again," *San Luis Obispo County Telegram-Tribune*, July 23, 1993. Reprinted by permission of Associated Press.

. . . . . . . . . . . . . . . . . . . . . . . . . . . . . . .

1.  The lead tells us that the featured "children" are
    a.  baby boomers—now in their thirties and forties
    b.  in their teens and early twenties
2.  The article is reprinted from a self-help magazine.
    a.  true
    b.  false
3.  The ideas are developed mostly through many quotations from individuals and through many short paragraphs.
    a.  true
    b.  false

```
┌──────────────────────────────────────────────────────────────┐
│  Sel. 5   P-Skim                  1. _____                     │
│  Time    :30 = 2,500 wpm          2. _____                     │
│  Score   _____%                   3. _____                     │
│     ▶ 100%                        Check answers on p. 350.     │
│  Score = number correct × 33.                                  │
└──────────────────────────────────────────────────────────────┘
```

## B. Rapid Reading

Write your starting time in the next answer box, or wait for the signal to begin your rapid reading. Try to finish in 3 minutes (= 417 wpm) or less.

1. The main idea seems to be that
   a. today's "adult children" are examining their childhoods more than past generations could do
   b. while these old problems are important, it is both essential and difficult to confront them constructively
   c. TV talk shows and "recovery" groups tend to exaggerate the conflicts and make them worse, not better
2. Places where these issues are being raised include
   a. private and group counseling
   b. 12-step and other support groups
   c. self-help manuals and books
   d. all of these
3. Several of the therapists cited think that parents of baby boomers
   a. had different stresses and opportunities from today
   b. usually did the best they could at the time
   c. both a and b
4. The last three paragraphs stress that both parents and grown children do best if they can
   a. be loving, hear each other, give a little on each side, and keep trying to understand the past
   b. put the past with its old hurts behind them, concentrate on the future, "get a life"
   c. realize that the parents always acted in the children's best interests

```
┌──────────────────────────────────────────────────────────────┐
│  Sel. 5   R-Read                  1. _____                     │
│  Finish  _____:_____              2. _____                     │
│  Start   _____:_____              3. _____                     │
│  Time    _____:_____              4. _____                     │
│              min    sec           Check answers on p. 350.     │
└──────────────────────────────────────────────────────────────┘
```

Rate____wpm                    **Record rate and score on p. 117.**

**Find rate on p. 343.**

**Score** _____%

▶ 75%

**Score** = number correct × 25.

 C.  For Discussion and Writing

1.  Dreyfous tries to cover the spectrum among therapists, from those who think nearly all parents do a poor job, to those who think the "children" need to grow up and take responsibility for their own lives. Group the individuals along this spectrum. Transition words such as *but* and *however* signal the shifting viewpoints.

2.  Do you belong to a generation or time when people were "raised to cope"? Or were they "raised to ponder" (paragraph 42)? Explain.

3.  What disappointments, resentments, and hurts do you retain from your childhood that you are sure you will never inflict on your own children? How can you be sure?

D.  Midpoint Evaluation—Rapid Reading

Time out! You are halfway through the Timed Selections for rapid reading. Pause here to evaluate how well you have done on speeded reading of these first five selections.

Update your scores on the Progress Chart, page 117. Can you see an overall upward trend, however gradual? Consider your progress in both rate and comprehension. Do you tend to complete the preview and the reading within the target times? Are your quiz scores usually within the target percentages?

If you need extra practice before moving to the rest of the selections, go back to any selection and mark key words, draw shortened margins, and use a finger or an index card to finish each selection within the time limit.

Selections 6–10 will be somewhat longer; this may help you "hit your stride" more consistently.

• • • • • • • • • • • • • • • • • •

## SELECTION 6

This selection offers a poignant look at family relations when illness becomes the family's focus. This very well written piece deserves a careful rereading after you have read it rapidly.

Follow these steps:

A.  Preview skim the article. Then answer the three-item quiz.

B.  Read the article rapidly. Then answer the four-item quiz.

## A. Preview Skimming

Take 45 seconds (= 1,867 wpm) to preview for the usual features.

### *LIFE IS PRECIOUS—EVEN AT THE END*

*by Gary Eisler (1,400 words)*

1 It hurt—I could tell. Bonnie lay on her hospice bed. She started to convulse: She thrashed in her bed and moaned in pain. I called for the nurse and ran to squeeze her morphine pump to get her past another crisis. But while I was fumbling with the drug-delivering gadget, her eye twitched briefly, and then it was over. Her labored breathing had stopped, and the bulging veins at her temples—thin and purple from months of chemotherapy—receded into her now waxy, bald head.

2 Bonnie, my wife of 28 years, had said she was not afraid of death, but she was afraid of dying. She was afraid it was going to hurt, and it certainly looked to me as if it did. She never had fear of anything, especially not physical pain, until after months and months of surgeries, radiation therapy, chemotherapy, shunts, catheters, infections, unconsciousness, and finally cancer in her brain. Then she was afraid.

3 I wonder at what point she would have elected to end her life had Ballot Measure 16, Oregon's Physician Assisted Suicide Law, been allowed to take effect. Now, less than two years later, I have my own terminal illness, and I wonder what I will do. So does everyone else in Oregon, as we vote by mail between now and Tuesday on Ballot Measure 51, which would repeal what we voted for in 1994.

### KNEES BUCKLED

4 Bonnie was diagnosed with breast cancer in May 1987. She was in the kitchen when she picked up the phone and got the word from her biopsy. Her knees buckled when she heard the word "cancer." Fortunately for me, I was sitting down in May 1997 when the surgeon called to tell me my biopsy showed a cancer of the lymphatic system. The day after the diagnosis, I stayed in bed. I figured, what's the use of getting up, since I'm just going to die anyway? So I lay there until I got bored. Life goes on, no matter how much time you think you have.

5 I went to see the same oncologist who had presided over my wife's death. He had a stern, unsmiling face. I looked for some break, the hint of a smile, some reassurance that things would be OK. There was none. He told me I have a non-Hodgkin's lymphoma, a slow-growing cancer that can't be cured. It felt just like I had been fired. I tried to bargain with fate, to no avail. I looked around at the walls, the light coming through the window, like someone drinking in familiar sights because he knows even these small things will soon be gone.

6 Oncologists have the most difficult job in the world. They have to guide people to accepting the unacceptable. The same doctor told my wife in November 1995 that her breast cancer had spread to her brain and that he was recommending all further treatment be stopped. She said: "Then what about the bone marrow transplant?" That had been her last hope, but all we could do was wait for the inevitable, which came two months later.

7 Would she have asked him to help her die right then? Would he have suggested it? If she had ended it instead of living those last two months, would we all have been better off?

8      Many things happened between the time treatment ended and when she died—wonderful things. Bonnie had longed to see a grandchild before she died. When our grandson was born that November, she was in the delivery room in her wheelchair, coaching our daughter. On Christmas Day she held a plastic basin to her chin, in case she got sick, while the three kids opened their presents. She always loved to see them happy, and she got to see it one last time. No sooner did they finish than she keeled over where she sat, lapsing into a coma.

9      The hospice sent round-the-clock care-givers. One of them told me sometime between Christmas and New Year's that Bonnie would not live another 24 hours. She was showing the signs of impending death—cool knees, apnea, bluing hands. But instead she rallied. We brought her to the hospice, where she lay, her eyes opening occasionally but not focusing.

10      But New Year's Day was different. Andrea, the exchange student from Brazil who had stayed with us years earlier, came to Portland. Directly from the plane, she came to see her American mother. Andrea took Bonnie's hands and rubbed them, smooched her on the face, called her name. Bonnie's eyes focused for the first time in days, and she smiled. Andrea's presence brought her back from the brink. She talked. She even ate. I had the honor of feeding her a last meal—she ate for me because she knew I wanted her to stay.

11      I sat by her bed that night and we talked. We shared old memories—little things that had happened a quarter-century ago that would be important to no one else. As in many long marriages, there were many unforgivable hurts between us that we somehow managed to live with.

12      "Do you forgive me for everything?" I asked.

13      "Everything happened so long ago, none of it matters now," she said. We exchanged words of love—the last words we ever spoke to each other.

14      Our last hours together were some of the most intimate and precious of our marriage, and I share them with everyone to illustrate a point:

"Reason" and "compassion" would have dictated that Bonnie's life be ended weeks earlier, but how much poorer everyone—including her—would have been. There was a closure, a perfection, a beauty about those last days.

15      Now, less than two years later, It's my turn. The doctors say I could be dead in six months, a few years, maybe eight or 10. Since I know it's going to end anyway, why not just conclude my affairs and get it over with? There's not a day that goes by that I don't relive Bonnie's final, painful passage. Do I really want to wait for the disease to overtake me, or do I want to be proactive?

16      I'm not in any particular pain now, and I wonder how I'll feel about the issue when I am. But I know I don't need a doctor to be involved if I decide to end it. The questions are: What is the right time, and is it my decision to make?

17      I fear that unless assisted suicide is repealed, it will not be long before the vultures begin circling. After all, more than half a million people die of cancer every year. It costs our medical insurance about $100,000 for the last couple of years of Bonnie's life. The American Cancer Institute estimates that in 1996 the total cost of cancer was $104 billion, including $35 billion in medical costs and $57 billion for death-related expenses. Imagine the billions that could be saved by shaving a few points off those figures. My wife never knew what her treatments were costing; if she had, she might well have felt she was a burden. If suicide were legally sanctioned, many conscientious people would choose that route rather than take the chance of being a millstone to their families.

## A SUSCEPTIBLE PLACE

18      Cancer enters a body at a weak or susceptible place, and maybe that's why Oregon is at the frontier of the assisted suicide movement. After only Alaska, Oregon is perhaps the least churched state in the country. Oregonians often see issues without the filter of religious guidance or doctrine; the Catholic Church, the leading opponent of the 1994 initiative, counts only 10% of Oregonians as members.

19      Oregon was one of the first to hop on the abortion bandwagon: Will it once again open the door for the rest of the country? When abortion was legal in some states but not others, women crossed state lines to have the procedure. Will there be pilgrimages of the dying to Oregon, or will voters' decision here next Tuesday eventually be extended to the rest of the country? Will what has been "optional" someday become "suggested"—and perhaps eventually required?

20      It's bad enough to hear your doctor say there is no hope for your life. It would be even worse to face pressure to end your life from your doctor, friends, relatives or simply from public discussion. Under such pressure, many depressed and frightened patients would opt to end their lives. If they do, who's to say what they and their loved ones would miss out on? If our lives are dramas, who is the author? Us? I don't want my final chapter bungled by amateurs.

Gary Eisler, "Life Is Precious—Even at the End," *Wall Street Journal*, October 31, 1997. Reprinted by permission of the Wall Street Journal © 1997. Dow Jones & Company, Inc. All rights reserved.

• • • • • • • • • • • • • • • • • • • • • • • • • • • • • •

1.  This selection was written in
    a.  1995
    b.  1996
    c.  1997
2.  The title suggests that this article will treat
    a.  the need to enjoy one's family on holidays
    b.  the need to take special care of one's children when they are young
    c.  the death of a family member
3.  This selection has no subheads to divide it up.
    a.  true
    b.  false

| | |
|---|---|
| **Sel. 6**   P-Skim | 1. _____ |
| **Time**  :45 = 1,867 wpm | 2. _____ |
| **Score** _____% | 3. _____ |
| ▶ 100% | **Check answers with your instructor.** |
| **Score** = number correct × 33. | |

## B. Rapid Reading

Write your starting time in the box, or wait for the signal. Now go back to the article and read rapidly in 2 or 3 minutes (= 700 wpm to 467 wpm). Answer the quiz without looking back at the selection.

1.  The writer is describing the fatal illness of his
    a.  wife
    b.  daughter
    c.  son

2. We learn that
   a. the daughter is in remission
   b. the son finally dies
   c. the writer has been diagnosed with lymphoma
3. Some of the unexpected joys that the couple experience include
   a. the birth of a grandchild
   b. the visit of their exchange student from Brazil
   c. a surprise family reunion
   d. both a and b
4. The author suggests that assisted suicide, or euthanasia, is a
   a. humane solution to a fatal illness
   b. last resort
   c. choice that prevents loved ones from experiencing their last moments together
   d. very complicated procedure

---

**Sel. 6   R-Read**          1. _____

**Finish** _____ : _____          2. _____

**Start** _____ : _____          3. _____

**Time** _____ : _____          4. _____

   min    sec          **Check answers with your instructor.**

**Rate** ____ **wpm**          **Record rate and score on p. 117.**

**Find rate on p. 343.**

**Score** _____ %

   ▶ 80%

**Score** = number correct × 25.

---

 C. For Discussion and Writing

1. What is the overall organizational pattern of this article? Locate three details that support your choice.
2. Reread paragraph 14. Summarize it. Why is it such an important part of this article?
3. Do you believe that assisted suicide is a viable option? Give reasons for your answer.

• • • • • • • • • • • • • • • •

# SELECTION 7

This selection is taken from a college textbook on the family. Imagine you are previewing and then rapidly reading, prior to serious study. Note how textbook authors help student readers by using clear, organized headings and subheads. Remember to pay attention to the various graphics—print styles and so forth.

Follow these steps in rapid reading this excerpt:

A. Preview skim, then answer the three-item preview quiz.
B. Read rapidly, then answer the five-item reading quiz.

## A. Preview Skimming

Preview the excerpt in 1 minute (= 2,300 wpm) or 1:30 (= 1,533 wpm), noting especially all headings.

• • • • • • • • • • • • • • • •

## MARRIAGE: WHEN AND WHY

• • • • • • • • • • • • • • •

*by Mary Ann Lamanna and Agnes Riedmann (2,300 words)*

1  A couple's happiness in marriage frequently depends on when and why they married. In this section, we will look first at the relationship between marital stability and age at marriage. Later we will discuss some reasons for marrying that are less likely than others to lead to happiness.

### THE STABILITY OF EARLY AND LATE MARRIAGES

2  In 1987 the median age for men at first marriage was 25.3; for women, 23.6 (U.S. National Center for Health Statistics 1990b). Statistics show that marriages are more likely to be stable when partners are in their 20s or older. Marriages that occur when the woman is over 30 may be slightly more stable than those that take place in the 20s, but the most significant distinction is between teenage and all other marriages (Norton and Moorman 1987).

3  Teenage marriages are twice as likely to end in divorce as marriages of those in their 20s (Norton and Moorman 1987). Social scientists generally maintain that people who marry young are less apt to be emotionally or psychologically prepared to select a mate or to perform marital roles (Lee, G. R., 1977, p. 494). Low socioeconomic origins, coupled with school failure or lack of interest in school, are associated with early marriages (Elder and Rockwell 1976, p. 35). Higher fertility and economic deprivation are also associated with early marriages (Otto 1979, pp. 117–18).

4  Age itself is probably not the key variable in determining the likelihood of a marriage succeeding (Knox 1975; Otto 1979). Rather, it seems likely that one's age at marriage is associated with other elements contributing to marital instability, such as "parental dissatisfactions accompanying precocious marriage, social and economic handicaps, premarital pregnancy or the female's attitude toward the pregnancy condition, courtship histories including length of acquaintance and engagement, personality char-

acteristics, and the rapid onset of parental responsibilities" (Otto 1979, p. 119; references deleted). According to one study, however, marrying before age 20 remained a significant predictor of divorce even after all of these factors were statistically controlled for or taken into consideration. Respondents often mentioned sexual infidelity as reason for conflict. As a result, the researchers hypothesized that teens who marry do so when their unmarried peers are experimenting sexually with more than one partner and before they are emotionally ready or willing to relinquish this behavior. In the words of the researchers:

5    It is striking that the role performance variable which best accounts for instability has to do with a lack of sexual exclusiveness. What is intriguing is that this perceived problem coincides with the peak in sexual interest, especially among males, hinting at the possibility that part of the instability experienced may have a biosocial origin. Perhaps individuals constrained to limit their sexual activity to a single individual at a time in their life when variety is important develop a pattern of acting out their impulses throughout much of their life. (Booth and Edwards 1985, p. 73)

6    Although one's age at marriage is only one factor contributing to marital stability or instability, age still is associated with maturity, and sociologist David Knox isolates *four elements of maturity that he does consider to be critical: emotional, economic, relationship, and value maturity* (Knox 1975 [italics added]).

7    **Emotional Maturity.**    The emotionally mature person has high self-esteem, which permits a greater degree of intimacy and interdependence in a relationship. Emotional maturity allows people to respond appropriately to situations. When conflict arises, emotionally mature people aim to resolve it, rather than becoming defensive or threatening to end the relationship.

8    **Economic Maturity.**    Economic maturity implies the ability to support oneself and a partner if necessary. Especially for teenagers who have had little formal training or other job preparation, economic problems can put heavy strains on a marriage. Without a decent wage, people's physical and emotional energy can be drained as they try to scrape together enough to live on. Developing a loving relationship under these conditions is extremely difficult.

9    **Relationship Maturity.**    Relationship maturity involves the skill of communicating with a partner. People with this kind of maturity are able to (1) understand their partner's point of view, (2) make decisions about changing behavior a partner doesn't like, (3) explain their own points of view to their partner, and (4) ask for changes in their partner's behavior when they believe this is appropriate. Without the willingness and skills to understand each other and to make themselves understood, it is difficult or impossible for a couple to maintain intimacy.

10    **Value Maturity.**    Value maturity allows people to recognize and feel confident about their own personal values. By their mid-20s most people have developed a sense of their own values. A high school senior or a first-year college student, however, may still have a number of years of testing and experiencing before he or she reaches value maturity.

11    Age, then, is an important variable in determining a relationship's potential for success. We can measure age objectively; that is, statistics can tell us how age relates to marital stability. Other factors are more subjective; they have to do with the explanations people give for marrying a certain person. But these reasons are also associated with the success of a relationship.

## REASONS FOR MARRYING

12    The reasons people give for marrying are far more complex than "because we were in love." It is a combination of many complicated situations and needs that motivates people to marry. We'll look at several common reasons—first, those that are less likely to lead to a stable marriage, and second, more positive reasons—and see how each relates to the probability of a marriage's success (Knox 1975, pp. 134–48).

13   **Premarital Pregnancy.**   One problematic reason for marriage is premarital pregnancy. Research indicates a consistent relationship between premarital pregnancy and unhappiness in marriage (for example, Norton and Moorman 1987). Ironically, as one study shows, teenage women who married to avoid single parenthood often found themselves to be single parents after all, as 60 percent of the marriages had broken up after six years (Furstenberg 1976). Research indicates that for black and white couples, a premarital birth is most associated with subsequent marital breakup, followed by premarital pregnancy and no premarital pregnancy, in that order (Glick and Norton 1979; Teachman 1983).

14   There are several reasons for such unhappiness or failure. First, the marriage is forced to occur at a time not planned. Often, pregnant brides are teenagers. At least two-thirds of all first births to teenagers were conceived out of wedlock. About 25 percent of teenage first births are legitimated by marriage prior to birth (U.S. Bureau of the Census 1986b). Second, babies are expensive, and a couple not financially prepared for the costs can be overwhelmed. Third, "babies shatter goals": Teenage parents, for example, are less likely to attain educational goals, whether high school or beyond; and they are more likely to have lower incomes and occupational status, to have more children than they would like, and to go on welfare (Hayes, C. D., 1987). Fourth, the in-law relationship may be marred if parents resent their child's marital partner for having brought about a marriage they did not want or viewed as too early. Finally, the couple may not ever have decided they were compatible enough for marriage and may resent each other, either overtly or subconsciously, during the marriage. Of course, other options—abortion, giving the child up for adoption, or raising the child as a single parent—also have an impact on the lives of the young couple. And values and emotions may vary widely among individuals. Still, it is difficult to be encouraging about young, pregnancy-inspired marriages, and some churches have been reluctant to sanction them unless the young couple is unusually mature.

15   There are certainly exceptions to this scenario. Factors that reduce the damaging effects of pregnancy-inspired or teenage marriage include having a supportive family (giving both financial and emotional support), being able to remain in school and then become steadily employed, controlling further fertility, and being older when the pregnancy occurs (Furstenberg and Crawford 1978; Presser 1978). One study found that families that had begun with a pregnancy had caught up financially in most respects after fifteen years (Freedman and Thornton 1979). But this recoupment took place in a period of financial expansion, and the study was limited to whites, many older than teenagers, who married before the birth—so it cannot be generalized regarding many of today's premaritally pregnant young people.

16   **Rebound.**   Marriage on the rebound occurs when a person marries very shortly after breaking up another relationship. To marry on the rebound is undesirable because the wedding occurs as a reaction to one's previous partner, rather than being based on real love for the new partner.

17   **Rebellion.**   Marriage for the sake of rebellion occurs when young people marry primarily because their parents disapprove. Social-psychological theory and research show that parental interference can increase feelings of romantic attraction between partners (Brehm 1966; Driscoll, Davis, and Lipetz 1972); this has been called the *Romeo and Juliet effect*. As with marriage on the rebound, the wedding is a response to someone else (one's parents) rather than to one's partner.

18   **Escape.**   Some people marry to escape an unhappy home situation. The working-class male who hasn't gone to college, for instance, may reason that getting married is the one way he can keep for himself any money he makes instead of handing it over to his parents. Or, denied the opportunity to go away to college, working-class youth often use marriage as an escape from parental authority (Rubin, L., 1976, p. 57).

19    **Physical Appearance.** Marrying solely because of the physical attractiveness of one's partner seldom leads to lifelong happiness. For one thing, beauty is "in the eye of the beholder," and if the beholder finds he or she really doesn't like the partner, that beauty is certain to diminish. Second, the physical beauty of youth changes as partners age. The person who married for beauty often feels she or he has been cheated. After a time, there is little left to be attracted to and love (Berscheid and Walster 1969).

20    **Loneliness.** Sometimes people, especially older adults, marry because they don't want to grow old alone. Marrying is not always the solution, for people can be lonely within marriage if the relationship isn't a strong one. In other words, it is the relationship rather than the institution that banishes loneliness.

21    **Pity and Obligation.** Some partners marry because one of them feels guilty about terminating a relationship: A sense of pity or obligation substitutes for love. Sometimes this pity or obligation takes the form of marrying in order to help or to change a partner, as when a woman marries a man because she believes that her loyal devotion and encouragement will help him quit drinking and "live up to his potential." Such marriages don't often work: The helper finds that his or her partner won't change so easily, and the pitied partner comes to resent being the object of a crusade.

22    **Social Pressure.** Parents, peers, and society in general all put pressure on singles to marry. The expectations built up during courtship exert a great deal of social pressure to go through with the marriage. As engagements are announced or as people become increasingly identified as a couple by friends and family, it becomes more difficult to back out. Still, breaking an engagement or a less formal commitment is probably less stressful than divorcing later or living together unhappily. About 100,000 couples decide to break their engagements each year (Bradsher 1990).

23    **Economic Advancement.** Marrying for economic advancement occurs in all social classes. Young divorced mothers may consider remarriage primarily because they are exhausted from the struggle of supporting and caring for their small children; and working single women often associate marrying with the freedom to stay home at least part of the time. Men, too, can marry for reasons of economic advancement. This can be especially true in some professions where social connections provide important business ties. In the words of one executive, marrying the right woman "open[s] up doors in the same way as going to the right college" (in Cuber and Harroff 1965, pp. 82–83).

24    Is marrying for economic advancement the right reason? The answer depends on the individuals. Certainly the thrust of this book is to encourage intimacy and a strong emotional relationship as a basis for marriage. A person going into a marriage mainly for economic reasons should be very honest with her or his partner, so that both know what the marriage means to the other.

25    **More Positive Reasons for Marrying.** We have seen that rebounding, rebellion, escape, physical appearance, loneliness, obligation, and social pressure are all unlikely bases for a happy marriage. What are some positive reasons? Knox (1975) lists three: companionship, emotional security, and a desire to parent and raise children.

26    Marriage is a socially approved union for developing closeness with another human being. In this environment, legitimate needs for companionship—to love and to be loved by someone else—can be satisfied. Marrying for emotional security implies that a person seeks the stable structure of marrying to help ensure the maintenance of a close interpersonal relationship over time. Although most people do not marry only to have children (and this alone may *not* be a positive reason for marrying), many regard children as a valuable part of married life. "The benefits of love, sex, companionship, emotional security, and children can be enjoyed without marriage. But marriage provides the social approval and structure for experiencing these

phenomena with the same person over time" (Knox 1975, p. 143).

27    It seems to us that the most positive motivation toward marriage involves the goal of making permanent the relationships of love and intimacy.

## IN SUM

28    Americans have been used to thinking of love and marriage as going together like a "horse and carriage," but this association is unique to our modern culture. Historically, marriages were often arranged in the marriage market, as business deals. Many elements of the basic exchange (a man's providing financial support in exchange for the woman's childbearing and child-rearing capabilities, domestic services, and sexual availability) remain.

29    What attracts people to each other? Two important factors are homogamy and physical attractiveness. Some elements of homogamy are propinquity, social pressure, feeling at home with each other, and the fair exchange. Three patterns of courtship familiar in our society are dating, getting together, and cohabitation.

30    Besides homogamy and the degree of intimacy developed during courtship, two other factors related to the success of a marriage are a couple's age at marriage and their reasons for marrying. People who marry too young are less likely to stay married; and there are several negative reasons for marrying that can lead to unhappiness or divorce.

31    If potential marriage unhappiness can be anticipated, breaking up before marriage is by far the best course of action, however difficult it seems at the time. A certain number of courting relationships will end in this fashion.

Mary Ann Lamanna and Agnes Riedmann, *Marriages and Families,* 4th ed. (Belmont, CA: Wadsworth, 1991), 241–46. Used by permission.

• • • • • • • • • • • • • • • • • • • • • • • • • • • • • • • •

1.  The introductory paragraph offers a series of questions.
    a.  true
    b.  false
2.  The title of this segment sets up the two major divisions, which may be paraphrased as (choose two)
    a.  rebellion
    b.  age at marrying
    c.  emotional and economic maturity
    d.  reasons for marrying
3.  There is a short summary at the end.
    a.  true
    b.  false

| | |
|---|---|
| **Sel. 7**   P-Skim | 1. _____ |
| **Time** _____:_____ = _____wpm | 2. _____ |
|         min    sec | 3. _____ |
| **Score** _____% | **Check answers on p. 351.** |
| ▶ 100% | |
| **Score** = number correct × 33. | |

## B. Rapid Reading

Write your starting time in the box, or wait for the signal to read. Aim for 5 minutes (= 418 wpm) or less. The quiz will ask for main ideas and important details only.

1.  Researchers agree that, regarding marriage, one's age is closely related to one's maturity.
    a. true
    b. false

2.  The authors give much more space to poor reasons for marrying than they do to good reasons.
    a. true
    b. false

3.  Of the poor reasons listed, premarital pregnancy/birth was discussed in considerable detail.
    a. true
    b. false

4.  The sociologist Knox lists four "elements" critical to the stability of a marriage. Was physical/sexual compatibility one of the four?
    a. yes
    b. no

5.  Throughout the piece, the main idea put forth by the authors and experts they cite is that marriage, to succeed, should be sought mainly for
    a. the economic and emotional stability it can provide for children
    b. a long-term, close, loving, secure relationship with another human being

| | |
|---|---|
| **Sel. 7**   R-Read | 1. ____ |
| **Finish** ____:____ | 2. ____ |
| **Start** ____:____ | 3. ____ |
| **Time** ____:____ | 4. ____ |
| min    sec | 5. ____ |
| **Rate**____wpm | **Check answers on p. 351.** |
| **Find rate on p. 343.** | **Record rate and score on p. 117.** |
| **Score** ____% | |
| ▶ 80% | |
| **Score** = number correct × 20. | |

## C.  For Discussion and Writing

1.  Reread the first paragraph and look over the subtopics of this selection. What is the overall organizational pattern of this piece?
2.  Reread the section on premarital pregnancy (paragraphs 13–15). List the authors' reasons for why premarital pregnancy can lead to unsuccessful marriages. Can you provide any other reasons?
3.  Reread paragraph 27. What conclusions do the authors come to regarding the reasons for a successful marriage? Do you agree? Can you think of any other reasons for a successful marriage?

• • • • • • • • • • • • • • • • • • • •

## SELECTION 8

This selection carefully examines the research of the sociologist Edward Shorter on European families in the eighteenth and nineteenth centuries. Many of his conclusions are startling. Read rapidly, but reread the selection if you want to study some of his findings.

Follow these steps:

A.  Preview skim. Then answer the three-item preview quiz.
B.  Read rapidly. Then answer the five-item reading quiz.

## A.  Preview Skimming

Preview the excerpt in 1 minute (= 2,900 wpm) or 1:30 (= 1,933 wpm).

• • • • • • • • • • • • • • • • • • •

## LIFE IN THE TRADITIONAL EUROPEAN FAMILY

• • • • • • • • • • • • • • • • • • •

*by Rodney Stark (2,900 words)*

1    Not until quite recently did social historians and sociologists of the family begin to dig out reliable data on family life in times past, and not until the late 1960s and the 1970s did substantial reports on these efforts begin to appear (Laslett, 1965, 1977; Rosenberg, 1975). Up to that time, our notions about family life in, for example, seventeenth-century Europe came from novels, letters, diaries, and autobiographies written at the time. The trouble with these sources is that they reflect a narrow stratum of society: the wealthy and literate. Although they may shed light on how the privileged few lived and felt, they tell us very little about the lives of the vast majority.

2    Europe's peasants and urban laborers left no literary traces. To discover what the life of an average family was like in past times and places, scholars have had to laboriously reconstruct the period from tax records; lawsuits; parish records of baptisms, weddings, and funerals; and even information on gravestones. These labors proved to be worthwhile. The picture of traditional fam-

ily life is far from the warm, intimate, loving, caring extended family that we have long celebrated.

3    For many sociologists, the first real fruits of these historical searches came with the publication of Edward Shorter's *The Making of the Modern Family* in 1975. In it Shorter combined the research of many scholars to depict the traditional family and contrast it with the modern family. Shorter's book changed sociologists' views about the family. Let's see what Shorter found out about the traditional European family.

## HOUSEHOLD COMPOSITION

4    The first step in assessing family life is to know who is living with whom—that is, what the usual composition of a household is. From many studies of different parts of Europe, Shorter discovered that the extended family living in a single household was not typical except for the wealthy, both urban and rural. As we shall see, the typical household did include more than a nuclear family, but the additional members were often only temporary members, such as lodgers and hired hands. Moreover, the traditional household was much smaller than had been assumed. While wealthy households often included ten or more people, most households had only five or six members.

5    We know that in those days women gave birth to many children, often as many as eight or ten. How, then, could the normal household be so small? One reason was high infant and child mortality. One of every three infants died before the age of 1, and another third died before reaching adulthood. Another reason is that children typically left the household to take full-time employment at ages that seem incredibly young to us.

6    In the eighteenth century, for example, children in western France left home to work as servants, shepherds, cowherds, or apprentices at age 7 or 8! By age 10, virtually all children had gone off on their own. In England at this same time, children did not begin to leave home until age 10, but by 15 nearly all of them had left. Keep in mind that people physically matured

later in this period. These were little kids who were having to go it alone.

7    Of course, not all the children left. Eldest sons stayed home or returned home after a period of working elsewhere, and one day took over the farm. In some places, daughters remained home until they married. Nevertheless, the traditional household is remarkable for the small number of children living in it, especially given the large number who were born.

8    In addition, the traditional household contained fewer adults than one might expect. High mortality meant that there were few elderly in the households, and many homes lacked either a father or a mother. In fact, female-headed households were as common in the past as they are today. The primary cause of such households today is divorce, and thus the father often continues to see the children and to provide financial aid. Back then, the cause was death. The average married couple had only about ten years together before one died. As a result, many people remarried; therefore, many children grew up with a stepparent and with half sisters and half brothers. Perhaps you've wondered why so many fairy tales involve wicked stepmothers: because she was such a common part of life back when parents weren't especially nice even to their own children.

9    Thus, the image of the large extended families of preindustrial societies is based on wealthy households. These households were large because their rate of mortality was lower (the rich were much more likely to live to see their grandchildren, and more grandchildren survived), because their children were not pushed out to fend for themselves at young ages, and because many servants were considered part of the household.

## CROWDING

10    Although the average traditional household was not large, even compared with modern households, it was crowded. The overwhelming majority of traditional European families lived in one room, where all indoor family activities took

place. Rural families usually shared their one-room houses with livestock and poultry, while urban families frequently had a lodger or some other nonfamily member sharing their living space. Usually, the one room wasn't even very large. At night, beds were arranged on the floor, and when people had mattresses, the beds were often crowded: Adults and children, males and females, family members and outsiders huddled together for warmth.

11    As late as the 1880s, when good census data were first recorded, half of the people in Berlin and Dresden still lived in one-room households. This situation seemed to be much more common throughout Europe earlier in the century. Far less crowding in households can still cause serious strains among family members. When American families have more than one person per room, husband-wife and parent-child relations become strained. With whole families crowded into one room, family relations in preindustrial times were simply terrible, as we shall see.

## "OUTSIDERS"

12    Though much smaller than had been believed, many traditional households contained nonfamily members. Many rural households contained male and female teenagers who served as hired hands. Such outsiders were particularly common during the peak of the farming season. Urban households frequently included lodgers who paid to eat and live with a family. Often, several unrelated families shared one-room urban homes, forced into a common residence by poverty. Moreover, there was a considerable coming and going by these live-in outsiders. Families tended to have people they did not know well living temporarily in their midst.

13    Clearly, the traditional family lacked privacy and a well-defined boundary. Family members ate, slept, gave birth, engaged in sex, and argued not only in full view of one another but also in full view of a changing audience of outsiders. And the traditional family was under close obser-

vation by neighbors, too. Even rural families did not live far apart, each on their own farm as in Canada and the United States, but in cramped farming villages. As we shall see, these crowded living conditions undermined feelings of family unity.

## CHILD CARE

14    We have seen that the traditional family was quick to send kids out on their own. This reflected more than mere economic necessity or the fact that unskilled children could perform productive labor in preindustrial economies. It also reflected an indifference toward children and neglectful child-care practices. Shorter put it bluntly: "Good mothering is an invention of modernization."

15    A good index of neglect and indifference is found in journals kept by local doctors. All of these doctors complained about parents leaving their infants and young children alone and untended for much of the day. Rashes and sores from unchanged swaddling clothes afflicted nearly all infants. Repeated accounts tell of children burning to death because they were left too close to an open hearth, and reports of unattended infants being eaten by barnyard pigs are frequent. In the part of France where silkworms were raised, a peasant proverb acknowledged that children were neglected during the busy season: "When the silkworms rise, the kids go to paradise." Indeed, throughout Europe, rural infants were most likely to die during the harvest season, when they were most neglected.

16    Even when parents were around their infants, they ignored them. Mothers rarely sang or talked to their infants when they tended them, nor did they play games with them as the children grew older. In fact, mothers didn't even refer to children by name, calling a child "it" or, in France, "the creature."

17    Mothers frequently were unsure of their children's ages (Shorter reports a mother who said her son was either 11 or maybe 14), failed to recall how many children they had given birth to,

and often gave the name of a child who died to the next one born.

18    Because of the high rates of infant mortality, it might be understandable that parents were somewhat reluctant to form intense emotional bonds with their babies. But in some parts of France, parents typically did not attend funerals for children younger than 5, and there is widespread evidence that infant deaths often caused little if any regret or sorrow. Instead, parents often expressed relief at the deaths of children, and many proverbs reflected this attitude. Moreover, dead and even dying infants were often simply discarded like refuse and were frequently noticed "lying in the gutters or rotting on the dungheaps."

19    Large numbers of legitimate infants whose parents were still living were abandoned outside churches or foundling homes. Some scholars suggest that as many as half of the children abandoned in parts of France during the eighteenth century were abandoned by intact families. Additional indifference and neglect is evident in the large numbers of infants sent off to wet nurses, despite the well-known fact that such children faced much higher probabilities of death. Indeed, wet nursing became a prominent cottage industry outside of major cities in the eighteenth and nineteenth centuries, as families, especially the poor, sent away infants so that the mother would not be tied down by nursing and child-care responsibilities. An estimated one-sixth or more of all babies born in Paris in 1777 were shipped out to wet nurses.

20    Once at the wet nurse's, infants were often not nursed at all but fed a paste of grain and water and given little attention. In truth, these homes were baby barns, crowded with infants. Parents seldom, if ever, visited. Deaths were often covered up so that payments could still be collected. But staggering numbers of these babies were never seen again. Nor, it seems, were they missed.

21    The extraordinary infant death rates in preindustrial Europe now become easier to un-

derstand. The general conditions of life and public health practices alone would have produced high mortality rates. But the actual rates were pushed even higher because of neglect and indifference. Indeed, as late as the 1920s, a government study in Austria attributed about 20 percent of infant deaths to "poor care."

22    Obviously, infants usually gained little emotional support from the preindustrial family. But what about other family members? What Shorter found seems as alien to us today as the idea of parents engaging in sex while sharing their bed with children and a lodger.

## RELATIONS BETWEEN HUSBANDS AND WIVES

23    Only in modern times have most people married for love. In the "good old days," most married for money and labor—marriage was an economic arrangement between families. How much land or wealth did the man have? How large a dowry would the bride bring to her spouse? Emotional attachments were of no importance to parents in arranging marriages, and neither the bride nor the groom expected emotional fulfillment from marriage.

24    Shorter (1975) noted an absence of emotional expression between couples and doubted that more than a few actually felt affection. The most common sentiments seem to have been resentment and anger. Not only was wife beating commonplace but so was husband beating. And when wives beat their husbands, it was the husband, not the wife, who was likely to be punished by the community. In France, a husband beaten by his wife was often made to ride through the village sitting backwards on a donkey and holding the donkey's tail. He had shamed the village by not controlling his wife properly. The same practice of punishing the husband was frequently employed when wives were sexually unfaithful.

25    The most devastating evidence of poor husband-wife relations was the reaction to death and dying. Just as the deaths of children often caused no sorrow, the death of a spouse often

prompted no regret. Some public expressions of grief was expected, especially by widows, but popular culture abounded with contrary beliefs. Shorter reported the following proverbs:

> The two sweetest days of a fellow in life,
> Are the marriage and burial of his wife.

> Rich is the man whose wife is dead and
> horse alive.

26    Indeed, peasants who rushed for medical help whenever a horse or cow took sick often resisted suggestions by neighbors to get a doctor for a sick wife. The loss of a cow or a horse cost money, but a wife was easily replaced by remarriage to a younger woman who could bring a new dowry.

27    Since women were in relatively short supply, would they not have been highly valued? Simply because men think of women as valuable "goods" does not mean they will love or even like their wives. Thus, in ancient Rome, where female infanticide resulted in far more extreme sex ratios than existed in preindustrial Europe, men found it difficult to relate to women, and many men preferred not to marry at all since prostitution flourished. As Beryl Rawson (1986) reported, "One theme that occurs in Latin literature is that wives are difficult and therefore men do not care much for marriage." In 131 B.C., the Roman censor Quintas Caecilius Metellus Macedonicus proposed that the senate make marriage compulsory because, although "we cannot have a really harmonious life with our wives," the society needed children and therefore men must marry (Rawson, 1986). As with the women in Athens, Roman women were hidden away as too valuable to associate freely. But they weren't often loved.

## BONDS BETWEEN PARENTS AND CHILDREN

28    Besides the lack of emotional ties to infants and young children, emotional bonds between parents and older children were also weak. First, most of the children left the household at an early age. Second, when they did so, it was largely a case of "out of sight, out of mind." If a child ventured from the village, he or she was soon forgotten, not just by the neighbors but by the parents as well. All traces were lost of those who moved away. According to Shorter, a French village doctor wrote in his diary in 1710 that he had heard about one of his brothers being hanged but that he had completely lost track of the others.

29    Finally, even those children who stayed at home in the village did not come to love their parents. Instead, they fought constantly with their parents about inheritance rights and about when their parents would retire, and they openly awaited their parents' deaths. Shorter concluded that dislike and hatred were the typical feelings between family members.

## PEER GROUP BONDS

30    Surely people in traditional societies must have liked someone. Unfortunately for our image of traditional family life, the primary unit of society and attachment was not the family but the peer group. The family provided for reproduction, child rearing (such as it was), and economic support (often grudgingly), but emotional attachments were primarily to persons of the same age and sex *outside* the family.

31    Wives had close attachments to other wives, and husbands to other husbands. Social life was highly segregated by sex and was based on childhood friendships and associations. For example, a group of neighborhood boys would become close friends while still very young, and these friendships remained the primary ties of these people all their lives. The same occurred among women. While this no doubt provided people with a source of intimacy and self-esteem, it hindered the formation of close emotional bonds within the family.

32    A woman would enter marriage expecting to share her feelings not with her husband but with her peers. Men reserved intimate feelings for their peers, too. In this way the weak boundaries defining the household were perforated by primary relations beyond the family. Thus, out-

siders determined much that went on within a household. Husbands and wives often acted to please their peers, not each other.

[33]    Of course, sometimes people loved their children, and some couples undoubtedly fell in love. But most evidence indicates that life in the preindustrial household was the opposite of the popular, nostalgic image of quiet, rural villages where people happily lived and died, secure and loved, amidst their large families and lifelong friends. It was instead a nasty, spiteful, loveless life that no modern person would willingly endure. Indeed, as industrialization made other options possible, the family changed radically because no one was willing to endure the old ways any longer.

Rodney Stark, *Sociology*, 7th ed. (Belmont, CA: Wadsworth, 1998), 360–366. Used by permission.

• • • • • • • • • • • • • • • • • • • • • • • • • • • • •

1.  The title suggests that this excerpt will consider
    a.  European life
    b.  European family life
    c.  traditional European family life
2.  This excerpt was published in
    a.  1996
    b.  1997
    c.  1998
3.  This excerpt is subdivided by only three subtitles.
    a.  true
    b.  false

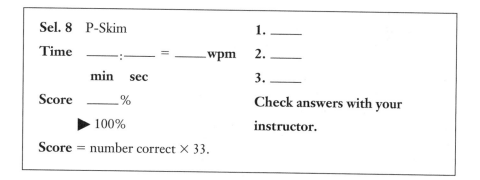

| Sel. 8   P-Skim | 1. _____ |
|---|---|
| **Time** _____ : _____ = _____ wpm | 2. _____ |
| min    sec | 3. _____ |
| **Score** _____% | **Check answers with your** |
| ▶ 100% | **instructor.** |
| **Score** = number correct × 33. | |

## B.  Rapid Reading

Write your starting time in the next box, or wait for the next signal. Though this is a long and carefully written selection, push yourself to read it quickly. Remember, you can always go back to reread more slowly. Take no more than 7 minutes (= 414 wpm) or, better yet, 6 (= 483 wpm) to rapidly read this piece on the family.

1.  Edward Shorter's *The Makings of Modern Life* was
    a.  a revolutionary sociological study
    b.  a traditional explanation of European family life
    c.  criticized by most sociologists specializing in the family
    d.  never published in the United States
2.  Which of the following is *not* one of Shorter's findings concerning the European family of the past?
    a.  These families were smaller than once imagined.
    b.  Children took jobs as early as the age of seven.
    c.  Many homes lacked both a mother and father.
    d.  Widows rarely remarried.
3.  The traditional European family tended to live
    a.  on a large farm
    b.  in one room
    c.  in crowded tenement buildings
    d.  all of these
4.  In regard to children, Shorter concludes that
    a.  they were raised with little love
    b.  the church was the center of their social life
    c.  they rarely attended school
    d.  fathers played an important role
5.  In earlier years in Europe, which unit provided the strongest emotional bond?
    a.  husband and wife
    b.  father and son
    c.  mother and daughter
    d.  peer group

---

**Sel. 8   R-Read**

**Finish** ____:____

**Start** ____:____

**Time** ____:____

      min    sec

**Rate**____**wpm**

**Find rate on p. 343.**

**Score** ____%

▶ 80%

**Score** = number correct × 20.

1. ____

2. ____

3. ____

4. ____

5. ____

Check answers with your instructor.

**Record rate and score on p. 117.**

## C. For Discussion and Writing

1.  What thesis does Shorter present?
2.  As you read this selection, which findings from Shorter surprised you most?
3.  In what ways does your understanding of today's American family differ from Shorter's descriptions of early European life? Like Shorter, be as specific as you can.

• • • • • • • • • • • • • • • • • • • •

# SELECTION 9

This next selection, taken from the same book the previous selection came from, examines how relationships have been altered by industrialization. The author explores changes in romantic love, kinship relationships, and divorce practices, and he refers again to some of the findings of Edward Shorter. As with the previous selection, this excerpt is thought provoking and should be reread after you have read it rapidly.

Follow these steps as you rapidly read this well-researched excerpt:

A.  Preview skim the selection. Then answer the three-item preview quiz.
B.  Read the report rapidly. Then answer the five-item reading quiz.

## A. Preview Skimming

Preview the excerpt in 1 minute (= 2,400 wpm) or 1:30 (=1,600 wpm). Carefully consider the title, study the subheads, and try to predict what topics will be covered.

• • • • • • • • • • • • • • • •

 ## MODERNIZATION AND ROMANCE, KINSHIP, AND DIVORCE

*by Rodney Stark (2,400 words)*

1    Here we shall point out that life in modern societies is not simply better than in preindustrial societies but also *different*.

2    Nowhere is this clearer than in the transformations in family life. Where once a "happy couple" meant an absence of mutual antagonism, today that phrase is reserved for people who feel strong positive sentiments. We do not hope for a tolerable marriage; we seek love. Nor do we think it enough that parents do not hate, abuse, or neglect their children; we expect parents to love, nourish, and encourage them. We expect people to grieve when their parents die, not to be relieved that they are out of the way. In short, we assume that families foster deeply felt emotional attachments. How did this transformation come about?

3    Quite simply, modernization radically changed the conditions of life, giving people the opportunity to seek individual happiness. Shorter

has sketched a number of these changes. First, industrialization freed individuals from depending on inheritance for their livelihoods. Eldest sons no longer had to wait for their fathers' land; daughters no longer had to wait for a husband with land. Both sons and daughters could seek wage-paying work, especially in the rapidly expanding urban industries. Soon young people were heading off to the cities in droves.

4    This change allowed people to make their own marital choices, free from both parental approval and concern about keeping property in the family. People no longer had to delay marriage until their parents died or retired, and property concerns no longer dominated the choice of a spouse. As these matters became less important, other concerns emerged. And as men and women began to select their marriage partners, they began to seek people who appealed to them. Romantic attraction rapidly became the basis for marriage. "I love you" became the precondition for asking, "Will you marry me?"

5    Of course, notions of romantic love were not discovered in modern times. Greek and Roman poets and dramatists wrote of love; indeed, the Trojan War was thought to have been fought because of Paris's all-consuming love for Helen. And love was a major theme of court poets and minstrels in the days of chivalry and knighthood. But until relatively modern times few could afford to let love be the basis for marriage selection. The Puritans in England were among the first to stress the importance of romantic sentiments between husbands and wives, and this reflected their status as members of a newly affluent middle class who could afford to marry for love.

6    In fact, affluence explains much of modern family life. The average modern family is wealthy beyond the dreams of preindustrial families. One of the first fruits of this affluence was space and privacy. As rapidly as economic circumstances permitted, families sought sufficient household space to gain privacy from one another and to shield themselves from outsiders. While married couples today routinely and openly express affection in ways unthinkable in the past, they are able to keep their most intimate relations private.

7    Moreover, the rise of romantic love in marriage redirected the primary attachments of the individual to within the household. Husbands and wives now expect their relationships to take priority over attachments to peers. A popular song at the turn of the twentieth century proclaimed, "Those wedding bells are breaking up that old gang of mine." With modernization came the expectation that husbands would not remain "one of the boys."

8    This redirection of primary attachments to family members was facilitated by mobility. People now seldom remain in the same place throughout their lives. As people become adults, they move away and break ties to their peers. Even if an individual does not go away, most of the peer group does. A common observation today is that if you want a lifelong friend, you had better marry one. Husbands and wives have become the only consistent, permanent emotional attachments.

9    Romantic love between spouses has also affected parent-child relationships. We now commonly believe that children must be wanted or they should not be engendered. By the late nineteenth century, child care and good parenting became a major topic in book publishing (Zuckerman, 1975). Attitudes toward children have changed so dramatically that it is now against the law to treat children in ways that were once customary.

## MODERNIZATION AND KINSHIP

10    One of the widely noted "symptoms" of the decline of the family in modern times is the erosion of kinship bonds. We have seen that these perceptions are based in part on nostalgic illusion; the preindustrial family was not the warm, secure nest we once thought it was. Yet for many North Americans and Europeans, the extended family remains an ideal standard against which the nuclear family is seen as wanting. Reiss (1988) has noted the irony that this should be so

even though most of these same people do not want to live with their parents or with their grown children.

11     Nevertheless, the question persists: Has kinship really taken on less importance among people in modern societies? To answer the question, we shall have to distinguish between the *quantity* and the *quality* of kinship bonds.

12     There can be no doubt that most Americans are much less likely to have as many close bonds to brothers and sisters, cousins, aunts and uncles, and nephews and nieces than was the case several generations ago. This is a simple result of the *decline in fertility*.

13     The preindustrial household contained relatively few people despite widespread impressions about family life in that period. However, in the nineteenth and early twentieth centuries, especially in the United States and Canada, the average woman had many more babies than she does today and, even with mortality considered, the average family was much larger. The result is that several generations ago the average person in the United States and Canada had many more relatives (Pullum, 1982). A simple example will make the point.

14     At the turn of the century, the average North American woman gave birth to more than three children, and when only those women who married are counted, their average was four children. So put yourself in an average family. If all members marry and each couple has the average number of children, then if you gave a party and invited your relatives, the gathering would include your two parents, twelve aunts and uncles (six by marriage), twenty-four cousins, three siblings, twelve nieces and nephews, and four children—a total of fifty-seven people.

15     In contrast, put yourself in an average family when the birth rate is two per female. Now your family reunion will draw two parents, four uncles and aunts (two by marriage), four cousins, one sibling, two nieces and nephews, and two children—a total of fifteen people. And that's part of what has happened to kinship bonds in modern life: There simply are far fewer of them.

Other things being equal, a person born at the turn of the century had *six times* the probability of forming a close bond with a cousin, for example. So modernization has greatly reduced the *quantity* of kinship bonds and, in that way, may have reduced the quality as well. But then again, maybe with so many kinship bonds the chances were reduced of having any one of them become really close.

16     Of American adults who have a living parent, one in ten spends nearly every evening with his or her parents, while another two of ten spend a social evening with their parents several times a week. Indeed, more than half of Americans with living parents see them at least once or twice a month. Another third only sees their parents once or twice a year—they probably live a long distance apart—and only one in ten seems to have broken off ties.

17     Americans are even more active in spending social evenings with relatives (often their sons and daughters). Those with siblings also see them often, although less frequently than they see parents and other relatives.

18     Finally, almost two-thirds of married Americans rate their marriage as "very happy," and only 2 percent say it was "not too happy."

19     The picture that emerges here is not one of weak family ties. The American family has grown much smaller, but it seems to have stayed rather tightly knit. Most Americans spend frequent social evenings with relatives, and most are happily married.

20     But, you may be asking, if people are so happy with their marriages, why are there so many divorces? Don't high divorce rates suggest a breakdown in ties between wives and husbands?

## MODERNIZATION AND DIVORCE

21     Ironically, a high divorce rate probably indicates that the marital relationship has become *much more important than it used to be*. Back when most couples had weak emotional ties at best, they seldom divorced; now, although couples marry for love, they often divorce in anger and

disappointment. Let's explore why divorce occurs and what it means for family life.

22    Divorce means the end of a marriage, but it does not necessarily mean the end of a family, because two-thirds of divorces occur between people who have children. One parent (usually the father) leaves the household, but a family remains. Moreover, divorce does not mean that many people experiment with marriage and then opt for a single life. Fewer than 5 percent of North American adults at any given moment report their current marital status as divorced; more than 80 percent who divorce remarry. Thus, millions of couples give up on their marriages but not on marriage itself. These statistics offer an important insight into *why* people get divorced.

23    Most people who get divorced report that their marriage ceased to provide adequate emotional satisfaction—that is, their relationship was no longer happy. That might mean that the current high divorce rate indicates a lot of unhappy marriages, but it could also mean that at any given moment the great majority of marriages are happy ones. How is this possible?

24    Over the past eighty years, divorce laws have become much less restrictive. The intention behind this legislation was to strengthen the family by permitting intolerable marriages to be dissolved. The rationale was that if the bad marriages are ended by divorce, most marriages will be good ones. Today, when many marriages end in divorce, it seems unlikely that people are enduring bad marriages to the same extent as when only a few got divorced. Indeed, it seems likely that people today become dissatisfied with marriages people would have deemed acceptable fifty years ago.

25    Marital satisfaction is partly a matter of comparison. In days when few people divorced, a couple comparing themselves with their friends might have rated their marriage as good. Today, the same couple might find theirs to be a poor marriage by comparison because the standard has risen: Marriages must be better to qualify as satisfactory when more unsatisfactory marriages are eliminated by divorce. Thus, as divorce rates rise, the average level of satisfaction in existing marriages should rise also. We have reason to suspect, however, that a substantial part of this perceived satisfaction is simply a "newness" or "variety" effect. That is, as people divorce and remarry, many may not find someone who suits them better but simply a replacement for a partner who had become too familiar.

### When Romance Fades

26    We have seen that romance has become the basis for marriage in modern times. People now expect deep romantic sentiments to lead them into marriage and to sustain their marriages. Unfortunately, these feelings can fade and be difficult to revive. Because so many adults rely on their spouses for their deepest emotional ties, immense weight is placed on these romantic feelings. Even small tensions are easily magnified, for any discontent or threat to this primary attachment provokes anxiety. Indeed, romantic sentiments may suffer from too frequent assessment, and the slightest doubts can easily shatter that "special feeling." So, too, can the simple passage of time, especially when sexual attraction is the focal point of romance.

27    Studies suggest that sexual attraction, in and of itself, is based partly on novelty and tends to decline with time (Pinco, 1961). If this is an intrinsic feature of sexual attraction and not just a temporary aspect of current sexual patterns, then a decline in sexual attraction and satisfaction will permanently threaten marriages based on sexual attraction. That is, if sexuality is a primary basis for emotional attachment between husbands and wives, then marriages will tend to weaken as familiarity causes a loss of fervor. In this sense, a good deal of divorce may reflect a form of swapping sexual partners.

28    In any event, clearly most people do not equate love with sexual thrills. While a decline in sexual novelty may be at the root of many divorces, many other couples find that their relationships improve the longer they live together. Research shows that marital satisfaction is higher

the longer a couple has been married (Campbell, 1975). Once again, this finding could partly reflect a bias of selection. As time passes, more of the less-satisfied couples get divorced. However, many couples report that their marriages have become more satisfying over time and that they are happier now than when they were just married.

Rodney Stark, *Sociology*, 7th ed. (Belmont, CA: Wadsworth, 1998), 366–371. Used by permission.

• • • • • • • • • • • • • • • • • • • • • • • • • • • • • • • • •

1. From the title, it appears that this selection will examine
   a. how modernization led to World War II
   b. how relationships have changed dramatically
   c. how modernization has saved humanity from destruction
2. The year of publication is
   a. 1996
   b. 1997
   c. 1998
3. The selection ends with a discussion of
   a. how friendships dissolve
   b. what happens when romantic love is no longer the main force in a marriage

| | |
|---|---|
| **Sel. 9**   P-Skim | 1. _____ |
| **Time** _____:_____ = _____**wpm** | 2. _____ |
| **min    sec** | 3. _____ |
| **Score** _____% | **Check answers on p. 351.** |
| ▶ 100% | |
| **Score** = number correct × 33. | |

## B. Rapid Reading

Write your starting time in the next box, or wait for the signal to begin reading. This excerpt is densely packed with details, so you need to push yourself to maintain a rapid pace. Take no more than 6 minutes (= 400 wpm); 5 would be better (= 480 wpm).

1. According to the author, what is modern society's attitude toward the family?
   a. It is quickly disintegrating.
   b. Families have created strong emotional bonds.

2. What is the key factor in the resurgence of romantic love?
   a. more affluence in the family
   b. less affluence in the family
   c. a movement away from traditional religious beliefs
3. According to the selection, modernization led to stronger ties between husband and wife and stronger ties among the spouses' friends.
   a. true
   b. false
4. The conclusion drawn regarding modern family ties is that they are
   a. weaker than those in the past
   b. stronger than those in the past
   c. no different than those in the past
   d. hard to assess because of conflicting evidence
5. According to the selection, what does a higher divorce rate in modern society indicate?
   a. Marriage has more importance today than in the past.
   b. Marriage has less importance today.
   c. Romantic love has less importance today.
   d. Today's marriages are more unhappy.

---

**Sel. 9   R-Read**

**Finish** ____:____

**Start**   ____:____

**Time**   ____:____

           min   sec

**Rate**____wpm

**Find rate on p. 343.**

**Score**   ____%

       ▶ 80%

**Score** = number correct × 20.

1. ____

2. ____

3. ____

4. ____

5. ____

Check answers on p. 351.

Record rate and score on p. 117.

---

 C. For Discussion and Writing

1. Reread paragraphs 5–7, on romantic love. Summarize the main points made here. What dominant organizational pattern emerges in these paragraphs?
2. List two or three surprising conclusions this selection makes regarding modern relationships. Do you agree or disagree with these conclusions? Give reasons for your answers.

3.  Reread the last subsection, "When Romance Fades." Summarize the author's understanding of sexuality's role in marriage and divorce. How important do you think sexual attraction is to a successful marriage?

## SELECTION 10

After three fact-filled selections in a row, you can finish with a long but more casual reading: a feature story taken from an urban newspaper.

Follow these steps in rapid reading this article:

A.  Preview skim as usual, then answer the three-item preview quiz.
B.  Read the article rapidly, then answer the five-item reading quiz.

### A.  Preview Skimming

Preview the article in 2 minutes (= 1,750 wpm) or more quickly.

## EVERYPLACE, ENEMIES OF THE FAMILY

*by Nina J. Easton (3,500 words)*

**While politicians talk of family values, beleaguered parents don't look to government for answers. But they find plenty of people to blame—from neighbors to themselves.**

1   SAN ANTONIO—More and more, politicians talk about The Family. But families talk about politicians less and less.

2   Here's George Bush during the State of the Union speech, concerned blue eyes fixed firmly on the TV cameras: "We must strengthen the family—because it is the family that has the great bearing on our future." Here's Democratic contender Bill Clinton, out on the campaign trail: "Our streets are meaner, our families are more broken. . . ."

3   Trisha and Dick Corrigan are worried about the rise of broken homes, too. But they do not see much of a role for direct government aid: They will settle for some tax breaks so the investments they set aside for three college educations will be worth something. Irene and Frank Aguero can barely cover the rent, food and utilities on their combined minimum-wage salaries. Thank God for Irene's mother and her good health, because the Agueros cannot afford day care for their two young daughters. But when asked what government could do to ease their family life, they draw a blank.

4   Most of the nearly 30 families interviewed in this South Texas town do not look to government to solve family problems. Issues like day care, parental leave and more flexible work hours rarely come up, even though large majorities of Americans support these initiatives when directly asked about them.

5   Americans still seem to view this messy business of family—with its own rhythms, bonds and strains—as an internal affair. They blame declining family values on their neighbors, on

"those people" across town, sometimes on themselves. "A lot of people nowadays are making choices without thinking," 41-year-old Robert Gonzales, a divorced father of two, says in a pointed reference to himself, as well as society. "And when they don't think things through, a lot of loose ends are left."

6    Still, politicians know that talk about the troubled family goes to the very soul of this country and its romanticized image of itself. A majority of Americans tells pollsters that they are satisfied with their own home lives, but when they look beyond their own front lawns they see family values in decline—and they worry that problems like crime and drugs and teen pregnancy are the result.

7    Those worries are evident in San Antonio, a mid-size city with small-town values. This is a place where you still pump first/pay later, where McDonald's has not yet squeezed out Murf's Better Burgers, where the cashiers hand-punching prices at the Handy Andy Supermarket know their regular customers.

8    Like other American cities, this one divides neatly between families who have managed to keep it all together—even if under siege from the pressures of modern life—and families that have crumbled under the weight. Economic status is one factor determining the survivors, but not the only one: San Antonio's gangs are more successful at recruiting middle-class members than low-income teens, notes Cynthia Test, who runs a gang-intervention program.

9    For Americans everywhere, family time together is at a premium, with parents under economic stress and usually holding down at least two jobs between them. Majorities of respondents across the country tell pollsters that parents today do not spend enough time with their children. One national survey found that one in five teen-agers had not had a 10-minute conversation with a parent in the past month. Another study found that parents in the 1980s spent 10 to 12 fewer hours per week with their children than parents did in 1960.

10    Meanwhile, single-parent households are on the rise—boosted by out-of-wedlock births. Nationally, 24 percent of children live with only one parent, usually the mother, and one in three of those households lives in poverty. Among urban minorities the situation is even more distressing: According to the Urban Institute, nearly 90 percent of black children born today will spend at least part of their childhood with a single parent.

11    "I see mothers daily who have given up," says Steve Johnson, the weary and frustrated principal of Mark Twain Middle School in the heart of San Antonio's barrio. "And there aren't enough people and places to help them."

12    Throughout the neighborhoods like the one Mark Twain serves are families disintegrating, parents afraid of their own children and throwing up their hands in disgust, or—like Mary Johnson—left dazed and confused by the truckload of troubles that came crashing through their front door. "I've asked myself 9,000 times, 'Where did I go wrong?'" says Johnson, who sent her gang-member son to a juvenile facility after he was shot three times within six months. "I beat my head against the wall, but I don't have an answer."

13    At the other end of the spectrum are families making a determined effort to build private buffers against what they see as an increasingly unstable and amoral outside world. One family moved to the country to lessen urban influences on their two boys; a couple in their 20s made wrenching financial sacrifices so the mother of their toddler could quit work; another set of parents keeps their children out of the school system as part of a growing trend toward home schooling.

14    Even among families with comfortable incomes, supportive relationships and children who appear to be well on the way to college and bright careers, there is a palpable fear of what the future holds. In the midst of a discussion about the challenges of being a single father, self-employed consultant Eduardo Gutierrez, 48,

suddenly stops and looks his interviewer hard in the eye. "You know what my nightmare is?" he asks. "That my kid might not do as well as me."

15  All this is a potent brew of political discontent. But so far in 1992, it remains unfocused, untapped.

16  Most of the cries for government help come from those representing the institutions forced into the vacuum left by broken families—the schools, the churches and a myriad of under-funded private and governmental family support agencies. They are the ones, like principal Steve Johnson, who daily pick up the pieces when a family becomes dysfunctional. They are over-burdened, angry at the country's political leadership and pessimistic about the future.

17  "We do not see the connection between families and children and developing our future work force, our leaders," says Gloria Rodriquez, executive director of Avance, a parenting program for San Antonio's low-income Latinos. "Families are the basic unit of society, and if you're not supporting that basic unit, society is going to crumble. It's a ticking time bomb ready to explode."

18  With Latinos making up half the population, San Antonio reflects the future of the American West, especially California. Immigrants who poured into town from Mexico in the early 1900s to sew shirts and shell nuts are clustered on the West Side in neighborhoods that look like a cross between East Los Angeles and a Western movie set. Chic enclaves to the north—where pristine storefronts suddenly materialize offering fresh roasted coffee and exotic flowers—are populated by Anglos. The city's small black population is concentrated on the poverty-stricken East Side.

19  The weed-choked asphalt lots and boarded-up storefronts of downtown San Antonio suggest better times gone by. But the military and tourism (this is home to the Alamo) spared the city from the economic free fall that took hold in Texas towns built on oil. Despite large pockets of poverty, San Antonio seemed insulated from the worst urban ills—until gangs

hit the headlines. Local leaders say the groups—many of them Los Angeles exports—have been active for six years. But last summer they started shooting, and the city has been in shock ever since.

20  To Cynthia Test, who runs the anti-gang program, the rise of gangs reflects the sorry state of San Antonio's families. "The gang becomes a family. They are great at communicating with each other. There is trust and respect. We should learn from them," she says.

21  Inside San Antonio, many families—like David and Julie Welch—are building their own Alamos against the destructive forces gnawing at the family. Until two years ago, Julie, 26, worked as a bookkeeper, and in many ways her life would be easier if she had kept her job. But when Amy was born, she and her husband, David, 31, decided she would stay home. "The first six months after she was born, we didn't know how we were going to do it," she says. "We're still late on a lot of bills."

22  Even that understates the sacrifices the Welches have made. As Julie sits on the floor of the nursery, passing brightly colored blocks to her toddler, she recounts how the couple once owned their own home (bought with Veterans Administration help). But when she quit work, they could no longer afford the payments so they moved to a small clapboard rental house nestled between an upscale country club neighborhood and a crime-infested commercial strip. When one of their cars was stolen, they were almost relieved. "We couldn't make the payment," she says. "The bank would have gotten it anyways."

23  David is starting to make money, running his own paint-and-body shop, but his hours are grueling. This night he will not get home until 10 p.m.; after she puts the baby to bed, Julie will push a dresser up against the back door so no intruders can break in.

24  The images of the stable, well-adjusted nuclear family in the '50s and '60s may have been largely the figment of TV producers' imaginations. How often in real life did that carefully

trimmed hedge at the end of the cul-de-sac conceal a family scarred by alcoholism, physical or emotional abuse, or simply a bad marriage?

25   But that does not stop many families in the 1990s from trying to re-create their own version of "Father Knows Best." Couples like the Welches are searching for stability in an unstable world. When she was a child, Julie recalls, her once close-knit family was torn apart when her older brother got into drugs. Her husband's mother abandoned the family when he was 5; he had a troubled childhood and adolescence. Now David is trying to build the kind of family he did not have.

26   And more couples would do the same if they could, Julie Welch insists. "The problem is the economy," she says. "It makes it real hard for mothers to stay at home. I know too many women who say, 'If we could afford it, I'd stay at home.' The cost of living is going up, but salaries aren't."

27   Landa Mabry, 42, had the luxury of being able to stay home, and she did. She and her husband, Bob, a 42-year-old food broker, went even further to ensure a stable home life by moving out to the country, north of San Antonio. A born and bred urbanite, she says the move was a culture shock. But the impact on her two boys—Matt, now 17, and Clint, 14—was worth it.

28   "We kept our kids from being exposed [to urban culture] longer than most," says Landa, whose elegant home provides sweeping vistas of the valley below. "You didn't have something on every corner. We were more prone to do things as a family."

29   Tim and Jill Thomas, both in their 20s, are sheltering their four young children, ages 1 to 7, from the harsher side of modern life in a different way—through home schooling. "A lot of what we do is integrate our beliefs," Jill Thomas says. "We do Bible readings and life skills on how it applies to your life."

30   Home schooling is on the rise, particularly among fundamentalist Christians. (It is legal in every state, though the degree of regulation varies.) One estimate put the number of home-schooled children in 1990 at between 250,000 and 350,000, roughly three times as many as in 1983. The Thomases say they know 30 other San Antonio families engaged in home-schooling.

31   Jill does the teaching while Tim covers the bills by waiting tables. Articulate and thoughtful, the Thomases make clear that their decision to home-school is more than a reaction to the lack of religious training in schools (though Tim blames today's adolescent social ills on the demise of school prayer). They complain that young children today are pushed too hard and that too often children are afterthoughts in their parents' hectic schedules.

32   "It's convenient for society to put them somewhere else," Jill says. "People want to give *things* rather than *self.*"

☐

33   These families and others in San Antonio are concerned about the influence of popular culture on their children. According to a 1991 poll by the Washington research firm Mellman & Lazarus, two-thirds of Americans believe that the entertainment industry—not parents or teachers or peers—has the most influence on the development of children's values today.

34   Gary Bauer, president of the Washington-based Family Research Center, says parents are particularly concerned that the values they try to teach their children are undermined by conflicting signals in the mass media. "They feel surrounded by hostile territory," he says.

35   Child-development experts also worry about the steady barrage of violence and explicit sex children receive through TV, movies and popular music. Last November, the National Commission on Children called on TV producers to exercise greater restraint in children's programming and advertising.

36   Popular culture is a key factor behind concerns over the country's moral standards and quality of life, Bauer argues. The Mellman/Lazarus survey, sponsored by the Massachusetts Mutual Life Insurance Co., found that 65% of

respondents worried that family values are declining, with the sharpest concerns found among the elderly, women, blacks and Latinos.

[37]    However, the same survey found that two-thirds of Americans are "very" or "extremely" satisfied with their own family life. And even the bleakest assessments of today's adolescents also note that most teen-agers go on to lead healthy, productive lives.

[38]    That was evident among San Antonio youths like 16-year-old Michael Gonzales, who says most of the talk about gangs and drugs on campus is overstated. Sporting a ponytail, glasses and a deadly serious demeanor, Gonzales—who intends to become a sound engineer—says the biggest pressure in his life is academic achievement.

[39]    Likewise, 17-year-old Matt Mabry seems most concerned about his future after college. He has worked three summers in his dad's food brokerage firm, but technological advances and competitive pressure are fast making the business obsolete. "I don't know if it will even be there," he says.

[40]    Seventeen-year-old Crissy Rivas, who attends a small private school, sees family communication as a serious issue. "Parents don't listen," she says. "Some of the kids are afraid of their parents."

☐

[41]    Although divorce rates have leveled off—and in many upper-middle-class San Antonio neighborhoods divorce is as rare as spring snow—ruptured marriages remain a fixture of American life. And many are troubled by that. "If the car gets dirty they get a divorce," complains Emily Jackson, a 70-year-old widow and grandmother of three. "They don't get married with the idea that it's going to work."

[42]    Rick Saldana, 28, assistant manager of a posh San Antonio restaurant, estimates that half of his friends are already divorced. "People think it's easier to get divorced than to break off an engagement," says Saldana, who recently broke off his own engagement because he was not ready for marriage.

[43]    Marriage did not work out for Robert Gonzales, a 41-year-old railroad switchman, but he is confident that he has softened the impact on his two children. Inside his modest apartment crammed with family photos, Gonzales paints an upbeat picture of his life as a father. Although the children live with their mother and his job demands long hours and travel, Gonzales says he sees his children frequently and maintains good communication. Private school tuition for 11-year-old Amanda, he says, is part of "an investment in my children."

[44]    That does not cover the emotional costs, though. When Amanda is asked about pressures in her life, she begins to cry. She chokes on the words as they haltingly spill out: "My . . . parents' . . . divorce." Then comes a flood of tears she cannot stop.

[45]    Outside, after the interview, Gonzales says, "I didn't know she felt that way." He and Amanda's mother have been divorced six years.

[46]    Experts are divided on the impact of divorce on the family and on American society.

[47]    Researchers note that divorce does not equal dysfunction: Many divorced parents remarry, and plenty of single parents are successful at raising their children. But, increasingly, men are missing from family life. According to surveys by University of Pennsylvania sociologist Frank Furstenberg and colleagues, nearly half of all children living apart from their fathers had not seen them during the previous year, and for those that did see them, the contact was sporadic.

[48]    Often, it is the schools that step in when the father is not around. Steve Johnson, the principal, recalls how one mother demanded that school authorities discipline her son for allegedly breaking her boyfriend's window. "She wanted us to punish him," Johnson recalls incredulously. "She sat in the room telling him he was worthless. After she left, he grabbed me and started bawling. Here was this big pathetic kid—he must weigh 200 pounds—crying on my shoulder."

[49]    Johnson is a firm believer that schools should pick up where troubled families leave off.

He has tried to restructure his own school to meet the social—as well as educational—needs of children. "I really feel that education is going to have to fill the vacuum," he says. "My dream was to have the school become a community center."

50    If that happens, it will not be here. Johnson's attempts to expand his school's role have run into resistance from the city's education Establishment. So Johnson is resigning this spring. "Some of my colleagues think I'm crazy to work on kids' social needs rather than their test scores," he says bitterly.

51    Churches also are trying to fill the gaps left by deteriorating families and communities. Popular among Roman Catholic churches in San Antonio, and nationwide, is a program called RENEW, in which parishes set up small faith-sharing and support groups. "One area where the church can make a difference is in creating smaller communities within the larger parish," says Sister Frances Briseno, associate director of San Antonio's RENEW program. "So, if I lose my job, this group is here to support me emotionally and financially. . . . Once people experience community, they really long for it. It fulfills them."

52    On San Antonio's West Side, Gloria Rodriquez has shaped her parent-teaching organization Avance into a kind of extended family—the barrio's grandmother and grandfather. A large portion of mothers in this community are raising families on their own. Aunts, uncles and grandparents who might have helped out a generation ago live in other cities, or are already overtaxed by their own problems of survival or are too angry with their children to be supportive.

53    Inside an Avance classroom—once a run-down housing project apartment—21-year-old Ruby Rodriguez, mother of two, is one of six women pasting together lesson books for toddlers. She says Avance has transformed her parenting style. "Now I talk to the kids," she says.

"You learn that mothers are the first teacher. Before, I thought they start learning when they go to school." Twenty-two-year-old Sylvia Gutierrez, mother of four boys, says, "I get mad less. You learn to be patient because you spend more time with the kids."

54    It is a paradox of modern times that Americans place more emphasis on child-rearing than ever before and yet are increasingly less able to devote time and attention to it. (As Juliet B. Schor notes in her book "The Overworked American," today's deep parent-child bonds are "very much a social construction" of [only] the past 200 years. Hiring wet nurses, swaddling infants to immobilize them, routinely leaving children in the house alone—these kinds of practices are the historical norm.)

55    In the 1990s, yuppies shell out money for classes on breast-feeding and diapering. Books on child-rearing fill the stores, and parents of all income levels in San Antonio were deeply concerned about how to rear their own children.

56    Modern times, however, demand modern child-rearing. A post-industrial country facing international competition requires a more educated work force. And children today are exposed to a variety of destructive societal pressures.

57    That is where political leaders should step in with policies that give parents the time and resources to be part of their children's lives, family advocates like Gloria Rodriguez argue. Moreover, as parents grow more isolated from their own families, many of them are forced to look to outsiders—such corporate- and government-funded programs as Avance—to show them the art of discipline and nurturing and teaching.

58    Rodriguez knows that her efforts will help only a fraction of the San Antonio families in need. But she does not let herself count that way. Neither does Sister Mary Boniface, who collects the remains of children who are pregnant, abused or drug-addicted at the Healy-Murphy Center across town.

59    "It's an evil, evil world," the elderly nun says in her twirling Irish brogue. But like others

filling in for family, Boniface does not have the luxury to despair, so that moment of hopelessness quickly passes. She walks over to her bookcase and picks up framed photos, one by one—of the boy who gave up drugs, of the young man who went on to politics, of the brightly smiling girl in her college cap and gown.

Nina J. Easton, "Everyplace, Enemies of the Family," *Los Angeles Times*, front page, March 1, 1992. © 1992 Los Angeles Times. Reprinted by permission.

• • • • • • • • • • • • • • • • • • • • • • • • • • • • • •

1. What is the source and date (year)? _____
2. As is common in feature articles, useful subheads are interspersed throughout.
   a. true
   b. false
3. It ends with two paragraphs about
   a. a politician's speech
   b. a social-activist nun

---

| | |
|---|---|
| **Sel. 10**   P-Skim | 1. _____ |
| **Time**   2:00 = 1,750 wpm | 2. _____ |
| **Score** _____ % | 3. _____ |
| ▶ 100% | **Check answers with your instructor.** |
| **Score** = number correct × 33. | |

---

## B. Rapid Reading

Try to read in 7:30 minutes (= 466 wpm), 7 (= 500 wpm), or more quickly.

1. From the title on, this feature story focuses on the stresses today's parents face as they try to raise their children safely and with "good family values."
   a. true
   b. false
2. The writer has interviewed and quoted members of thirty families in San Antonio, Texas, many of them Latino(a).
   a. true
   b. false
3. Adults interviewed by the writer feel that families are "under siege from the pressures of modern life." What "pressures" are cited?
   a. divorce
   b. effect of popular culture (TV, etc.)
   c. gang recruitment and activities

      d. fear of what the future holds

      e. having less time to spend with children

      f. all of the above

      g. all except b

4. In San Antonio, some individuals and organizations are trying to help. Which one of the following is definitely not looked to for help, at least by these families presently?

      a. a parent-teaching organization called Avance

      b. a gang-intervention program

      c. state/federal programs, such as day care and parental leave

      d. the public schools

      e. church-run support centers

5. Some families are trying such solutions as

      a. living on one income even though poor

      b. home schooling

      c. moving to the country

      d. all of these

---

**Sel. 10  R-Read**

**Finish** ——:——

**Start** ——:——

**Time** ——:——

         **min    sec**

**Rate**——**wpm**

**Find rate on p. 343.**

**Score** ——%

   ▶ 80%

**Score** = number correct × 20.

1. ——

2. ——

3. ——

4. ——

5. ——

**Check answers with your instructor.**

**Record rate and score on p. 117.**

---

 C. For Discussion and Writing

1. In two places—paragraphs 6 and 36–37—statements are made that most Americans are satisfied with their own families but think that family values are declining "out there." How do you account for this paradox?

2. Experts continue to argue about the impact of the entertainment industry on children, especially in terms of violence and sex. Reread paragraph 33. Explain why you agree or disagree with the "two-thirds of Americans" cited in the poll.

3. Paragraphs 47–48 bring up a topic we met in Selection 2: the role of men in U.S. culture. In your opinion, what has resulted from the fact that in U.S. families today, "increasingly, men are missing"?

## Follow-Up

Now that you have read ten rapid-reading selections on the family, you may want to consider how your understanding of this issue has changed and how your rapid-reading abilities have improved. Individually, in small groups, or in large groups, you may want to consider the following questions.

### On the Family

1. What factors do you now think are key to a healthy family life?
2. Which factors contribute to an unhappy family life?
3. How do today's families differ from those in the eighteenth and nineteenth century?
4. After rapidly reading these selections and writing about them, how has your understanding of the family changed?

### On Rapid Reading

5. Of the rapid-reading techniques in this chapter, which one seems most helpful to you? Why?
6. Which area(s) of rapid reading do you still need to practice further?
7. Consider the selections you read rapidly. Which types of readings are easy for you to read rapidly?
8. Which types of readings are difficult for you to read rapidly?

## Internet Activity

Use the Internet to find out more information about rapid reading and the family. Break up into groups of four or five. To answer the following questions, use the given web site and InfoTrac College Edition. Then return to your group with your information.

If you cannot access this web site or InfoTrac College Edition, research the Internet to find information on rapid reading and the family to answer these questions.

### On Rapid Reading

Go to the web site entitled "Virginia Polytechnical Institute Study Skills Self-Help Information" and look for material on rapid reading. Then answer the following questions.

1. What new information on rapid reading did you find?
2. How does this information differ from what you learned about rapid reading in this chapter?
3. Describe how you located this information.

**On the Family**

If you have access to InfoTrac College Edition, use this research tool to learn more about the family to complete the following activities:

1. Locate and print an article of interest related to the family.
2. Summarize this article.
3. Describe how you located this information.

## How to Record Your Scores on the Progress Chart

After you have finished a timed selection and have entered your time and score in the score box:

1. Find the correct selection number on the top row of the chart. Transfer your rate (wpm) to the chart, under the selection number. Make a dot, X, bar, or other mark. (If you know your time only, not your rate, you must first look up your wpm in the Rate Table in Appendix B. Then mark that number on the chart.) Note that the acceptable or "target" rates for the featured skill are shaded. Do your rates fall within the target area?
2. Transfer your Rapid Reading (R-Read) comprehension score to the top blank on the chart. Note that the acceptable or "target" percentage for that selection is printed underneath the blank. Does your score meet—or surpass—the target percentage?
3. Connect the rate marks with a line to see your progress clearly. Remember, though, that your scores will not necessarily rise steadily. The different selections contain too many variables—difficulty, your interest in or familiarity with the topic, and so forth.

# PROGRESS CHART: RAPID READING

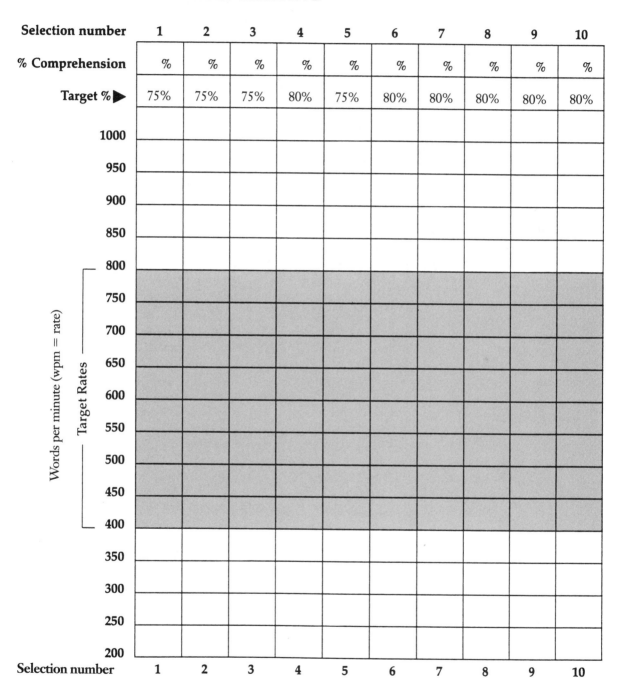

| Selection number | 1 | 2 | 3 | 4 | 5 | 6 | 7 | 8 | 9 | 10 |
|---|---|---|---|---|---|---|---|---|---|---|
| % Comprehension | % | % | % | % | % | % | % | % | % | % |
| Target % ▶ | 75% | 75% | 75% | 80% | 75% | 80% | 80% | 80% | 80% | 80% |

Words per minute (wpm = rate) — Target Rates

1000
950
900
850
800
750
700
650
600
550
500
450
400
350
300
250
200

| Selection number | 1 | 2 | 3 | 4 | 5 | 6 | 7 | 8 | 9 | 10 |

# Overview Skimming

$\mathcal{C}$hapter 4 presents a second kind of time-pressured, speeded reading: overview skimming for main ideas. The proficient, flexible reader will find it just as practical as the rapid reading taught in Chapter 3. Once again, you must make sure that your materials (the What) and your purpose (the Why) are appropriate for this high-speed treatment. Overview skimming is the closest thing in this book to the so-called speed reading taught in commercial courses.

As in the previous chapter, *it is essential that you do not browse or read ahead in any timed sections.* When you do move to the separate, timed sections—practices or longer selections—please follow very carefully all directions for timing.

The subject for most practices and all timed selections is "work."

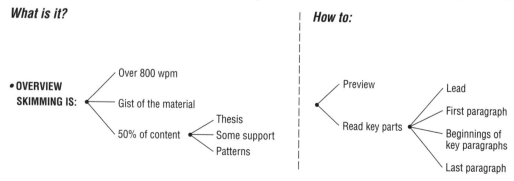

**What is it?**

- OVERVIEW SKIMMING IS:
  - Over 800 wpm
  - Gist of the material
  - 50% of content
    - Thesis
    - Some support
    - Patterns

**How to:**

- Preview
- Read key parts
  - Lead
  - First paragraph
  - Beginnings of key paragraphs
  - Last paragraph

# INTRODUCTION TO OVERVIEW SKIMMING

- - - - - - - - - - - - - - - - - - - - -

## CHECKLIST OF SYMPTOMS

Do you often

_____ 1. wonder at and secretly envy the speed-reader, who turns a page every ten seconds yet seems to get the gist of the book?

_____ 2. wish that you could grasp the main point of an article, a business letter, a report, or an essay without reading the entire thing?

_____ 3. believe that it's impossible to get the main ideas of a selection without reading all of it?

_____ 4. believe that it *is* possible, but don't know which parts to skip and which to read?

_____ 5. wish you could sometimes process print even faster than you did in Chapter 3, where the top speed was 800 wpm?

If you checked one or more of these symptoms, you should be interested in the next reading technique, overview skimming. When you have mastered it, you will be able to skim prose of average difficulty at rates over 800 wpm and still grasp and retain all the main ideas.

We hope that the introduction, practices, and timed selections of Chapter 3 brought about some behavioral changes in you, especially if you began as a typical compulsive reader. For example, did you rid yourself of the 100 percent compulsion, accepting comprehension scores of 70 to 80 percent? Did you manage to let go of occasional words—to infer them through your use of peripheral vision, soft focus, and shortened margins? We hope so, because we shall now ask you to settle for only 50 percent comprehension and to let go of entire paragraphs, sections—even pages!

In this book, overview skimming is the third time-pressured technique, preceded by preview skimming (of all materials) in Chapter 2 and rapid reading (of general materials) in Chapter 3.

Once again you will be timing yourself in order to build efficiency, and once again you will start with the first step, previewing. In some other respects, however, overview skimming differs from the other two speeded methods. Before comparing the three methods, we shall define our terms.

- - - - - - - - - - - - - - - - - - - - -

## WHAT IS OVERVIEW SKIMMING?

First, what does *skimming* mean? You already know from your study of previewing and rapid reading that anything called "skimming" must take place at high rates, over 800 or 900 wpm. At these rates, the eyes cannot see and "read" all the print on the page, so they must read selectively, skipping over some of it. This is true of overview skimming. You will be aiming at overall rates of 800 to 1,000 wpm and up, but you will not attempt to read all the print—only selected portions of it. Some readers actually learn to overview skim for main ideas at 1,500 wpm or better, which translates into four to five paperback pages per minute (= 12–15 seconds per page).

Second, what does *overview* mean? An overview is a general, holistic view of the content. You aim for only the *gist* of the reading material—the main idea(s), the core, the outline—plus some of the major supporting details. True, your goal will be to understand and retain 100 percent of the main ideas, but you will ignore most of the details. You will not be reading and grasping the entire selection, as you did in rapid reading. On average, a skimmer comprehends only about 50 percent of the total content. This selective process takes practice and discipline, because the details often make up the most interesting and accessible parts of an article, news story, or other nonfictional work. Only by skipping them and focusing on the main ideas, though, can you reach the overall high rates that characterize skimming.

How does overview skimming compare with the speeded techniques you have already practiced?

1. Like rapid reading, it is used on one-dimensional prose—easy to moderate difficulty—or where your purpose is not analysis and study but a surface understanding only. As in all comprehension, you must be familiar with basic literal comprehension. You must know the vocabulary, distinguish between main ideas and details, and pay special attention to all the writer's signals: titles, transitions, and key words. Organizational patterns also become crucial as you move through prose at high speed, trying to understand the main ideas without reading all the support.
2. Overview skimming is much like preview skimming in that you carefully read the same key parts of the passage: titles, beginnings, and endings. However, whereas previewing prepares you to go back to the material for a more thorough reading, *overviewing is the only reading you will do on it.* Therefore, you must spend a little more time and read the key parts more thoughtfully than you would if you were only previewing.

What do you learn through overview skimming? How does your comprehension compare with that in careful reading or rapid reading?

First, like a preview, a good overview can tell you whether you want to read the material more carefully. Second, by itself it can give you the thesis, the main support for the thesis, and the organizational patterns, but not many details. For example, it can tell you what the Supreme Court's latest ruling is, but not how the justices arrived at it. A good overview can tell you the overall style, the main characters, and the plot outline of a novel, but you will not get to enjoy the clever dialogue or beautiful descriptions. It will tell you the main features of your insurance policy but not whether it will cover that peculiar little accident you had last week. As with rapid reading, overview skimming may not do justice to many fine pieces of writing, but it is better than not reading at all. For many of your reading purposes and materials, it is a handy technique.

In fact, you have done this kind of skimming already, many times—whenever you have looked over a page of the daily newspaper, flipped through an article while waiting in a checkout line, looked through last year's magazines before throwing them out, or reviewed textbook chapters already studied. In all these situations, you were skimming for overview—to get the gist, the main ideas. So, now all you must do is learn how and when to use this skill most effectively.

• • • • • • • • • • • • • • • • • • •

# HOW TO OVERVIEW SKIM—IN GENERAL

When you preview skim, you raise questions about the reading material. When you overview skim, you gain answers—about the main points in an argument, the conclusions of a research study, the outcome of a trial, the story line of a novel. How is it possible to find these answers at rates over 800 wpm?

You can do it because, as we said at the start of Chapter 1, all professional writing has structure, whether or not it is immediately obvious. Prose writers in particular work from outlines or plans. When you decide to skim a piece, you should imagine that you are reading for only the major headings of the outline (or the big print and big boxes of a "study map"). For example, an outline for a typical essay, editorial, chapter, or article might look like this:

I. Introduction
   A. Definitions: *chemical, poisons*
   B. Public perceptions—distorted?
   C. Scientific fields involved
II. Risk Management
   A. How toxicity of substance is determined
   B. Problems of assessing danger
      1. Humans vary more than lab animals do
      2. Chronic vs. acute reactions
      3. Chemicals *not* "toxic" vs. "nontoxic"
      4. Many chemicals are *mixtures*
   C. "Bottom line"
III. Transport of Toxic Substances in the Body
   A. Inhalation
      1. Types of airborne toxic substances: gases/vapors; solids/liquids
      2. How humans breathe
         Examples: carbon monoxide; hydrogen cyanide
      3. Effect of toxic substances on blood, lungs
         Examples: asbestos; mining dust
   B. Skin Absorption
   C. Ingestion—and so on.*

---

*Outline adapted from Hamid R. Kavanian and Charles A. Wentz, Jr., *Occupational and Environmental Safety Engineering and Management* (Belmont, CA: Wadsworth, 1990), 86–90.

As usual, the Roman numerals precede topics, capital letters point to major details, and numbers and examples indicate relatively minor details. If you were overview skimming, you would try to concentrate on the main ideas, toward the left—the I and II, the A and B—and skip over the details, examples, repetitions, and filler. (Remember, if your purpose—the Why—is to enjoy the style or memorize the details of a piece, you should elect to do slow reading, not skimming.)

Where does a writer place these headings or main ideas in his or her written work? By now, you know the answer: in the title, subtitle, lead (explanatory note under the title), subheads throughout the selection, and all beginnings and endings. A skimming reader will slow down and notice beginnings of paragraphs, sections, and chapters, and any summary or concluding part, whether it is one sentence or several pages.

A good overview skimmer must also notice writing patterns. As you learned in Chapter 1, organization is always an integral part of content; how something is developed or supported is essential to basic literal comprehension. So, patterns are especially important to a skimmer, who is trying to grasp the outline of the ideas, not only accurately but also quickly. To do this, of course, the skimmer must not miss any transitions or other signals. For example, if the passage seems to follow a strong cause-effect pattern, the skimmer makes sure to grasp all the causes and all the effects and to follow the writer's argument linking the two.

Recognizing the organizational pattern also helps increase your skimming speed, because it helps you sort essential from nonessential material more easily. For example, if you have grasped a writer's main point and reinforced it by reading one specific example, you can skip the next five *for example*s and *for instance*s. Some reading experts think that 60 percent of one's skimming skill lies in the ability to recognize patterns immediately.

Remember that a key transition may be very short—like *but*. Or it may be as long as entire sentences, even paragraphs.

• • • • • • • • • • • • • • • • • • • •

# HOW TO OVERVIEW SKIM—IN DETAIL

Imagine that you have before you a newspaper or magazine article, a chapter of an easy paperback book, a long memo or report, or an editorial. You do not have time to read it slowly—or even rapidly. You want to know the thesis and all the main ideas, with some of the important details (about 50 percent of the total content). The next six points will show you how to do it.

## 1. PIF—Preview It First—Even Before Overview Skimming

Do a *minimal* preview, since you do not intend to return for a complete reading. Take only a few seconds to focus your mind on the passage and raise questions. As usual, check out the length, title, subtitle and lead (if any), source and date, author, divisions or subheads, graphics and photos, and difficulty level.

Some titles, for example, "Yesterday" or "Bears," help a reader very little because they do not indicate the topic. Other titles state the general topic: "Farm Subsidies" or "Farm Subsidies in the 1990s." However, if the title reads, "Time to Reevaluate Farm-Subsidy Giveaways," the writer has provided both the topic and the main idea. In other words, a good title prepares you for the content. Such anticipation is invaluable for better comprehension and, ultimately, speed.

Turn to Practices 4.1 and 4.2, beginning on page 130. At high speed, you will try to discriminate between those titles/subtitles that reflect main ideas and those that are too broad or vague to be useful.

## 2. Go Back and Read Selectively for the Writer's Main Ideas

You must select and read the key areas carefully, for you have already decided to skip other areas completely. Sometimes you may need to reread a key part to grasp the gist of the piece. Needless to say, you must remain alert and focused on the material.

After the title and subtitle, key parts usually include

a.  lead, if any
b.  the entire first paragraph or introduction
c.  the beginnings of each key paragraph, as indicated by signal words and phrases, plus one or two important details
d.  the entire last paragraph or conclusion

Like all rules, you should use these flexibly. You will have to adapt them to fit the subject matter, the length of your material (from one page to an entire book), and the writer's style. For example, unless the selection has a strong time-sequence or step-by-step pattern, you may choose not to skim the piece in one direction from beginning to end, but to jump around from part to part, constructing the "big picture" from bits and pieces. Or, you may want to read the ending before you read the beginning. Many professional writers save their thesis until the end. So, skimming backward in a selection is not as zany as it sounds.

Especially notice any *lead*—a short summary by a writer or an editor, often in italics, that follows the title or the subtitle. It is a good indicator of what will follow, and it sometimes provides a complete summary of the article or report. All you have to do then is skim the body for organization and major details.

Always use the typographical aids given you by the writer and the editor. For instance, watch for paragraphs. Also notice any breaks in the print that indicate new sections. John Hersey used an extra line space in his nonfiction book, *Hiroshima*, to signal a shift from one of his six interviewees to another. Even fiction writers may employ breaks or spacing meaningfully to show shifts in time, place, or point of view.

In long works, such as novels (fiction) or nonfiction books, try reading carefully the beginning and ending of each chapter. You may be surprised at how much these parts tell you about the book. You can often get a broad but quite accurate view of topics covered, style, place and time settings, where the book starts and where it ends, and major characters.

Of course, there are exceptions to this rule about the importance of beginnings and endings. Though writers of informative articles usually state their thesis in the opening paragraphs, they also tend to entice the stray reader with a "hook"—a personal-interest story or a minor but colorful detail.

Nowadays, even straight news items may begin with an individual's name and story rather than the traditional, factual "Five W's and H" (Who-What-When-Where-Why, plus How). For instance, not many people would want to read, or even skim, an article that began, "Yet another dreary tax-reform package is winding its way through Congress this spring." But what if the first paragraph began, "Joe Manteca stared down at the five dollars in his billfold. How would he ever pay for the paperback required for his college reading course?" By empathizing with Mr. Manteca, we have been lured into the intricacies of tax reform and have spent a lot of time merely getting interested. However, skimmers are smart and in a hurry. They learn to skip over poor Joe and slow down only when they find the true introduction to the body of the article, in this case, the prospect for tax reform.

Similarly, endings often fail to provide helpful information. News items and minor articles often simply stop where the editor chopped them off to fit the available space. However, editorials, feature articles, and "opinion pieces" continue to save the clearest summary of their message for the very end, the conclusion—as do most essays, works of fiction and nonfiction, and even sermons.

Turn to Practice 4.3 on page 132. Distinguish between the professional writer's "hook" and the thesis statement, which signals the body of the article.

Now that you know where the main body of a work begins, you might ask, "How does a reader know which paragraphs in the body are the most important?" Often, a paragraph does not express the content of a selection. It may be a bridge (transition) linking one group of paragraphs with another, a digression, or the umpteenth repetition of an idea. A skimmer, of course, tries to skip over these paragraphs. A good writer will indicate through various signals, usually in the opening words, that a paragraph is, or is not, important.

Turn to Practice 4.4, beginning on page 133, and try to discriminate among paragraph openings.

## 3. Time Yourself Rigorously

If you find yourself reading all the details and all the middles of paragraphs, and if your rate falls below 800 wpm, then you are probably reading too much to be skimming. To keep yourself skimming, simply watch the clock. If necessary, reskim a selection until you finish it within the skimming time limit (900 wpm or faster).

As in every reading task, your mind-set is all-important. Keep reminding yourself that you want *only* the main ideas, that the details must wait for another kind of reading. Keep aiming for only about 50 percent of the total content. If you discover you are retaining 80–90 percent of the details, you have slipped from skimming to reading.

## 4. Use a Highly Variable Rate Within the Material Itself

When you overview skim correctly, you read key parts carefully (maybe even reread them), race past unimportant material, then slow down and read carefully, and so on. In other words, the high skimming rates do not result from a super-fast reading of all the words, as most beginners believe. Rather, they result from what is not read at all.

As you learn to skim, you may find you cannot achieve this slow-fast-slow pace with your eyes alone. The habit of reading at an even pace, whether fast or slow, is hard to break. If this applies to you, then you need a "crutch."

*Crutch 1:* Use your fingers to point out key passages, such as the beginning of a group of paragraphs. Read carefully. Then run your hand down lines, paragraphs, or even pages if necessary, and point to the next key passage. Make your eyes and your brain follow your hand. This way, you cannot dally on the interesting trivia.

*Crutch 2:* Read aloud, or at least mumble, the key passages as you point them out.

*Crutch 3:* If you still tend to read it all rather than skim, try highlighting the key passages in a bright color first. Then go back and make sure you read only what is highlighted. You can try these three tips on the last practice or on the timed selections. Eventually, you will be able to skip over, then read, then skip over, at will.

Of course, the real problem when you skim is not where your hand or your eyes go, but thinking so you can sift through material and locate the gist very rapidly. It takes an alert mind; it also takes repeated timed practice.

Turn to Practice 4.5, beginning on page 134. Here you will practice discriminating among details of support for various topics. In skimming complete works, you would expect to read the relevant details carefully and skip over the less relevant ones.

## 5. Use Your Eyes in the Most Efficient Way for Skimming Long Passages

Of course, key passages must be read carefully and thoroughly. But as you are looking down a page for these passages, try moving your eyes in a slow, wide-ranging spiral down the lines. The soft focus, floating manner you learned in rapid reading works here, as well as the concept of shortening your margins. The whole idea is to prevent yourself from reading everything, including unessential details, at the same rate.

Again, if your eyes seem to want to see and read every word on every line, use your hand to direct your vision down the page. Remember to keep alert for topic sentences, key transitions and other signals, breaks, spacing, capital letters, and other essential signs of the main ideas and the structure. Stop immediately and read *slowly* when you see such elements.

Turn to any timed selection in Chapter 3; with your teacher's direction, practice skimming down a page.

## 6. Use Your Eyes Efficiently when Skimming Through Single Key Paragraphs

If a paragraph seems important by itself, read to find the topic sentence. Usually (70–90 percent of the time, according to the experts), it will be the first or the second sentence in the paragraph. Read this sentence carefully. Rather than skip over the rest of the paragraph entirely, check it out—use soft focus to pass rapidly through it. Watch for any important detail or signal. You may either spiral through or force your eyes through on a slant. This takes only a few seconds, but it can either confirm your first impression of the paragraph's main point or uncover an important shift in, or addition to, the main point.

Turn to Practice 4.6 on page 135 and see how these eye movements work as you skim one paragraph at a time.

With all this emphasis on speed, you may wonder about other aids, such as the mechanical gadget or a hand-held index card recommended in Chapter 3 for rapid reading. Students often imagine that if they can keep a card moving over print steadily at a high enough rate—900–1,500 wpm, for example—they will be overview skimming very effectively. However, a moment's thought will show that this is not the case. The slow-fast-slow, variable rate required for skimming would be greatly hampered by any method that promoted an even rate, however rapid.

Perhaps we have been overstressing the pitfalls and problems of overview skimming. Actually, in much of the prose you will come across, the "writer's path" is clearly written out and carefully constructed, with headings, topic sentences, beginnings, endings, and transitions—all the things that lend themselves to skimming. Textbook writers pride themselves on this kind of writing. On the whole, you will find overview skimming a wonderful tool for learning a great deal in a short time. In fact, many business and professional people learn to skim simply to keep up with the flood of memos, reports, and journals that land on their desks.

To see how overview skimming can work for you in typical expository prose, read the following outline of an article, drawn from the first sentences of the paragraphs. Notice how you can get the gist of the article just by reading these selected sentences carefully. They represent about one-fifth of the original article. Remember, don't speed or skip anything—these *are* the key parts. And do not time yourself. The numbers refer to the order in which the paragraphs appeared in the article.

1. (Thesis) In my opinion, students should pay a higher parking fee than they do now.
2. The current fee is fairly low—about one-half the fee at three nearby colleges.

3. We need to develop a fund to pay for construction of a new parking garage.
4. Residents near the college are becoming angrier every year, as they lose all their parking spaces to students.
5. Some residents are threatening to hire an attorney and sue the college.
6. The state will no longer pay half the costs of new parking facilities, as in the past. Where will the money come from?
7. Therefore, I propose doubling the present $20/month fee.

You have probably become an expert on this local issue just by reading these key sentences.

Turn to Practice 4.7, page 137, to overview skim an entire personal essay on your own. Once you have finished, you will be ready to skim the series of timed selections that follow the practices.

# SUMMARY

Overview skimming is a speeded technique designed to give a reader the gist of a passage or the outline of a selection's main ideas from just one pass. Like rapid reading, overview skimming is best used for general reading—that is, easy to moderate nonfiction—but it can also give the reader some idea of the content of difficult material, such as textbooks. It can never substitute for careful, analytical reading.

Overview skimming is slower and more thorough than preview skimming, faster and less thorough than rapid reading. The skimmer aims for about 50 percent of the total content—but *all* the main ideas of a work. Overviewing requires an *uneven pace*, not a steady one as in most reading. The overall high rate for any given selection—800–1,500 wpm—results from the material that is skipped. The skimmer continues to read the key parts carefully. The challenge in overviewing is to distinguish, under considerable time pressure, key parts from unimportant ones.

When you skim, you must pay special attention to titles, leads, headings, graphic devices, transitions, patterns of organization, and beginnings and endings—any parts likely to contain the thesis and the main ideas. For single paragraphs, you read the topic sentence, if stated, and glance through the rest of the paragraph. In longer works, you may read only beginnings and endings of sections or chapters. You rely on soft focus, shortened margins, and floating on a slant or an **S** curve as you pass rapidly through less important material.

To skim well, you must be physically and mentally alert. Do not decide to overview skim books at bedtime or next to a swimming pool! You have to constantly synthesize the writer's ideas from a few sentences and paragraphs and translate these bits into a meaningful whole without missing key parts or distorting the whole. Skimming is rather hard to do if the material is fiction, if the style is disorganized or indirect (requiring much inference), or if the subject is unfamiliar to you. But you can skim fairly easily if the material (the What) is clearly organized, loaded with signals, and on a familiar topic.

Pragmatically, skimming enables you to get through the morning paper in twenty minutes, an average article in about ten minutes, an entire magazine in an hour, and a paperback in a few hours.

Last, overview skimming requires a certain debonair attitude toward the parts you skip. That attitude will be fully justified the day you return to some work you originally skimmed, read through it slowly, and realize you are gaining little additional content—you have already grasped most of it.

## Summary Box: Overview Skimming

| What? | Why? | Acceptable Comprehension | Acceptable Rates |
|---|---|---|---|
| General materials, light-to-moderate difficulty, familiar topics and fields, supplemental reading, newspapers and magazines, general business mail (prior to discarding it) | For overview, outline, thesis, main idea plus major details, structure; general idea of style; passing acquaintance with best-sellers | 50–60% (But *all* the main ideas!) | 800–1,500 wpm |

# PRACTICES:
## OVERVIEW SKIMMING

These practices present the art of skimming from its easiest elements to its most difficult. Please do the practices in the order presented in the introduction. Time yourself rigorously—skimming requires pressure.

Answers are not provided in the key, so please check them with your instructor.

4.1 GOOD TITLES VS. POOR TITLES
4.2 MORE GOOD TITLES VS. POOR TITLES
4.3 DISTINGUISH THE "HOOK" FROM THE THESIS STATEMENT
4.4 RECOGNIZE KEY (TOPIC) SENTENCES
4.5 RECOGNIZE IMPORTANT DETAILS OF SUPPORT
4.6 USE YOUR EYES EFFICIENTLY—PARAGRAPHS
4.7 OVERVIEW SKIM A COMPLETE ESSAY

### 4.1 GOOD TITLES VS. POOR TITLES

A skilled skimmer begins thinking ahead to possible main ideas, starting from the beginning of a work—that is, from the title (and subtitle, if any). In each of the following items, one title contains strong clues about the content of the article. Read down the list as fast as you can, putting a checkmark (√) by the helpful titles. Leave the others blank. Be able to explain your choices.

Try to finish the following list in 60 seconds.

*Example:* a. _____ The 1990s Job Market
b. _____ Job Hunting in the 1990s
c. _____ Tips for Finding the Right Job

The most general is a.—it could cover almost anything to do with work. The most specific is c.—"the *right* job" implies "for *you*." Also, even more than b., it suggests a personal *how-to* or process pattern and prepares you to skim through a list of concrete "tips."

1. a. _____ Summer Jobs for College Students
   b. _____ Summer Jobs for Animal Lovers
2. a. _____ Mr. Jones's Matchbook Collection
   b. _____ The Hobby That Became a Hazard
3. a. _____ Surrogate Motherhood
   b. _____ When Surrogate Mothers Change Their Minds
   c. _____ A Major Problem with Surrogacy
4. a. _____ A Discussion About Growth Hormones
   b. _____ Dr. Yule B. Biggar, Advocate of Growth Hormones
5. a. _____ Elvis Disciple Says He Has No Problem with Identity
   b. _____ Interview with Houston's Most Visible Elvis Fan
   c. _____ Elvis Look-Alikes

6. a. _____ The New Leader of Granola
   b. _____ The Perils of Democratic Elections
   c. _____ Did Granolans Vote Themselves a New Dictator?
7. a. _____ Returning to the Wreck to Find Out Why
   b. _____ Diving Expedition Planned in Lake Superior
   c. _____ Sinking of Ore Boat Still Unsolved
8. a. _____ Tough Lessons in a Tough Place
   b. _____ Rehabilitation: A Prison Psychologist Explains His Goals
   c. _____ Reality Therapy: Inmates Must First Accept Responsibility for What They Did
9. a. _____ Colleges Inconsistent in Assigning Student Aid
   b. _____ National Survey: How Colleges Assign Student Aid
   c. _____ The Student Aid Picture in Colleges Today
10. a. _____ Triathlete Prefers Solitude When He Trains
    b. _____ Greg Clarke's Training Methods
    c. _____ Professional Triathlete Training Locally

Time: _____ : _____

Number correct of 10 _____

Check answers with your instructor.

## 4.2   MORE GOOD TITLES VS. POOR TITLES

Do the next ten the same way you did Practice 4.1, but work faster this time. Aim for 40 seconds.

1. a. _____ Living with Three Parrots
   b. _____ The Macaw Mafia in Our House
2. a. _____ Latino Groups Not Single Voting Bloc
   b. _____ Latino Groups in the U.S.
   c. _____ Politics Among Latino Groups
3. a. _____ Morality and the Arts
   b. _____ Public Funding of the Arts: Whose Morality?
4. a. _____ "U.S. English"—A Hidden Agenda?
   b. _____ The Campaign for English as Our Official Language
5. a. _____ Amtrak
   b. _____ What's Wrong with Amtrak
   c. _____ An Analysis of Amtrak Today
6. a. _____ Traveling in the 1990s
   b. _____ How to See America on $30 a Day
7. a. _____ Marvel Maids: Good Clean Profits from a Dirty Business!
   b. _____ An Unusual Small Business in Our Area
   c. _____ Housecleaning Service Available
8. a. _____ Another Look at Inner-City Graffiti
   b. _____ Tagging and Graffiti: What It Means
   c. _____ Tagging—Kids Speak Out About Its Meaning

9. a. _____ Computers Analyze Murderers' Handwriting
   b. _____ Another Innovative Use for Computers
   c. _____ The Handwriting of Criminals
10. a. _____ Beloved Bugs: Recent Studies
    b. _____ Status of the Firefly
    c. _____ No Gentle Fireflies in Our Future?

Time: _____ : _____

Number correct of 10 _____

Check answers with your instructor.

## 4.3 DISTINGUISH THE "HOOK" FROM THE THESIS STATEMENT

Here are typical first sentences of paragraphs in articles, essays, feature stories, and editorials. Put a checkmark (√) before those that probably signal the body or thesis of the work. Leave the detailed "hook" or human-interest sentences blank.
    Try to finish in 30 seconds or less.

1. a. _____ Store owner Marty Jones still talks about that summer evening two years ago, when a crowd of celebrating college students turned ugly outside his liquor store.
   b. _____ College officials unveiled a plan this week that will, they believe, prevent the violence that erupted after the Spring Royale festival two years ago.
2. a. _____ Susan Birch and Margaret Taylor have been neighbors for 16 years, but they have not spoken to each other for the past 8.
   b. _____ Much of the current controversy over abortion arises over differing views of when a human life actually begins.
3. a. _____ Can a woman's beauty actually work against her in a business career?
   b. _____ Could it be, she asked herself, that she was being passed over for promotions because she was too pretty?
4. a. _____ Do you seethe when you get a lower grade in a course than you think you deserved?
   b. _____ Do you wish grades were abolished, because you know that a professor's evaluation paragraph would more truly reflect your real abilities?
   c. _____ National surveys have shown that the "written evaluation" method tried in the 1970s created more problems than benefits for students, especially when they entered graduate schools.
5. a. _____ Brad H., 12, has lain in a coma at Eastside Hospital for three months; his bills have totaled over $200,000. Stevie W., 6, was killed last year when a car barely tapped his bicycle as he rode home from school.
   b. _____ The new state law mandating helmets for all bicycle riders under age 15 would have prevented both accidents.

c. _____ Even proponents of strict helmet laws concede that they raise the question: How far should government go to protect citizens against themselves?

Time: _____:_____

Number correct of 5 _____

Check answers with your instructor.

## 4.4   RECOGNIZE KEY (TOPIC) SENTENCES

Read through the following sentences rapidly. Imagine that they are the first (topic) sentences of paragraphs in editorials or articles. If the entire sentence would be important to read as you overview skim, underline all of it. If only a part of the sentence would be important, underline that part.

1. Forest fires in Yellowstone and Yosemite may look tragic, but, after all, wildfire is just part of the natural cycle.
2. Wildfire may be part of the natural cycle, but still, the forest fires in Yellowstone and Yosemite are tragic for our disappearing wilderness habitat. (Notice the position of these opposing ideas in the two sentences. Also notice the word choice: *after all* versus *but still, may look* versus *are.*)
3. After weeks of divisive campaigning, the students have finally elected a slate of conservative officers.
4. The students have elected a slate of conservative officers, but unfortunately the weeks of divisive campaigning have taken their toll.
5. Admittedly the lead guitarist took a certain energy with him when he left, but the group obviously retains its distinctive Euro sound.
6. The group still has a distinctive sound; however, the loss of the lead guitarist and his special energy is all too obvious.
7. Whereas some law enforcement agencies favor the ban on assault weapons, many continue to voice a strong opposition to it.
8. Whereas a few law enforcement agencies oppose the ban on assault weapons, many, if not most, voice strong support for it.
9. Restaurant owners insist they have lost considerable business as a result of the city's controversial antismoking ordinance; in fact, one cafe has filed for bankruptcy.
10. Restaurant owners admit they have lost little business as a result of the city's popular antismoking ordinance; in fact, two cafes report increased business.

Time: _____:_____

Number correct of 10: _____

Check answers with your instructor. Count as correct any item in which your underlinings are *largely* similar to the instructor's answer key.

## 4.5 Recognize Important Details of Support

You have discriminated among titles, paragraph beginnings, and parts of key (topic) sentences. Now try to discriminate among subtopics included within a selection.

Here are five main-idea statements drawn from pamphlets, magazines, and newspapers. Each one is followed by a list of subtopics or details of support. As fast as possible, read each statement and keep it firmly in mind as you read the list. Most details will be important; put checks (✓) before those. However, *one* detail in each list will be *unimportant* or *irrelevant to the main idea;* you would skip over it if you were overview skimming. Leave that detail blank.

Try to do each list in 20 seconds or less. Finish all five in 2 minutes or less.

*Example:* Main idea: A cat makes a better pet than a dog, for students or working singles.

    a. _____ Cats can be left home alone more easily than dogs.

    b. _____ Like all pets, cats require loving care and attention every day.

    c. _____ Cats can be trained to use a litter box.

    d. _____ Cats don't have to be walked when you get home.

Which *one* detail is not essential to a busy student looking for reasons to keep a kitten? _____

1. Main idea: Dogs make better pets for a family than do cats.

    a. _____ Dogs warn of intruders; do you know a cat that will?

    b. _____ Cats claw furniture; dogs just lie on it.

    c. _____ Dogs actually crave petting and play from family members, especially the children.

    d. _____ Most dogs need obedience training, which takes time and effort.

2. Main idea: This college has many advantages.

    a. _____ It's cosmopolitan—students come from all walks of life and from many foreign countries.

    b. _____ Our parking permits are simply hunting licenses; they don't guarantee a parking space.

    c. _____ Noted artists, writers, musicians, and dancers visit the campus, offering free lectures and performances.

    d. _____ It offers students a chance to study abroad for one semester.

3. Main idea: The deaths of the ten "smoke-jumpers" in this week's wildfire resulted from several factors.

    a. _____ The Safety Officer, coming from another fire, had not arrived yet.

    b. _____ Firefighters interviewed for this story showed grief but vowed to continue in their jobs.

    c. _____ The wind unexpectedly shifted 180 degrees and increased to 35 mph.

    d. _____ The fire "blew out" across the line and overtook them as they ran.

4. Question-answer topic: Why should an employer be concerned about the child-care problems of employees?

    a. _____ Even in the 1990s, many employers still think that family life has nothing to do with work.

b. _____ Mothers have become a large and permanent part of the work force, and fathers have begun to share in child-care responsibilities.

c. _____ Child-care worries on top of rigid work schedules create many problems for both worker and employer: stress, less productivity, and more absenteeism.

d. _____ Employers should have a positive influence on employee family life and on the upbringing of the country's future work force.

5. Main idea: There are several reasons why mothers work outside the home.

a. _____ Like fathers, most mothers work in order to provide their families with a good standard of living.

b. _____ Women have had to work to maintain this standard, because real wages (adjusted for inflation) declined by 20 percent between 1973 and 1989.

c. _____ Women's wages still have not caught up with men's; even in management and the professions, the "glass ceiling" is apparent, and elsewhere, a woman earns 60 cents for each dollar a man earns.

d. _____ A recent study found that the parents of many "latchkey children" are well-to-do professionals, so these mothers have reasons other than financial need for holding outside jobs.

Time for all 5 _____:_____

Number correct of 5 _____

Check answers with your instructor.

Do you now feel you could skip over parts of your reading that do not directly pertain to the thesis or main ideas? If so, you have the mind-set necessary for overview skimming at 900 wpm and up.

## 4.6 USE YOUR EYES EFFICIENTLY—PARAGRAPHS

Practice skimming through the body of each of these next six paragraphs, in a spiral or on a slant, rapidly and easily. Slow down for only the italicized sections—topic sentences, key phrases, and so on. You may use your finger or hand on the print, if it helps. Be alert for any shift or contrasting element. Then, underneath each paragraph, identify which writing pattern it seems to follow. You may want to review the various writing patterns on pages 8–16 before you begin this practice.

1. It's a little before 6 A.M. It's so early, the sun hasn't even come up. *So who in their right mind would be up at such a ridiculous hour? The "morning people."* About two of every five people are early birds. During the wee hours of the morning, while others are still sleeping, these early birds are up and gabbing at coffee klatches, studying, watching cable TV, shopping for groceries, jogging around their neighborhoods, and jumping up and down in aerobics classes. "I like getting up at hours when most people are asleep. It's so quiet and peaceful during the morning hours. Now, some people can lie in bed,

but not me. Once I've rolled out of bed and my feet hit the floor, I'm ready to go," says Maria Sullivan, a morning workout regular.

Pattern: _____

2. *Are these morning people nuts? "Not at all,"* says Charles Ehret, an authority on circadian rhythms (our inner clocks). "It's not unusual for most morning people to get out of bed very early and still feel alert and able to function. They're the types who bounce out of bed, feeling bright-eyed and energetic. They go on to have very productive mornings. But they usually begin winding down by midafternoon, and some of them retire to bed before 9 P.M."

Pattern: _____

3. *Typically, all humans* have a low body temperature between 4 and 5 A.M., followed by a sharp temperature rise before they wake; a morning person simply has his inner clock set a few hours earlier than the rest of us. As Dr. Srinath Bellur, a neurologist with a sleep-disorder clinic, says, *"This helps explain why the true morning person always wakes up feeling ready to go. It's because his temperature is already high, and his metabolism is in full swing." In other cases, a person's occupation* can be responsible for putting him on a different timetable. About 20 percent of Americans work late shifts that lapse into early-morning hours at factories, hospitals, police departments, and radio and television stations. Eventually, the enforced pattern becomes an inner pattern.*

Pattern: _____

4. Flocks of songbirds arrive in our cities and countryside each spring. The windows of our homes and our nice clean cars get messy. The chattering and singing of small feathered critters wake us up at dawn. Lots of birds, right? Maybe *too many birds*, we mutter darkly to ourselves. *But appearances are deceptive. All is not well on the bird front.* If birds act like the early-warning canary in the old coal mines, we may all be in a really deep mess. According to a British study of international bird populations, 70 percent of the world's species are on the decline. *One cause* is the wild-bird trade, up to eight million exotic lovelies per year, that flourishes out of Southeast Asia. *Other causes* can be traced to the global spread of human populations. Forests are cleared, wetlands are drained and paved over, cattle overgraze in many places, and deserts are slowly but steadily expanding.

Pattern: _____

5. It is only in recent years that stress has surfaced as an issue affecting workers at every level and in every occupation. Even though intuitive awareness of stress in the workplace is now virtually universal, *the definitions and formal concepts of "stress" are still tentative and evolving. Decades ago,* psychologists told us that certain external events—illness, death in the family, financial worries, divorce, high-profile jobs, etc.—caused us to suffer physical and emotional damage. *More recently,* researchers decided that the key factor was not the situation, but our reaction to it. Habitual worriers, "Type A" personalities, and other superachievers were said to create the problem for themselves; therefore they could be trained to handle life's irritations and crises

*Paragraphs 1, 2, and 3 adapted from Clarence Moore, "Morning People Driven by the Beat," *San Luis Obispo County Telegram-Tribune*, December 25, 1991, 9.

more positively. *Now some experts are questioning this last view,* wondering if it is not too simplistic, unrealistic, and sometimes actually harmful.*

Pattern: _____

6.  *Sometimes the outside observer may not immediately spot the real cause of the worker's stress. For example,* a Latino groundskeeper at a local college was constantly fretting and complaining about "the boss." Yet, counsellors felt he had an ideal, healthful, secure job. He seemed to be "making his own stress." In middle age, for no obvious medical reason, he developed high blood pressure and a heart condition, suffered a heart attack, and finally had to quit on disability at age 50. He died at 52. Later, an unrelated inquiry discovered that the *worker's supervisor* had a history of bias against Latinos and *probably had been applying subtle pressure against his groundskeeper for years.*

Pattern: _____

Check answers with your instructor.

## 4.7    OVERVIEW SKIM A COMPLETE ESSAY

This is the last practice before you begin the longer timed selections. Try out all your previous skills on this personal essay.

Time yourself carefully for both steps.

### Step A
PIF—preview it first in 20 seconds (= 2,460 wpm), then think about the content. (There is no quiz on the preview.)

## A DAY IN THE LIFE OF A VETERINARIAN

*by Janet Foley (820 words)*

[1]    What is a typical day in the life of a veterinarian? First, I must tell you that since graduating from Wilson College in 1982 and Virginia Tech in 1986 (DVM), the one thing I have learned is that there is (almost) never such a thing as a typical day. However, each day we try to start out with what we hope will be a plan for a "typical" day.

[2]    First, meet our staff. The clinic is staffed by four doctors: Dr. Lucy Rhymes, also known as the owner; Dr. Eddie Hunter, a classmate from LSU; myself and my husband, Dr. Jordan Kocen from the University of Missouri. Thankfully, we also have Cindy, Ashley, Sharon, Linda (a 1992 Wilson alum), and Rita, our five very capable veterinary technicians. Without them, our lives would be hell. There's also our receptionist staff, supervised by the very capable Kim; plus countless kennel attendants; Jackie, our office manager, who pays the bills and keeps our shelves stocked; and Ruth, who keeps our files straight.

---

*Paragraph 5 adapted from Eugene V. Martin, "Worker Stress: A Practitioner's Perspective," *Stress Management in Work Settings,* U.S. Department of Health and Human Services, NIOSH, 1987, 149–151.

3    Together, we start the day. The clinic opens at 7 A.M. every morning except Sunday. At this time, the receptionists admit all animals for surgeries and dentistries, along with any boarders and animals needing baths and flea treatments. The technicians sort through the stacks of charts, and record temperatures, heart and respiratory rates on all the patients. The first doctor in each morning is usually the surgery doctor. (We each rotate through surgery during the week.) Our goal is to try to get surgery started before the other doctors arrive. Since the treatment area is small, four doctors in there at once can be an entertaining if not a chaotic experience. To avoid this, I usually arrive last in the morning, and my first goal is coffee.

4    Our appointments run each day from 9:30 A.M. to noon, and 3 to 6 P.M. We also schedule later shifts for the convenience of our working and commuting clients. Although many of our appointments are for routine checkups and vaccines, a typical afternoon can include patients who are vomiting, are in congestive heart failure, have urinary or upper-respiratory infections, and so much more. In addition, Dr. Kocen treats many patients with acupuncture, Chinese herbs, and homeopathy. His treatments have especially helped us with some of our geriatric patients, when all conventional options have been exhausted.

5    If we are lucky and have a typical day, by 7 P.M. everyone is happy and healthy, clean and flea-free, and we go home.

6    But remember, we (almost) never have a typical day. There are days when we have no appointments scheduled all day, and we read magazines and gossip. Just as we get ready to leave, the emergency arrives. Then, we all stay to help. Sometimes it's a bitch in labor and she needs a C-section, sometimes a dog has been hit by a car, or a dog has eaten something it shouldn't.

7    Sometimes we have to coax an owner to bring a dog in, because we really feel it needs to be seen and the owner doesn't. Often, people expect us to make the diagnosis over the phone, which of course we can't. I'll never forget the client who held her dog up to the phone while he was coughing, and then asked me what I thought it was. Occasionally, owners take their dog's medicine and give the dogs their medicine and suddenly, we have two intoxications to deal with at once.

8    Holidays are often our most exciting times. At Christmas, we have the fun of seeing all the new puppies and kittens. We also see the dogs that have poisoned themselves on chocolates hidden for Christmas stockings or Easter baskets.

9    Harder still are the sad times. Sometimes the emergency is too severe, and we have to counsel the client on the hard decision of when to let a beloved pet go. This never gets any easier for me to do, and having been at this practice for eight years, I've known some of these animals a long time. Many nights when I go home to my full household of two cats, one dog, and a cockatiel, I can't help thinking of those people going home to an empty house, and I just feel sad.

10    A veterinarian who is successful and practices good medicine all day, gives a lot of herself/himself to the patients and clients. By the end of the day, we sometimes feel as if there is nothing to give the next day. But we always come back. For all the sadness, there is a tremendous amount of joy. I delight in the break I get in my afternoons to play with the Boston terrier puppies in Dr. Kocen's exam room. Every new kitten or puppy is exclaimed over in our hospital. And when a chronically ill patient gets the thumbs up to go home, sometimes we can't resist—we all walk to the door to wave goodbye.

11    Overall, I'm glad to be a veterinarian.

Janet Foley, "A Day in the Life of a Veterinarian," *Wilson College Magazine*, Spring 1994, 10. Chambersburg, PA. Reprinted by permission.

Your quick preview should have answered these typical questions: Topic? Length? How current (year published)? Style? Any divisions or subheads? Are you curious? Interested? Now for the second step. . . .

## Step B

Go back and overview skim in 45 seconds (= 1,093 wpm) or at the most, 1 minute (= 820 wpm). You'll be tested on your skimming comprehension, but only for main ideas. Please cover these questions, so you can't peek, and don't look back at the essay when you answer them.

Informal skimming quiz—write in or circle answers:

1.  In your own words, write a summary of Dr. Foley's essay in one sentence. What question did the writer begin with? What, in general, was her answer to it?

    _____

    _____

2.  Which one of the following was *not* a major detail of support?
    a.  description of the clinic and staff
    b.  impact of her career on her marriage
    c.  both happy and sad events
3.  Overall, what dominant pattern(s) does the writer use?
    time sequence _____ examples _____ compare-contrast _____
    spatial-geographic _____
4.  Write the name of any staff person mentioned in the essay, besides the author: _____

Check answers with your instructor.

If you hit the right places in your preview, could skim the essay in less than one minute, and could answer most of the questions, you are doing well. If you answered the *last* question correctly, you are reading too much, too carefully. Individual names are not important here; speed up and miss more details!

If you did well on these last three selections, you are ready for carefully timed skimming of longer selections.

# TIMED SELECTIONS:
## OVERVIEW SKIMMING

The ten timed selections in this chapter follow much the same format as do those in Chapter 3. You may do them in class with an instructor or outside of class on your own. In either case, be sure to follow the step-by-step instructions carefully. Please do not skip any step or change the order. Also, exact timing is a must when you are learning to skim. If you allow yourself a minute or two more for a selection, you are not skimming anymore—you are reading too much. So, watch the clock and do not pad your time.

Do not preread any selection. We have set up a rigorous procedure for you to follow, from preview through overview skimming to close reading. If you have already read a selection on your own, you will find it more difficult to improve your reading habits, and you will not be learning how to overview skim new material.

Throughout, neither preread the quiz questions nor refer back to the selection for answers. Of course, you are welcome to read the selection more slowly later. In fact, you are required to do so for the "Writing and Discussion" section.

Compared with the preparation for rapid reading in Chapter 3, the preview step for overview skimming will be minimal because you will be returning not to read the selection but to skim it for main ideas.

Answers to odd-numbered selections are listed on page 351. Answers to even-numbered selections are not provided; ask your instructor for them. We expect 100 percent scores for the preview skim quizzes. Our questions are mainly designed to keep you previewing correctly. Please place your answers to each quiz in the box that follows it.

If your preview and skim times differ from those recommended, use the rate table at the back of the book to determine your words per minute. Finally, when you have finished the timed part of the selection, record your rate and score on the chart on page 192.

The general subject of these selections continues to be "work"—from part-time, minimum wage jobs to highly professional careers to retirement.

Before you begin these selections, you may want to consider the following general questions on work. Answering these questions will help you uncover the knowledge that you and your peers already have concerning work. You may want to respond to these questions individually or discuss them in small or large groups in class:

1. What kinds of work do you think provide the most satisfaction?
2. What kinds of work do you think provide the least satisfaction?
3. Do you think that women are discriminated against in the work force today?
4. What qualities do you believe make a good worker?
5. How do you think workers should plan for their retirement?

## TIMED SELECTIONS: OVERVIEW SKIMMING

. . . . . . . . . . . . . . . . . .

## *SELECTION 1*

This selection was originally a speech about two professions related to books. This clearly written presentation relies on many of the author's personal experiences. As a short selection, you can successfully skim it quickly.

Remember—neither to preread the quiz questions nor to look back at the selection for answers. Follow these steps:

A. Preview skim the article. Then answer the three-item preview quiz.
B. Overview skim the article for main ideas. Then answer the four-item overview quiz.

### A. Preview Skimming

Take no more than 30 seconds (= 1,400 wpm) to preview the entire article.

. . . . . . . . . . . . . . . . . .

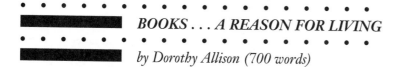

## *BOOKS . . . A REASON FOR LIVING*

. . . . . . . . . . . . . . . . . .

*by Dorothy Allison (700 words)*

[1] When I was eleven years old, I wanted to die.

[2] Now there are a lot of ways for an eleven-year-old girl to die. I could have managed it, but I did not. One reason why is simple. I walked into a bookstore and found a way to live. I traded one of my momma's John D. MacDonald mysteries for the first book I could afford—a paperback without a cover. I took it home and read it. Reading, I began to imagine the possibility of justice. Reading gave me an idea of the worth of my own life. Books did that, writing.

[3] I don't think writing is a small thing. I don't think books are objects of marketing. I don't think of bookstores as the place to push product. I believe in the possibility of changing

the world, and I think that writers give us a way to imagine that—the world we deeply need and want.

4    I keep a sign over my desk, a quote from Grace Paley. It reads, "I write for the still, small possibility of justice." Underneath it I have listed names, my reasons to write. I write to save my dead. I got a lot of dead. Not just in my family, but a nation of people disappeared, lost, not honored, not understood—men, women, children, those who lost their lives because no one knew the full story. Books are a small gesture toward the full story.

5    Understand me. What I am here for is to tell you stories you may not want to hear. What I am here for is to rescue my dead. And to scare the hell out of you now and then. I was raised Baptist, I know how to do that.

6    Now it may be true that, as George Bernard Shaw once said, we become writers because we don't have to get dressed to go to work. I think one of the reasons I began to write was because to do it I did not need to be pretty, did not even have to be interesting. All I needed was to be able to write something pretty and interesting. But the truth is that people become writers out of need. People begin to write in order to create what they have not found and, a little bit, to give something back. Toni Morrison, James Baldwin, Angela Carter . . . my life has been saved over and over again by picking up a book in which someone captured the whole experience of being despised and not dying.

7    I'm going to write a lot of books if I live long enough. Each and every one of them is going to be about being despised and not dying. Each and every one of them is going to be a small gesture toward the possibility of justice.

8    Where I live, the tiny bookstore downtown just disappeared. The rent got too high and a realtor made a better offer. In the next town over the same thing is happening. We keep losing bookstores and getting more realtors—evidence of how very hard it is to keep bookstores alive. But this is what I believe: I believe that when we lose bookstores we are losing the vital—that bookstores are not just places where people go to drink coffee or get a bargain. People don't even go to bookstores just to get a book. Sometimes people go to bookstores to find what they sometimes cannot find at home.

9    I believe that in the absence of what I started out with in my life—women's centers and rape crisis centers—bookstores are community centers. That little bookstore downtown is where you go to be reassured that you are not crazy, to be reassured that the world changes, to be told hard truths and, occasionally, reassured with a little laughter.

10    What I need to say to you as booksellers is very simple. Don't go away. I know how difficult the work can be, but please, don't go away. And thank you. I need to say thank you. For the eleven-year-old girl that I was and the forty-six-year-old woman that I am. Because of you I am still here, here with my three-year-old who loves to be read to and my partner who is building me more bookshelves while I stand here talking to you. As a writer and a woman, I am going to live forever. You are why.

Dorothy Allison, "Books . . . A Reason for Living" (Speech delivered at the annual convention of the American Booksellers Association, Chicago, IL, June 1996), 5. Used by permission of Frances Goldin, Inc.

•   •   •   •   •   •   •   •   •   •   •   •   •   •   •   •   •   •   •   •   •   •   •   •   •   •   •   •

1. The year of publication is
   a. 1995
   b. 1996
   c. 1997
2. There are no major subdivisons in this selection.
   a. true
   b. false
3. The title suggests that books are
   a. not an important part of the author's life
   b. an important part of the author's life
   c. an extremely important part of the author's life

---

**Sel. 1**   P-Skim            1. _____

**Time**   :30 = 1,400 wpm     2. _____

**Score**   _____ %            3. _____

▶ 100%                         **Check answers on p. 351.**

**Score** = number correct × 33.

---

## B. Overview Skimming

If possible, overview skim the article in 45 seconds (= 933 wpm). For faster rates, time yourself to the nearest 15 seconds on page 344 in Appendix B. Then take the skimming quiz without referring to the article.

1. The selection begins with a strong, shocking statement.
   a. true
   b. false
2. The author is a
   a. writer
   b. teacher
   c. actor
   d. none of these
3. This article deals with all of the following *except*
   a. the problems the writer had learning to read
   b. how books influenced the writer's childhood
   c. why the writer must write
   d. the importance of booksellers to a society
4. This article ends with a strong, surprising statement. What is it?
   a. "I plan to die tomorrow."
   b. "I am going to live forever."
   c. "I must live through my books."

---

**Sel. 1   O-Skim**                        1. ____

**Time**  ____:____  =  ____wpm      2. ____

     **min    sec**                  3. ____

**Score**  ____%                         4. ____

   ▶ 75%                          **Check with your instructor.**

**Score** = number correct × 25.      **Record rate and score on p. 192.**

---

## C. For Discussion and Writing

1. What is the dominant organizational pattern of this selection? Give evidence for your answer.
2. What are your childhood memories of bookstores? How do they compare with those of the author?
3. What do you think the author is suggesting when she says in paragraph 10 that she is "going to live forever"? How does this relate to her argument?

• • • • • • • • • • • • • • • • • •

# SELECTION 2

Because it presents findings of a detailed study, this second article will challenge your skimming ability. Do not let the numbers detract you or slow you down. You will have time later to read more carefully for those supporting details.

Follow these steps:

A. Preview the article. Then answer the three-item quiz.
B. Overview skim the article. Then answer the four-item quiz.

## A. Preview Skimming

Take no more than 45 seconds (= 1,600 wpm) to preview skim the article.

# WORK-FORCE STUDY FINDS LOYALTY IS WEAK, DIVISIONS OF RACE AND GENDER ARE DEEP

*by Sue Shellenbarger (1,200 words)*

1    NEW YORK—A broad new survey of American workers depicts a work force that has little loyalty to employers and is deeply divided by race and gender.

2    The study, the most comprehensive look so far at employees' lives, also reflects broader-than-expected conflict between work and family life. It suggests that workers place high value on flexible scheduling, attention to personal needs and management recognition for work well done—and that they are willing to make trade-offs, including changing jobs, to get them.

3    The privately funded National Study of the Changing Workforce by the Families and Work Institute, the first installment of a planned quadrennial survey of U.S. workers' attitudes about their work and personal lives, dwarfs similar efforts since a 1977 federally funded Quality of Employment Survey. The institute, a non-profit New York research and consulting concern, held hour-long telephone interviews with a nationally representative sample of 2,958 wage and salaried workers on issues ranging from relationships with their bosses to household chores.

## LESS LOYAL TO EMPLOYERS

4    The results paint a picture of American workers less loyal to employers than in the past. That isn't surprising: 42% of those surveyed had been through downsizing, 28% had seen management cutbacks at their companies, and nearly 20% said they fear being fired.

5    The study was financed by 15 companies and foundations: **Salt River Project,** a Phoenix utility; **Sears, Roebuck** & Co.'s Allstate Insurance unit; **American Express** Co.; **American Telephone & Telegraph** Co.; Commonwealth Fund; **Dupont** Co.; General Mills Foundation; **International Business Machines** Corp.; **Johnson & Johnson; Levi Strauss** & Co.; **Merck** & Co., **Mobil** Corp.; **Motorola** Inc.; the Rockefeller Foundation; and **Xerox** Corp.

6    The study challenges the notion that younger workers are better equipped to cope with a more diverse workplace. Instead, employees under 25 show no greater preference than older employees for working with people of other races, ages or ethnic groups. Just over half of surveyed workers of all ages said they prefer working with people of the same race, sex, gender and education.

7    Employees who had greater experience living or working with people of other races, ethnic groups and ages showed a stronger preference for diversity in the workplace. But few employees have such experience. The study shows that even workers under 25 had little contact in the neighborhoods where they grew up with people of different ethnic and cultural backgrounds.

8    "The workplace is the main social arena" for racial and ethnic interaction, the study says. "Perhaps even more than school, it is the front line in our nation's efforts" to assimilate diverse workers, "and it's unlikely we will succeed unless employers assume strong leadership."

9    The study also reflects widespread perceptions of racial and sexual discrimination in the workplace. Asked to rate their own chances for advancement against those of members of other racial and ethnic groups, employees of all kinds agreed that minority workers' chances were poorer than those of non-minority workers. (White men and white women rated minorities'

chances of advancement higher than minority workers did.) Minority men and women and white women also rated white men's chances of advancement higher than white men did themselves.

10    Perceptions of discrimination take a heavy toll on job performance, the study suggests. More than one-fifth of minority workers reported that they had been discriminated against by their current employers. Those beliefs correlated with a higher tendency to feel "burned out," a reduced willingness to take initiative on the job and a greater likelihood of planning to change jobs, the study showed.

11    And despite a 20-year flood of women into the work force, women managers surveyed were more than twice as likely as men to rate their career-advancement opportunities as "poor" or "fair," with 39% choosing those labels, compared with 16% of men. In contrast, 84% of men rated their promotion chances "good" or "excellent," compared with 60% of women.

12    Women who said they saw little opportunity for career advancement also tended to be less loyal, less committed and less satisfied on the job, the survey showed.

## EXPLODES GENDER STEREOTYPES

13    The study explodes some popular stereotypes about gender roles, however. Most workers surveyed didn't see much difference in the way men and women manage, for instance—though women managers were viewed as a little more sympathetic to family or personal problems. On other criteria, including keeping workers informed, offering recognition and support and being fair, men and women managers were rated the same.

14    "Despite myths to the contrary, there is no difference, as judged by workers, between men and women supervisors," says Chip U'Ren, associate general manager of Salt River Project, one of the sponsors of the study. The finding should help companies "find ways to . . . break through the glass ceiling," he says.

15    The survey also disputes the notion that an emerging generation of 20-something males will help out their employed partners by doing more chores at home. Men under 25 aren't any more likely to help with cooking, cleaning, shopping or bill-paying than their older counterparts, the study shows. The only area in which younger men surpassed older men was in doing repairs around the house.

16    Not unexpectedly, surveyed employees expressed greater commitment to their jobs than to their employers. While 57% strongly agreed with the statement, "I always try to do my job well, no matter what it takes," only 28% strongly agreed that they were "willing to work harder than I have to help my [employer] succeed."

## WORK ENVIRONMENT

17    But employees also said they placed high value on the quality of their work environment, suggesting that efforts to improve communication, reduce work-family conflict and create a more supportive environment might rekindle flagging loyalty. Surveyed employees who had changed jobs in the past five years, for instance, said they rated such workplace characteristics as open communications, management quality and impact on family life even higher than pay in choosing an employer.

18    Employees also assigned great importance to benefits they thought would help them achieve a better balance between job and personal life. About one-quarter of employees without flexible scheduling or the right to work at home said they would change jobs to gain those opportunities; 47% of those who lacked the right to time off to care for sick family members said they would take a cut in pay or benefits to get it.

19    Such nontraditional benefits also correlate with greater feelings of loyalty and commitment to helping the employer succeed, the study shows—though traditional benefits, such as health insurance, don't have the same impact.

## JOB-FAMILY CONFLICTS

20    The survey reflects surprisingly broad conflict between workers' job and family responsibilities. Nearly half of those surveyed have responsibility for caring for dependents, whether

elderly or disabled relatives or young children. And 87% reported having at least some day-to-day family responsibilities at home, suggesting that work-family policies such as flexible scheduling and dependent-care help "shouldn't be viewed as special assistance for a small group of workers, but as general assistance for virtually all employees," the study says.

21    The results "make you catch your breath," says Faith Wohl, director of human resource initiatives for DuPont, another sponsor of the study. The results suggest work-family programs should be broadened and integrated with quality-improvement efforts, she says. "Ultimately, what makes your company family-friendly is to be worker-friendly," she says.

22    When work and family clash, a worker's family is more than three times more likely to suffer than his or her job performance, the study shows. When problems erupt at work, employees reported that they were far more likely to give up time with their families, leave housework undone or experience bad moods than to refuse overtime or business travel, cut their output or quarrel with their bosses.

23    Two-thirds of surveyed employees with children said they lack adequate time with them. "Especially for workers with children, the picture is of individuals in gridlock," says Dana Friedman, co-president of the institute. "People feel strongly about doing a good job at work. They also yearn to spend more time with their families but arrive home exhausted."

Sue Shellenbarger, "Work Force Study Finds Loyalty Is Weak, Divisions of Race and Gender Are Deep," *Wall Street Journal*, September 3, 1993. Reprinted by permission of *The Wall Street Journal* © 1993 Dow Jones & Company, Inc. All rights reserved.

• • • • • • • • • • • • • • • • • • • • • • • • • • • • • • • • • •

1.  This article is from
    a. a union newsletter
    b. a business newspaper
    c. a psychology text
2.  The title is
    a. long, and a good summary of the contents
    b. short, but followed by a long, useful lead
3.  Which of the following is truer?
    a. Every paragraph in this article is loaded with details and figures—it's impossible to skim.
    b. There are some general conclusions in the article, so it's skimmable.

| | |
|---|---|
| **Sel. 2**   P-Skim | 1. \_\_\_\_ |
| **Time**   :45 = 1,600 wpm | 2. \_\_\_\_ |
| **Score**   \_\_\_\_ % | 3. \_\_\_\_ |
| ▶ 100% | **Check answers with your instructor.** |
| **Score** = number correct × 33. | |

## B. Overview Skimming

Now go back and overview skim for the main ideas in 1 minute (= 1,200 wpm), if possible, or up to 1:30 (= 800 wpm). Remember to focus on broad conclusions, not on exact percentages.

1. Which subhead was not in the article? Or were they all present?
   a. Job-Family Conflicts
   b. Explodes Gender Stereotypes
   c. Less Loyal to Employers
   d. All were present
2. The main conclusion reached by this massive study is that American workers value pay incentives—money—above all other factors in their jobs.
   a. true
   b. false
3. This privately funded study is
   a. the most comprehensive one in many years
   b. fairly small, but conducted each year
4. The ending section (prime placement) of the article deals with
   a. the trauma of being laid off
   b. problems arising from work-family conflicts
   c. the importance of job recruiting

| Sel. 2   O-Skim | 1. _____ |
|---|---|
| **Time** _____:_____ = _____**wpm** | 2. _____ |
| min    sec | 3. _____ |
| **Score** _____% | 4. _____ |
| ▶ 75% | **Check answers with your** |
| **Score** = number correct × 25. | **instructor.** |
| | **Record rate and score on p. 192.** |

##  C. For Discussion and Writing

1. Were you surprised, like many employers and the study's architects, at the importance workers assigned to conflicts between their work and their families? Why or why not?
2. The article also gives much space to the subtopics "gender" and "race/ethnicity" in the workplace. Give your reactions to and opinions on either subtopic.
3. Imagine you own a business or factory. After reading this survey of workers' perceptions, you want to "assume strong leadership" (paragraph 8) in helping your workers accept diversity among their co-workers. How would you go about it?

## SELECTION 3

This next selection, a typical feature story from a daily newspaper, has short paragraphs that make it harder to skim than journal articles with fully developed paragraphs. Nonetheless, skimming newspapers is a marvelously useful skill. Practice it on this piece.

A. Preview skim. Then answer the three-item quiz.
B. Overview skim. Then answer the four-item quiz.

### HER CAREER FROM "CUTIE" TO "CAPTAIN"

*by Phil Dirkx (1,300 words)*

**Helen Smith spent 25 years in the Navy breaking longtime gender barriers.**

1    PASO ROBLES—When Helen Smith was a young ensign in the Navy, her male superior officers called her "Tootsie," "Sweetie Pie," and "Cutie." But for the past few years she's been called Capt. Smith.

2    She retired from the Navy in July [1993] after 25 years' service and now lives in the Rancho Paso mobile home park. . . .

3    Those early nicknames didn't bother her, she said. "It was nothing like sexual harassment. All those guys acted like our big brothers and fathers."

4    That first duty assignment was at the Key West Naval Air Station in Florida. Later she did encounter sexual harassment and other obstacles elsewhere, but she still strongly recommends the Navy as a career for women.

5    Smith was born in San Rafael 47 years ago. She graduated from San Fernando Valley State University (now Cal State Northridge) in 1968 with a degree in geography.

6    She signed up for the Navy that spring, but wasn't to report for duty until September. So she went to Sitka, Alaska, that summer with a Pres-byterian volunteer and missionary program.

7    As a sideline she learned to scuba dive in the 40-degree water and became one of the only three scuba divers in southern coastal Alaska. She also did some underwater demolition for the Navy in the removal of an old rotting pier and got a state license as a powder monkey.

8    In September she entered the Navy and went directly to the women's officer candidate school at Newport, R.I., which was separate from the men's. In fact, it was upstairs over the chaplains' school, she said.

9    Smith told the school commandant she wanted to be a Navy SEAL. SEAL stands for Sea, Air and Land teams, which do combat underwater demolition and clandestine commando operations.

10    The commandant, who was a woman, said, "Miss Smith, ladies are not SEALS." So the first assignment she got was as assistant administrative officer for a fighter squadron at Key West. She was one of two women officers in the outfit.

11    That was 25 years ago, and women officers didn't object to being called "Tootsie" or being the "coffee makers and note takers," she said.

12    "We were thrilled these guys really liked us. We were making our way in a man's world.

They treated us as they knew how to treat the other women in their lives—their wives, mothers, sisters."

13 She and the other woman officer found they got all the administrative duties. "The men just wanted to get into those airplanes and fly all they could," she said. "They didn't want to do paperwork."

14 The men hadn't discovered yet that they had to learn to do paperwork to get ahead, so the women got promoted first, she said. The women officers learned to do personnel and legal work and had picked up the training they needed to become department heads and commanding officers.

15 "A whole generation of male officers discovered too late they were behind the power curve," she said.

16 From Key West, she was transferred to Moffett Field where she was the administrative officer and only woman in a simulated aircraft training unit. There she ran into sexual discrimination. When she got her fitness report, she found her commanding officer had placed her 13th among the 13 lieutenants in the unit.

17 "He told me, in fact, I was the best in the whole command, but he said, 'These men will go on to command and you won't. They need good ratings.' It was very demoralizing. No matter what I did, I'd be ranked lowest. Why should I try?"

18 In those days the Navy didn't have rules and procedures for appealing sexual discrimination, she said. "There was no recourse, no one to talk to."

19 About that time she came down with severe rheumatoid arthritis and was hospitalized for a year and on temporary disability retirement from 1973 to 1976. She believes the arthritis was brought on by her stress over the fitness report, although it is also genetically linked. She eventually recovered, and her arthritis is now medically managed.

20 In 1977 she was assigned to an American naval base in Spain. That's where she ran into sexual harassment. She said her male superior

officer indicated to her and the other female officers that "if you're willing to sleep with me, I'll see that you get a medal."

21 She was in a teaching unit there, where she developed workshops on race relations and on women in the Navy, and programs to teach Navy personnel how to get around in foreign countries. "It led to some good fitness reports," she said, "but never a medal."

22 Her next assignment was at Pearl Harbor, Hawaii. By that time she had become a lieutenant commander and was administrative officer for the naval station. One of her jobs there was to set up and oversee a family service center for Navy personnel. It provided such services as marriage and family counseling, budgeting workshops, and single-parenting workshops. The program was a success and gained national recognition, she said.

23 But it also created a problem for Smith's career, when the wife of one of Smith's superiors asked for help because he was abusing her. Smith sought the assistance of the husband's commanding officer, but he didn't discipline the husband or urge him to get counseling. Instead the commanding officer told the husband, "You better squash these people because they'll ruin your career."

24 Fortunately his wife got other help and left him, Smith said, but the husband was still Smith's superior and he "put one of those faintly damning remarks in my fitness report that guarantees you will never be promoted."

25 She had just been promoted to commander, but that report caused her to be passed over three times for command assignments. If you miss three times, she said, you're out of the Navy.

26 After the third time, she wrote a letter to the Selection Board explaining that she'd had a problem with an individual in her chain of command. The board reviewed her record and assigned her to a command post. "I was able to break through the good-old-boy network," she said.

27 After that she made her way up the career ladder, and in 1991 she was promoted to captain,

which is equivalent to a full colonel in the Army. At that time she was one of the 25 women captains on general duty in the Navy. By contrast, in the spring of this year [1993], she said, the Selection Board picked 25 women to be promoted to captain.

28    In 1991 she was transferred to the faculty of the Armed Forces Staff College at Norfolk, and after one month there she was appointed the base commander for the college.

29    That was the same year as the Tailhook Association convention in Las Vegas, which caused a scandal that rocked the Navy. Smith didn't attend the convention, but she knows women who did.

30    Time Magazine reported that the official investigation of the 1991 convention found "83 women and seven men were forcibly groped, stripped, bitten on the buttocks, or made to drink from the phallus of a fake rhinocerus."

31    "It took more than a year for the system to say it was wrong; we'll change things," she said. "It [Tailhook] exposed a lot of lip service about the issue of equality. I think the Navy is better for it."

32    Smith is confident that the Navy is changing for the better, and she emphatically recommends it as a career for women. She believes the modern armed services offer more opportunity for women than do civilian employers.

33    "Increased opportunity is almost guaranteed," she said, "if you work hard and learn."

34    And the problems she experienced have been ended, she said, by the new rules and regulations that spell out women's rights and hold people responsible for enforcing those rights.

Phil Dirkx, "Her Career from 'Cutie' to 'Captain,'" *San Luis Obispo County Telegram-Tribune*, November 10, 1993. Reprinted by permission of the publisher.

• • • • • • • • • • • • • • • • • • • • • • • • • • • • • • • •

## A.  Preview in 30 seconds (= 2,600 words)

1.  The text is broken up by several useful subheadings.
    a.  true
    b.  false
2.  The item focuses on the experiences of one woman.
    a.  true
    b.  false
3.  Given its subject matter, the article is reasonably current: _____ (year).

| | |
|---|---|
| **Sel. 3**   P-Skim | 1. _____ |
| **Time**   :30 = 2,600 wpm | 2. _____ |
| **Score**   _____ % | 3. _____ |
| ▶ 100% | **Check answers on p. 351.** |
| **Score** = number correct × 33. | |

## B. Overview Skimming

Take 1 minute (= 1,300 wpm) or 1:30 (= 867 wpm) to skim this selection for the story of one woman's Navy career and the conclusions she drew from it. Then take the quiz without looking back at the text.

1. Captain Smith makes clear that she had to fight blatant sexism in the Navy from the beginning to the very end of her career.
   a. true
   b. false
2. The account of the captain's training and her background shows that
   a. she developed various skills after her college years
   b. she had a strict, military-type upbringing
3. Over the years, her assignments were
   a. varied in location and duties
   b. limited to two U.S. locations and dull paperwork
4. The piece concludes with her belief that
   a. women considering a Navy career should realize that sexism will probably always be a major obstacle
   b. the Navy is changing its ways and can be a good career choice for women

---

| **Sel. 3   O-Skim** | **1.** _____ |
| **Time**  ____:____  =  ____**wpm** | **2.** _____ |
| min   sec | **3.** _____ |
| **Score**  ____% | **4.** _____ |
| ▶ 75% | **Check answers on p. 351.** |
| **Score** = number correct × 25. | **Record rate and score on p. 192.** |

---

 ## C. For Discussion and Writing

Reread or refer back to the article as needed.

1. What is the dominant organizational pattern of this article? What is its thesis?
2. Using evidence from the interview, explain what qualities enabled Captain Smith to rise through the various Navy ranks.
3. Women are succeeding at previously nontraditional careers: firefighters, engineers, and bodybuilders. Similarly, men are succeeding as registered nurses, kindergarten teachers, and grief counselors. Have you ever been interested in a career in a nontraditional field? If so, which one?

# SELECTION 4

Here is another newspaper article of general interest, with the same short-paragraph format. The topic, "excellence in a chosen field," relates directly to the chapter topic, though the article does not evaluate specific jobs.

Follow the usual steps:

A.  Preview skim the article. Then answer the three-item quiz.
B.  Overview skim the article. Then answer the four-item quiz.

## A.  Preview Skimming

Do the usual minimal preview: headlines, subheads, length, and so on. Spend no more than 30 seconds on this (= 3,000 wpm).

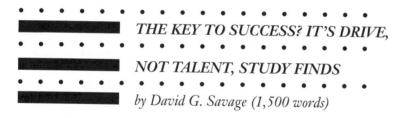

*THE KEY TO SUCCESS? IT'S DRIVE,*

*NOT TALENT, STUDY FINDS*

*by David G. Savage (1,500 words)*

1   A five-year study of 120 of the nation's top artists, athletes and scholars has concluded that drive and determination, not great natural talent, led to their extraordinary success.
2   "We expected to find tales of great natural gifts," said University of Chicago education professor Benjamin Bloom, who led the team of researchers who studied the careers of America's top performers in six fields: concert pianists, Olympic swimmers, sculptors, tennis players, mathematicians, and research neurologists.
3   "We didn't find that at all. Their mothers often said it was their other child who had the greater gift," Bloom said.
4   The most brilliant mathematicians often said they had trouble in school and were rarely the best in their classes. Some world-class tennis players said their coaches viewed them as being too short ever to be outstanding, and the Olym-

pic swimmers said they remember getting regularly "clobbered" in races as 10-year-olds.

ANONYMOUS INTERVIEWS
5   The foundation-supported research team conducted in-depth, anonymous interviews with the top 20 performers in the six fields, as judged by national championships or similar honors.
6   They also interviewed their families and teachers, hoping to learn how these individuals developed into extraordinary performers.
7   Instead, the researchers heard accounts of an extraordinary drive and dedication through which, for example, a child would practice the piano several hours daily for 17 years to attain his goal of becoming a concert pianist. A typical swimmer would tell of getting up at 5:30 every morning to swim two hours before school and

then two hours after school to attain his or her goal of making the Olympic team.

8    Bloom, an eminent educational researcher, said his findings "remind me of the old joke about the young man walking down a New York street who stops to ask a little old lady, 'How do I get to Carnegie Hall?' And she looks up and says, 'Practice, young man. Practice.'"

9    Although practice and motivation seemed to explain their success, the top performers, regardless of their field, appeared to follow a similar course of development, the researchers found.

10    In practically every case, the parents played the key role, first by exposing their children at an early age to music, sports or learning. The vast majority of the parents were not themselves outstanding musicians, athletes or scholars. For example, fewer than half of the parents of the distinguished pianists had ever played any musical instrument.

## VALUED COMPETITION

11    But the parents of the swimmers and tennis players did enjoy sports and valued competition, Bloom reported. The families of the pianists and sculptors appreciated art and music, while the parents of the research scientists displayed a great love for learning.

12    The parents of the mathematicians and research neurologists reported that their children showed both an unusual curiosity about how things work and an "independent nature" that allowed them to play or work alone for hours.

13    Although it is not uncommon for children to ask repeatedly "why?," "what appears to make the parents of the (scientists) unique is the nature of their response to their children's questions," Bloom wrote. "They responded to the questions seriously, often encouraging even more questions."

14    Beyond specific attitudes or interests, the parents also taught their children to value hard work and competition.

15    "These parents placed great stress on achievement, on success, and on doing one's best at all times. They were models of the 'work ethic,' believing that work should come before play and that one should always work toward distant goals," Bloom said. The results of the research will be published this week in a book entitled Developing Talent in Young People.

16    The families said in the interviews that they wanted their sons and daughters to have "normal" childhoods and that they had no inkling that the children would achieve unusual success.

## PARENTS ENCOURAGED THEM

17    But once a child displayed an interest and enthusiasm in a particular area, these parents encouraged them at every step and were willing to spend countless hours shuttling them to and from piano, tennis, or swimming lessons.

18    "Even in homes where money was tight, no sacrifice was too great in order that the child have whatever he needed to learn to become a musician. 'My parents didn't have nickels to rub together,' Bloom quoted one pianist as saying. "'Those were the bad old days. But there was always money for music.'"

19    Several of the families reported moving to new homes just to get their children in better academic environments or to be closer to a coach or instructor.

20    Bloom's study also found that these extraordinary achievers, all of whom were younger than 40 when interviewed, appeared to have gone through three distinct stages of development, regardless of their field.

21    At first, the parents exposed the children to playing a piano, tinkering with scientific games or hitting a tennis ball, but it was just fun. They played tennis with their families, for example, and developed the habit of regular practice. Usually, the children also had some outside instruction—perhaps a neighbor who gave piano lessons or an uncle who was a good tennis player.

22    Then, at some point, they began to gain recognition for their ability. A 7-year-old would play the piano for a school performance. An 8-year-old would beat all the other children at his local tennis or swimming club.

23    "Within two to five years, most of the individuals in our study began to see themselves in terms of the talent field," Bloom wrote. "They began to see themselves as 'pianists' and 'swimmers' before the age of 11 or 12, and 'mathematicians' before the age of 16 or 17."

24    "Most of our talented individuals had very good experiences with their initial teachers, and many had developed a very comfortable relationship with them," Bloom wrote.

25    At the second stage of development, as a child's rapid progress became apparent, the parents usually sought out a more expert instructor or coach.

26    Typically, the new teachers "were perfectionists who demanded a great deal of practice time for the student and looked for much progress in a relatively short period of time," Bloom wrote. They usually stressed the refining of the child's technique, whether it be their fingers on the keyboard or their strokes in the water or on the tennis court.

27    In the middle years, these young people first tasted extraordinary success. Some set national swimming records as adolescents. The pianists got opportunities to perform with symphony orchestras. The future mathematicians and neurologists were already doing independent research projects and winning science fairs. The tennis players were winning state championships.

## GREATER COMMITMENT

28    At this point, their commitment to their field escalated one step further. The subjects said they began "living" for swimming, or tennis or the piano and devoted hours each day to practice. They also sought out the nation's best coaches or teachers, those who were recognized masters at training the best.

29    Sixteen of the world-class pianists reported having studied at some time with one of five master teachers. The mathematicians and scientists, who often had become attached to a special teacher or gained the attention of a local university professor, gravitated to the nation's top universities in math and science.

30    At this final stage of development, the focus was less on technique than on developing a personal style. The swimmers and tennis players said their master teachers helped them with strategy and psychology. The pianists said they learned about expressing their own interpretation of the music.

31    "During these years the student was completely committed to the talent field. Now most of the motivation was internal and related to their larger goals," Bloom wrote.

32    Few of the talented individuals expressed any regret about devoting so much of their time to pursuing a single goal.

33    "I loved tennis. To me, it was productive," said one former player. "To sit in a (fast-food) parking lot in a car with four or five 16-year-olds didn't interest me a bit. I never felt I missed that."

34    A few swimmers reported a great feeling of letdown after the Olympics ended and their swimming careers were over. Most of the top achievers, even those who had left their field, said they had retained a feeling of pride in their accomplishments.

35    Bloom said the study convinced him that talent must be carefully nurtured over many years.

36    "The old saw that 'genius will win out' in spite of the circumstances just doesn't hold up," he said.

37    Because natural talent seemed to play such a minor role in the development of these performers, Bloom said he was also convinced that a large number of individuals could achieve at extraordinary levels if given the right encouragement and training.

38    The research "points to the enormous human potential available in each society and the likelihood that only a very small amount of this human potential is ever fully developed," he concluded. "We believe that each society could vastly increase the amount and kinds of talent it develops."

David G. Savage, "The Key to Success? It's Drive, Not Talent," *Los Angeles Times*, February 17, 1985. Copyright 1985, Los Angeles Times. Reprinted by permission.

• • • • • • • • • • • • • • • • • • • • • • • •

1.  The article and lead of the news story sum up the main idea: the results of the research study.
    a. true
    b. false
2.  The article concerns individuals who have been successful in scholarship, the arts, and sports.
    a. true
    b. false
3.  One inserted subheading is
    a. Parents Encouraged Them
    b. Money Not a Factor

---

**Sel. 4**   P-Skim                              1. _____

**Time**   :30 = 3,000 wpm                       2. _____

**Score**   _____%                               3. _____

▶ 100%                                           **Check answers with your instructor.**

**Score** = number correct × 33.

---

## B. Overview Skimming

Take no more than 1:30 minutes (= 1,000 wpm) to skim the article for main ideas. Of course, if you can skim it in 1 minute (= 1,500 wpm), that's fine, too. For any faster or slower times, look up your wpm rate on page 344. Then take the quiz without looking back at the article.

1.  The study took five years, analyzed 120 people in six fields, and was directed by the University of Chicago.
    a. true
    b. false
2.  The results of the study seem to prove that high achievement in various fields results from
    a. great teachers or coaches at a crucial phase of development
    b. unusual natural talents or gifts present at birth
3.  The study also shows that extremely successful people
    a. shared much the same background and phases of development
    b. cannot be categorized one way or another
4.  The article ends with Bloom's conviction that
    a. "genius will win out," regardless of outside forces
    b. the human potential for success is enormous and largely untapped

**Sel. 4**   O-Skim                        1. _____

**Time** _____:_____ = **1,500 wpm**      2. _____
                 min    sec               3. _____

**Score** _____%                          4. _____

        ▶ 75%                    **Check answers with your**

**Score** = number correct × 25.   **instructor.**

                              **Record rate and score on p. 192.**

 C. For Discussion and Writing

Read or refer back to the article as needed.

1.  What is the dominant writing pattern of this article?
2.  Using phrases or sentences, outline the "three distinct stages of development" of the high achiever.
3.  This study and its published results are several years old. Does this invalidate the findings, in your opinion? Why or why not?
4.  Assuming that Bloom's conclusions are valid, what meaning does this study have for you? For children growing up in families everywhere?

# SELECTION 5

This interview is one of a series of interviews about work by Studs Terkel, a famous Chicago journalist. In this selection, the interviewee gives ample reasons for choosing his profession. As an interview, it reads quickly. Later, you may want to savor the interesting details that Bob Freeman presents concerning his job.
    Follow these steps:

A.  Preview skim. Then take the three-item quiz.
B.  Overview skim. Then take the four-item quiz.

## A. Preview Skimming

Spend 1 minute (= 1,700 wpm) previewing this interview. Get to know Bud Freeman generally—his personality and a little bit about the job he loves.

• • • • • • • • • • • • • • •
## BUD FREEMAN
• • • • • • • • • • • • • • •
*by Studs Terkel (1,700 words)*

1    *He is sixty-five years old, though his appearance and manner are of William Blake's "golden youth." He has been a tenor saxophone player for forty-seven years. Highly respected among his colleagues, he is a member of "The World's Greatest Jazz Band." It is a cooperative venture, jointly owned by the musicians, established jazz men.*

2    *"I'm with the young people because they refuse to be brainwashed by the things you and I were brainwashed by. My father, although he worked hard all his life, was very easy with us. Dad was being brainwashed by the people in the neighborhood. They'd come in every day and say, "Why don't your boys go to work?" So he made the mistake of awakening my brother at seven thirty. I pretended to be asleep. Dad said, "You're going to get up, go out in the world and get jobs and amount to something." My brother said, "How dare you wake us up before the weekend?" (Laughs.) I don't recall ever having seen my father since. (Laughs.)*

3    I get up about noon. I would only consider myself outside the norm because of the way other people live. They're constantly reminding me I'm abnormal. I could never bear to live the dull lives that most people live, locked up in offices. I live in absolute freedom. I do what I do because I want to do it. What's wrong with making a living doing something interesting?

4    I wouldn't work for anybody. I'm working for me. Oddly enough, jazz is a music that came out of the black man's oppression, yet it allows for great freedom of expression, perhaps more than any other art form. The jazz man is expressing freedom in every note he plays. We can only please the audience doing what *we* do. We have to please ourselves first.

5    I know a good musician who worked for Lawrence Welk. The man must be terribly in need of money. It's regimented music. It doesn't swing, it doesn't create, it doesn't tell the story of life. It's just the kind of music that people who don't care for music would buy.

6    I've had people say to me: "You don't do this for a living, for heaven's sake?" I was so shocked. I said, "What other way am I going to make a living? You want to send me a check?" (Laughs.) People can't understand that there are artists in the world as well as drones.

7    I only know that as a child I was of a rebellious nature. I saw life as it was planned for most of us. I didn't want any part of that dull life. I worked for Lord and Taylor once, nine to five. It was terribly dull. I lasted six weeks. I couldn't see myself being a nine-to-five man, saving my money, getting married, and having a big family—good God, what a way to live!

8    I knew when I was eight years old that I wasn't going to amount to anything in the business world. (Laughs.) I wanted my life to have something to do with adventure, something unknown, something involved with a free life, something to do with wonder and astonishment. I loved to play—the fact that I could express myself in improvisation, the *unplanned.*

9    I love to play now more than ever, because I know a little more about music. I'm interested in developing themes and playing something creative. Life now is not so difficult. We work six months a year. We live around the world. And we don't have to work in night clubs night after night after night.

10    Playing in night clubs, I used to think, When are we going to get out of here? Most audiences were drunk and you tended to become lazy. And if you were a drinker yourself, there went your music. This is why so many great

talents have died or gotten out of it. They hated the music business. I was lucky—now I'm sixty-five—in having played forty-seven years.

11    If jazz musicians had been given the chance we in this band have today—to think about your work and not have to play all hours of the night, five or six sets—God! Or radio station work or commercial jingle work—the guys must loathe it. I don't think the jazz man has been given a fair chance to do what he really wants to do, to work under conditions where he's not treated like a slave, not subject to the music business, which we've loathed all our lives.

12    I've come to love my work. It's my way of life. Jazz is a luxurious kind of music. You don't play it all day long. You don't play it all night long. The best way to play it is in concerts. You're on for an hour or two and you give it everything you have, your best. And the audience is sober. And I'm not in a hurry to have the night finish. Playing night clubs, it was endless.

13    If you're a creative player, something must happen, and it will. Some sort of magic takes place, yet it isn't magic. Hundreds of times I've gone to work thinking, Oh my God, I hate to think of playing tonight. It's going to be awful. But something on a given night takes place and I'm excited before it's over. Does that make sense? If you have that kind of night, you're not aware of the time, because of this thing that hits you.

14    There's been a lot of untruths told about improvisation. Men just don't get up on the stage and improvise on things they're not familiar with. True improvisation comes out of hard work. When you're practicing at home, you work on a theme and you work out all the possibilities of that theme. Since it's in your head, it comes out when you play. You don't get out on the stage and just improvise, not knowing what the hell you're doing. It doesn't work out that way. Always just before I play a concert, I get the damn horn out and practice. Not scales, but look for creative things to play. I'll practice tonight when I get home, before I go to work. I can't wait to get at it.

15    I practice because I want to play better. I've never been terribly interested in technique, but I'm interested in facility. To feel comfortable, so when the idea shoots out of my head I can finger it, manipulate it. Something interesting happens. You'll hear a phrase and all of a sudden you're thrown into a whole new inspiration. It doesn't happen every night. But even if I have a terrible night and say, "Oh, I'm so tired, I'll go to sleep and I'll think of other things," the music'll come back. I wasn't too happy about going to work last night because I was tired. It was a drag. But today I feel good. Gonna go home and blow the horn now for a while.

16    Practicing is no chore to me. I love it. I really do love to play the horn alone. They call me the narcissistic tenor (laughs), because I practice before the mirror. Actually I've learned a great deal looking in the mirror and playing. The dream of all jazz artists is to have enough time to think about their work and play and to develop.

17    *Was there a time when you were altogether bored with your work?*

18    Absolutely. I quit playing for a year. I met a very rich women. We went to South America to live. We had a house by the sea. I never realized how one could be so rich, so unhappy, and so bored. It frightened me. But I did need a year off. When I came back, I felt fresh.

19    The other time was when I had a band of my own. I had a name, so I no longer worked for big bands. I was expected to lead one of my own. But I can't handle other people. If I have a group and the pianist, let's say, doesn't like my playing. I can't play. I don't see how these band leaders do it. I can't stand any kind of responsibility other than the music itself. I have to work as a soloist. I can be the custodian only of my own being and thinking.

20    I had this band and the guys were late all the time. I didn't want to have to hassle with them. I didn't want to mistreat them, so I said, "Fellas, should we quit?" I wouldn't let them go and stay on myself. We were good friends. I'd say I'd quit if they didn't come on time. They started

to come on time. But I wasn't a leader. I used to stand by in the band! A bit to the side. (Laughs.) Now we have a cooperative band. So I have a feeling I'm working for myself.

21    I don't know if I'll make it, but I hope I'll be playing much better five years from now. I oughta, because I know a little bit more of what I'm doing. It takes a lifetime to learn how to play an instrument. We have a lot of sensational young players come up—oh, you hear them for six months, and then they drop out. The kid of the moment, that's right. Real talent takes a long time to mature, to learn how to bring what character you have into sound, into your playing.* Not the instrument, but the style of music you're trying to create should be an extension of you. And this takes a whole life.

22    I want to play for the rest of my life. I don't see any sense in stopping. Were I to live another thirty years—that would make me ninety-five—

why not try to play? I can just hear the critics: "Did you hear that wonderful note old man Freeman played last night?" (Laughs.) As Ben Webster† says, "I'm going to play this god-damned saxophone until they put it on top of me." It's become dearer to me after having done it for forty-seven years. It's a thing I need to do.

23    *Mme. Lotte Lehmann often spoke of art and age. She recalled a wistful conversation with Maestro Bruno Walter. In his eighties, he reflected on the richness and wisdom of the aged artist and of the long way the young virtuoso had to go—"but he's less tired." It is said that Arturo Toscanini, in his last years, often was thus reflective.

24    †The eminent tenor sax man whose highly creative years were with Duke Ellington.

. . . . . . . . . . . . . . . . . . . . . . . . . . . .

1.   This interview was published in
    a.  1970
    b.  1974
    c.  1984
2.   This interview begins with
    a.  a physical description of Bud Freeman and a general description of his job
    b.  all the things Bud dislikes about his job
    c.  an explanation of where this interview took place
3.   Bud Freeman is a
    a.  sculptor
    b.  television actor
    c.  saxophone player

| **Sel. 5**  P-Skim | 1. _____ |
|---|---|
| **Time**   1:00 = 1,700 wpm | 2. _____ |
| **Score** _____ % | 3. _____ |
| ▶ 100% | **Check answers on p. 351.** |
| **Score** = number correct × 33. | |

## B. Overview Skimming

Take 2 minutes (= 850 wpm) or fewer to overview skim this interview for main ideas. Then take the quiz without looking back at the interview. For faster times, look up your wpm on page 344.

1.  The main point that Bud Freeman makes concerning his job is that
    a. playing the saxophone is one of many jobs he had in his career
    b. playing the saxophone is often too tedious a job
    c. he cannot see himself doing anything but playing the saxophone
    d. drug use makes up a large part of the music profession
2.  Which of the following does *not* describe Bud Freeman's character?
    a. He is rebellious.
    b. He enjoys the business aspect of music.
    c. He enjoys practicing his saxophone.
    d. He wakes up late.
3.  Bud Freeman brags that he has never been bored with his work.
    a. true
    b. false
4.  When does Bud Freeman plan to retire?
    a. at sixty-five
    b. at seventy
    c. after his last child finishes college
    d. never

| | |
|---|---|
| **Sel. 5**   O-Skim | 1. _____ |
| **Time** _____:_____ = _____ **wpm** | 2. _____ |
| min    sec | 3. _____ |
| **Score** _____ % | 4. _____ |
| ▶ 75% | **Check answers on p. 351.** |
| **Score** = number correct × 25. | **Record rate and score on p. 192.** |

 C. For Discussion and Writing

Reread the interview as needed.

1.  Reread this interview to determine the sort of person Bud Freeman is. How does his personality seem to fit his job choice?
2.  Job dissatisfaction is a common complaint we hear today, yet Freeman is satisfied with his work. Select at least three reasons why Freeman continues

to love his work. Do these reasons describe any other people you have known who also love their work?

3. What do you think causes job satisfaction? What causes job dissatisfaction?

## D. Midpoint Evaluation—Overview Skimming

Did you preview and overview skim Selection 5 effectively? That is, were your skimming times and quiz scores on target?

In the preview skim, you should have noticed both when this interview was published and the peculiar nature of its organization—italics for the interviewer's questions and introductory background to Bud Freeman and regular print for the transcript of Freeman's responses. Did you also notice that there were no clear subdivisions?

Early in the overview skim, you should have noticed some of the key bits of information regarding Freeman's job and the immense pleasure he derives from playing the saxophone. You should have then spiraled your eyes through the paragraphs to locate details about why Freeman loves his job and formed a general picture of his independent personality. By the end, you should have had a clear, though general, picture of this saxophone player's lengthy and fulfilling career.

If you had trouble with any of these concerns, take time now to skim this article again, making sure to finish within the recommended time.

• • • • • • • • • • • • • • • • • • •

## SELECTION 6

The term *service industry* usually brings to mind fast food and dry cleaners, with their large numbers of minimum wage jobs. However, *service* also means domestic service. Individuals with estates often employ a domestic staff—including butlers, who comprise so precious a breed that they command high salaries.

Kazuo Ishiburo's novel *The Remains of the Day* chronicles the life of a repressed English butler before World War II. You may have seen the award-winning 1993 film. Here is an inside look at modern-day butlering as practiced in California.

Follow these steps.

A. Preview skim. Then take the three-item quiz.
B. Overview skim. Then take the four-item quiz.

## A. Preview Skimming

Spend 1 minute (= 1,900 wpm) or 1:30 (= 1,267 wpm) previewing the article for any subtitle, lead, or subheads, and for length and difficulty level. Then answer the preview quiz without referring back to the article.

## AT YOUR SERVICE

by Leslie Gregory (1,900 words)

1 In a time when millionaires are becoming commonplace, there are still those very few whose net worth stretches nine or 10 digits. These are the people who make an easy million in a matter of weeks or those who were born knowing they would never, ever have to worry about making a dime.

2 They are the privileged few who live in mansions at the end of winding driveways hidden behind iron gateways—the mysterious passengers in the back seats of limousines with darkened windows. Seldom glimpsed. Rarely addressed.

3 At the heart of many of these households there lives a man whose very purpose is to know everything that goes on, making sure that each need is met, each comfort provided for. He is the butler and, though he is of a rare breed, he still thrives in a modern world that shuns tradition and propriety. And, there at the center of this private world, he knows precisely what is going on behind closed doors.

4 Most of us can only fantasize about what it would be like to live among the creme de la creme of society, traveling to the most exotic corners of the world in the lap of luxury, bantering with royalty or witnessing dinner conversations that determine the price of gold or the strange bedfellows among the powerful. For the butler, these privileges are part of daily life, and he often grows as familiar with enormous wealth as his employer.

5 Anthony Ivory is one of a handful of top butlers on the Westside. Ivory's mother was a cook and his father a butler in a number of fine houses in England. At 16, Ivory left home and went to sea, serving in the British Merchant Navy and eventually working his way to tending the captain and crew on the Queen Mary. "I've met a lot of people," he says. "I've traveled the world and lived in some of the most beautiful homes on earth."

6 Ivory's most recent position was head butler for a woman whose family amassed a great fortune in the steel industry. Like most in his position, Ivory was careful to protect the woman's name. His duties in that home consisted of supervising the household staff, caring for the silver, choosing the finest wines and generally tending to anything and everything that kept the household in perfect order.

7 "From six in the morning (the house) went like a clock up until when dinner was finished and the alarms were put on. You make sure you don't run out of catsup, caviar or lavatory paper—the very important things," Ivory explains with a mischievous gleam in his eye.

8 Though the butler's position keeps him subtly removed from the family, his duties often involve close interaction with his wealthy employer. "This woman (his previous employer) wouldn't let anybody feed her but me until the day she died," he recalls. "Still you don't feel part of the family. I remember that this is their home."

9 Anthony Beckett, also born and bred in England, agrees, explaining his butler position as intimately close to his employer while keeping his distance as propriety dictates. "The Southern California lifestyle is very relaxed," he says. "But you can't be if you're in a formal household. It's very difficult sometimes. Everyone may be in bathing suits and diving in the pool and you're sweating in your suit thinking, 'Oh, I'd love to get in that pool.' But you don't. Quite often they'll say, 'Go ahead and have a swim.' But I've found that I can't just change and put on a costume and dive into their pool because it's not my home, even though I'm living there."

10     Matthew Riley, founder of the English Butler Service and an instructor of a course on butlering in the Learning Network, recalls his position as butler for one of the foreign royal families living in Los Angeles. "The Prince's dinner entertainment would last all night long most every night," he says. "The butler is the one who keeps a straight head while everyone else is enjoying themselves. It's the butler's image. You don't let your hair down. Not while you're at work."

11     Most of the best butlers are trained in England, apprenticing in the finer hotels or even Buckingham Palace. They come from a very old tradition that originated in France in the 12th or 13th century, according to Robert Mann of the Sandra Taylor Agency, a Westside placement agency. "They were originally 'buteliers'—trained in the vineyards in wine tasting then passed down from family to family. Today, wherever there is great wealth, there are a few formal households with full domestic staffs."

12     A butler's primary duties involve supervising the household help which, in a few cases, includes up to 30 people—butlers, footmen, ladies' maids, chefs, cleaning staffs and chauffeurs. He makes sure the lady of the house never has to tend to domestic problems. The butler greets guests at the door and answers the telephone. Many employers prefer English butlers because the British accent nicely complements these duties.

13     It is the butler who plans the menu with the chef and the lady of the house and serves the meals with strict adherence to codes of etiquette. When guests arrive, he has made sure the house is stocked with the particular favorites of each guest. Anthony Ivory explains how he makes a mental note of the people who have been to the house before, recalling who prefers lime with their Perrier, which gentleman loves Dunhill cigarettes or which lady is constantly on a diet. "You tend to the one thing that will make each person think, 'Oh, I'm being looked after.'

14     "I have the feeling that when I'm looking after someone they are very lucky that I'm doing it. I do know how people should be looked after. No, I don't feel servile. I think we're all looked after in one way or another."

15     Robert Mann put in one word as the single most important feature in a good butler: "Discretion." It's a word that surfaces in any conversation on the art of butlering. Ivory agrees. "If I walk in the bedroom in the afternoon and Madam has her gigolo in bed, or say it's the morning and I walk in with the coffee tray. Well, I merely get another cup and saucer and put it down. Perhaps just draw the curtains. You often become the confidant. But I feel the less they know about me, the better. Basically, nobody is really interested in you. So, you don't draw onto them your life or what makes you tick—better to keep that a mystery."

16     Doris Romeo runs her own agency out of Beverly Hills, placing butlers and domestic help from all over the world in the finest homes in the United States. "The butler knows all the household secrets and where the skeletons are buried," she explains. "And I hear all the gossip. Sometimes I know when someone has died even before their families know.

17     "You've got to be the creme de la creme to have a butler," she explains. "Some of these people have a billion dollar net worth."

18     It is a world peopled with events too fantastic for the commoner to comprehend. Anthony Ivory, who is in the process of wrapping up his late employer's household, is in charge of cleaning up many of her domestic affairs. "I just handed over thousands and thousands and thousands of dollars worth of jewels," he says. "Mind boggling jewels. Black pearls like this," he curls his fingers into a circle, leaving a pingpong ball-sized hole, "and blood red rubies the size of pigeon eggs. It was amazing."

19     Anthony Beckett has similar stories of his days working for a notorious English woman who began as a hat sales girl and, through three well-chosen marriages, became a titled Lady. Beckett butlered aboard her 1,000 foot yacht as it sailed the Mediterranean. "We would go to the South of France, Cannes, Monte Carlo, Capri.

We'd be out of England for six months of the year. It was great adventure.

20    "In my time off the chauffeur and I went around the South of France in a gold-plated car. The rest of the staff was afraid of Madam. But I found the inner woman charming and very courteous. I used to dance down the hallway with her. I knew her fairly well. We used to talk sometimes an hour at a time. I always knew when she had gone through the house because of her perfume. If you wanted to know if she was in the lounge, you just went into the hallway to smell her perfume. She wore some beautiful perfumes and she had more than 20 wardrobes."

21    Tending to the lives of the rich and powerful may mean great personal sacrifice for a butler. Live-in help usually has one or two days off a week. When they are working, their job is 24 hours each day. "Personal life? It goes way down," Anthony Beckett stresses. "I find work more demanding in the United States because people often have no idea of what your life should be—only theirs."

22    Still, the butler is recognized as a strategic element in a well-ordered household. "I have seen powerful men—billionaires—leave board meetings to take care of domestic staff matters. Anything to keep the household running smoothly," says Robert Mann. "One director I know in New York stopped everything—he was filming a movie—to meet two new butlers coming in from London."

23    Though a good butler enjoys some status, he rarely receives much personal recognition. "You just blend in with everything," Ivory explains. "Madam (his former employer) used to look up and she'd say, 'Divine.' That meant the food was divine. We had nine chefs in one year. At the other home (where I worked) the prior

cook committed suicide. He jumped in the pool. Put heavy stones at the end of ropes on his arms and feet. It was his final statement, I would say."

24    Some butlers are compensated quite well for their work. Doris Romeo mentions one butler who was set up for life when his employers, the owners of a major department store chain, willed him $50,000 a year and an indefinite stay in her mansion following her death.

25    But some might argue that no amount of money could compensate for the butler's personal sacrifice as he dedicates his lifetime to giving careful attention to the details of an opulent household which does not belong to him. Many have places of their own to retreat to during their minimal free time.

26    Beckett says he has saved his earnings to acquire finery of his own. "I like the best. When you are raised in surroundings with scrub top tables with newspapers for tablecloths, sharing with nine other children, you choose the other world. You do learn to appreciate a lot of things more because you are not able to get them yourself. They are at your fingertips, but they're not actually yours. I always wanted my own Waterford (crystal). I do entertain—with my own china and my Waterford."

27    Anthony Ivory has built a very different kind of home away from his work. His is a retreat where he can go and relax. "My place is very simple, and I would say very chic, because it is so simple. I would say, my place has more warmth and more comfort than the mansion."

28    And who would know more about comfort than a butler?

Leslie Gregory, "At Your Service," *Evening Outlook*, Santa Monica, CA, June 25, 1985. Reprinted by permission.

•  •  •  •  •  •  •  •  •  •  •  •  •  •  •  •  •  •  •  •  •  •  •  •  •  •  •  •  •

1. Several subheads throughout the article help highlight the content.
   a. true
   b. false
2. According to the citation at the end, the writer of the article is married to a butler.
   a. true
   b. false
3. The article focuses on
   a. one real-life butler exclusively
   b. several real-life butlers

---

**Sel. 6   P-Skim**

**Time** _____ : _____ = _____ wpm
　　　　　　 min　 sec

**Score** _____ %

▶ 100%

**Score** = number correct ×33.

1. _____
2. _____
3. _____

**Check answers with your instructor.**

**Record rate and score on p. 192.**

---

## B. Overview Skimming

Take 2 minutes (= 950 wpm) or fewer to overview skim this article for main ideas. Then take the quiz without looking back at the article. For faster times (to the nearest 15 seconds), look up your wpm rate on page 344.

1. The main idea seems to be that
   a. the typical butler is fairly content with the restrictions and rewards of his demanding career
   b. unlike Europeans, wealthy Americans do not value their butlers properly
   c. the ancient breed of first-rate butlers is slowly dying out in these democratic times
2. The last few paragraphs indicate that
   a. most butlers secretly envy the wealth and freedom of their superrich patrons
   b. butlers know how to live well in their own homes, too
   c. butlers are often tempted to get rich by "telling all" to the media
3. According to the interviews, whereas a butler must be outwardly discreet and formal, he is also intimate with the family he serves.
   a. true
   b. false

4.  Although the setting is Southern California, England is mentioned in several paragraphs.
    a.  true
    b.  false

| | |
|---|---|
| **Sel. 6**   O-Skim | 1. _____ |
| **Time** _____:_____ = _____wpm | 2. _____ |
| min   sec | 3. _____ |
| **Score** _____% | 4. _____ |
| ▶ 75% | **Check answers with your** |
| **Score** = number correct × 25. | **instructor.** |
| | **Record rate and score on p. 192.** |

 C. For Discussion and Writing

Reread or refer back to the article as needed.

1.  What dominant writing pattern does the writer use in this article?
2.  In paragraph 23, Anthony Ivory tells a tragic story in an oddly low-key way. Study the paragraph, consider the rest of the article, and infer what Ivory seems to be saying about domestic service, especially in that household. (To review how to infer, see p. 6.)
3.  Much of this article describes the paradoxical position of a butler: to live in and run a household not one's own. Find several specific examples of this dual life and state them in your own words.
4.  Do you think you could do the work of a butler? Why or why not?

• • • • • • • • • • • • • • • • • • • •

## SELECTION 7

This and the following selection examine welfare and work. As newspaper articles, they have some very short paragraphs. When you finish skimming this selection, you may want to read it carefully to understand how the current welfare laws influence how the unemployed find work.

Follow these steps:

A.  Preview skim the article. Then answer the three-item quiz.
B.  Overview skim the article for the general story line and how it relates to the new welfare and work laws. Then answer the four-item quiz.

## A. Preview Skimming

Glance through the article in 1 minute (= 1,600 wpm). By now you know what to look for as you preview: title, leads, subheads, length, and difficulty.

# ADULT LITERACY HEADS CLASS IN
# WELFARE-TO-WORK REFORM

*by Melissa Healy (1,600 words)*

1    CANTON, Ohio—After three years of adult-literacy classes, Mary Bowman still labors to read a newspaper or understand a form letter. She puzzles over sale prices because doing fractions in her head remains difficult. She and her teachers are resigned to the fact that Bowman will never pass the test for a high school equivalency certificate.

2    Yet by the evolving standards of adult educators across the nation, Mary Bowman is a success story.

3    The 40-year-old Bowman, who left school in the eighth grade to care for a little brother, helps her four young children with their homework. She looks you in the eye when she talks to you. She negotiates a bus system to get to work every day. And she juggles her children's school schedules with her full-time job as a maintenance worker in a nursing home.

4    In short, Bowman has dramatically improved her ability to function as a parent, worker and community member. And for that, the Canton City School system proudly graduated her in June from its widely hailed adult-literacy program, Canton's Even Start.

5    These may seem like unexpectedly low standards for adult-literacy educators to embrace. But two words explain the shift: welfare reform.

6    Having nudged most of their most-employable (and better-educated) recipients into work since reforms were enacted two years ago, many states now face a welfare population with daunting roadblocks to employment, including low levels of literacy. In Wisconsin, a state that has posted steep declines in its welfare rolls, 83% of those still receiving public assistance do not have high school diplomas. In Ohio, about half lack them.

7    Here in Canton, those who run adult-literacy classes have retooled for the new era. In doing so, they have formed a unique partnership with the state's welfare administrators.

8    The federal government spent $124 million in 1998 on an array of family literacy programs, all of them under the Even Start umbrella. Critics say that their effectiveness has not been tested. But Canton's program has become a model for other communities. In a campaign next month to promote innovation in welfare reform, Vice President Al Gore plans to praise Canton's program, which draws half its funds from the federal government and half from local sources.

## FOCUS CHANGES TO FINDING JOBS

9    The idea of training workers to read instructions and balance checkbooks rather than enjoy the cerebral pleasures of Charles Dickens or appreciate the intricacies of higher math is attractive to employers. To compete in today's economy, they insist on workers who have an ability to learn and adapt. So if jobs are to be found for the 3 million people still on welfare across the nation, educators have concluded that they must adjust their goals. And fast.

10    In Canton, educators had always been extremely proud of their family literacy program for adults. It might take as many as five years with some students. But with grit and persistence, Canton's teachers dragged many of the city's most educationally challenged to successful completion of their high school equivalency certificates.

11    "We had a peach of a program, an award-winning program," said Jane Meyer of the Canton adult education program in place until the spring of 1997. "But in the scheme of welfare reform, we realized, it wasn't going to work." Teaching literacy to adults with fewer skills would require some outside-the-box thinking.

12    So working with the state's Department of Human Services and local businesses, Canton school officials crafted a program designed to serve some of the welfare roll's most difficult cases.

13    One key new element was to make "work experience" a part of the curriculum. Along with two hours a day of classroom learning, the adult student works four hours at his or her child's school—as a teaching assistant, cafeteria worker, janitor or office clerk. This satisfies the state's requirement that welfare recipients work at least 20 hours a week. But officials believe it also promotes family literacy.

## KEEPING CHILDREN IN THE EQUATION

14    Mothers—most recipients are women—walk or ride the bus to school with their children and spend part of the day there. Officials believe that recipients gain self-confidence working with teachers and school administrators. And, as their academic skills increase, they are more likely to read and do homework with their children, boosting the children's academic performance.

15    To drive home these indirect benefits, Canton's Even Start teachers consistently address family matters in the classroom. Adult students keep detailed family journals, including a log of books that they have read with their children. During class time, home visits and scheduled parent-and-child play sessions, specially trained teachers offer their adult students a steady stream of parenting and homemaking advice.

16    "Many of our students are second- and third-generation welfare recipients," said Even Start coordinator Meyer. "What we wanted to do was break the cycle of welfare dependency, first with them and then with their children. . . . And the last thing we needed was to do things that pull these moms away from their families for more time than we had to."

17    Critics have questioned whether programs that aim to affect the academic performance of parents and children at the same time are effective at either goal. Some scholars of federal education efforts, like the University of Michigan's Maris A. Vinovskis, have complained that Even Start programs have not been subject to rigorous outside review.

18    In programs like Canton's Even Start, however, the task of measuring effectiveness is complicated. What, in an era of welfare reform, constitutes success or failure? Since the new program was inaugurated, 29% of participating parents have passed the General Equivalency Development test and 21% either secured a job for the first time or got a better one. It will take years to know whether the children of students like Bowman performed better in school because of their mother's participation. In the meantime, she has something to brag about.

## PRACTICAL LESSONS FOR EVERY DAY

19    On a recent day, Even Start teacher Michelle Miller deftly coaxed a classroom of 12 welfare mothers through a lesson in time management.

20    Miller opened by inviting students to name the major activities—sleep, child care, housekeeping, school and free time—that fill 86,400 seconds of each day (though it took some prompting before students remembered time spent in school and at work). She urged students to think of time as a resource that can be wasted or used productively every day. Then Miller asked the women to estimate how they spend a routine 24-hour period and write it down.

21    In the back-and-forth banter that ensued, Miller and her students discussed the pros and cons of time spent in front of the television, pondered the stresses in their lives and looked ahead at how a job would complicate the picture. Then, using long division and geometry, they

calculated their activities as fractions of 24 hours and made pie charts of their typical days.

22  In coming weeks and months, students will return to the lesson, writing in journals and contemplating ways to streamline their lives, make time for their children and incorporate their jobs into the picture. In the process, teachers hope, they will learn valuable lessons not only in math and literacy but also in planning their time around competing demands.

23  In addition, students will work together on group projects that involve planning, budgeting, teamwork and follow-through. The projects range from organizing a special "math night" for their children's school to making curtains for a sun-drenched classroom. While the team projects provide welcome services for their children's school, the adult students gain something more: a rare opportunity to develop workplace skills.

24  When Even Start graduates like Bowman go to a prospective employer, lessons like these form an important part of the job pitch. On the strength of lessons like Miller's time management exercise, Bowman could advertise to a prospective employer her ability to "organize time and resources to be punctual and maintain consistent attendance." That, and many other "soft skills" that Canton's program teaches, go into a "career passport," a resume of sorts, prepared by students on a computer and tucked neatly into a bound packet with references, awards and letters from Even Start teachers.

25  To her enduring sadness, Bowman never could pass the test to get her high school equiva-lency certificate. "I wanted to get my GED," she said at her home recently. "It was a big disappointment when I realized last year I couldn't. . . . Working became my goal, but what I wanted was my GED."

26  But in the eyes of some employers, Bowman's career passport holds something of almost greater luster: Tucked in the folder's back pocket is an award for outstanding attendance.

27  Bowman gives her children, who dragged her to school when her will flagged, some of the credit. But she cannot stifle her pride in her achievement and says that it was the key to landing the job she has now held for three months.

28  Today, Bowman still relies on a small welfare check to supplement a full-time job that pays $7.20 an hour. And she worries about the day that that small measure of help will end. But when asked what her future holds, she clutches a framed photograph of herself at summer's Even Start graduation in a new blue dress with certificate in hand.

29  Bowman has not passed a GED test. But as her photograph and her "career passport" prove, she has succeeded at something. And she'll find a way to make it through, she said.

30  "It'll be hard. But I'll still be working."

Melissa Healy, "Adult Literacy Heads Class in Welfare-to-Work Reform," *Los Angeles Times*, December 26, 1998, A1, A30–A31. Copyright 1998, Los Angeles Times. Reprinted by permission.

• • • • • • • • • • • • • • • • • • • • • • • • • • •

1. This article came from
   a. the *New York Times*
   b. the *Los Angeles Times*
   c. the *Wall Street Journal*
2. The title suggests that
   a. welfare recipients read poorly
   b. adult literacy classes are not successfully preparing welfare recipients for work
   c. adult literacy classes are a successful part of the welfare-to-work program

3. There are no subheads in this article.
   a. true
   b. false

---

| | |
|---|---|
| **Sel. 7**  P-Skim | 1. _____ |
| **Time**  1:00 = 1,4600 wpm | 2. _____ |
| **Score** _____ % | 3. _____ |
| ▶ 100% | **Check answers on p. 351.** |
| **Score** = number correct × 33. | |

---

## B. Overview Skimming

Now go back and overview skim for the main points made in the narrative and for the ways this story relates to the welfare-to-work program. Take no more than 2 minutes to overview skim (= 800 wpm). If you go over or under this time, check your rate in Appendix B on page 344.

1. This article is a
   a. compare-contrast piece
   b. narrative piece
   c. piece with many facts and figures
   d. series of five interviews
2. Mary Bowman's single failure in the literacy program was that she
   a. could not attend all of the classes
   b. could not pass the history class
   c. did not get her high-school diploma
   d. failed to teach her children to read
3. One goal of this particular literacy and work program is to get
   a. the parents involved in their children's learning at school
   b. tutors for the children of the welfare recipients
   c. the welfare recipients employed within six months
4. What one achievement most impressed the employers interested in Mary?
   a. She quickly learned to work their computers.
   b. She received a perfect attendance certificate from her literacy program.
   c. She wanted her children to attend college.
   d. She presented them with an impressive resume.

---

| | |
|---|---|
| **Sel. 7**  O-Skim | 1. _____ |
| **Time** _____:_____ = _____wpm | 2. _____ |
|      min    sec | 3. _____ |

**Score** _____%

▶ 75%

**Score** = number correct × 25.

4. _____

**Check answers on p. 351.**

**Record rate and score on p. 192.**

 C. For Discussion and Writing

Reread or refer back to the article as needed.

1. The author has taken the basic aspects of an Ohio welfare-to-work program and interspersed them throughout the narrative of Mary Bowman's education and job search. Read over the article, then summarize the three most important elements of this welfare program.
2. In paragraph 17, the author comments that some critics of the program question how a welfare education program can involve both parents and children effectively. Why do you think program planners aimed at making welfare parents more active in their children's education?
3. Why do you believe education matters in today's job market, even for entry-level jobs not requiring college training?

• • • • • • • • • • • • • • • • •

## SELECTION 8

This newspaper article examines how welfare recipients today enter the job market. Again, this article focuses on personal experiences—the job-search trials of a married couple. As with the previous selection, some of the paragraphs in this newspaper article are quite short.

Follow these steps:

A. Preview skim the article. Then answer the three-item quiz.
B. Overview skim the article. Then answer the four-item quiz.

• • • • • • • • • • • • • • • • •

### WELFARE REFORM MEETS REAL LIFE

*by Carla Rivera (1,900 words)*

**Although federal law requires that aid rolls be cut, one young couple with two children illustrates the problems and, sometimes, setbacks of the national effort.**

1    Maybe this story began 44 years ago on a windblown Canadian farm when a young man of 20 pondered his future and felt adrift in a sea of bewildering choices.

2   At that moment, Phil Jakobi began to take note of the fearful pressures and duties of adulthood. He remembered that feeling years later when he read a story about David and Veronica Marquez, urban teenagers a world removed from his bucolic upbringing but compelled by circumstances of poverty and parenthood to be grownups too soon.

3   He thought the young family deserved a chance. So in 1997 he hired David from the ranks of welfare, placed him in the shipping and receiving department of his Long Beach machine shop and laid out a slow course of training and development that he hoped would lead to success.

4   A year later, it appeared that it had. David was a good worker and a quick study. He had begun to master the precision machinery and had gotten a raise. His bosses wanted the young homeboy who hadn't gone past the ninth grade to study advanced math and blueprint reading to further his climb at the company.

5   The couple's welfare caseworker was exultant. Nineteen-year-old Veronica, shy and soft-spoken, was spurred to keep pace with her husband and entered a nursing program.

6   Jakobi was pleased that his patience was paying off. Here was the perfect example of welfare reform's potential: an employer with a sense of responsibility working to help a deprived young couple achieve self-sufficiency.

7   But life is rarely so simple.

8   In the midst of everyone's optimism, David made a serious misjudgment at work and was fired. The sense of triumph turned into one of betrayal for Jakobi and of misunderstanding for David.

9   The fairy tale became a parable: The progression of human lives is mostly made in fits and starts. It is a lesson that welfare workers on the front lines must deal with day in and day out. Behind the mandate for reform and the numbers are real people whose lives are not so tidily managed.

10   Cases like the Marquezes' present a daunting challenge to local officials who must put public aid recipients to work and do it quickly. Under federal law, two-parent families—either individually or in combination—must be engaged in 35 hours of work or job training each week to continue receiving some sort of aid.

11   The law imposes deadlines on states to place such couples into the work force—75% of them this fiscal year, 90% next year—at the risk of losing welfare funding. In California, only about 22% of these families meet the work requirements. Many other states are in a similar boat, and federal authorities are trying to determine how strictly to enforce the penalties.

12   Thus, here and around the nation officials are expending an enormous amount of energy providing supportive services to couples like the Marquezes. The government pays for child care, school tuition, books and uniforms for them. A county job counselor, Frank Mora, has been working closely with them, assessing their needs, ferreting out possible jobs or training opportunities.

13   He suggested that Veronica consider becoming a nursing assistant and found a program for her at Cal State Long Beach. Mora's investment in David has become almost personal, with monthly meetings that have turned into rap sessions akin to those between a caring uncle and his brash young charge.

14   The welfare department's job counselors must also prevail upon, cajole and induce employers to hire large numbers of recipients if goals are to be met.

## OFFERING A CHANCE

15   Jakobi needed no persuading. He bought Delco Machine and Gear eight years ago and nurtured its growth from nine workers to 100 employees who produce gears and other components for aircraft, space shuttles and the International Space Station.

16   Jakobi, 64, with graying hair and round spectacles, hails from just outside Windsor, Canada, and recalls his own rocky transition to adulthood.

17   "I grew up on a farm and, until I was 20, didn't know what I wanted to do," he said, sitting

in a small office hung with pictures of swooping jet fighters. "A buddy of mine happened to start as a tool-and-die apprentice and said why don't I come down and take the test. People have been willing to train me all my life."

18    He has tried to give back in kind, advising young students, being mindful of the harmful pressures heaped on urban youths, exhorting fellow business owners to get with the program.

19    "Rather than sit wringing our hands and saying we can't find skilled machinists, we better go out and find people and train them," he said.

20    After reading a 1997 Times article about the Marquez family, Jakobi hired David.

21    There had been a few missteps. David was still young and immature. He was not used to criticism and could show sparks of anger. He needed to be reminded that his supervisor was not the enemy. But Jakobi's son-in-law, also in training, was working closely with David and he seemed to be making progress.

22    "If we're going to make that commitment to him staying, we should bend over backwards to make sure it works," Jakobi had vowed. David was being paid $8 an hour, and Jakobi was sure that within two years he could be earning $12 or $14.

23    But those hopes crumbled practically overnight. David left work early one afternoon and had a colleague clock him out at normal quitting time so that his pay would not be docked. He was suspended. Jakobi says David then confronted the worker who told on him and that threats were made. David denies this, but in October he was fired.

24    Jakobi sees it as a clear-cut case of insubordination.

25    "He left an hour early and didn't tell anyone he was leaving. Some of the guys wanted to terminate him right there, but I said, no, let's give him another chance. He didn't want to admit he did anything wrong, and then he threatened people for ratting on him."

26    There would be no final encounter. Like anyone else, David was let go by his immediate supervisor. That was part of the lesson to be learned.

27    "I'm sure if I would have sat down with him, it might have had more impact, but he has to learn to deal with everyone he touches within the organization," Jakobi said.

28    Yes, he left early, admits David. But it was only by about 10 minutes, not an hour. He might have gone to his bosses and asked to leave but said he did not want to give up any pay. He couldn't afford to.

29    But why would he risk getting caught to shave 10 minutes? He says it was David Jr.'s birthday and he wanted to pick his son up early from the baby sitter for a surprise party. As to the threats, there was a time when he let his fists do the talking. But he has left that life behind, he says.

30    "I didn't raise my hand to anyone, but said in a mad but respectful way, 'Hey man, why'd you do something like that?'"

31    He was both hurt and angry that his boss wouldn't tell him to his face he was fired.

32    But ultimately, it was not worth losing his job.

33    "I feel mad at myself because I was learning something," he said. "If I could go back and say I'm sorry, I would, but it's already done."

## PENALTY IS STEEP

34    It wouldn't work with Jakobi, who had already angered some of his workers with his kid glove treatment of David. Guys had begun joking that he had adopted the new kid. Now he feels betrayed.

35    "What seemed to be going so well, ended up going down the tubes," he said tersely.

36    It was never going to be easy for David and Veronica. When they first walked into Mora's office a year ago, they were both teenagers, struggling to provide for their two children, David Jr., now 4, and Michael, 2, saddled with bills and constricted by their lack of education.

37    They are not quite back at square one, but for everyone there is the sense that they will have to work doubly hard to rebuild the gains they had made.

38    During the week that David was dismissed from Delco, the couple completed a move into a new, less cramped apartment. They have a bedroom, where Michael also sleeps in a crib. David Jr. sleeps in the living room, in a fold-down bed.

39    The move boosted their rent from $400 to $515 monthly at a time when they could least afford it. Although the new place is not far from their old neighborhood, they are closer to relatives and feel safer.

40    It didn't help that the couple's welfare benefits were reduced from $625 to $498 monthly, said David. Their Food Stamp allotment was also lowered, and they applied for and received $370 in emergency funds to tide them over for the month. The family, he said, was directed to a pantry or church for extra food.

41    Behind David's usually broad smile and cheerful disposition lies an undercurrent of desperation.

42    The monty never lasts long enough to cover all the bills or the food and milk needed for two growing boys. The children walk into a store and want everything they see, and then David feels ashamed when he can't afford to buy them the kinds of toys other children get.

43    "I feel like I have all this responsibility, and it fills up to my head," he said, pointing to his forehead. "Sometimes I feel like it's going to come to the end of the world. I get really down."

44    David is painfully aware that history may be repeating itself. His own father was a teenage parent and never seemed to overcome the odds, always struggling to hold his life together.

45    "I know what it's like . . . and I don't want it to be that way with me," he said. "I had them too early, but I can't take it back now."

## LOOKING BACK, AND AHEAD

46    Jakobi and the Marquezes have parted ways but not without leaving sharp imprints.

47    Within a week of David's departure, Jakobi hired "another young gentleman" sent from the welfare office. Jakobi learned some lessons too. He surmises that a lot of inexperienced young people need more lecturing on how to develop a good work ethic, to work as a team and to respond to criticism.

48    "If I had it to do over again, I would spend an awful lot of time with David emphasizing what to expect, rather than just going through the motions," he said. "We've changed our ways here a little bit."

49    He still feels a stake in what happens to his former recruit.

50    "Yes, I'm interested in knowing what develops. If he shows he's able to adapt in the work place . . . give it some time and show me how he's progressed in the next six months. Maybe there's another shot."

51    And the Marquezes are pondering fresh opportunities.

52    Veronica is training to become a certified nursing assistant, about which she is clearly excited. At 19, with two children and no high school diploma, she is finally getting a chance to consider alternatives to the clouded future that once seemed ordained.

53    Job counselor Mora is sure the couple will rebound. He advised David to call him when he gets the urge to do something "crazy."

54    Mora has already helped David find a new job doing assembly work at 75 cents an hour less than his old job.

55    "He has a chance to start again and move up," Mora said. "I tell him he's lucky he has skills people like. He's a good worker, mechanically skilled. He's in demand.

56    "He told me the other day he loved his job at Delco. David needs to grow up, and our objective is to see to that. David and Veronica are growing up together, and I can tell you—'cause I've been married a long time—that will help. They have to help each other."

## A. Preview Skimming

Glance through the article in 1 minute (= 1,900 wpm), focusing on its organization.

1. Three subheads divide this article.
    a. true
    b. false
2. The article focuses on the employment experiences of
    a. David
    b. Veronica, David's wife
    c. both a and b
3. The title and lead suggest that this article will address
    a. the ease with which welfare recipients can enter the job market
    b. difficulty welfare recipients face when they attempt to enter the job market
    c. successful of welfare reforms over the past five years
    d. failed welfare reforms over the past five years

---

| | |
|---|---|
| **Sel. 8** P-Skim | **1.** _____ |
| **Time** 1:00 = 1,900 wpm | **2.** _____ |
| **Score** _____ % | **3.** _____ |
| ▶ 100% | **Check answers with your instructor.** |
| **Score** = number correct × 33. | |

---

## B. Overview Skimming

Take 2 minutes (= 950 wpm) or 2:15 (= 844 wpm) to overview skim the article for the experiences this couple has in finding and keeping work.

1. Phil Jakobi
    a. is unemployed
    b. owns a machine shop
    c. hired David Marquez
    d. both b and c
2. David Marquez
    a. was an excellent worker
    b. was a promising worker who left work early one day and was fired
    c. is a college graduate
    d. only finished high school
3. Toward the end of the article, we learn that David
    a. is still unemployed
    b. found a job for less pay doing assembly work

    c. left his wife and went to live with his parents
    d. began in the same training program that his wife entered
4. It seems that this welfare-work program stresses
    a. gradual transition into work
    b. high educational requirements
    c. job placement as soon as it seems that the welfare recipient can keep a job

| | |
|---|---|
| **Sel. 8**  O-Skim | 1. _____ |
| **Time** _____:_____ = _____wpm | 2. _____ |
|      **min**  **sec** | 3. _____ |
| **Score** _____% | 4. _____ |
| ▶ 75% | **Check answers with your** |
| **Score** = number correct × 25. | **instructor.** |
| | **Record rate and score on p. 192.** |

 C. For Discussion and Writing

Refer back to the article, as instructed.

1. Reread the reason David was fired. Do you agree with his boss? What do you think David learned from this experience?
2. In paragraph 44, David describes his general family history. Why do you think children born into welfare tend to have children of their own who need welfare assistance?
3. Are you in favor of the current welfare laws mentioned in the last two selections? Do you believe they are too lenient? Too strict? Why or why not?

•  •  •  •  •  •  •  •  •  •  •  •  •  •  •  •  •

# SELECTION 9

The aging of the world affects all people, from young workers to the elderly themselves. Change always requires new thinking. As such, start with the title and what it implies.
    Follow these steps:

A. Preview skim the article. Then answer the three-item quiz.
B. Overview skim the article for thesis and main support. Then answer the four-item quiz.

## A. Preview Skimming

Glance through the article in 1 minute (= 2,300 wpm) or 1:15 (= 1,840 wpm). Preview the title, subtitle, lead, subheadings, length, and difficulty level. Unfortunately, we could not include the five striking photographs of these elders, but their comments are reprinted at the outset.

## THE END OF RETIREMENT

*by Susan Champlin Taylor (2,300 words)*

**From the South of France to the hills of Cameroon, we're grappling with the meaning of work—and whether we can ever afford to stop.**

"Civil servants in this country must retire when they are 60. This is not fair, because most people are still very strong and alert at that age. Besides, most politicians who rule the country are far older than 60."—Peter Mba Muyu Tebe, 57, principal agricultural assistant, Bamenda, Cameroon

"I would like my life as it is now to continue. I would not want to be weak or dependent even if I feel that my children would take care of me. I don't want to be a burden or a nuisance to anyone."—Monique Jourdan-Gassin, 62, painter, Nice, France

"In the past, people relied on the system; they had no worries about older life. Now, that's not true. We couldn't live without hope, but we can't see the future. We don't know if what the government is doing is good or bad."—Nina Persidskaya, 65, musicology professor, Kiev, Ukraine

"I am enjoying the best of life. No problems of old age. This is part of life. I take it in my stride. I am a God-fearing man and say my prayers regularly. That way, I am sure, God will look after us even 20 years hence."—Gian Singh, 62, retired civil servant, New Delhi, India

"I don't think you have to be a member of a volunteer organization to be a productive member of society. I weed the streets around my home, which is a small thing, but which is a kind of volunteer activity. Taking care of my husband also contributes to society. These things add up."—Sumiko Yoshida, 56, housewife, Tokyo, Japan

1    In the grassy highlands of Bamenda, Cameroon, Peter Mba Muyu Tebe reaches into his small black bag and pulls out a fistful of polished brass medals. These are his rewards for loyal service to the Ministry of Agriculture, where he's worked for 35 years, driving into the hinterlands to demonstrate farming techniques and equipment. He reaches into the bag again and his hand emerges holding a necklace with a star-shaped pendant, a gift from "the President of the Republic himself." He nods in a small gesture of self-praise.

2    After all these years, Muyu Tebe looks forward to his retirement three years down the road. He has it all mapped out: "Rest, a lot of travel, and pleasure in a Swiss city or on a Mediterranean beach." Oh yes, and caring for his late father's three elderly wives, educating his 15 children by his own three wives, running two large plantain and coffee plantations in his native village 20 miles away, overseeing the houses he rents out in Bamenda, heading the PTA, championing school reforms, and working with the Credit Unions, Farmers' Cooperative, and the Pipe-borne Water Project.

3    It should be a very relaxing retirement, indeed.

4    Muyu Tebe is riding the wave of the future: what you might call the end of retirement as we know it. The world's over-60 population numbered nearly 500 million in 1991; by 2020 it is expected that figure will surge to a full billion older people. This startling shift in demographics leads many experts to predict huge financial and cultural problems down the road—unless we rethink our notions of work and retirement.

5    The crisis mentality that attends these population figures rests on old assumptions: that the "retired" are dependent, sucking up nations' scarce resources and giving nothing in return; that they have no vital role in, and make no valuable contribution to, their societies.

6    "You will always have the older old—the fourth age—and yes, more of these people will be dependent," says Julia de Alvarez, one of the Dominican Republic's deputy ambassadors to the United Nations. "But there is no reason to discard a person just because he or she turns 60."

7    Rather than seeing seniors as an economic burden, adds Mukunda Rao, an international consultant on social-development issues, it's crucial to view them as an untapped resource, not only for themselves, but for the broader society. "Today," he says, "industrialized societies with their outmoded ideas about retirement are wasting their precious resources."

8    When it originated in the 1800s, the idea of "retirement" was actually intended in part to do the opposite—to *avoid* wasting resources, human and financial. Forcing (or strongly encouraging) retirement phased out older, more expensive workers and brought in younger, cheaper ones.

9    In 1889, Germany's "Iron Chancellor," Otto von Bismarck, instituted the first pensions on a national scale. He set an initial eligibility age of 70, later changed to 65. (Bismarck was not entirely the altruist this would make him seem; life expectancy then was about 45.) Other countries have adopted different age limits, but the arbitrary nature of retirement ages today—when life expectancy has increased significantly—renders them not only meaningless but wasteful in the extreme. Over the years, the age of retirement has come to symbolize an end to productivity, even when there is no physical or mental reason for it.

10    "I think this idea of old age linked to retirement, with a sudden dropping-off from the workforce, is an unfortunate product of the industrial revolution," Rao says. "It needs to be rethought." For one thing, in developed countries the need to make room for younger workers will no longer exist; in fact, quite the opposite: The "birth dearth" that followed the baby boom means that fewer young workers will be entering the workforce. Older workers may well become hot commodities. Secondly, we simply can't afford to maintain retirement and pension plans as they've traditionally existed. Finally, the outdated notion of retirement as a withdrawal into some utopian idyll does not play in a rapidly changing world.

11    Industrialized nations with expansive social-welfare systems are already feeling the cash crunch. Realizing that their systems will prove far too expensive in the future, these countries (primarily in Europe) are having to think about scaling them back—though politically acceptable ways of doing so are hard to come by. In an effort to reduce the cost of public retirement benefits several countries, including the United States, have started by raising the eligibility age; more draconian measures may be down the road.

12    The potential costs of health care are also frightening countries with socialized medicine. As a small first step many European countries are leaning more heavily on volunteers, families and creative problem-solving: e.g., Sweden's use of rural mail carriers to look in on the isolated elderly people on their routes.

13    While money woes are cutting into industrialized nations' ability to care for the old, the globalization of culture and communications is undermining the traditional support networks of developing countries.

14    "You sit in a remote village in India and you can watch CNN," says Rao. "Is that a good thing or a bad thing? On the one hand, you get

instant news; on the other, you get MTV. It projects different values. From a young person's perspective, what comes from outside—especially from the West—is always better."

15    With so many outside influences, young people's respect for tradition and for older generations decreases. Peter Mba Muyu Tebe is a well-respected assistant in Bamenda's Ministry of Agriculture. Yet at home he is alarmed by the cultural gap growing between himself and his 15 children. His boys refuse to attend the traditional ceremonies in which elders pay respect to their ancestors, and they will not dress traditionally. "They always want to be in three-piece suits, while the girls are not ashamed to wear trousers like men," Muyu Tebe laments. "Worst of all, they talk of boyfriends or girlfriends and quite often shamelessly kiss before my very eyes. What an abomination books and TV have brought into our culture."

16    In families where reverence for the elderly remains strong, it is geographic, rather than cultural, separation that may determine whether the younger generations can care for the older. Says Julia de Alvarez, "Years ago, people didn't migrate that much. Now you have young people migrating from developing countries to the already-developed ones, or from rural areas to the cities, where they may have small apartments and can't take care of the elderly. It's not that they don't want to; they're just not in a position to do it."

17    In Tokyo, housewife Sumiko Yoshida is in the midst of changing cultural expectations. "Today's children are focusing almost entirely on education and getting into good schools, whereas they used to spend time with their grandparents learning about the old days and learning to care about them," she says. "I can see already on the train that young children are happy to sit while old people remain standing." Yoshida herself helps her brother and widowed sister care for their blind 92-year-old mother, yet she does not expect her own 25-year-old daughter, Kyoko, to look after her and her husband in their old age. Though Yoshida's husband used to say he wanted Kyoko "close enough so that the soup doesn't get cold," he is changing his mind, and the couple already discuss plans to move into a new retirement home two blocks from their house.

18    Similar cultural upheavals are forcing many nations to rethink the whole idea of retirement. In so doing, developing and developed nations can learn from each other. "Industrial countries are moving away from the concept of retirement for economic reasons, but it never really operated in developing countries at all," says Sandeep Chawla, Ph.D., co-author with Marvin Kaiser, Ph.D., of a U.N. study on the implications of population aging in the Dominican Republic, Chile, Sri Lanka and Thailand.

19    Christine Fry, Ph.D., professor of anthropology at Loyola University of Chicago, notes that in Botswana, among the !Kung Bushmen and Herero of the Kalahari Desert—as in many traditional societies—the notion of retirement is nonexistent. One works until one is no longer physically able.

20    "There's also no retirement in Hong Kong," Fry adds. "People start out having steady work, then get laid off or fired; they may not be able to find another full-time job, so it turns part-time. Then they just gradually withdraw from the workforce."

21    If people want to remain economically productive and have no physical limitations, however, why not make full use of their skills to benefit society? Julia de Alvarez, for example, helped set up a program in the Dominican Republic in which 12 teachers were brought out of retirement to run a preschool program in the rural mountain area near the Haitian border.

22    "Without exception these teachers say they feel 'reborn,'" says De Alvarez. "This has added joy to their existence, as well as being economically good for them."

23    Working after "retirement" for spiritual and economic reward is also a goal of microenterprises—small businesses—run by older people. Such endeavors can provide one alternative for developing nations that can't afford

large-scale social-welfare programs for their senior populations. "Microenterprises allow people to be engaged and productive while contributing to their own economic security," says Marvin Kaiser.

24    Economics isn't everything, however. Focus exclusively on older people working for pay and you miss the many other kinds of contributions they make: to their families, their communities and their cultures.

25    "Ironically, we measure productivity solely in terms of cash," says Christine Fry. "That means when you're not compensated in cash, you're not productive, which doesn't make much sense."

26    In many places where generations live together, older people play vital roles such as cooking, cleaning or providing childcare. When living in Kiev, Ukraine, Igor Persidsky, M.D., his wife, Lena Krushniruk, and their four-year-old daughter, Marina, shared what Persidsky calls "an informal support network" with their 75-year-old neighbor, Maria Skripnik. "She looked after Marina when we were busy after work," says Persidsky. "And when Maria needed medical attention, I was happy to provide it. Neither of us would ever take money from the other." A standard economic measure would consider Maria Skripnik unproductive. But to Persidsky, the dollar value of her services was, in fact, substantial.

27    Seemingly invisible contributions like housework and childcare can no longer be ignored, says Charlotte Nusberg, outgoing secretary-general of the International Federation on Ageing: "If you define economic productivity to include unpaid support activities for family and friends, and volunteer activities, then most older people certainly are productive"—even when they're allegedly "retired."

28    Consider retiree Gian Singh. On a sultry afternoon in the sprawling New Delhi suburb of Janak Puri, he sits in the shade of a neem tree in a local park playing a game of sweep, sipping a Campa-Cola, and joking with his retired friends. The genial, bearded Sikh is enjoying himself; he

is not, however, just killing time. After he retired from government service four years ago at age 58, Singh and his friends formed an informal social club that—besides playing cards—takes on local problems.

29    "For example," Singh explains, "if there is an inflated electricity or telephone bill, we meet the officials concerned. This way we have solved a number of our day-to-day problems." Though club members receive no money for their efforts, Singh says he is "rather happier than when I was in government service and used to go to an office every day." In fact, he adds, outsiders who don't belong to the club "envy our lot."

30    Similar volunteer efforts—both informal and organized—will be critical in the future, says Mark Gorman, development director of London-based HelpAge International, a multinational coalition of service organizations for the elderly. "Many of our member organizations run different versions of 'good neighbor' programs that show how older people are going to cope in the absence of government support. Basically, it's going to have to be self-help."

31    In the Mediterranean island nation of Malta, volunteers run an eldercare version of Neighborhood Watch: they look out for each other and quickly spot signs of trouble. If an elderly neighbor fails to show up for church, for example, a volunteer goes out to check on the person.

32    "These are not high-cost programs at all," says Gorman, "and they're an effective way to maintain people in their own communities and homes so they don't end up institutionalized."

33    This notion of self-reliance strikes a responsive chord with Mukunda Rao. Government, community and family have vital roles to play in aging issues, Rao says, but the individual is the final key component. "Older people have to develop some real understanding of their own resources. They need to assess their skills and knowledge and adapt themselves to different types of work and employment patterns," he says. "And they need to reassess their own attitudes. Sometimes they look to the past and say,

'This is what was valid before.' They need to see things as they are today."

34    Armed with this consciousness, Rao says, "Older people need to make their case known—to make known their importance to national development itself."

35    In this way the alleged "problem" of an aging population becomes its own answer. As Julia de Alvarez says, "Every time I go to talk to poli-cymakers, they say, 'Here she comes again with a problem.' I tell them, 'I'm not bringing a problem—I'm bringing a solution.'"

Susan Champlin Taylor, "The End of Retirement," *Modern Maturity*, October–November 1993, 32–39. Reprinted with permission. © 1993, American Association of Retired Persons.

• • • • • • • • • • • • • • • • • • • • • • • •

1. The source of the article is
   a. a magazine for mature U.S. citizens
   b. an urban daily newspaper
   c. an international newsletter
2. The writer offers the reader
   a. a useful lead
   b. several useful subheadings throughout
   c. neither a nor b
3. The date of publication is
   a. 1980
   b. 1988
   c. 1993

---

**Sel. 9**   P-Skim

**Time** ____:____ = ____wpm

**Score** ____%

▶ 100%

**Score** = number correct × 33.

1. ____
2. ____
3. ____

**Check answers on p. 351.**

---

## B. Overview Skimming

Now go back and overview skim for the writer's main ideas regarding work, aging, and retirement. Take less than 3 minutes for skimming: 2:00 (= 1,150 wpm), 2:15 (= 1,022 wpm), or 2:30 (= 920 wpm).

1. The writer has set up her article as a classic _____ piece.
   a. problem-solution
   b. spatial-geographic
   c. time-sequence

2. Both developed and undeveloped nations are having to rethink their traditional ideas of retirement because of
   a. the costly dependency of all old people
   b. the increasing proportions of old people
   c. changing cultural attitudes toward the elderly
   d. both b and c

3. Maunder and other international experts urge nations to see their senior citizens as
   a. an untapped resource
   b. a growing, mind-boggling problem

4. At present, in many countries the people over age sixty are
   a. still working
   b. doing volunteer work for their communities
   c. organizing to help care for each other
   d. providing indispensable family care
   e. all of the above

---

| | |
|---|---|
| **Sel. 9**  O-Skim | 1. _____ |
| **Time** _____:_____ = _____ **wpm** | 2. _____ |
| min    sec | 3. _____ |
| **Score** _____ % | 4. _____ |
| ▶ 75% | **Check answers on p. 351.** |
| **Score** = number correct × 25. | **Record rate and score on p. 192.** |

---

 C. For Discussion and Writing

Reread or refer back to the article as needed.

1. Find one or more paragraphs that show a strong "reasons why" pattern. Find other paragraphs in which the examples pattern prevails. Summarize the content of these paragraphs.

2. Now that you have reread the article, do you think the lead provides an entirely accurate summary of the content?

3. Recall the startling shift in demographics noted in paragraph 4—that, by the year 2020, 1 billion people will be over 60 (out of a projected world population of 7 billion). How do you imagine this scenario will affect your life in the year 2020?

• • • • • • • • • • • • • • • • • •

# SELECTION 10

This last selection is based on an interview with a couple who answered the writer's questions with perfect ease. The writer discovered that a month earlier, a university student had asked many of the same questions for a senior project. Evidently, quite a few people are interested in starting a small franchise business or working for one.

For good reason: The service industry is one of the few sectors of the U.S. economy that continue to expand. *Service* in this sense doesn't mean domestic service, as in Selection 6, but businesses that help ordinary people do ordinary things like eat, maintain their persons and homes, and mail their packages.

Follow these steps:

A.  Preview skim the article. Then answer the three-item quiz.
B.  Overview skim the article. Then answer the five-item quiz.

## A.  Preview Skimming

Take 1 minute (= 2,900 wpm) to preview this article.

• • • • • • • • • • • • • • • • • •

## HOW TO SUCCEED IN BUSINESS BY REALLY TRYING

• • • • • • • • • • • • • • •

*by Anne G. Phillips (2,900 words)*

1    On the well-heeled, newer side of a small city is a well-designed, newer shopping plaza. It's one story, it's sunny and clean, and it's small enough that you will never lose your car in the parking lot. Except for the chain supermarket and drugstore, the shops are locally owned. There's a beauty salon with two tanning rooms, a quite good Chinese restaurant, a tiny bank, a kiosk selling fresh flowers, a yogurt shop, a pet store, a small independent bookshop, a vitamin store—all the essentials for middle-class living.

2    In this continuing recession, several of the sites are empty. There isn't much demand for oddly colored popcorn or hand puppets made of real sheepskin. But one business has been consistently lively for eight years: the Pak Mail store.

3    Walk past Pak Mail any time it's open ("9:00 A.M.–6:00 P.M. weekdays, 9:00 A.M.–4:00 P.M. Saturday, closed Sunday"), and someone is either pulling in to park or just leaving. Through the plate-glass front, you can see people visiting their postal boxes, running off a few photocopies, standing at the counter to mail a package to Boston or a money order to Mexico. There's little stress in the air: customers gossip with friends they've met there. Or they chat with the owners, Jeff and Jo Sprawls. If one or the other is absent, the counter is staffed by a serious young man or woman. They look like students. And they usually are.

4    The Sprawls are a relaxed, attractive couple in their early 40s. They have one dog, a quiet

cocker spaniel named Crista, who hangs out in back. And they have this one store, a franchise they bought three years ago. Pak Mail is one of many national chains of "service" outlets that provide pesonalized help with packing, mailing, minor photocopying, and related concerns.

## STARTING OUT: MINUSES AND PLUSES

5    For Jeff and Jo, as for most people who start a small business for the first time, buying a franchise was a daunting adventure. Married only two years, they knew it would entail sacrifice, risk, and change. There would be no paychecks coming in, a startup period of unknown duration, no vacations and—worst of all—maybe not enough demand. They had to collect the usual financial cushion to see them through the start-up period.

6    It is common knowledge that most novice entrepreneurs begin with too much hope and too little capital. Was this true of them?

7    "Actually," says Jo, "the amount of capital you need varies a *lot*, according to the business. But in every case, there are opening costs and loan-servicing costs. It usually takes you six to twelve months just to reach a break-even point. And then you can expect to work one to two years more *with no profit*. How do you manage? Well, you use up all your savings, you take out loans just to exist."

8    A special problem for the Sprawls was that for six months Jo would have to run the business pretty much by herself. Jeff could only be a "silent partner," helping out only on weekends, since he still held his corporate job. (He expected to be laid off the following year.) In this difficult period, they played it safe. They continued the previous owner's patterns, with no innovations.

9    But apart from these negatives, Jeff and Jo had several positives going for them. First, there was the happy fact that their abilities were not only complementary, but tailor-made for a service business like Pak Mail. Jeff, a West-Coast native, came from a management background. He was the one with the ideas, the interest in long-range plans. So, he has turned out to be the "project person." Jo, an Easterner, was experienced in sales. She loves people, detail, and daily organization, she follows through on the plans—so she is the "maintenance person." A hard look at their different modes convinced them that the partnership would work.

## BUYING A FRANCHISE

10    A second advantage lay in the franchising system itself. Instead of starting a business from scratch, the Sprawls were going to get help from the parent company. And in their opinion, Pak Mail is one of the better franchisors.

11    "Some of them only want to sell the contracts and leave the buyers to sink or swim," Jo explained. "Pak Mail wants each store to *succeed*. It wants to generate a good royalty stream."

12    Just how expensive is this "stream" for franchise holders like Jeff and Jo? Each store must give up a total of 6 percent of its receipts to Pak Mail: 1 percent to a fund for national advertising and 5 percent to royalties. But the Sprawls think this is a fair price to pay for the company's direction and expertise. Pak Mail offers a one-week crash course in operating a franchise and a trained assistant for the first week of operation after the store opens. There is a "bible": ten giant notebooks of questions and answers, which Jeff and Jo keep in the back of the store and consult often. There are regional conventions, a hot line—in fact, it's a total operating system. They both agree that it is much harder to start this kind of business on one's own.

13    And they say Pak Mail is less restrictive than some franchisors; owners can be more independent in design and services. When customers go into a McDonald's, anywhere in the world, they are paying for that dependable sameness. In contrast, Pak Mail mandates only six or seven services, which allows owners the freedom and flexibility to offer other services.

14    They had a third, major advantage in their venture: they were not opening a new store but taking over a franchise that had done well for five years. According to the Sprawls, owners starting in a brand-new location must expect a shakier

start. There will be less volume at first, the cash flow will build more slowly, and the initial financial cushion must be fatter. But in their case the clientele was already there. People were used to dropping by en route to the Chinese restaurant or the supermarket.

## THE "GENERAL STORE" TOUCH

15    But they did have to figure out how to retain these previous customers. They needed to offer patrons a sense of continuity, make them feel comfortable with the change of owners. To smooth the transition (and also to help learn the ropes), Jo kept the former store manager on for one month.

16    In part, their concern over customer relations was simply a shrewd business tactic, essential to the success of any retail business.

17    As Jeff explains it: "The service field is different from retailing. We can't offer special sales on our products. Also we can't create demand—the demand has to be there in the public, to start with. So what can we add, to keep attracting customers? First of all, complete expertise, so we can help people with their decisions, present alternatives to them.

18    "For instance, a person will come in with something to mail and ask, what's the best way to send this? Of course, what the person really means is, what's the cheapest way to send it? So we have to know what we're doing!"

19    But good customer relations, for them, is more than just a good business tactic. One senses immediately, from talking with Jeff and Jo and from the atmosphere of their store, that their warmth is genuine, a natural part of their personalities. "These service businesses are the hands-on type," says Jo. "You've got to *like people and like to serve them*. You either love that idea, or you hate it—there's no middle ground. And if you want to succeed, you'd better love it!

20    "Customers have to *enjoy* being in your store. All the surveys show that people won't go across town just to buy something a little cheaper. They'll buy where they feel comfortable—and of course, where they think the staff

knows its product. We try to provide all that—it's almost like having an old-time general store. People meet other people they know here. It's funny, but one woman told us, if she's in a hurry to mail something, she'll sit in her car and fill out the forms. Because if she comes in, she'll see a friend here and talk, and it will take up too much time."

21    "We both like doing this," says Jeff. "It's fun."

## DEMANDS OF A SMALL BUSINESS

22    The Sprawls also talk about the special reward that comes from making or breaking it all by yourself, which is the case when you are your own boss. "It's a little like being in sales," says Jo, who speaks from experience. "Beyond a certain level that your company expects of you, you're in control of how much or how little you make. And that's exciting."

23    But the flip side of that excitement is the anxiety of having no hourly wage, no paycheck coming in from the government or a company. Jeff and Jo smile at each other, remembering how they began.

24    "Of course there are ups and downs, especially at the beginning," they say. "If you're not selling, or if profits are down, you can get pretty depressed, have self-doubts. But this is true of *any* business, not just the service or franchise types. Every owner has times when she or he asks, 'Am I crazy to start this project? Or to keep on with it?' If they deny it, they're lying! And eventually, if you hang in there, you can sense that the business is smoothing out and the highs and lows can be averaged."

25    We have all heard that small-business owners must work very hard to be successful. Yes, the Sprawls do admit to working hard. Anyone contemplating this kind of livelihood *has* to really like it. Adds Jo with a grin, "And don't forget the old saying 'YOU will be the most difficult person you have ever worked for!'"

26    How do the hard work, long hours, and scant vacation time affect their private lives? Here again, we've all heard that these can be ma-

jor drawbacks for couples who run small businesses, manage motels, and so on. But Jeff and Jo have ready answers.

27    "No problem! We see a lot of each other, much more than if we worked two different jobs like we used to. So we don't have to take a two-week vacation in order to be together, like other couples do. And hey, if happiness in your marriage depends on that annual big trip to Hawaii or Florida, you're both in deep trouble already! Sometimes we take vacations separately, and it works out fine. After all, we see more of each other than most couples do, in our work."

28    Each has different outside interests, and each is willing to take turns in the store to enable the other to pursue them. As for interests they share: after three years, they've finally reached the point where they can trust one or two of their part-time workers to manage without them for a few hours. But they're really not free to leave for more than a day at a time. Part-timers can't handle the variety of demands that surface in a Pak Mail store for very long. So have they thought of hiring a store manager?

29    "Yes, but so far we're not ready," says Jeff. "If we ever expand and own two or more stores, then we'd hire a manager, just to give us some time off. But as long as we have just this one store . . . studies show that a hired manager is *never* as successful as an owner/manager. Also, it's expensive. We'd have to train them extremely well, and then pay a good salary, maybe even offer incentives like profit-sharing to insure they'd manage the business properly. Of course, that's one more reason we decided to operate this store together. If one person tried to do it alone, he or she *would* have to hire a manager."

30    So far then, Jeff and Jo have relied only on part-timers to help run their store.

## STUDENT EMPLOYEES
## MIXED SUCCESS

31    The Sprawls are astonished at the applicants they draw for this minimum-wage work—in the current recession, even Ph.D.'s! However, most applicants are young, and in this small city, many are students at the university or the community college.

32    The couple would sum up their three years' experience with student workers as a "mixed success." According to them, too many students make it clear that "I'm willing to do *only this much* for $5 an hour." Jeff and Jo are understanding. But that attitude just doesn't work in a service business. Customers are not likely to compute the competence and attention they receive in the same way. The Sprawls give each new employee a three-month training period, then a 90-day evaluation period, as they are required to do by the terms of the Pak Mail franchise. And yet, reluctantly, they sometimes have to let the person go.

33    On the other hand, many students have become excellent employees: interested and willing to learn about the business and teach themselves. They're not just making a few dollars to help with expenses, they're developing good job skills that will sustain them in any kind of job later in life.

34    The best student workers, of course, are the ones who share the owners' attitudes toward people—they like people and deal well with them. "Dealing well" means being poised and calm at the counter. And here is where Jeff and Jo have discovered something that surprises them: young workers often make big mistakes when left alone to serve at the counter.

35    "And these are clerks who never made a mistake during the training period, or when being tested, or when working alongside their employers," says Jo, laughing. "It isn't the mistake that bothers us—any mistake can be fixed later. It's that when we ask *why* it happened, the worker doesn't seem to know—and doesn't seem to wonder why he/she doesn't know!"

36    Having discussed this phenomenon at home, the Sprawls have come up with a reason. They think it's a matter of *poise*. At the counter, young people feel stressed out, easily intimidated by customers who are older or very demanding.

37    "Some workers get so nervous, they speak too fast," says Jo. "Sometimes they panic, actually

seem to *freeze!* And panic doesn't look good—people want to feel you know your business. You should act as if you know the answer and the solution—even when you don't."

38    How can shy, inexperienced young people gain the poise needed for jobs that involve a lot of public contact? Both Jeff and Jo urge all college students to take speech or drama classes, or join a debate team. "Join *any* organization where you have to speak in public, learn to project yourself and your voice and to be self-confident. Then you'll be ready for anyone who walks in the door."

## TRULY "MOM AND POP" BUSINESS?

39    Hiring young workers sometimes gives rise to another difficulty, almost as important as their tendency to panic: Jeff and Jo get cast as substitute parents. Students are often living away from home for the first time and can become dependent on the all-knowing owners during the 90-day training period. Then the Sprawls have to cut out some of the dependency.

40    At other times, students bring their personal problems to work, saying, "I can talk to you—I wish you were my parents!" To which Jo replies, sensibly enough: "That's just why you *can* talk to us—because we *aren't* your parents." Then the Sprawls have to cut out some of the counseling role.

## DOWN THE LINE . . .

41    How do they see their future? Would they keep this Pak Mail Center for ten more years, twenty years? Jeff and Jo answer this one immediately, with one voice: "*Absolutely not!*" Well . . . maybe if they were to expand and buy other Pak Mail stores. But once the challenge and growth of this first store is gone, they say, there would be no fun left, and they would want to switch to some other line.

42    So far, after three years as partners in a small service business, Jeff and Jo look happy and fit. So far, the challenge and growth continue. And so far, they say, running a Pak Mail franchise with their dog Crista and student help in a small plaza on the west side of a small city has been—actually—fun.

Anne G. Phillips, unpublished article, June 1994.

• • • • • • • • • • • • • • • • • • • • • • • • • • • • • • • • • •

1.  Which of these structural items does not appear in the article?
    a.  frequent direct quotes
    b.  long, helpful lead after the title
    c.  subheads throughout
2.  Topics that are discussed include
    a.  staking $100,000
    b.  location, location, location
    c.  hiring minorities
    d.  none of the above
3.  The piece ends with
    a.  the Sprawls' future plans
    b.  the Sprawls' regrets
    c.  the word *fun*
    d.  both a and c

---

**Sel. 10**   P-Skim                        1. _____

**Time**   1:00 = 2,900 wpm               2. _____

**Score** _____ %                         3. _____

▶ 100%                                    **Check answers with your instructor.**

**Score** = number correct × 33.

---

## B.  Overview Skimming

Go back and overview skim for main ideas in 2:30 minutes (= 1,160 wpm) or fewer—but no longer than 3 (= 967 wpm). The style and content are simpler than those of some of the previous selections, so skim with confidence.

1.   The main idea of this article is that
  a.  any business major with enough money can run a franchise successfully
  b.  this couple has what it takes to run a service business—and they have fun doing it
  c.  with the decline of values in America, "You probably can't find good workers anymore!"

2.   The interview covers the couple's business experience from the time they opened their Pak Mail store to the present.
  a.  true
  b.  false

3.   The success of this store impresses the writer because
  a.  the owners are only in their twenties
  b.  the recession has caused other stores to close
  c.  student help is often unreliable
  d.  Pak Mail does not offer enough incentives to owners

4.   Jeff and Jo try to draw and keep customers through
  a.  a friendly "general store" atmosphere
  b.  weekly specials
  c.  colorful decor

5.   According to the ending,
  a.  the couple expect to enjoy running this one store for decades
  b.  the hard work and the long hours are finally getting to them
  c.  Jeff and Jo Sprawls might buy other outlets eventually

| Sel. 10   O-Skim | 1. _____ |
| --- | --- |
| Time  _____ : _____ = _____wpm | 2. _____ |
| min    sec | 3. _____ |
| Score  _____% | 4. _____ |
| ▶ 80% | 5. _____ |
| Score = number correct × 20. | **Check answers with your instructor. Record rate and score on p. 192.** |

 ## C. For Discussion and Writing

Read the article or refer back to it as needed.

1. Would this article encourage or discourage you from owning and operating your own small business, whether a franchise or some other kind? Explain.
2. From your personal job experience, would you say that the Sprawls' assessment of "good" and "poor" part-time workers is fair and convincing?
3. Whether young, middle-aged, or older, many people struggle with the problem of lack of poise. Comment on the Sprawls' ideas for helping overcome shyness in public or on the job.

## Follow-Up

Now that you have read ten overview selections on "work," you may want to consider how your understanding of this issue has changed and how your overview skimming abilities have improved. Individually, in small groups, or in large groups, you may want to consider the following questions.

### On Work
1. What qualities do you think a person needs to succeed at work?
2. Why do you think people become dissatisfied with their work?
3. How has your understanding of retirement changed?
4. Has this set of readings given you any new ideas about a career you might want to pursue?

### On Overview Skimming
1. Which overview skimming technique has helped you the most? Why?
2. Which area(s) of overview skimming do you still need to practice?

3. Consider the selections you overview skimmed. Which types of reading material are easy for you to overview skim?
4. Which types of reading material are still difficult for you to overview skim?

## Internet Activity

Use the Internet to find out more information about overview skimming and work. Break up into groups of four or five. To answer the following questions, use the Wadsworth web site and InfoTrac College Edition. Then return to your group with your information.

If you cannot access this web site or InfoTrac College Edition, research the Internet to find information on overview skimming and on work to answer these questions.

### On Overview Skimming
Go to the online Writing Center at Marist College and find information on skimming. Then answer the following questions.

1. What new information on overview skimming did you find?
2. Describe how you located this information.

### On Work
1. Locate and print an article of interest related to work.
2. Summarize this article.
3. Describe how you located this information.

## How to Record Your Scores on the Progress Chart

After you have finished a timed selection and have entered your time and score in the score box:

1. Find the correct selection number on the top row of the chart. Transfer your rate (wpm) to the chart, under the selection number. Make a dot, X, bar, or other mark. (If you know your time only, not your rate, you must first look up your wpm in the rate table in Appendix B. Then mark that number on the chart.) Note that the acceptable or "target" rates for the featured skill are shaded. Do your rates fall within the target area?
2. Transfer your overview skimming (O-Skim) comprehension score to the top blank on the chart. Note that the acceptable or "target" percentage for that selection is printed underneath the blank. Does your score meet or surpass the target percent?
3. Connect the rate marks with a line to see your progress clearly. Remember, your scores will not necessarily rise steadily. The different selections contain too many variables—difficulty, your interest in or familiarity with the topic, and so forth.

• • • • • • • • • • • • • • • • • • • •

# PROGRESS CHART: OVERVIEW SKIMMING

| Selection number | 1 | 2 | 3 | 4 | 5 | 6 | 7 | 8 | 9 | 10 |
|---|---|---|---|---|---|---|---|---|---|---|
| % Comprehension | % | % | % | % | % | % | % | % | % | % |
| Target % ▶ | 75% | 75% | 75% | 75% | 75% | 75% | 75% | 75% | 75% | 80% |

Words per minute (wpm = rate)

Target Rates

| | 1 | 2 | 3 | 4 | 5 | 6 | 7 | 8 | 9 | 10 |
|---|---|---|---|---|---|---|---|---|---|---|
| 2000 | | | | | | | | | | |
| 1900 | | | | | | | | | | |
| 1800 | | | | | | | | | | |
| 1700 | | | | | | | | | | |
| 1600 | | | | | | | | | | |
| 1500 | | | | | | | | | | |
| 1400 | | | | | | | | | | |
| 1300 | | | | | | | | | | |
| 1200 | | | | | | | | | | |
| 1100 | | | | | | | | | | |
| 1000 | | | | | | | | | | |
| 900 | | | | | | | | | | |
| 800 | | | | | | | | | | |
| 700 | | | | | | | | | | |
| 600 | | | | | | | | | | |
| 500 | | | | | | | | | | |
| 400 | | | | | | | | | | |

| Selection number | 1 | 2 | 3 | 4 | 5 | 6 | 7 | 8 | 9 | 10 |
|---|---|---|---|---|---|---|---|---|---|---|

# CHAPTER 5

# Study Reading

*T*his chapter may well be crucial to your success in college. You will learn here the SQ3R study system, which helps you understand and remember textbook material. We also introduce "mapping," a popular visual approach to learning. You can begin applying both methods immediately to all your college textbook reading.

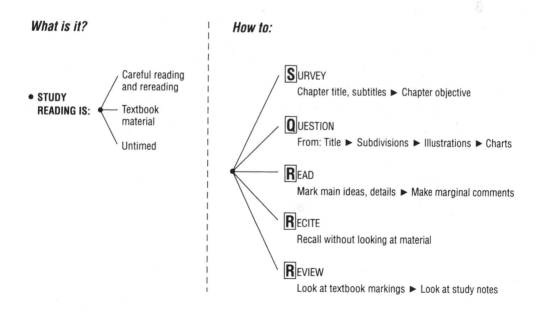

**What is it?**

- **STUDY READING IS:**
  - Careful reading and rereading
  - Textbook material
  - Untimed

**How to:**

**S**URVEY
Chapter title, subtitles ▶ Chapter objective

**Q**UESTION
From: Title ▶ Subdivisions ▶ Illustrations ▶ Charts

**R**EAD
Mark main ideas, details ▶ Make marginal comments

**R**ECITE
Recall without looking at material

**R**EVIEW
Look at textbook markings ▶ Look at study notes

# INTRODUCTION TO STUDY READING

· · · · · · · · · · · · · · · · · · ·

## CHECKLIST OF SYMPTOMS

Do you often

\_\_\_\_\_ 1. get bored or fall asleep when reading a textbook chapter?

\_\_\_\_\_ 2. feel that you haven't remembered a thing after you finish reading a chapter?

\_\_\_\_\_ 3. get poor grades in those courses that require reading textbook material?

\_\_\_\_\_ 4. get poor grades on chapter tests when you think that you knew the material?

\_\_\_\_\_ 5. spend several hours rereading a chapter in a textbook?

If you checked one or more of these symptoms, you need to read this introduction carefully. If you learn to use the system that we present, you will improve your reading of textbook material.

As you know, much of your college reading consists of reading and learning the information in textbooks. Though not the most interesting books to read, they are often the most predictable. Sections are clearly divided and subdivided into boldface print and italics; study questions often come at the end of the chapter; charts and illustrations usually represent the most important facts and concepts discussed in the chapter; and usually the style of textbook material is straightforward. With the right system, reading textbook material can be an efficient experience.

· · · · · · · · · · · · · · · · · · ·

## THE SQ3R STUDY SYSTEM

One consistently successful program that learning experts have developed for reading textbooks is called *SQ3R*, which stands for Survey, Question, Read, Recite, and Review. Many other study systems have emerged since SQ3R, yet all seem to follow the SQ3R format. You need to understand each step of this reading system before you can successfully apply it to your study reading. As such, read and, if necessary, reread the following steps until you understand how the SQ3R method works.

### Step 1: Survey

This first step is similar to the preview skimming that you were introduced to in Chapter 2. Surveying is a major study-reading step, because, like preview skimming, it prepares you for what you will read. Educational studies consistently show that surveying a textbook improves your comprehension, because you can better *predict*, or anticipate, what you will be reading, and prediction is the practice most significant in reading accurately. Also, surveying activates your *background knowledge*, or that knowledge you already have of a particular subject. So, by predicting the structure of the textbook chapter and by activating what you already know about its subject, you are much better prepared to understand and remember the textbook material than if you had done nothing.

**Surveying the Entire Text.**    Before you read a given textbook for the first time, get to know it by doing the following:

1.  Read the preface. It gives the author's reasons for writing the book, the topics covered, and the book's intended audience—information that will help you read the chapters efficiently.
2.  Study the table of contents to see how the book is organized. Look at its divisions and subdivisions. The textbook's overall organization will help you understand how the author thinks about the material that she or he is presenting. Textbooks today often provide a shorter version of the contents called "Contents in Brief," as well as a complete table of contents. Surveying both is helpful.
3.  Thumb through the index to see the number and types of words listed.
4.  Look for a glossary or an appendix. See if you will need to refer to terms, charts, or graphs as you read various chapters of the book.
5.  Note any answer keys at the end of the book or each chapter. Are answers given to all problems or only to odd- or even-numbered ones?
6.  Note any computer-related materials or information offered. Textbooks often direct you to web sites that provide supplemental information. Further, many textbooks in technical fields such as chemistry and physics actually attach software to the front or back cover. The CD-ROMs offer exercises as well as samples, quizzes, and examinations.
7.  Read through a few pages at the beginning, middle, and end of the textbook to get a sense of the author's style and the book's level of difficulty. Do you find the vocabulary difficult? Are the sentences complicated and hard to follow?

**Surveying a Specific Chapter.**    Once you have surveyed the entire textbook, you are ready to survey a specific chapter. Assume that you are reading an environmental science textbook chapter entitled "Ecosystems: What Are They and How Do They Work?" In your survey, you should do the following:

1.  Study the title. Do you know what an "ecosystem" is? If not, look it up in the glossary, if the textbook provides one, or in a dictionary.
2.  Read the general objectives or outline to the chapter found at the beginning. This section will provide you with the major topics this chapter will address.
3.  Read over the subdivisions, noting words and phrases in boldface and italics. These are the terms you will need to learn once you finish the chapter.

Check the margins for any definitions of important terms and for important questions that pertain to a given page; read these over.

4. Glance at any illustrations and charts. How do these visual statements help explain the ecosystem and help answer the questions posed in the general objectives?

5. Skim the chapter summary and discussion questions at the end of the chapter to see what the author considers the most important issues for you to learn. If there is a chapter quiz or examination at the end of the chapter, review the questions to see what you need to study.

6. See if computer support is mentioned at the end of the chapter, particularly web sites you can access after you have studied the material.

## Step 2: Question

The second step—formulating questions from the chapter survey—is crucial. If you have questions to answer, your reading is more directed. For most textbooks, the questioning step is simple, because questions are provided either at the beginning or at the end of each chapter. Read these questions over carefully, and choose four or five that seem most important to you and that you intend to answer as you study read. Remember that questioning what you read makes reading more interactive—you ask a question, then the textbook chapter provides an answer.

If there are no questions at the beginning or end of the chapter, review the boldface or italicized words and phrases and make up your own questions from them. In a subdivision entitled "The Biosphere and Ecosystems," for example, you can create two questions: "What is the biosphere?" "What are ecosystems?"

Asking the right kinds of questions is one of the most important skills an educated reader can develop. In fact, many researchers suggest that the right question is more important than the right answer, because the right question encourages further study. As you continue to read your textbook, the quality of your questions will improve along with your understanding of the material. Soon you may find that the questions you ask are the same as those your professor asks in class and on examinations.

## Step 3: Read

You are finally ready to read. But now you will be reading with a purpose because you know the chapter's organization and you have asked key questions about the chapter. Because you will need to read with concentration, find a quiet area. Always choose the time of day when you are most alert, whether the morning or evening.

As you read, mark your textbook. Underline or highlight only main ideas and supporting details in each paragraph—do not fill the page with too many markings. Make marginal notes when a phrase or sentence is confusing; when you want to identify a definition, step, cause, or effect; and when you are struck by an insight that the book does not state directly. If you cannot understand a phrase or sentence in the first reading, reread it as well as the sentence before and after it. Finally, keep your questions in mind, and answer them as you move through the chapter.

Be diligent. Do whatever you have to do to make sense of the chapter—read silently, read aloud, reread passages, and jot down notes.

**Reading Tips.**    Here are nine tips that should help you in marking and underlining textbook material.

1.  Mark main ideas with a double or a curved line, or use a highlighter. Underline or highlight only the key parts of the main idea, not the entire sentence. If you find any main ideas that are related, number them to underscore this relationship.

2.  Mark a major detail with a single line, or use a highlighter (perhaps of a different color than the one used for main ideas). Mark only the important details in each paragraph, and only mark the important parts. If any details are related, use a numbering system similar to the one you used in relating the main ideas.

3.  Place an asterisk (*) in the margin to emphasize a very important point. The asterisk will help you study this significant point when you review the material.

4.  When you think it matters, identify a detail as an example, step, cause, effect, or characteristic by writing an appropriate abbreviation in the margin. By doing so, you will have a better chance of remembering the detail and relating it to the main idea.

5.  Mark carefully all sections that define terms. Definitions are essential to learning any subject. You may want to circle the key parts of a definition to make them stand out from the main ideas and major details you have underlined.

6.  When you cannot understand a particularly difficult passage after rereading it, place a question mark in the margin. When you return to study this material, the question mark will alert you to those sections you did not understand. Remember, you are never expected to understand all textbook material, so noting what you do not know is a helpful practice.

7.  As you read, write a few comments in the margins. Place them anywhere in the margins: right or left, top or bottom. These comments could be summaries, rewordings of difficult sentences, or original insights.

8.  Do not begin marking your textbook until you have read through several paragraphs. Remember that if your markings are incorrect, you will have difficulty erasing them. Some students quickly read through the entire chapter without marking anything. Then, in their second reading, they begin to mark the chapter. See your textbook marking as a process you continue to reshape as you reread and study the chapter.

9.  Be consistent in your markings. You may use the system we have suggested, or you may design your own. Either way, be sure that when you study your markings, you can easily separate main ideas from major details, you can identify particular organizational patterns, and you can easily read your comments and see how they relate to the chapter.

*Ecological Questions* {

What plants and animals live in a forest or a pond? How do they get the matter and energy resources needed to stay alive? How do these plants and animals interact with one another and with their physical environment? What changes will this forest or pond undergo through time?

Ecology is the science that attempts to answer such questions. In 1866 German biologist Ernst Haeckel coined the term *ecology* from two Greek words: *oikos*, meaning "house" or "place to live," and *logos*, meaning "study of." Literally, then *ecology is the study of living things or organisms in their home.*

*Def.*  In more formal terms, **ecology** is the study of interactions among organisms and between organisms and the physical and chemical factors making up their environment.

*Def.*  This study is usually carried out as the examination of **ecosystems**: forests, deserts, ponds, oceans, or any self-regulating set of plants and animals interacting with one another and with their nonliving environment.

*Def.*  This chapter will consider the major nonliving and living components of ecosystems and how they interact. The next two chapters will consider major types of ecosystems, and the changes they can undergo as a result of natural events and human activities.

## THE BIOSPHERE AND ECOSYSTEMS

## The Earth's Life-Support System

What keeps plants and animals alive on this tiny planet as it hurtles through space at a speed of 66,000 miles per hour? The general answer to this question is that life on earth depends on two fundamental processes: *matter cycling* and the *one-way flow of high-quality energy* from the sun, through materials and living things on or near the earth's surface, and into space as low-quality heat (Figure 4-1).

*Def. 1*  All forms of life depend for their existence on the multitude of materials that compose the **(1)** solid **lithosphere**, consisting of the upper surface or crust of the earth, containing soil and deposits of matter and energy resources, and

*Def. 2*  an inner mantle and core, **(2)** the gaseous **atmosphere** extending above the earth's surface, **(3)** the **hydrosphere**, containing all of the earth's moisture as

*Def. 3*  liquid water, ice, and small amounts of water vapor in the atmosphere, and

*Def. 4*  **(4)** the **biosphere**, consisting of parts of the lithosphere, atmosphere, and hydrosphere in which living organisms can be found.

*Def.*  Human life and other forms of life whose existence we can threaten also depend on the **culturesphere**: the use of human ingenuity and knowledge based on past experience to extract, produce, and manage the use of matter, energy, and biological resources to enhance human survival and life quality.

*Imp. pt.*  A major input of ecology into the culturesphere is that all forms of life on earth are directly or indirectly interconnected. This means that to enhance long-term human survival and life quality, we must not blindly destroy other forms of plant and animal life—we must learn to work with, not against, nature.

The biosphere contains all the water, minerals, oxygen, nitrogen, phosphorus, and other nutrients that living things need. For example, your body consists of about 70% water obtained from the hydrosphere, small amounts of nitrogen and oxygen gases continually breathed in from the atmosphere,

**Figure 5-1a**   *Example of a well-marked page of text.*

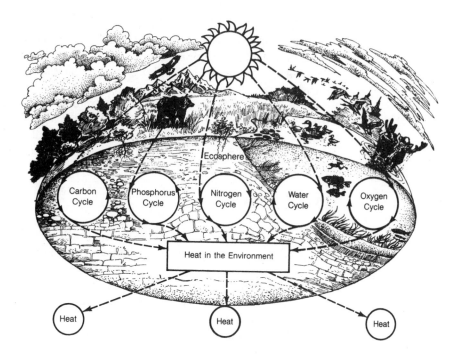

and various chemicals whose building blocks come mostly from the lithosphere. If the earth were an apple, the biosphere would be no thicker than the apple's skin. Everything in this "skin of life" is interdependent: air helps purify water and keeps plants and animals alive, water keeps plants and animals alive, plants keep animals alive and help renew the air and soil, and the soil keeps plants and many animals alive and helps purify water. *The goal of ecology is to find out how everything in the biosphere is related.*

## The Realm of Ecology

Ecology is primarily concerned with interactions among five of the levels of organization of matter, organisms, populations, communities, ecosystems, and the biosphere. An **organism** is any form of life. Although biologists classify the earth's organisms in anywhere from 5 to 20 categories, in this book it is only necessary to classify organisms as plants or animals. Plants range from microscopic, one-celled, floating and drifting plants known as phytoplankton to the largest of all living things—the giant sequoia trees of western North America. Animals range in size from floating and drifting zooplankton (which feed on phytoplankton) to the 14-foot-high, male African elephant and the 100-foot-long blue whale.

*Def.*

G. Tyler Miller, Jr., *Living in the Environment*, 5th ed., 68–69. © 1988 by Wadsworth, Inc. Reprinted by permission of the publishers.

**Figure 5-1b**   *Life on earth depends on the cycling of critical chemicals (solid lines) and the one-way flow of energy through the biosphere (dashed lines).*

These suggestions clearly show how study reading is an active process. After study reading effectively, you should be able to demonstrate that you understand the main points and major details of a chapter, that you can follow the organization and logic of the chapter, and that you can make appropriate inferences about the chapter. Passively underlining passages in a chapter is *not* study reading.

Figure 5-1 (pp. 198–199) provides an example of a successfully marked page from an environmental science textbook. Study it to see how it effectively incorporates many of the nine suggestions we have just explained.

Turn to Practice 5.1 on page 208. Then see Practice 5.2 on page 209.

## Step 4: Recite

By itself, careful reading will not ensure that you have adequately learned a chapter of your textbook. If you cannot remember what you have read, if you cannot *recite* the material that you have studied, you have not learned the material.

In the beginning of the recite step, stop after ten minutes of study reading and review all that you have marked. Then open your notebook, and, in your own words, write down the main points you have learned. If you are unhappy with what you have written, return to the material you have read, and review your marginal notes and underlinings. As you continue to recite, extend your concentrated reading to fifteen minutes, then twenty, each time reviewing your marking, then jotting down the significant points after each reading session. After a semester of practice, you should be able to study-read for an hour at one sitting and accurately summarize what you have read. These summaries may prove most helpful when you study for exams.

Your recite notes should be placed in a separate section of your notebook entitled "Study Reading" or "Reading Notes." You should have a separate study-reading section for each of your courses. Title each entry with the chapter title or subtitle, the pages read, and the date (for example, "Human Population Growth," pp. 2–8, 9/2/99). By including such information, you will know which pages of the textbook you have put in your own words and the date you completed this reading activity.

**Note Taking.**    Write your notes in any style that works for you. The two most common note-taking formats are the numeral-letter and the indenting formats. In the numeral-letter system, you use Roman numerals and capital letters: The Roman numerals indicate main ideas; the capital letters, major details. Study the following example:

> *"The Biosphere and Ecosystems," pp. 68–9 9/2/99*
>
> > I.   *What keeps plants and animals alive?*
> >
> > > A.   *Matter cycling: movement of chemicals necessary to life*
> > >
> > > B.   *Energy from the sun*

The main ideas and major details can either be in phrases or sentences. The main idea, indicated by the Roman numeral I, is to the left; the major details, A and B, are indented to the right.

The indenting format follows the same left-right pattern. Main ideas are to the left, major details to the right:

*"The Biosphere and Ecosystems," pp. 68–9 9/2/99*

    *What keeps plants and animals alive?*

        *Matter cycling: movement of chemicals necessary to life*

        *Energy from the sun*

In both formats, skip a line between main ideas so that in your review you can easily distinguish different types of information.

A third technique some students find effective is writing short paragraphs:

*"The Biosphere and Ecosystems," pp. 68–9 9/2/99*

*There are two ways to keep plants and animals alive on earth. The first is matter cycling, or the movement of chemicals necessary for life. The second is using the energy from the sun.*

In all three systems, only main ideas and significant details are noted. Thus, as in all effective summaries, the minor details have been omitted in favor of the important general and specific statements.

**Concept Maps.** Once you have read several chapters and begin to study them for a midterm or final, you may want to format all of the information in clear visual representations. Known as *concept maps* or *study maps*, these visual representations should be used when you have had time to restudy or rethink a chapter and to organize the material in the most economical way you can. Educational researchers have demonstrated that the mind remembers best when material is learned several ways: through what you hear, what you read, what you write, and what you see. Placing your study reading material in a visual pattern can therefore help you learn.

Concept maps often use geometric shapes such as circles, squares, rectangles, and triangles, as well as radiating lines and arrows, to place information in order. Each concept map requires a separate sheet of paper and should emanate from the center of the page. Many learning theorists contend that the mind remembers much more if you place the most important material in the center with additional information moving outward rather than if you place subordinate ideas to the left or to the right only.

Three geometric structures are commonly used as the basis for study maps. In the first structure, known as a *line map*, the topic is boxed in the center. The main points then radiate from the center as lines, and details are added to each radiating line. See Figure 5-2.

A version of the line map is known as a *semantic web*, which also places the most general concept in the center. Subtopics, also called *web strands*, radiate from this major concept in double lines. Details for each subtopic emanate from it in single lines known as *strand supports*. See Figure 5-3 for an example of a semantic web.

A variation of both the line map and the semantic web is known as the *tree study map* or hierarchical map. The topic comes first. Branching from the topic are main ideas; branching down from these are major details. See Figure 5-4.

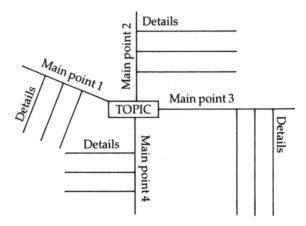

**Figure 5-2**   *Diagram of a line map.*

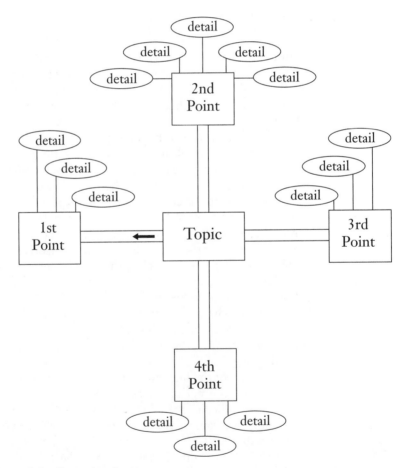

**Figure 5-3**   *Semantic web.*

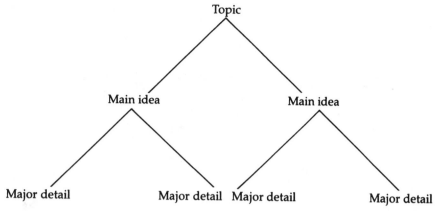

**Figure 5-4**  *Tree study map.*

A fourth structure for placing information into a visual pattern is the *flow-chart*. Sometimes more complicated than the other structures, this map works effectively with cause-and-effect and series of time sequences or procedures. In the flowchart, arrows tend to go left, right, up, and down to show the relationship of steps in a particular procedure or event.

The flowchart in Figure 5-5 shows how poverty, malnutrition, and disease work in relation to each other. Note how certain processes such as malnutrition and decreased resistance to disease move from left to right and down, showing that they affect two processes at the same time. Also, see how the decreased ability to work moves from right to left, affecting the original cause—poverty. Finally, note how much information, how many cause-effect relationships, are economically portrayed in this flowchart. A student studying this flowchart would likely remember much complicated information because it is expressed economically on one page and it has a visual structure.

Often, you will come across small bits of information you can express well visually by using small study maps—radiating lines, arrows, or intersecting circles. For example, let's say that an environmental science textbook mentions three disciplines concerned with the environment: chemistry, biology, and physics. Your recite notes could look like the study map shown in Figure 5-6. This concept map expresses the relationship among the four disciplines more effectively than would a sentence in a notebook.

In another example from environmental science, see how the statement "Environmental science often relies on studies in biochemistry, or experts in biology and chemistry" is nicely expressed in a concept map using intersecting circles (see Figure 5-7).

Finally, cause-effect statements can be expressed in recite notes via arrows. See how the following information about the use of carbon dioxide is easily represented with arrows that indicate a cause-effect relationship: "Carbon dioxide in the atmosphere is used by plants in the photosynthesis process, which in turn creates stored chemical energy for the plants to use."

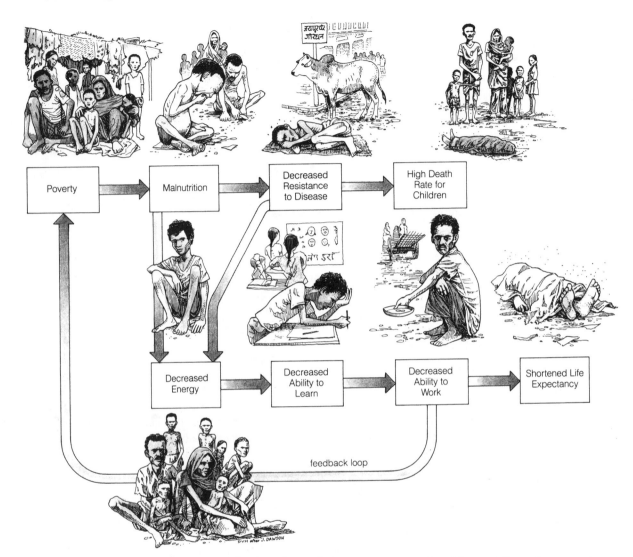

**Figure 5-5**   *Flowchart. Interactions among poverty, malnutrition, and disease form a tragic cycle that perpetuates such conditions in succeeding generations of families.*

G. Tyler Miller, Jr., *Living in the Environment*, 5th ed., 243. © 1988 by Wadsworth, Inc. Reprinted by permission of the publishers.

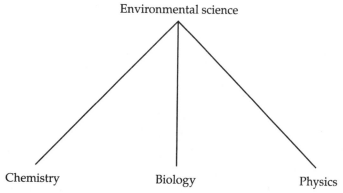

**Figure 5-6**  *Student study map.*

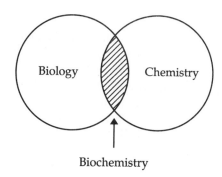

**Figure 5-7**  *Small study map.*

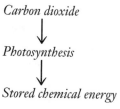

In summary, your recite notes from textbook material can be expressed in several ways: (1) through traditional note-taking techniques, (2) through summaries written in paragraph form, and (3) through concept maps expressing major or minor concepts from a textbook. No matter what note-taking styles you choose, keep in mind that recite notes are very important because they place textbook information into your own voice or point of view. Only when you have translated textbook material into your own, accurate summaries can you begin to understand the material you have read.

Turn to Practice 5.3 on page 211.

## Step 5: Review

Once you have successfully completed the previous four steps in the SQ3R system—survey, questions, read, and recite—you are ready for the last step—review. Reviewing is an essential step in the SQ3R system because it allows you to make the information your own, or to *rehearse* it, as educational psychologists put it. Reviewing allows you to move what you have study-read from *short-term* to *long-term* memory. Long-term memory allows you to call up information several days after you have reviewed it, such as for an exam.

You now know what to review for your exam on ecosystems.

1. Review your underlinings: main ideas and supporting details.
2. Carefully review all your marginal notes—your inferences and questions about the textbook material.
3. Study your recites carefully so you can recall on your examination most of what you have written in your notes.
4. Give yourself several days before the exam date to review your notes and underlinings. In some cases, you may need to review a page in the textbook or a topic in your notes several times before it becomes material you can easily recall. Like study reading, reviewing is an active process. Educational psychologists call studying over a set period of time *learning in spaced intervals*, and they have demonstrated that spacing your studying, compared with cramming, allows more information to stay in long-term memory.
5. Reflect on what you have read. See how the chapter you have reviewed fits into what you have read before and what you will be studying next. Further, ask yourself how this material has changed your attitude toward the subject under study. By reflecting on your study material, you can both recite what you have learned and evaluate it.

• • • • • • • • • • • • • • • • • • •

# *SUMMARY*

You can now see why efficient learning requires concentration and planning. Textbooks are dense, presenting much information concisely. The passive reader cannot begin to learn textbook material, whereas the active reader of textbooks

1. knows when to reread
2. knows how to summarize
3. can make appropriate inferences from the material she or he reads
4. can take accurate, concise, and easy-to-read notes

To study-read textbooks efficiently, you must learn to use the following steps effortlessly: survey, question, read, recite, and review.

Apply this SQ3R system to the practices and study selections that follow.

## SUMMARY BOX: STUDY READING

| What? | Why? | Acceptable Comprehension | Acceptable Rates |
|---|---|---|---|
| Textbooks in all fields | To understand the material; recall material for exams and job-related tasks, get better grades, save time studying | 80–90% | 100– 300 wpm |

# PRACTICES:
## STUDY READING

Answers to these questions are not provided in the answer key. Check your work with your instructor.

5.1 UNDERLINING A TEXTBOOK EXCERPT
5.2 UNDERLINING AND MARKING A TEXTBOOK EXCERPT
5.3 MAPPING SHORT STATEMENTS
5.4 UNDERLINING, MARKING, AND MAPPING A TEXTBOOK EXCERPT

### 5.1   UNDERLINING A TEXTBOOK EXCERPT

Here is a five-paragraph excerpt from an environmental science textbook. It is from the introduction to a chapter entitled "Environmental Problems and Their Causes." Read the five paragraphs through carefully, then go back to underline the main ideas twice and the major details once. Remember to underline only important parts of the main ideas and major details. If any main ideas or details are particularly important, be sure to place an asterisk in the margin.

## FROM "ENVIRONMENTAL PROBLEMS AND THEIR CAUSES"

*G. Tyler Miller, Jr.*

### WHAT ARE SOLAR CAPITAL, EARTH CAPITAL, AND SUSTAINABILITY?

1    Our existence, lifestyles, and economies depend completely on the sun and the earth. We can think of energy from the sun as **solar capital,** and we can think of the planet's air, water, soil, wildlife, minerals, and natural purification, recycling, and pest control processes as **earth capital.** The term **environment** is often used to describe these life-support systems.

2    Environmentalists and many leading scientists believe that we are depleting and degrading the earth's natural capital at an accelerating rate as our population and demands on the earth's resources and natural processes increase exponentially. Others, mostly economists, dis-

agree. They contend that there are no limits to human population growth and economic growth that can't be overcome by human ingenuity and technology.

3    There are two basic issues: First, are we impairing the sustainability of the planet's life-support systems for both humans and other species? Second, how can we live more sustainably by replacing actions that degrade life and the earth with actions that sustain them?

4    A **sustainable system** is one that survives and functions over some specified time and that attains its full expected life span. A **sustainable society** manages its economy and population size without exceeding all or part of the planet's ability to absorb environmental insults, replenish

its resources, and sustain human and other life over a specified period—usually hundreds to thousands of years. During this period, it satisfies the needs of its people without degrading or depleting earth capital and thereby jeopardizing the prospects of current and future generations.

5     Living sustainably means living off of income and not depleting the capital that supplies the income. Imagine that you inherit $1 million.

If you invest this capital at 10% interest, you will have a sustainable annual income of $100,000; that is, you can spend up to $100,000 a year without touching your capital.

G. Tyler Miller, Jr., *Living in the Environment*, 10th ed., 5–6. © 1998 by Wadsworth, Inc. Reprinted by permission of Brooks/Cole Publishing.

• • • • • • • • • • • • • • • • • • • • • • • • •

Score: Underlinings will vary.

Ask your instructor for sample underlinings.

## 5.2   UNDERLINING AND MARKING A TEXTBOOK EXCERPT

Here is an excerpt on the earth's resources from an environmental science textbook, the same textbook you read from in Practice 5.1. As in that practice, read through the excerpt carefully, then underline main ideas twice and major details once. Be sure that you underline only important parts of these sentences. Make marginal comments regarding organizational patterns and write any insights that you have while reading. Remember not to make too many marginal comments. You may want to review Figure 5-1 for an example of a successfully marked text.

• • • • • • • • • • • • • • • • • • •

 *"RESOURCES," FROM* **LIVING IN THE ENVIRONMENT**

• • • • • • • • • • • • • • • • • • •

*G. Tyler Miller, Jr.*

## WHAT IS A RESOURCE?

1     In human terms, a **resource** is anything we get from the environment (the earth's life-support systems) to meet our needs and desires. However, all forms of life need resources such as food, water, and shelter for survival and good health.

2     Some resources, such as solar energy, fresh air, wind, fresh surface water, fertile soil, and wild edible plants, are directly available for use by us and other organisms. Other resources, such as petroleum (oil), iron, groundwater (water occurring underground), and modern crops, aren't

directly available. They become useful to us only with some effort and technological ingenuity. Petroleum, for example, was a mysterious fluid until we learned how to find it, extract it, and refine it into gasoline, heating oil, and other products that could be sold at affordable prices. On our short human time scale, we classify material resources as renewable, potentially renewable, or nonrenewable.

## WHAT ARE RENEWABLE RESOURCES?

3     Solar energy is called a **renewable resource** because on a human time scale this solar

capital is essentially inexhaustible. It is expected to last at least 6 billion years while the sun completes its life cycle.

4      A **potentially renewable resource*** can be replenished fairly rapidly (hours to several decades) through natural processes. Examples of such resources include forest trees, grassland grasses, wild animals, fresh lake and stream water, groundwater, fresh air, and fertile soil.

5      One important potentially renewable resource for us and other species is **biological diversity,** or **biodiversity,** which consists of the different life-forms (species) that can best survive the variety of conditions currently found on the earth. Kinds of biodiversity include **(1)** *genetic diversity* (variety in the genetic makeup among individuals within a single species), **(2)** *species diversity* (variety among the species found in different habitats of the planet), and **(3)** *ecological diversity* (variety of forests, deserts, grasslands, streams, lakes, oceans, wetlands, and other biological communities).

6      This rich variety of genes, species, and biological communities gives us food, wood, fibers, energy, raw materials, industrial chemicals, and medicines—all of which pour hundreds of billions of dollars into the world economy each year. The earth's vast inventory of life-forms and biological communities also provides free recycling, purification, and pest control services.

7      Potentially renewable resources, however, can be depleted. The highest rate at which a potentially renewable resource can be used *indefinitely* without reducing its available supply is called its **sustainable yield.** If a resource's natural replacement rate is exceeded, the available supply begins to shrink—a process known as **environmental degradation.** Several types of environmental degradation can change potentially renewable resources into nonrenewable or unusable resources.

*Most sources use the term *renewable resource*. I have added the word *potentially* to emphasize that these resources can be depleted if we use them faster than natural processes renew them.

## CONNECTIONS: RENEWABLE RESOURCES AND THE TRAGEDY OF THE COMMONS

8      One cause of environmental degradation is the overuse of **common-property resources,** which are owned by no one but are available to all users free of charge. Most are potentially renewable. Examples include clean air, the open ocean and its fish, migratory birds, Antarctica, gases of the lower atmosphere, the ozone content of the stratosphere (the atmosphere's second layer), and space.

9      In 1968, biologist Garrett Hardin called the degradation of common-property resources the **tragedy of the commons.** It happens because each user reasons, "If I don't use this resource, someone else will. The little bit I use or pollute is not enough to matter." With only a few users, this logic works. However, the cumulative effect of many people trying to exploit a common-property resource eventually exhausts or ruins it. Then no one can benefit from it, and therein lies the tragedy.

10     One solution is to use common-property resources at rates below their sustainable yields or overload limits by reducing population, regulating access, or both. Unfortunately, it is difficult to determine the sustainable yield of a forest, glassland, or an animal population, partly because yields vary with weather, climate, and unpredictable biological factors.

11     These uncertainties mean that *it is best to use a potentially renewable resource at a rate well below its estimated sustainable yield.* This is a *prevention or precautionary approach* designed to reduce the risk of environmental degradation. This approach is rarely used because it requires hard-to-enforce regulations that restrict resource use and thus conflict with the drive for short-term profit or pleasure.

G. Tyler Miller, Jr., *Living in the Environment*, 10th ed., 11–14. © 1998 by Wadsworth, Inc. Reprinted by permission of Brooks/Cole Publishing.

Score: Underlining and marking will vary.

Ask your instructor for sample underlinings and markings.

## 5.3    MAPPING SHORT STATEMENTS

Use any mapping system that seems appropriate to visually represent the following statements. Your maps may vary from those your instructor shows you.

1.  There are three types of resources in our environment: a renewable resource, one that is depleted but can be replaced; a perpetual resource, one that will always be available; and a nonrenewable resource, one that exists in fixed amounts.
2.  Examples of nonrenewable resources include (1) fossil fuels, (2) metallic minerals, and (3) nonmetallic minerals.
3.  There seem to be three major causes of environmental pollution: (1) development of technology, (2) overpopulation, and (3) natural occurrences such as fires and volcanic eruptions.
4.  The world can be divided into two types of countries: (1) less developed countries (LDCs) and (2) more developed countries (MDCs).
5.  Overpopulation has created many problems. First, it has led to the overuse and depletion of many natural resources. Also, in some parts of the world, it has led to famine and the spread of communicable diseases. These diseases have caused the deaths of millions. Occasionally, famine has caused disputes among organizations in more powerful countries over decisions either to help or to ignore the starving countries. Finally, the increase in human population has led to habitat loss for other species; as a result, many plant and animal species face extinction in the coming years.

Score: Answers will vary.

Ask your instructor for sample maps.

## 5.4    UNDERLINING, MARKING, AND MAPPING A TEXTBOOK  EXCERPT

Read the following science textbook excerpt on pollution. Reread, then underline main ideas and major details. Make marginal comments on (1) organizational patterns and (2) points that you consider important.

When you have finished marking and underlining the passage, use the numeral-letter format to summarize the key points in the excerpt. Finally, from these recite notes, make a study map that represents these points visually.

## "POLLUTION," FROM LIVING IN THE ENVIRONMENT

*G. Tyler Miller, Jr.*

### WHAT IS POLLUTION, AND WHERE DOES IT COME FROM?

1    Any addition to air, water, soil, or food that threatens the health, survival, or activities of humans or other living organisms is called **pollution.** The particular chemical or form of energy that causes such harm is called a **pollutant.** Most pollutants are solid, liquid, or gaseous byproducts or wastes produced when a resource is extracted, processed, made into products, or used. Pollution can also take the form of unwanted energy emissions, such as excessive heat, noise, or radiation.

2    In other words, a pollutant is a chemical or form of energy in the wrong place in the wrong concentration. For example, ozone is a natural and important component of the stratosphere (the atmosphere's second layer), where it shields the earth from most of the life-destroying ultraviolet radiation emitted by the sun. In the trophosphere (the layer of the atmosphere closest to the earth), however, ozone is a dangerous air pollutant.

3    Pollutants can enter the environment naturally (for example, from volcanic eruptions) or through human (anthropogenic) activities (for example, from burning coal). Most pollution from human activities occurs in or near urban and industrial areas, where pollutants are concentrated. Industrialized agriculture is also a major source of pollution. Some pollutants contaminate the areas where they are produced; others are carried by winds or flowing water to other areas. Pollution does not respect local, state, or national boundaries.

4    Some pollutants come from single, identifiable sources, such as the smokestack of a power plant, the drainpipe of a meat-packing plant, or the exhaust pipe of an automobile. These are called **point sources.** Other pollutants come from dispersed (and often difficult to identify) **nonpoint sources.** Examples are the runoff of fertilizers and pesticides (from farmlands, golf courses, and suburban lawns and gardens) into streams and lakes, and pesticides sprayed into the air or blown by the wind into the atmosphere. It is much easier and cheaper to identify and control pollution from point sources than from widely dispersed nonpoint sources.

### WHAT TYPES OF HARM ARE CAUSED BY POLLUTANTS?

5    Unwanted effects of pollutants include **(1)** disruption of life-support systems for humans and other species; **(2)** damage to wildlife; **(3)** damage to human health; **(4)** damage to property; and **(5)** nuisances such as noise and unpleasant smells, tastes, and sights.

6    Three factors determine how severe the harmful effects of a pollutant will be. One is its *chemical nature*—how active and harmful it is to living organisms. Another is its **concentration**—the amount per unit of volume of weight of air, water, soil, or body weight.

7    A concentration of **one part per million (1 ppm)** corresponds to one part pollutant per one million parts of the gas, liquid, or solid mixture in which the pollutant is found; **one part per billion (1 ppb)** refers to one part of pollutant per one billion parts of the medium it is found in; and **one part per trillion (1 ppt)** means that one part of pollutant is found in one trillion parts of its medium. Table 1-1 shows some equivalents for these units of concentration. In a gas mixture the reference is usually to ppm, ppb, or ppt by *volume*; in liquids and solids the reference is generally to ppm, ppb, or ppt by *weight*.

8    Parts per million, billion, or trillion may seem like negligible amounts of pollution. Nevertheless, concentrations of *some* pollutants at such

low levels can have serious effects on people, other animals, and plants.

One way to lower the concentration of a pollutant is to dilute it in a large volume of air or water. Until we started overwhelming the air and waterways with pollutants, dilution was *the* solution to pollution. Now it is only a partial solution.

[9] The third factor is a pollutant's *persistence*— how long it stays in the air, water, soil, or body. **Degradable,** or **nonpersistent, pollutants** are broken down completely or reduced to acceptable levels by natural physical, chemical, and biological processes. Complex chemical pollutants broken down (metabolized) into simpler chemicals by living organisms (usually by specialized bacteria) are called **biodegradable pollutants.** Human sewage in a river, for example, is biodegraded fairly quickly by bacteria if the sewage is not added faster than it can be broken down.

[10] Many of the substances we introduce into the environment take decades or longer to degrade. Examples of these **slowly degradable,** or **persistent, pollutants** include the insecticide DDT and most plastics.

[11] **Nondegradable pollutants** cannot be broken down by natural processes. Examples include the toxic elements lead and mercury. The best ways to deal with nondegradable pollutants (and slowly degradable pollutants) are to not release them into the environment at all or to recycle or reuse them. Removing them from contaminated air, water, or soil is an expensive and sometimes impossible process.

[12] We know little about the possible harmful effects of 90% of the 72,000 synthetic chemicals now in commercial use and the roughly 1,000 new ones added each year. Our knowledge about the effects of the other 10% of these chemicals is limited, mostly because it is quite difficult, time-consuming, and expensive to get this information. Even if we determine the main health and other environmental risks associated with a particular chemical, we know little about its possible interactions with other chemicals or about the effects of such interactions on human health, other organisms, and life-support processes.

[13] A major problem in dealing with pollution and its effects is that people differ on the definition of a pollutant and on acceptable levels of pollution—especially if they must choose between pollution control and their jobs. As the philosopher Hegel pointed out nearly two centuries ago, tragedy is not the conflict between right and wrong, but the conflict between right and right.

G. Tyler Miller, Jr., *Living in the Environment,* 10th ed., 16–18. © 1998 by Wadsworth, Inc. Reprinted by permission of Brooks/Cole Publishing.

• • • • • • • • • • • • • • • • • • • • • • • • • • • • • •

Score: Answers for underlinings, mapping, and summary will vary.

Ask your instructor for sample responses.

**Table 1-1**  *Equivalents of Some Trace Concentration Units*

| Unit | 1 part per million | 1 part per billion | 1 part per trillion |
|---|---|---|---|
| *Time* | 1 minute in 2 years | 1 second in 32 years | 1 second in 320 centuries |
| *Money* | 1¢ in $10,000 | 1¢ in $10,000,000 | 1¢ in $10,000,000,000 |
| *Weight* | 1 pinch of salt in 10 kilograms (22 lbs.) of potato chips | 1 pinch of salt in 10 tons of potato chips | 1 pinch of salt in 10,000 tons of potato chips |
| *Volume* | 1 drop in 1,000 liters (265 gallons) of water | 1 drop in 1,000,000 liters (265,000 gallons) of water | 1 drop in 1,000,000,000 liters (265,000,000 gallons) of water |

# SELECTIONS: STUDY READING

The four selections in this chapter may be done in class or out of it. In either case, be sure to follow the step-by-step directions carefully. Please do not skip any step or change the order.

In this set of selections on environmental studies you will use the SQ3R system to read text material. You will begin by surveying each one. After taking a five-item survey quiz, you will write five questions of your own that will direct your study reading. With these in mind, you will read, underline, mark, and recite as part of the process of understanding what you read. Then you will take a ten-item study quiz, testing your understanding of what you have read. Next you will work on five questions for discussion and writing. Here you will return to reread and rethink the selection. You may answer these questions either alone or in small groups. Only the survey section is timed.

Each selection concludes with a self-evaluation whereby you rate your success in the various exercises and read some additional suggestions about how to study-read in that particular discipline.

Any unusual, important words will be defined at the beginning of the selection. For context, we also include quotations from the selection that include a given word.

The answers to odd-numbered selection quizzes are on page 352. Your instructor will provide the answers to even-numbered selection quizzes.

Before you begin study reading these four selections, consider the following questions on environmental studies. Because all of the selections will be dealing with some aspect of this issue, answering these questions will help uncover what you and your peers already know about this important social topic. You may want to respond to these questions individually or discuss them in small or large groups in class.

1. How would you define the word *environment*?
2. How have people treated the environment in the last 200 years?
3. What do you think are the greatest threats to the environment?
4. How do you think U.S. society is responding to the pollution problem?
5. Do you think that the pollution problem is serious? Why? Why not?

## SELECTIONS: STUDY-READING

. . . . . . . . . . . . . . . . . . . . .

# *SELECTION 1*

**Vocabulary**

*estuaries:* partly enclosed coastal areas at the mouth of a river, where its fresh water mixes with seawater; "ocean or marine life zones (such as estuaries, coastlines, coral reefs, and the deep ocean)"

*phytoplankton:* small, drifting plants, mainly algae and bacteria; "floating and drifting *phytoplankton,* most of them microscopic"

*nucleic acids:* structural units in cells formed as long chains of four different kinds of organic compounds; "and nucleic acids in plant tissues"

*aquifers:* underground rock bodies that can yield a large amount of water; "down in aquifers within volcanic rocks"

*fungi:* multicelled organisms that get nutrients by secreting enzymes on other organisms; "mostly certain types of bacteria and fungi"

*salinity:* salt content in water; "salinity and the level of dissolved oxygen are also major chemical factors"

This excerpt comes from an environmental science textbook. Like most environmental science material, this piece relies heavily on the organizational patterns of definition and cause-and-effect. The sentence structure and style are fairly easy to follow; however, you may find it hard to keep track of and use the several definitions you come across. Be sure to reread any definitions that are not immediately clear to you and to make appropriate marginal notes.

Because it presents the central terms of environmental studies, this excerpt will provide you with an important introduction to the field's general issues. As such, it will help make the next three selections easier to understand. Besides being introduced to several definitions of environmental studies, you will see how these terms are interrelated and learn which major natural processes environmental studies describe.

**Reading Practices.**   To read this excerpt effectively, use the following practices:

1.  Circle the key parts of the definitions, or highlight them in a way that separates them from the rest of the material.
2.  See how the various definitions relate to each other—for example, those of *organism, species,* and *population; habitat, ecosystem,* and *ecotone;* and *biotic* and *abiotic* components of the environment.
3.  Note in the margins the important process patterns, particularly the steps involved in photosynthesis and chemosynthesis and those steps leading to recycling in the environment.

## A. Survey

Take 2 minutes to survey the excerpt. Read the chapter title, the headings, the terms in boldface print, and the words and phrases in italics. If time permits, begin reading the first and last paragraph or two.

When your time is up, answer the five questions without looking back at the excerpt. Place all your answers in the answer box.

• • • • • • • • • • • • • • • •

## ECOSYSTEM COMPONENTS
### by G. Tyler Miller, Jr. (2,253 words)

## WHAT IS ECOLOGY?

1     The term *ecology* was coined in 1869 by German biologist Ernst Haeckel, but the discipline of ecology was created about 100 years ago by M.I.T. chemist Ellen Swallow. **Ecology,** (from the Greek *oikos*, "house" or "place to live," and *logos*, "study of") is the study of how organisms interact with one another and with their nonliving environment (including such factors as sunlight, temperature, moisture, and vital nutrients). The key word in this definition is *interact.* Ecologists focus on trying to understand the interactions among organisms, populations, communities, ecosystems, and the ecosphere (Figure 5.8).

2     An **organism** is any form of life. Organisms can be classified into **species**—groups of organisms that resemble one another in appearance, behavior, chemistry, and genetic endowment. Organisms that reproduce sexually are classified in the same species if, under natural conditions, they can actually or potentially breed with one another and produce live, fertile offspring.

3     We don't know how many species exist on the earth. Estimates range from 5 million to 100 million, most of them insects and microorganisms. So far biologists have identified and named only about 1.75 million species. Biologists know a fair amount about roughly one-third of the known species, but the detailed roles and interactions of only a few.

4     Each identified and unknown species is the result of a long evolutionary history, involving the storage of an immense amount of unique and irreplaceable genetic information about how to survive under specific environmental conditions. According to biologist E. O. Wilson, if the genetic information encoded in the DNA found in the approximately 100,000 genes of a house mouse were translated into a printed text, it would fill all of the books in each of the 15 editions of the *Encyclopedia Britannica* published since 1768.

5     A **population** consists of all members of the same species occupying a specific area at the same time. Examples are all sunfish in a pond, all white oak trees in a forest, and all people in a country. In most natural populations, individuals vary slightly in their genetic makeup, which is why they don't all look or behave exactly alike—a phenomenon called **genetic diversity.** Populations are dynamic groups that change in size, age distribution, density, and genetic composition as a result of changes in environmental conditions.

6     The place where a population (or an individual organism) normally lives is known as its **habitat.** It may be as large as an ocean or prairie or as small as the underside of a rotting log or the intestine of a termite. Populations of all the different species occupying and interacting in a particular place make up a **community,** or **biological community**—a complex network of interacting plants, animals, and microorganisms.

7     An **ecosystem** is a community of different species interacting with one another *and* with their nonliving environment of matter and energy. The size of an ecosystem is somewhat arbitrary; it is defined by the particular system we

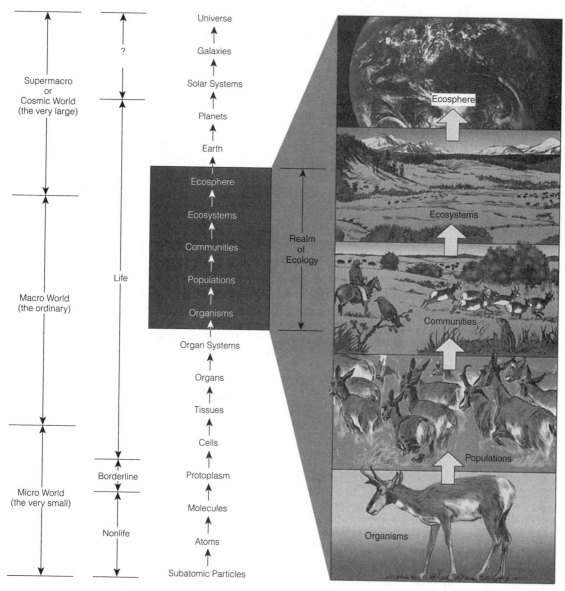

**Figure 5-8**  *Conceptual model of levels of organization of matter in nature. Note that ecology focuses on five levels of this hierarchical model.*

wish to study. The unit of study may be relatively small, such as a particular stream or field or a patch of woods, desert, or marsh. Or the units may be large, generalized types of terrestrial (land) ecosystems such as a particular type of grassland, forest, or desert. Ecosystems can be natural or artificial (human-created). Examples of human-created ecosystems are cropfields, farm ponds, and reservoirs or artificial lakes created behind dams.

8    To be *sustainable* for some specified period of time, an ecosystem must contain the energy and nutrient resources needed to support its resident organisms and to dispose of and recycle their wastes. All of the earth's ecosystems together make up what we call the *biosphere*, or *ecosphere*.

9    For convenience, scientists usually consider an ecosystem under study to be an isolated unit. However, natural ecosystems rarely have distinct boundaries and are not truly self-contained, self-sustaining systems. Instead, one ecosystem tends to merge with the next in a transitional zone called an **ecotone,** a region containing a mixture of species from adjacent regions and often species not found in either of the bordering ecosystems. For example, a marsh or wetland found between dry land and the open water of a lake or ocean is an ecotone. Another example is the zone of grasses, small shrubs, and scattered small trees found between a grassland and a forest. An ecotone often contains both a greater number of species and a higher population density than in either adjacent ecosystem; this is known as the **edge effect.**

10    **Climate**—long-term weather—is the main factor determining what type of life, especially what plants, will thrive in a given land area. Viewed from outer space, the earth resembles an enormous jigsaw puzzle consisting of large masses of land and vast expanses of ocean. Biologists have divided the terrestrial (land) portion of the ecosphere into **biomes,** large regions (such as forests, deserts, and grasslands) characterized by a distinct climate and specific life-forms—especially vegetation adapted to it. Each biome consists of many ecosystems whose communities have adapted to differences in climate, soil, and other factors throughout the biome.

11    Marine and freshwater portions of the ecosphere can be divided into **aquatic life zones,** each containing numerous ecosystems. Aquatic life zones are the aquatic equivalent of biomes. Examples include freshwater life zones (such as lakes and streams) and ocean or marine life zones (such as estuaries, coastlines, coral reefs, and the

deep ocean). The earth's major land biomes and aquatic life zones are discussed in more detail in Chapter 7.

## WHY IS BIODIVERSITY SO IMPORTANT?

12    As environmental conditions have changed over billions of years many species have become extinct, and new ones have formed. The result of these changes is **biological diversity, or biodiversity**—those forms of life that can best survive the variety of conditions currently found on the earth. As you learned in Chapter 1, biodiversity includes **(1) genetic diversity** (variability in the genetic makeup among individuals in a single species, **(2) species diversity** (the variety of species in different habitats on the earth), and **(3) ecological diversity** (the variety of biological communities that interact with one another and with their nonliving environments).

13    We are utterly dependent on this mostly unknown *biocapital*. This rich variety of genes, species, and ecosystems gives us food, wood, fibers, energy, raw materials, industrial chemicals, and medicines—and it pours hundreds of billions of dollars yearly into the global economy.

14    The earth's life-forms and ecosystems also provide recycling, purification, and natural pest control. Every species here today contains genetic information that represents thousands to millions of years of adaptation to the earth's changing environmental conditions and is the raw material for future adaptations. Biodiversity is nature's insurance policy against disasters.

15    Some people also include *human cultural diversity* as part of the earth's biodiversity. The variety of human cultures represents numerous social and technological solutions that have enabled us to survive and adapt to and work with the earth.

## WHAT ARE THE MAJOR LIVING COMPONENTS OF ECOSYSTEMS?

16    The ecosphere and its ecosystems can be separated into two parts: **(1) biotic,** or living,

components (plants, animals, and microorganisms—sometimes referred to as *biota*); and **(2) abiotic,** or nonliving, components (water, air, nutrients, and solar energy).

17   Living organisms in ecosystems are usually classified as either *producers* or *consumers*, based on how they get food. **Producers**—sometimes called **autotrophs** (self-feeders)—make their own food, from compounds obtained from their environment. On land, most producers are green plants. In freshwater and marine ecosystems, algae and plants are the major producers near shorelines; in open water the dominant producers are floating and drifting *phytoplankton*, most of them microscopic. Only producers make their own food; all other organisms are consumers, which depend directly or indirectly on food provided by producers.

18   Most producers capture sunlight to make sugars (such as glucose, $C_6H_{12}O_6$) and other complex organic compounds from inorganic (abiotic) nutrients in the environment. This process is called **photosynthesis.** In most green plants, *chlorophyll* (a pigment molecule that gives plants their green color) traps solar energy for use in photosynthesis and converts it into chemical energy. Although a sequence of hundreds of chemical changes takes place during photosynthesis, the overall reaction can be summarized as follows:

carbon dioxide + water  + **solar energy** → glucose  + oxygen

$$6\,CO_2 \quad\quad + 6\,H_2O + \textbf{solar energy} \rightarrow C_6H_{12}O_6 + 6\,O_2$$

19   Green primary producers absorb only about half of the light energy falling on them and reflect or transmit the rest. Plants then manage to convert only about 1–5% of this absorbed energy into chemical energy, which is stored in complex carbohydrates, lipids (fats), proteins, and nucleic acids in plant tissues.

20   A few producers, mostly specialized bacteria, can convert simple compounds from their environment into more complex nutrient compounds without sunlight, a process called **chemosynthesis.** In one such case, the source of energy is heat generated by the decay of radioactive elements deep in the earth's core; this heat is released at hot-water (hydrothermal) vents in the ocean's depths, where new crust is constantly being formed and reformed. In the pitch darkness around such vents, large populations of specialized producer bacteria use this geothermal energy to convert dissolved hydrogen sulfide ($H_2S$) and carbon dioxide into organic nutrient molecules. These bacteria in turn become food for a variety of aquatic animals, including huge tube worms and a variety of clams, crabs, mussels, and barnacles.

21   In 1995, researchers found bacteria subsisting on rock and water about 1,000 meters (3,200 feet) down in aquifers within volcanic rocks near the Columbia River in Washington. They survive by getting dissolved $CO_2$ from the groundwater and appear to get energy by using hydrogen ($H_2$) generated in a reaction between iron-rich minerals in the rock and groundwater.

22   All other organisms in an ecosystem are **consumers** or **heterotrophs** ("other-feeders"), which get their energy and nutrients by feeding on other organisms or their remains. There are several classes of consumers, depending on their primary source of food. **Herbivores** (plant eaters) are called **primary consumers** because they feed directly on producers. **Carnivores** (meat eaters) feed on other consumers; those called **secondary consumers** feed only on primary consumers (herbivores). Most secondary consumers are animals, but a few (such as the Venus's-flytrap plant) trap and digest insects. **Tertiary (higher-level) consumers** feed only on other carnivores. **Omnivores** are consumers that eat both plants and animals; examples are pigs, rats, foxes, bears, cockroaches, and humans. These types of consumers typically hunt and kill live prey.

23   Other consumers, called **scavengers,** feed on dead organisms that were either killed by other organisms or died naturally. Vultures, flies, crows, hyenas, and some species of sharks, beetles, and ants are examples of scavengers. **Detritivores** (detritus feeders and decomposers) live off **detritus** (pronounced di-TRI-tus)—parts of

dead organisms and cast-off fragments and wastes of living organisms. **Detritus feeders,** such as crabs, carpenter ants, termites, earthworms, and wood beetles, extract nutrients from partly decomposed organic matter in leaf litter, plant debris, and animal dung.

24    **Decomposers,** mostly certain types of bacteria and fungi, are consumers that complete the final breakdown and recycling of organic materials from the remains or wastes of all organisms. They recycle organic matter in ecosystems by breaking down dead organic material (detritus) to get nutrients and releasing the resulting simpler inorganic compounds into the soil and water, where they can be taken up as nutrients by producers. In turn, decomposers are important food sources for worms and insects living in the soil and water. When we say that something is **biodegradable,** we mean that it can be broken down by decomposers.

25    Both producers and consumers use the chemical energy stored in glucose and other organic compounds to fuel their life processes. In most cells, this energy is released by the process of **aerobic respiration,** which uses oxygen to convert organic nutrients back into carbon dioxide and water. The net effect of the hundreds of steps in this complex process is represented by the following reaction:

glucose   + oxygen  → carbon dioxide + water  + **energy**

$$C_6H_{12}O_6 + 6\,O_2 \rightarrow 6\,CO_2 \qquad + 6\,H_2O + \textbf{energy}$$

Although the detailed steps differ, the net chemical change for aerobic respiration is the opposite of that for photosynthesis, which takes place during the day, when sunlight is available; aerobic respiration can happen day or night.

26    Some decomposers get the energy they need through the breakdown of glucose (or other nutrients) in the absence of oxygen. This form of cellular respiration is called **anaerobic respiration** or **fermentation.** Instead of carbon dioxide

and water, the end products of this process are compounds such as methane gas ($CH_4$), ethyl alcohol ($C_2H_6O$), acetic acid (the main component of vinegar, $C_2H_4O_2$), and hydrogen sulfide ($H_2S$, when sulfur compounds are broken down).

27    The survival of any individual organism depends on the *flow of matter and energy* through its body. However, an ecosystem as a whole survives primarily through a combination of *matter recycling* (rather than one-way flow) and *one-way energy flow*. Decomposers complete the cycle of matter by breaking down detritus into inorganic nutrients that are usable by producers. Without decomposers, the entire world would soon be knee-deep in plant litter, dead animal bodies, animal wastes, and garbage. Most life as we know it would no longer exist.

## WHAT ARE THE MAJOR NONLIVING COMPONENTS OF ECOSYSTEMS?

28    The nonliving, or abiotic, components of an ecosystem are the physical and chemical factors that influence living organisms. Some important physical factors affecting land ecosystems are sunlight, temperature, precipitation, wind, latitude (distance from the equator), altitude (distance above sea level), frequency of fire, and nature of the soil. For aquatic ecosystems, water currents and the amount of suspended solid material are major physical factors.

29    Important chemical factors affecting ecosystems are the supply of water and air in the soil and the supply of plant nutrients or toxic substances dissolved in soil moisture (or in water in aquatic habitats). In aquatic ecosystems, salinity and the level of dissolved oxygen are also major chemical factors.

G. Tyler Miller, Jr., *Living in the Environment*, 10th ed., 95–103. © 1998 by Wadsworth, Inc. Reprinted by permission of Brooks/Cole Publishing.

•  •  •  •  •  •  •  •  •  •  •  •  •  •  •  •  •  •  •  •

1. This excerpt begins with
   a. a definition of population
   b. the difference between habitat and ecosystem
   c. a description of an ecosystem
   d. a definition of ecology
2. The author lists
   a. several definitions relating to ecology
   b. several books on environmental studies
   c. the most important species known to scientists
   d. the world's endangered species
3. This excerpt includes one figure.
   a. true
   b. false
4. In order to highlight key terms and concepts, this excerpt uses
   a. italics
   b. terms in boldface
   c. underlining
   d. both a and b
5. This excerpt ends with
   a. an illustration
   b. a section on nonliving parts of the environment
   c. a bibliography
   d. a summary of the excerpt

| | |
|---|---|
| **Sel. 1**  Sur | 1. _____ |
| **Score** _____ % | 2. _____ |
| ▶ 80% | 3. _____ |
| **Score** = number correct × 20. | 4. _____ |
| | 5. _____ |
| | **Check answers on p. 352.** |

## B. Question

Having surveyed the excerpt, list here five questions you intend to answer when you study-read. Make up questions from the title, the headings, and the words and phrases in italics.

1. _____
2. _____
3. _____

4. _____

5. _____

See sample questions on p. 352.

## C. Read

With all these questions in mind, read the selection carefully. You may want to read it through once before you begin marking. When you do begin to mark, re-member to underline only parts of sentences if possible and to write sparingly.

## D. Recite

Without looking back at the excerpt, write down in note-taking or paragraph form the important points made in the excerpt. When you have finished your summary, compare it with the excerpt. How accurate were you?

## E. Review

Now review all of your material: underlinings, marginal comments, and recite notes. You may now want to organize this information into one or more con-cept maps.

## F. Study-Reading Questions

When you have carefully studied the excerpt and your notes, answer the follow-ing ten questions without looking back. Place all your answers in the answer box.

1.  The fact that human beings do not look the same can be attributed to
    a. habitat
    b. genetic diversity
    c. the edge effect
    d. the differences among species
2.  One characteristic of ecosystems is that they
    a. are never large
    b. are never small
    c. are never made by humans
    d. vary in size
3.  A sustainable ecosystem must be able to
    a. support the organisms that live in it
    b. decompose and recycle its wastes
    c. continue to grow
    d. both a and b
4.  A biosphere is
    a. larger than an ecosystem
    b. another word for ecosystem
    c. smaller than an ecotone
    d. never sustainable

5. The edge effect describes
   a. aquatic life zones
   b. long-term weather in an ecosystem
   c. how an ecosystem is more diverse than an ecotone
   d. how an ecotone is more diverse than an ecosystem
6. Which of the following is most similar to a biome?
   a. genetic diversity
   b. population
   c. aquatic life zone
   d. edge effect
7. *Biodiversity* is a larger term that includes all but which *one* of the following?
   a. genetic diversity
   b. biological diversity
   c. species diversity
   d. ecological diversity
8. What does it mean that "biodiversity is nature's insurance policy against disasters" (paragraph 14)?
   a. Biodiversity allows human beings to protect themselves against dangerous pests.
   b. Biodiversity ensures natural recycling and genetic adaptation.
   c. Biodiversity relies on human beings to purify the world's waters.
   d. Biodiversity provides each species with genetic information.
9. An example of an autotroph is a
   a. meat eater
   b. green plant
   c. plant eater
   d. cockroach
10. Where do the decomposers fit into the process of breaking down organic material?
   a. They come before the scavengers.
   b. They come after the scavengers.
   c. They work at the same time as the scavengers.
   d. They are not part of this process.

| | |
|---|---|
| **Sel. 1**  S-Read | 1. _____ |
| **Score** _____ % | 2. _____ |
| ▶ 80% | 3. _____ |
| **Score** = number correct × 10. | 4. _____ |
| | 5. _____ |
| | 6. _____ |
| | 7. _____ |
| | 8. _____ |

9. _____

10. _____

**Check answers on p. 352.**

 G. For Discussion and Writing

1. How are populations, habitats, and biological communities related?
2. Reread paragraph 9. Provide reasons why a marsh can be considered an ecotone.
3. Explain why the survival of living things depends on biodiversity.
4. Reread paragraphs 18–20, then describe the differences between photosynthesis and chemosynthesis.
5. In paragraph 27, the author emphasizes the importance of decomposers in the survival of living things. In your own words, define *decomposers*. Then discuss their function. Finally, explain why they are central to the recycling process.

## Self-Evaluation—Environmental Science

Answer the following questions by circling yes or no. Your responses will help you assess your study-reading abilities in environmental science.

1. yes   no   Was your score in Section F, Study-Reading Questions, below 80 percent?

2. yes   no   Did you miss either question 6 or 7, which deal with the organizational pattern of definition?

3. yes   no   Did you miss question 10, which deals with the process organizational pattern?

4. yes   no   Did you have difficulty recalling the definitions of key terms presented in this excerpt?

5. yes   no   Did you have difficulty remembering the steps of various environmental processes, such as photosynthesis?

Scoring:   If you answered yes to two or more of these questions, you probably need more practice in reading environmental science material.

Follow-up:   To improve your skills in reading environmental science material, consider these suggestions:

1. When you come across a definition in your study reading, circle or underline the key elements in the definition and write *def.* in the margins. Understanding definitions is central to learning environmental science material.

2.  Realize that the process pattern is central to the structure of most environmental science material. In your reading, carefully identify the various steps in an environmental process. Determine how each step relates to the other, and see if you can remember the correct sequence of these steps.

3.  Whenever you can, relate a newly learned definition to a real-life environmental situation familiar to you.

# SELECTION 2

### Vocabulary

*leaching:* the removal of nutrients from the soil by the movement of water; "this promotes leaching of nutrients . . . on steep slopes"

*transpiration:* water evaporation from stems and leaves; "shifting rates of evaporation, transpiration, and runoff"

*biomass:* the combined weight of all organisms at a specific feeding level in an ecosystem; "carbon stored in their biomass"

*continental shelves:* the submerged shelves of land from the edge of a continent to where the steep descent to the ocean bottom begins; "and other fragile environments, such as continental shelves"

*greenhouse effect:* a natural effect that traps heat in the atmosphere; "and adds to the greenhouse effect"

*isotopes:* elements that have the same number of protons but different numbers of neutrons in their nuclei; "the remaining isotopes are still lethal"

"Changes in the Land" is an excerpt from a biology text. In this part of the textbook, the author focuses on how human beings have altered the world's landforms and forests. Like most biology material, this excerpt relies heavily on three organizational patterns: definition, cause-and-effect, and process. As you study-read this excerpt, be sure to reread any material structured by these three patterns.

Whereas the previous excerpt introduced key concepts in environmental studies, "Changes in the Land" focuses specifically on how life forms are affected by the way humans cultivate and mine the earth's various landforms. You will note that terms like *biome,* which was used in the previous excerpt, are used here as well.

### Reading Practices.
To read this material successfully, consider the following practices:

1.  Circle the key parts of a definition, or highlight them in a way that separates them from the rest of the material. Make appropriate marginal notes.

2.  See how the various definitions relate to each other—particularly, those of *desertification, deforestation,* and *shifting cultivation.*

3.  Note in the margins the major process and cause-and-effect patterns you find, especially the results of deforestation treated in paragraphs 5 and 9; the

effects of shifting cultivation in paragraph 7; and what occurs when the rates of evaporation, transpiration, and runoff change, analyzed in paragraph 8.

## A. Survey

Take 2 minutes to survey the excerpt. Read the chapter title, the headings, the terms in boldface print, and the figures. If time permits, begin reading the first paragraph or two as well as the last few paragraphs. When your time is up, answer the five questions without looking back at the excerpt. Place all your answers in the answer box.

## CHANGES IN THE LAND
### by Cecie Starr and Ralph Taggart (1,535 words)

### DESERTIFICATION

1    **Desertification** refers to the conversion of large tracts of grasslands, rain-fed cropland, or irrigated cropland to a more desertlike state, with a 10 percent or greater drop in agricultural productivity. In the past fifty years, 9 million square kilometers worldwide have become desertified. People are converting at least 200,000 square kilometers annually. Prolonged drought can accelerate the process, as it did in the American Great Plains many years ago. Today, overgrazing on marginal lands is the main cause of large-scale desertification.

2    In Africa, for example, there are too many cattle in the wrong places. Cattle require more water than the wild herbivores that are native to the region. This means the cattle have to move back and forth between grazing areas and watering holes. As they do, they trample grasses and compact the soil surface. By contrast, gazelles and other native herbivores get most (if not all) of their water from plants. They also are better water conservers; they lose little in feces, compared to cattle.

3    In 1978 a biologist, David Holpcraft, formed a ranch composed of antelopes, zebras, giraffes, ostriches, and other native herbivores.

He raised cattle as "control groups" in order to compare costs and meat yields on the same land. His initial results exceeded expectations. Native herds increased steadily and yielded meat. Range conditions improved rather than deteriorating. Vexing problems remained. African tribes have their own idea of what constitutes "good" meat, and some tribes view cattle as the symbols of wealth in their society.

### DEFORESTATION

4    The world's great forests profoundly influence the biosphere. Like giant sponges, forested watersheds absorb, hold, and gradually release water. By intervening in the downstream flow of water, forests help control soil erosion, flooding, and sediment buildup in rivers, lakes, and reservoirs.

5    **Deforestation** is the removal of all trees from large tracts of land for logging, agricultural, or grazing operations. The loss of vegetation cover exposes the soil, and this promotes leaching of nutrients and erosion, especially on steep slopes. Figure 50.12 provides views of deforestation in South America's Amazon basin.

6    In the tropics, clearing forests for agriculture leads to a long-term loss in productivity.

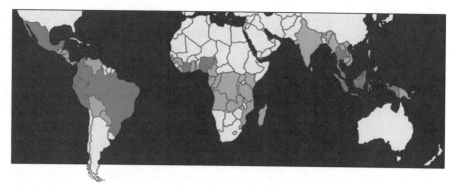

**Figure 50.12**  *Countries permitting the largest destruction of tropical forests. Red shading denotes where 2,000 to 14,800 square kilometers are deforested annually.* Orange *denotes "moderate" deforestation (100 to 1,900 square kilometers).*

The irony is that tropical forests are one of the worst places to grow crops and raise pasture animals. The high temperatures and heavy, frequent rainfall favor decomposition. In intact forests, organic remains and wastes decompose too fast for litter to build up. The forest trees and other plants absorb and assimilate nutrients as they become available.

7    **Shifting cultivation** (once called slash-and-burn agriculture) disrupts the forest ecosystem. People cut and burn trees, then till the ashes into the soil. The nutrient-rich ashes sustain crops for one to several seasons. Then, as a result of leaching, the cleared plots become infertile and are abandoned. Shifting cultivation on small, widely scattered plots may not damage forest ecosystems much, but fertility plummets when large areas are cleared and when plots are cleared again at shorter intervals.

8    Shifting rates of evaporation, transpiration, and runoff may even disrupt regional patterns of rainfall. Between 50 and 80 percent of the water vapor above tropical forests alone is released from the trees. Without trees, annual precipitation declines. Rain rapidly runs off the bare soil. As the region gets hotter and drier, soil fertility and moisture decline even more. In time, sparse grassland or even desertlike conditions prevail instead of a rich tropical forest.

9    Widespread tropical forest destruction may have global repercussions. These forests absorb much of the sunlight reaching equatorial regions of the earth's surface. When the forests are cleared, the land becomes shinier, so to speak, and reflects more incoming energy back into space. Also, by their photosynthetic activity, the great numbers of trees in these vast forest biomes help sustain the global cycling of carbon and oxygen. When trees are harvested or burned, carbon stored in their biomass is released to the atmosphere in the form of carbon dioxide—and this may be amplifying the greenhouse effect.

10    Almost half the world's tropical forests have been destroyed for cropland, grazing land, timber, and fuelwood. Deforestation is greatest in Brazil, Indonesia, Colombia, and Mexico. If clearing and destruction continue at present rates, only Brazil and Zaire will have large tropical forests in the year 2010. By 2035, most of their forests will be gone.

## A QUESTION OF ENERGY INPUTS

11    Paralleling the J-shaped curve of human population growth is a steep rise in total and per capita energy consumption. It is due to increased numbers of energy users and to extravagant consumption and waste. For example, in one of the most pleasant of all climates, a major university

constructed seven- and eight-story buildings with narrow, sealed windows. The windows can't be opened to catch prevailing ocean breezes. The buildings and windows were not designed or aligned to use sunlight for passive solar heating and breezes for passive cooling. Massive energy-demanding cooling and heating systems were installed.

12    When you hear talk of abundant energy supplies, keep in mind that there is a huge difference between the *total* and the *net* amounts available. Net energy is that left over after subtracting the energy used to locate, extract, transport, store, and deliver energy to consumers. Some energy sources, such as direct solar energy, are renewable. Others, such as coal and petroleum, are not. Currently, 83 percent of the energy stores being tapped are in the second category (Figure 50.13).

## Fossil Fuels

13    Forests that existed hundreds of millions of years ago gave us **fossil fuels.** Their carbon-

containing remains became buried and compressed in sediments, then were transformed into coal, petroleum (oil), and natural gas. They are nonrenewable resources.

14    Even with strict conservation, known petroleum and natural gas reserves may be used up in the next century. As known reserves run out in accessible areas, we explore wilderness areas in Alaska and other fragile environments, such as continental shelves. Net energy declines as costs of extraction and transportation to and from remote areas increase. Environmental costs of extraction and transportation escalate. The long-term impact of the 11-million-gallon spill from the tanker *Valdez* off Alaska's coast is still not understood.

15    What about coal? In theory, world reserves can meet the energy needs of the human population for at least several centuries. But coal burning has been the main source of air pollution. Most coal reserves contain low-quality, high-sulfur material. Unless sulfur is removed before or after burning, sulfur dioxides are released into the air. They add to the global problem of acid deposition. Fossil fuel burning also releases carbon dioxide and adds to the greenhouse effect.

16    Extensive strip mining of coal reserves close to the earth's surface carries its own problems. It removes land from agriculture, grazing, and wildlife. Restoration is difficult and expensive in arid and semiarid lands, where much of the trip mining is proceeding.

## Nuclear Energy

17    **Nuclear Reactors.** As Hiroshima burned in 1945, the world recoiled in horror from the destructive force of nuclear energy. By the 1950s, nuclear energy was being viewed as an instrument of progress. Many energy-poor industrialized nations, France included, now depend heavily on nuclear power. Yet new nuclear plants have been delayed or cancelled in most other countries. Since 1970, in the United States alone, plans for 117 nuclear power plants were cancelled. Other plants were abandoned before

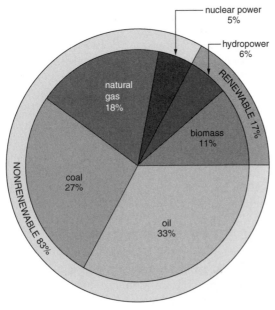

**Figure 50.13**   *World consumption of nonrenewable and renewable energy sources in 1991.*

completion. A few are being converted at great cost to fossil fuel burning.

18    Questions surround nuclear energy's costs, efficiency, safety record, and environmental impact. By 1990 in the United States, it cost slightly more to generate electricity by nuclear energy than by using coal. Energy from electricity now costs less. By the year 2000, solar energy with natural gas backup also should cost less.

19    What about safety? Less radioactivity and carbon dioxide normally escape from nuclear plants than from coal-burning plants of the same capacity and emit no sulfur dioxide. The danger lies with a potential for **meltdown.** As nuclear fuel breaks down, it releases considerable heat. Typically, water circulating over the fuel absorbs heat and produces steam that drives electricity-generating turbines. Should a leak develop in the circulating water system, water levels might plummet around the fuel, which might then heat past its melting point. On the generator floor, melting fuel would instantly convert the remaining water to steam. Together with other reactions, the formation of steam could blow the system apart and release radioactive material. Also, an overheated reactor core could melt through its thick concrete containment slab and contaminate groundwater.

20    Is this scenario far-fetched? The *Focus* essay suggests not, but this is a controversial issue.

21    **Nuclear Waste Disposal.**  Unlike coal, nuclear fuel cannot be burned to harmless ashes.

The fuel elements are spent after about three years, but they still contain uranium fuel and hundreds of new radioisotopes formed during the reactions. The wastes are extremely radioactive and dangerous. As they undergo radioactive decay, they become extremely hot. They are plunged at once into water-filled pools. The water cools them and keeps radioactive material from escaping. After being stored for several months, the remaining isotopes are still lethal. Some must be isolated for at least 10,000 years. If one kind of plutonium isotope ($239^{Pu}$) is not removed, the wastes must be kept isolated for a quarter of a million years!

22    After nearly fifty years of research, scientists still cannot agree on the best way to store high-level radioactive wastes. Even if they could do so, there is no politically acceptable solution. No one wants radioactive wastes anywhere near where they live.

23    Finally, following the Soviet Union's breakup, underpaid workers of a Russian nuclear power plant have been selling fuel elements on the black market. The buyers appear to be developing nations that want to produce nuclear weapons—and possibly put them in the hands of terrorist organizations.

Cecie Starr and Ralph Taggart, *Biology: The Unity and Diversity of Life*, 7th ed., 902–905. © 1995 by Wadsworth, Inc. Reprinted by permission of Brooks/Cole Publishing.

• • • • • • • • • • • • • • • • • • • • • • • • • • • • • • • • • • •

1.  The first paragraph discusses
    a.  deforestation
    b.  shifting cultivation
    c.  desertification
    d.  all of these terms
2.  Which of the following topics is *not* covered in the excerpt?
    a.  desertification
    b.  deforestation
    c.  fossil fuels
    d.  acid rain

3. In this excerpt, most key terms are
   a. underlined
   b. placed at the top of each page
   c. put in quotation marks
   d. put in boldface
4. The figures concern
   a. the destruction of tropical rain forests
   b. world consumption of energy
   c. nuclear reactors throughout the world
   d. both a and b
5. The excerpt ends with a discussion of the strip mining of coal.
   a. true
   b. false

---

**Sel. 2**   Sur

**Score** \_\_\_\_\_ %

      ▶ 80%

**Score** = number correct × 20.

1. \_\_\_\_\_
2. \_\_\_\_\_
3. \_\_\_\_\_
4. \_\_\_\_\_
5. \_\_\_\_\_

**Check answers with your instructor.**

---

## B. Question

Having surveyed the excerpt, list here five questions you intend to answer when you study-read. Create these questions from the title and headings.

1. _____
2. _____
3. _____
4. _____
5. _____

Ask your instructor for sample questions.

## C. Read

With all these questions in mind, read the selection carefully. You may want to read it through once you begin marking. When you do begin to mark, remember to underline only parts of sentences if possible to write sparingly.

## D.  Recite

Without looking back at the excerpt, write down in note-taking or paragraph form the important points made in the excerpt. When you have finished your summary, compare it with the excerpt. How accurate were you?

## E.  Review

Now review all of your material: underlinings, marginal comments, and recite notes. You may want to organize this information into one or more concept maps.

## F.  Study-Reading Questions

When you have carefully studied the excerpt and your notes, answer the following ten questions without looking back. Place all your answers in the answer box.

1.  The main cause of desertification is
    a.  drought
    b.  rain
    c.  grazing by antelopes
    d.  overgrazing
2.  Deforestation leads to
    a.  erosion and leaching of soil
    b.  more rainfall
    c.  lowering of temperature
    d.  more snowfall
3.  Why are tropical forests poor places to grow crops?
    a.  Litter decomposes too fast for trees to absorb it.
    b.  There is too little oxygen.
    c.  It is too humid.
    d.  all of these
4.  What is *shifting cultivation*?
    a.  Crops are rotated to other fertile areas every year.
    b.  Trees are cut and burned, and their ashes are worked into the soil.
    c.  Plots of land are fertilized with cow manure.
    d.  Mountain terrain is used to grow crops.
5.  Which of the following statements is *not* true of tropical forests?
    a.  They absorb much of the sunlight coming into the region.
    b.  They help to cycle carbon and oxygen throughout the world.
    c.  They are being destroyed at an alarming rate in Indonesia.
    d.  When their trees are chopped down, this action prevents the release of carbon dioxide into the atmosphere.
6.  Which of the following statements is *not* true about the use of coal as a fuel?
    a.  It is a major cause of air pollution.
    b.  It has a low sulfur content.
    c.  Its burning has helped create the greenhouse effect.
    d.  It has destroyed some land that could have been used for agriculture.

7. A meltdown is
   a. the burning of radioactive material
   b. the explosion of an atomic bomb
   c. the accidental melting of a nuclear reactor's core
   d. how nuclear reactors produce energy
8. The most negative aspect of using nuclear energy is that it
   a. is too expensive
   b. creates a greenhouse effect in the atmosphere
   c. emits too much carbon dioxide in the atmosphere
   d. produces radioactive wastes that are dangerous to store
9. Of the following energy sources, which one is *unlike* the others?
   a. coal
   b. the sun
   c. natural gas
   d. oil
10. Which energy source is the *least* used?
   a. nuclear energy
   b. hydropower
   c. natural gas
   d. coal

| | |
|---|---|
| **Sel. 2**  S-Read | 1. _____ |
| **Score** _____ % | 2. _____ |
| ▶ 80% | 3. _____ |
| **Score** = number correct × 10. | 4. _____ |
| | 5. _____ |
| | 6. _____ |
| | 7. _____ |
| | 8. _____ |
| | 9. _____ |
| | 10. _____ |
| | **Check answers with your instructor.** |

## G. For Discussion and Writing

1. Define *desertification* and *deforestation*. How are these processes similar? How do they differ?
2. Why does it seem that cattle do more damage to the land than do gazelles? Why is this particularly troublesome for the meat consumption practices of such countries as the United States?
3. Reread paragraph 8. List the four results of a change in evaporation, transpiration, and runoff.
4. Reread paragraph 9. Explain the two global effects of tropical forest destruction.
5. Of the three energy sources discussed in this excerpt—petroleum and natural gas, coal, and nuclear reactions—which source wields the greatest damage to the environment? Why?

## Self-Evaluation—Biology

Answer the following questions by circling yes or no. Your responses will help you assess your study-reading abilities in biology.

1. yes   no   Was your score in Section F, Study-Reading Questions, below 80 percent?

2. yes   no   Did you miss questions 1 and 2, which deal with the organizational pattern of cause-and-effect?

3. yes   no   Did you miss questions 4 and 7, which deal with the organizational pattern of definition?

4. yes   no   Did you have difficulty recalling the definitions of key terms presented in this excerpt?

5. yes   no   Did you have difficulty visualizing the major processes related to desertification and deforestation?

6. yes   no   Were the figures difficult for you to understand?

Scoring:       If you answered yes to three or more of these questions, you probably need more practice in reading biology texts.

Follow-up:     To improve your skills in reading biology texts, consider these suggestions:

1. When you come across a definition in your study reading, circle or underline the key elements of the definition and write *def.* in the margin. Understanding definitions is crucial to understanding biology.

2. Make careful marginal notes listing the major causes and effects of a biological process. Have the correct sequence clearly in mind before you take an exam on the subject.

3. Realize that understanding the cause-and-effect pattern is key to reading texts in biology. Carefully separate cause

from effect. Also determine if several factors causes an effect, such as the influences of deforestation and shifting cultivation on climatic changes.

4.   Whenever possible, try to visualize the biological or physical processes discussed in your reading, such as the processes involved in tropical forest destruction. Visualizing is an important aid to remembering material in biology.

•  •  •  •  •  •  •  •  •  •  •  •  •  •  •  •  •  •  •

# SELECTION 3

**Vocabulary**

*synthetic:* not of natural origin; "synthetic chemical compounds"

*compost:* to make a mixture of decaying organic matter; "a program that composts grass clippings"

*greenhouse effect:* a natural effect that traps heat in the atmosphere; "to counteract the greenhouse effect"

*ballasts:* heavy materials used to provide stability; "energy-efficient ballasts"

*antitrust laws:* laws concerned with breaking up huge businesses or monopolies; "by government antitrust laws"

This excerpt comes from the textbook *Introduction to Business*. In this excerpt, the authors discuss the strategies that industries have recently used to help clean up the environment and protect their consumers. Unlike the previous two selections, which are scientific, this excerpt presents political and economic perspectives on the environment: How do businesses respond to the government's environmental and consumer legislation? How effective is this response? Also, unlike Selection 2, this passage presents a more optimistic picture of environmental cleanup, although the authors admit that industry continues to pollute.

The authors' style is characterized by fact-filled sentences, such as discussions of percentages and metric tons to show how industry is responding to environmental legislation. Like most business readings, this excerpt has three organizational patterns: definition, problem-solution, and examples. You have already seen definitions in the previous selections. In this excerpt, you will see how the examples pattern gives the authors various ways to prove their point. In studying the problem-solution pattern, you will be able to examine how business professionals go about solving a problem.

**Reading Practices.**   To read this excerpt successfully, consider the following practices:

1.   When you come across a definition printed in boldface, circle or highlight the key parts of it. Write *def.* in the margin next to the term. As you continue reading, try to see how one definition is related to a subsequent definition. When you finish, make sure you have marked the following terms: *hazardous waste, recycling,* and *consumerism.*

2.  Note the several uses of the problem-solution pattern by identifying them in the margin. You may even want to include marginal comments at the top or bottom of the page, as follows: X (problem) → Y (solution). This will help you see how businesses respond to the following issues: (1) hazardous wastes, (2) solid wastes, (3) environmental maintenance, (4) energy conservation, and (5) consumer protection. Also note that most business material concentrates on the success or failure of its solutions.

3.  See if you can understand the figure and table. You may want to make marginal comments to highlight the significant points and conclusions about pollution reduction that the figure and table suggest.

4.  Before reciting this information, see if you can define the key terms out loud and can present three or four significant contributions industry has made to help the environment and the consumer.

## A. Survey

Take 2 minutes to survey the excerpt. Read the chapter title, headings, terms in boldface print, sections in italics, as well as the figure and table. If time permits, begin reading the first paragraph or two. Place all your answers in the answer box.

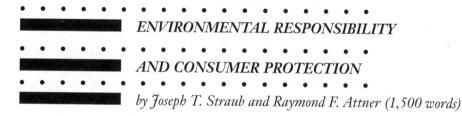

## ENVIRONMENTAL RESPONSIBILITY
## AND CONSUMER PROTECTION
*by Joseph T. Straub and Raymond F. Attner (1,500 words)*

## ENVIRONMENTAL RESPONSIBILITY

1   Environmental preservation, maintenance, and restoration must rank high on any corporation's list of social concerns. The advent of synthetic chemical compounds and materials and of exotic manufacturing processes means that the environment has become polluted. Actions have to be taken to eliminate the causes, and firms that are responsible must be held accountable. With this realization, there has been much environmental progress. Since Earth Day 1970, when Americans first began to "think green":

*   Miles of polluted rivers and streams have been brought back to life.

*   The number of cities with adequate sewage treatment plants has more than doubled.

*   The pumping of sewage sludge into the ocean has ceased.

*   Major air pollutants have been considerably reduced, as shown in Figure 2.4.

2   The business sector must continue its commitment. There are still problems in the areas of hazardous and solid waste and environmental maintenance.

### Hazardous Wastes

3   The problem with **hazardous wastes**—*waste materials containing toxic substances*—is one common to land, water, and air pollution.

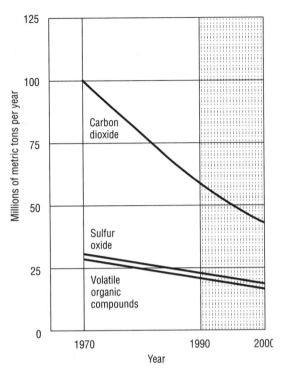

**Figure 2.4**   *Reducing air pollution.*

| Company | Millions of Pounds of Pollutant Released | |
|---|---|---|
| | **1987** | **1992** |
| American Cyanamid, Westwego, LA | 213.4 | 142.0 |
| Shell Oil Company, Norco, LA | 194.2 | 2.6 |
| Monsanto, Alvin, TX | 175.6 | 54.8 |
| Kennecott-Utah-Copper, Bingham Canyon, UT | 158.7 | 16.3 |

Source: Environmental Protection Agency.

**Table 2.2**   *A report card on the big polluters.*

According to recent estimates, industrial operations produce more than 50 million tons of hazardous waste each year, an average of 14.2 tons for each square mile of land mass in the forty-eight contiguous states. While generating products that benefit consumers in various ways, many manufacturing processes produce toxic chemical waste faster than it can be disposed of. Farsighted business leaders see this situation and give more than lip service to environmental concerns.

4    Recent data from the Environmental Protection Agency show that the toxic releases of U.S. manufacturers are falling. What's more, chemical makers that pump out the largest share of these poisons cut their emissions by 35 percent between 1987 and 1992, as shown in Table 2.2.

5    One factor that has led to this decrease is the chemical industry's voluntary program to reduce toxic air pollutants below the standards set by the 1990 Clean Air Act. Nine of the nation's biggest polluters, including Du Pont and Monsanto, signed on with the understanding that they could use the technology of their choice. At the same time, the Chemical Manufacturer's Association committed to pollution control. The results speak for themselves.

**Solid Wastes**

6    Besides hazardous waste, there is the basic problem of solid waste generated through packaging, bottling, and product construction. Experience and mistakes with waste disposal over the last three decades have shown that waste cannot be simply thrown away. About 64 percent of the country's growing mountain of waste is paper and paperboard, metals, glass, and plastics.

7    In response to difficulties with solid waste disposal, organizations have attempted to provide alternative packaging that can help in the decomposition of products. Another area of emphasis has been to limit the manufacturing of new products by **recycling,** *the practice of reclaiming or producing materials from previously manufactured products and using them to make other items.* At the present time only 11 percent of solid waste is recycled.

8    Recycling opportunities exist in all areas of a business. Instead of discarding its cocoa-bean hulls, Hershey Foods Corporation reportedly

grinds them up and sells them as garden mulch. Fiberboard and pressboard made from sawdust and wood chips enable economy-minded forest products firms to convert virtually every splinter of a tree into a salable product. In some manufacturing plants, heat from production processes is cycled through the heating system to heat the building. The Adolph Coors brewery once generated most of its needed electricity from recycled waste materials. The cumulative effects of recycling are impressive:

- Mississippi River water is used at least eight times on its journey to the Gulf of Mexico.
- Forty percent of all new copper is made from recycled copper.
- Twenty percent of the glass we use comes from recycled scraps and shards that are melted down and mixed with new material.

9   Organizations that have committed to recycling are varied:

- Gardner's Supply, a mail order company in Burlington, Vermont, committed to a program that composts grass clippings and leaves for free in the local area. The program has been so successful that it collects 3,000 to 4,000 tons per year.
- Yakima Products, Inc., a car-rack maker in Arcata, California, was unable to avoid using plastic and foam in packing its high-end roof-rack systems. The company created a way for customers to easily mail the packaging materials back—free. It then reuses the foam and polyethylene-shell portions of the container and recycles the outer chipboard.
- The Boston Park Plaza Hotel has become immersed in recycling. Wooden pallets on which food is delivered to the hotel—up to 100 each week—are now returned to the vender and reused. The housekeeping staff makes chefs' aprons from damaged tablecloths. And, guests' returnable bottles are recycled—resulting in the purchase of several new vacuums.

**Environmental Maintenance**

10   In addition to solid waste problems, industry has another major social concern: overall environmental maintenance of water, air, and land. Business has begun to address this area. For example:

- E&J Gallo Winery gave $250,000 to the American Forestry Association's Global Relief Program, whose goal is to plant 100 million trees in the United States to counteract the greenhouse effect.
- Apple Computer donated $40,000 worth of computer equipment to Earth Day 1990.
- Timberland Shoes gave $250,000 to the Wilderness Society to assist in accomplishing its goals.
- Du Pont voluntarily spends $50 million each year on environmental projects beyond what the law requires, such as the $15 million it spent at a Texas plant to reduce the risk of dangerous gases being released.

## ENERGY PROGRAMS

11   Companies have approached the energy situation from two directions: internal consumption efficiency and public programs. In the first area, organizations have attempted to use alternative means of energy, if possible, but many more have focused on developing or purchasing more efficient equipment. For example, Fox River Mills, a manufacturer of gloves and athletic socks, spent $40,000 on measures to improve energy efficiency and reduced the company's monthly utility bill by about $3,000. The company installed energy-efficient ballasts in 600 fluorescent lights, moved the lights closer to the work being performed, added six inches of insulation to outside walls, installed white steel inner walls to reflect light, and directed wasted heat from air compressors and boilers inside its facility to heat part of the building in cold months.

12   In the second area, firms have encouraged the use of van pooling. This public program has a twofold benefit: it reduces the amount of fuel consumed by using one vehicle instead of six, and

it reduces traffic congestion on already snarled streets and freeways.

## CONSUMER PROTECTION

13    In recent years another major area of concentration for businesses has been **consumerism**—*activities undertaken to protect the rights of the consumer.* To genuinely partner with society, businesses cannot simply produce a product and place it on the market. Consumer protection involves consumer rights: the right to product safety, to be informed, to choose, and to be heard.

### Product Safety

14    Businesses have spent time and money to improve the safety of products. Spurred on by the fear of lawsuits and consumer action, they have initiated a number of innovative ideas to ensure product safety.

15    Companies spend millions of dollars researching product safety. The auto industry has developed padded dashboards, shock-absorbing steering columns, and stronger gasoline tanks. Many companies have delayed the release of products until conclusive results of testing have been obtained, have initiated product recalls when their testing has discovered problems, and have attempted to identify product purchasers to make recalls less difficult.

### Consumer Information

16    Consumers have the right to have access to complete information about a product before they buy it, including information on potential dangers associated with the product. In response, companies have provided specific information on labels of food containers, and tags on clothing contain information on fabric composition and care. In addition, companies have co-sponsored, with retailers, workshops or clinics where consumers can see demonstrations of products and receive answers to their questions. Companies have produced extensive operating instructions, safety procedures, and practical uses of products to be provided to consumers at the time of purchase.

### Product Choice

17    Consumers have the right in the marketplace to choose between products offered by competing producers and marketers. This right is assured through the competition in the private enterprise system and by government antitrust laws.

### Voicing Concerns

18    Consumers have the right to be listened to and to have action taken when it is justified. A number of manufacturers have developed systematic programs to deal with consumer issues. A number of companies have established toll-free numbers for consumers to use to solve operating problems or receive product advice. Maytag introduced Red Carpet Service to improve its response to repair problems. General Electric operates the GE Answer Center, which handles consumer inquiries twenty-four hours a day, seven days a week, via a toll-free number. It receives 3 million calls each year. The center responds to questions from potential consumers and do-it-yourselfers and tries to resolve complaints from disgruntled customers.

• • • • • • • • • • • • • • • • • • • • • • • • • • • • • • • • •

1.   This excerpt focuses on
   a.  the environment
   b.  the government
   c.  how business attempts to protect the environment
   d.  pollution

2. The figure focuses on
    a. the amount of pollution in the United States
    b. money lost by industries that pollute
    c. the reduction of air pollution
    d. the number of industries that do not pollute
3. This excerpt is broken up into _____ main section(s) set off by full capitalization.
    a. one
    b. two
    c. three
    d. more than three
4. Definitions
    a. are placed at the end of the selection
    b. are set off in boldface print
    c. are defined in italics
    d. both b and c
5. This excerpt will *not* discuss industry's response to
    a. hazardous wastes
    b. recycling
    c. maintaining the environment
    d. Bill Clinton's energy conservation proposals

---

**Sel. 3**   Sur                    1. _____

**Score**  _____%                   2. _____

          ▶ 80%                     3. _____

**Score** = number correct × 20.    4. _____

                                    5. _____

Check answers on p. 352.

---

## B. Question

List here five questions you intend to answer when you study-read. Compose them from the title, headings, and words and phrases in italics that you surveyed.

1. _____
2. _____
3. _____
4. _____
5. _____

Find sample questions on page 352.

## C. Read

With all these questions in mind, read the excerpt carefully. You may want to read it once through before you begin marking. When you do begin to mark the excerpt, remember to underline only parts of sentences if possible and to write notes sparingly.

## D. Recite

Without looking back, write down in note-taking or paragraph form the important points of the excerpt. After you have finished your summary, compare it with the excerpt. How accurate were you?

## E. Review

Now review all your material: underlinings, marginal comments, and recite notes. You may want to organize this material into one or more study maps.

## F. Study-Reading Questions

When you have carefully studied the excerpt and your notes, answer the following ten questions without looking back. Place all your answers in the answer box.

1. The authors admit that industry often
   a. produces more toxic waste than it can eliminate
   b. eliminates all the toxic waste that it produces
   c. disobeys the government's toxic-waste legislation
   d. works with other industries to sidestep environmental laws
2. The industries that produce the most toxic waste are
   a. plastics companies
   b. chemical manufacturers
   c. automobile manufacturers
   d. paper manufacturers
3. In the figure on air pollution, which substance has been reduced the most in the atmosphere?
   a. volatile organic compounds
   b. sulfur oxide
   c. carbon dioxide
   d. lead
4. Which of the following is *not* mentioned as a solid waste that industry produces?
   a. wood
   b. paper
   c. glass
   d. plastics
5. One of business's solutions to solid waste that the authors mention is
   a. alternative packaging
   b. chemical decomposition

      c. burning

      d. dumping

6. The authors note that the Adolph Coors brewery once created its electricity by

      a. building a hydroelectric plant

      b. recycling waste products

      c. harnessing solar energy

      d. harnessing wind energy

7. Which action is *not* an example of business helping maintain the environment?

      a. Gallo Winery gave a monetary contribution to the American Forestry Association.

      b. Apple Computer contributed to Earth Day 1990.

      c. Timberland Shoes supported the Wilderness Society.

      d. Maytag introduced the Red Carpet Service to help its customers with their repair problems.

8. The authors note that businesses have improved the safety of their products because

      a. they fear lawsuits by consumers

      b. they have been given financial assistance from the federal government

      c. they want to increase their profits

      d. they want to compete with other consumer-conscious corporations

9. Which is an example of business's response to consumer protection?

      a. Fox River Mills spent $40,000 to improve energy efficiency.

      b. General Electric operates the GE Answer Center.

      c. Wooden pallets in the Boston Park Plaza Hotel are being reused.

      d. Hershey Foods grinds cocoa-bean hulls into garden mulch.

10. This excerpt generally depicts U.S. industry as being

      a. the leader in environmental protection

      b. reluctant to enforce consumer protection laws

      c. hostile to environmental legislation

      d. supportive of environmental legislation

---

**Sel. 3    S-Read**

**Score** _____ %

▶ 80%

**Score** = number correct × 10.

1. _____
2. _____
3. _____
4. _____
5. _____
6. _____
7. _____
8. _____

> 9. ____
>
> 10. ____
>
> **Check answers on p. 352.**

 G. For Discussion and Writing

1. In paragraphs 3–5, the authors discuss how industry is solving the hazardous waste problem. Choose three of the most convincing facts from these paragraphs and from the table to show industry's success in dealing with hazardous waste. Do you think these examples are impressive? Why or why not?
2. In paragraphs 6–9, the authors discuss industry's response to recycling. Select three examples of industrial recycling mentioned in this excerpt and show why they are intelligent recycling methods or not.
3. Study Figure 2.4, "Reducing air pollution." In a paragraph, analyze what this figure states and suggests.
4. In paragraphs 11–12, the authors discuss energy programs sponsored by industry. What energy programs do they mention? Provide three other energy programs of your own that industry could employ to conserve energy.
5. Examine the evidence the authors use to support their contention that industry is protecting the environment. Which examples from the excerpt do you find *least* convincing? Why?

## Self-Evaluation—Business

Answer the following questions by circling yes or no. Your responses will help you assess your study-reading abilities in business material.

1. yes   no   Was your score in Section F, Study-Reading Questions, below 80 percent?

2. yes   no   Was it hard to remember the definitions of key terms?

3. yes   no   Did you have a hard time seeing how the various environmental terms related to each other?

4. yes   no   Did you find it difficult to remember the various ways business responded to a particular environmental problem?

5. yes   no   Were the figure and table difficult for you to understand?

Scoring:       If you answered yes to three or more of these questions, you probably need more practice in reading business textbooks.

Follow-up:     To improve your skills in reading business material, consider these suggestions:

1. Watch for problem-solution patterns in your reading of business material. Accurately identify the problem and re-

state its solutions, then carefully consider these various solutions.

2. Business material also relies heavily on the definition pattern. You must know the meanings of business terms before you can discuss the material intelligently. To learn each term, circle the key parts of the definition and write *def.* in the margins. By the time you review, you should be able to define the key terms without looking back at the text.

3. You will find many graphs and tables in business textbooks. To read graphs, you must clearly understand what the horizontal and vertical lines represent, as well as their relation to each other. As you study-read, refer to the graph to help explain concepts presented in the text. When you study tables, be sure to understand the topic and all categories identified in the table. Then, study the numbers in each column to see how they relate to each other and whether they make a significant conclusion. Often, business writers can condense several pages of material into one graph or table, which provides an efficient visual summary.

4. Business material is result oriented; that is, it often presents facts and figures to support the success or failure of a particular project. You need to evaluate these results to see if they are convincing—if, in fact, the examples support the author's claims. For example, as you read about business and the environment, you would ask the following questions: Do the examples support the claim that the company has significantly contributed to environmental cleanup? Are the results long- or short-term? What are the company's future plans for environmental cleanup?

• • • • • • • • • • • • • • • • • • •

# SELECTION 4

### Vocabulary

*postnatal:* referring to events occurring after birth; "normal postnatal human beings have moral standing"

*anencephalic:* referring to that which has no brain; "anencephalic or (less but) radically defective infants"

*comatose:* being in a coma, or unconscious; "irreversibly comatose humans"

*divine providence:* God's plan; "according to divine providence"

*callousness:* insensitivity; "humans may learn callousness"

*unconditional:* without qualification; "because of their unconditional worth"

*anthropocentric paradigm:* the view that the human being is the center of the universe; "to challenge the anthropocentric paradigm" *sentience:* a state in which an organism can perceive through its senses; "mere consciousness or sentience"

*correlative:* a relationship in which one implies the other; "rights can be correlative with duties"

This excerpt is part of the introduction to an environmental ethics textbook, which discusses philosophical perspectives on environmental pollution. Here, you will consider what philosophers have said about how human beings should relate to their environment. Two writing patterns predominate: definition and time sequence. The authors present the arguments of renowned philosophers such as Aristotle, Thomas Aquinas, and Immanuel Kant. Each philosopher uses specific terminology to explain the environment and carefully sequences his arguments to support a pro- or anti-environmental position.

**Reading Practices.**    To read this excerpt successfully, consider the following practices:

1. Circle or highlight the key parts of important definitions. In marginal notes, show how various terms relate to one another.
2. Read each philosopher's argument carefully; in marginal or study notes, present the key steps in each argument.
3. Compare each philosopher's argument and his definitions of related terms. See where these philosophers agree or disagree.
4. By the end of your reading, you should be able to determine how each philosopher defines a human being, an animal, and an inanimate object.

## A. Survey

Take 3 minutes to survey the excerpt. Note the boldface print as well as the words and phrases in italics. If time permits, read the first few and the last few paragraphs in the excerpt.

## *THE ENVIRONMENT AND ETHICAL THEORIES*

*by Donald VanDeVeer and Christine Pierce (2,700 words)*

### HUMAN ORGANISMS

1    Talk of environmental ethics, ecological ethics, the preservation of nature calls to mind concerns about protection of individual animals or rare species; preserving clean air, wilderness areas, groves of redwood trees; avoiding the destruction of the wonders of nature such as the Grand Canyon; or the sense of loss when woods and pastures are transformed into concatenations of steel, concrete, plastic, and neon. It is a bit surprising, then, when the suggestion is made that there is a link between some of the basic issues in environmental ethics and certain perplexing issues often classified as matters of bio-

medical ethics such as abortion. Given our prior discussion, however, the link is more evident. If we agree that normal postnatal human beings have moral standing, whether "all things human" do is a matter of some dispute. Several sorts of entities deserve special consideration: (1) human fetuses, (2) anencephalic or (less but) radically defective infants, (3) irreversibly comatose humans, (4) newly dead human bodies. Let us use *NPH* to stand for these nonparadigmatic humans. Do any or all NPH have moral standing? If so, what sorts of duties are directly owed to NPH? Must we make equally stringent efforts to preserve or protect (or somehow "respect") such beings—as are required in our dealings with normal humans?

2    If the familiar contrast between "man and nature" is to be understood as one between normal neonatal humans and things that cannot be so classified, that is, everything else, then NPH are a part of "nature." As noted, according to one view what is part of nature (other than paradigm humans) can be used as a natural resource, for example, for the benefit of (paradigm) humans. Reasoning rather like this may be behind the view that we ought to put to good use, for example, aborted fetuses, the recently dead (where all respiratory and circulatory functions have irreversibly ceased), or those in a persistent vegetative state (sometimes described as brain-dead). There is a great need for organs for transplantation, a need for blood, for growth hormone, and so on. Hence, some regard the failure to "mine" NPH (or some subset) as a shameful waste—given the scarcity of resources valuable to paradigmatic humans. Disputes about these matters depend in part on ascertaining the appropriate criterion of moral standing. As we have noted, if by *natural resource* what is meant is "what it is morally permissible to use to benefit those with moral standing," one theoretical (and practical) connection of environmental ethics and biomedical ethics is clear. If we are to reassess or query *What's so important about animals?* Or rare species, jungles, wilderness, mountains, or redwoods? it is not out of place to consider *What's so important about people?*—Or nonparadigmatic humans—as well.

## TRADITIONAL ETHICAL THEORIES
### Natural Law Morality and Judeo-Christian Morality

3    Traditional morality is often associated with the view that there is a certain natural and morally defensible hierarchy of beings. There is, it is claimed, a natural order according to which inanimate objects are to serve animate ones; further, plants are here for the sake of animals, and animals for the sake of humans. It is, thus, right and proper, for the "higher" to use the "lower," as the former see fit. Throughout history this view has rarely been questioned. It is a view implicit in much (at least) of natural law theory dating back to Aristotle (384–322 B.C.) and in Thomas Aquinas's (1225–1274) theological revision of Aristotelianism. In theological versions, of course, the natural order is seen as part of the divine order—and people are around for the sake of God—and are to function within the constraints laid down by divine purposes.

4    In *The Politics* Aristotle says,

> plants exist for the sake of animals. . . . all other animals exist for the sake of man, tame animals for the use he can make of them as well as for the food they provide; and as for wild animals, most though not all of these can be used for food and are useful in other ways; clothing and instruments can be made out of them. If then we are right in believing that nature makes nothing without some end in view, nothing to no purpose, it must be that nature has made all things specifically for the sake of man.

Elsewhere in *The Politics* Aristotle compares the function of women to that of animals in an effort to explain the low position of each in the hierarchy of being:

> As between male and female the former is by nature superior and ruler, the latter inferior and subject. . . . Wherever there is the same wide discrepancy between two sets of human beings as there is between mind and body or between man and beast, then the inferior of the two sets, those whose condition is such that their function is the

use of their bodies and nothing better can be expected of them, those, I say, are slaves by nature.

In short, those with less rationality exist to serve the needs, interests, or good of those with more. One's place in the hierarchy of being reflects Aristotle's judgment concerning one's rational abilities.

5    Aquinas, like Aristotle, makes it clear that to kill and otherwise use animals for human purposes is part of the natural order of things. In the *Summa Contra Gentiles*, Aquinas says,

> we refute the error of those who claim that it is a sin for man to kill brute animals. For animals are ordered to man's use in the natural course of things, according to divine providence. Consequently, man uses them without any injustice, either by killing them or by employing them in any other way. For this reason, God said to Noe: "As the green herbs, I have delivered all flesh to you." (Genesis 9:3).

6    In Aquinas's view, animals have no independent moral standing or intrinsic goodness. Aquinas thought that we ought not to be cruel to animals, not because animals have an interest in not suffering, but because if such cruelty is allowed, humans may learn callousness and inflict it on their fellow humans:

> Man's affections may be either of reason or of sentiment. As regards the former, it is indifferent how one behaves towards animals, since God has given him dominion over all as it is written, "thou has subjected all things under his feet." It is in this sense that St. Paul says that God has no care for oxen or other animals. . . . As to affection arising from sentiment, it is operative with regard to animals. . . . And if he is often moved in this way, he is more likely to have compassion for his fellow-men. . . .

7    According to Genesis, God has given human beings dominion over the earth: "Be fruitful and multiply, and replenish the earth, and subdue it; and have dominion over the fish of the sea, and over the fowl of the air, and over every living thing that moveth upon the earth." There is, in the recent literature on animal liberation and environmental ethics, a dispute over the interpretation of the biblical notion of dominion. Some say that (1) dominion permits humans to do whatever they want with animals, plants, rivers, and rocks. Others claim that (2) dominion means stewardship. According to this view God expects us to exercise some responsibility toward the earth. The earth belongs to God and we are commanded to take care of it and the creatures that dwell therein.

8    A stewardship interpretation may be committed to an acceptance of a traditional private property view. That is, humans should not ruthlessly exploit the earth because the earth is God's. If we ought to treat the earth in a responsible and virtuous way, it is not because the earth and its creatures have independent moral standing or intrinsic goodness, but because it is God's property. It is important to note that this result—the lack of independent moral standing on the part of any being except humans—seems to follow from either interpretation of dominion. This is not a surprising outcome. In the history of ethics, Aristotle and Aquinas exemplify what is called *virtue ethics*. In this tradition, for example, if one is not cruel to animals, it is because one believes that cruelty is a vice. It was too early in the history of thought for the notion of a right, that is, for the idea that there is something about the being or entity toward whom (or which) we act that must be respected, that makes it or them not simply the beneficiaries of our good character.

## Natural Rights Theory

9    **The Kantian Argument.**    It is generally accepted that persons are the sorts of being that have rights. Immanuel Kant, a German philosopher (1724–1804), provided the original argument that explains what persons are and why they have rights.

10    Kant explicates what a person is by distinguishing persons from things. Persons are rational, autonomous beings who are capable of formulating and pursuing different conceptions of the good. That is, persons have ends of their

own; things or objects in the world do not. For example, suppose I walk into a classroom and decide to break up all the chairs in order to use them for firewood. If I do this, it does not matter to the chairs. Now, there may be many reasons why I should not destroy the chairs. The next class may be planning to sit on them. Presumably, somebody owns the chairs and does not want me to destroy them. However, I cannot give as a reason for refraining from breaking the chairs that it matters to the chairs. It can even be said that it is in the interests of chairs not to be broken (or in the interests of lawnmowers not to be left out in the rain), but this is not the same as claiming that chairs or lawnmowers have interests of their own if we mean by this that chairs or lawnmowers care about how they are treated. Persons care about how they are treated; things do not. According to Kant, things can be used to suit the purposes of persons, but persons are not to be used as if they were mere things, as if they had no ends or purposes of their own. Persons have rights because of their unconditional worth as rational beings, whereas the worth of things is relative to the ends of persons.

11    Conceptually, it is difficult, if not impossible, to extend rights to environmental objects such as rocks and streams on a Kantian analysis of rights. This is so for the following reason: According to this analysis, rights are designed to protect persons from being treated as things. Rocks and streams are paradigm cases of things or objects; they are incapable of formulating ends. *Thing*, in Kant, is a technical term. Something is a *thing* if it is incapable of autonomy in the Kantian sense which entails self-rule, that is, formulating and following rational principles. Hence, inanimate objects do not have rights in Kant's view. Nonetheless, we may have duties regarding inanimate objects. These duties, Kant maintained, are indirect duties toward human beings, as the following quotation shows:

> Destructiveness is immoral; we ought not to destroy things which can still be put to some use. No man ought to mar the beauty of nature; for what he has no use for may still be of use to some one else.

He need, of course, pay no heed to the thing itself, but he ought to consider his neighbor.

12    Animals are also considered "things" in Kant's scheme. In his *Lectures on Ethics*, he referred to animals as "man's instruments." Despite Kant's innovative work on the subject of rights, many older notions persist in his philosophy. The idea that animals, like any tool, exist for the use of human beings is one example. Likewise, we find in Kant the idea that our treatment of animals is a matter of our virtue. For example, in the *Lectures*, he says, "A master who turns out his ass or his dog because the animal can no longer earn its keep manifests a small mind."

13    Some human beings are not autonomous, yet Kant accorded them rights. Since Kant defined persons as rational, autonomous beings and not merely as human beings, he had the philosophical ammunition, so to speak, to challenge the anthropocentric paradigm. That is, a little reflection shows that a rational being in the Kantian sense and a human being, that is, a member of the species *Homo sapiens*, are not one and the same. Some human beings are not rational: fetuses, infants, the permanently comatose; some rational beings may not be human beings. For example, some animals may be autonomous in the Kantian sense, even though Kant denied it. Moreover, as mentioned earlier, there may be extraterrestrial beings, like the movie character E.T., who are rational beings, but not members of our species. Not only did Kant treat *human being* and *rational being* as interchangeable (thereby attributing rights to all and only human beings); he also attributed all the traditional rights (liberty, property, and so on) to rational beings. Although autonomy may be necessary for possession of a right to liberty, one might ask why a being must be autonomous in order to have a right not to be tortured? The failure to take seriously the relevant criteria for the various rights is considered a serious weakness in classical rights theories by many contemporary philosophers.

14    **Taking Qualifications Seriously.**  The new literature on animal liberation and animal

rights has caused many to rethink the claim that humans have rights solely because they are human. If we no longer rely on this kind of argument, then right-holders must possess some morally relevant features that may turn out to be shared by humans, animals, and environmental objects alike. The method employed is to identify the morally relevant qualifications for the possession of specific rights in order to determine what rights, if any, a being or entity has. With respect to some rights, a plausible case can be made that certain qualifications are morally relevant. To do this, however, one needs to know the specific purpose of each right. For example, the right not to be tortured protects the basic interest certain beings have in not suffering. The right to liberty protects the interest in directing one's life as one sees fit without unjustified interference from others. If a being is capable of suffering, but not capable of autonomy or self-rule, it can have a right not to be tortured, but not a right to liberty. On this model, the right to life must protect some specific interest or desire. One plausible candidate, suggested by Michael Tooley, is a desire to continue into the future, that is, to continue to live.

15    The desire for continued existence presupposes the capacity to have a concept of oneself as a continuing self—as an entity existing over time. Of course, each right, according to the view we have been developing, presupposes some morally relevant capacity. The right not to be tortured presupposes a capacity for suffering. The right to liberty presupposes a capacity for autonomy. Once we figure out the morally relevant capacity for any given right, only those beings or entities that have the relevant capacity have the right. Thus, only sentient beings have a right not to be tortured, only autonomous beings have a right to liberty, and only self-conscious beings have a right to life. Most adult human beings can meet the self-consciousness requirement, as may some animals. However, as Tooley points out, some adult human beings do not have the requisite capacity, nor do human fetuses or newborn infants. It is worth noting that the self-

consciousness requirement is a fairly sophisticated one. According to a view like Tooley's, mere consciousness or sentience may be sufficient for having a right not to be tortured, but not for having a right to life.

16    According to the above approach to rights, many animals fare rather well. Some animals most certainly have a right not to be tortured, and quite possibly a right to life. Environmental objects, such as rocks and plants, however, appear to fare rather badly. For example, it would be absurd to claim that rocks have a right not to be tortured if they are incapable of suffering. If environmental objects are not sentient or conscious, it is hard to see how they would qualify for any rights. Peter Singer claims that plants have no conscious experiences, and thus I do nothing seriously wrong if I pull out weeds from my garden. Nonetheless, some people believe that plants have feelings, and some, like Christopher Stone, think that the entire planet is at some level conscious. So, there are matters of disagreement about who or what has certain capacities, but the important point here is that the challenge to the anthropocentric paradigm has changed the character of the rights debate into one about capacities and the moral relevance of capacities.

17    **Rights and Duties.**    Rights can be correlative with duties. For example, correlated with my duty not to kill you is your right not to have me kill you. Some philosophers claim there can be duties toward another without that other's possessing correlative rights; others claim that a being can possess rights without others owing that being duties. Moreover, some philosophers claim that only those who can perform duties or act from a sense of duty can have rights; others claim that beings or entities (such as animals and trees) can have rights even if they cannot act from a sense of duty.

18    It is doubtful that animals can act from a sense of duty. Promise keeping is a paradigm of a duty or obligation. Suppose I say to my cat as I leave in the morning, "I want you to meet me here at 5:00 P.M." Can I seriously expect her to

make and keep a promise? Animals kill and eat one another (and occasionally us). As unfortunate as this may be, it does not seem to make sense to say that animals have duties not to do this.

19    In arguments about the correlativity of rights and duties, it is often pointed out that infants and retarded persons may be incapable of duties, yet they may have rights. If this is so, an animal's inability to perform duties does not imply that it cannot have rights. If the only requirement for rights is to be capable of having certain interests, then beings that have those interests have rights whether or not they can meet additional requirements for being able to perform duties. But this is simply to say that rights and duties are two different things. Acting out of a sense of duty presupposes certain rational capacities, whereas possession of the right not to be tortured, for example, presupposes a capacity to suffer.

20    If animals cannot perform duties, it is even less plausible to suggest that the "environment" can be morally responsible for the disasters it causes. Rivers overflow and damage property, forest fires destroy lives, sinkholes swallow up Porsches. The interest argument, which tenably can allocate rights (or, at least some rights) to animals, cannot do the same, with comparable ease, for environmental objects. Trees and streams not only lack the rational capacity required for duties, they appear to lack interests as well at least in the Kantian sense of caring about how one is treated. If a wilderness is destroyed to make a home for Mickey Mouse, it does not matter to the wilderness.

Donald VanDeVeer and Christine Pierce, *People, Penguins, and Plastic Trees,* 9–13. © 1986 by Wadsworth, Inc. Reprinted by permission.

• • • • • • • • • • • • • • • • • • • • • • • • • • • • • •

1.  This selection presents several excepts from philosophical works.
    a.  true
    b.  false
2.  Which philosopher is *not* mentioned in this excerpt?
    a.  Aristotle
    b.  Aquinas
    c.  Plato
    d.  Kant
3.  How are subheads highlighted?
    a.  italics
    b.  boldface
    c.  underlining and capitals
    d.  both a and b
4.  This excerpt will likely focus on
    a.  the ethical considerations involved in environmental decisions
    b.  how Aristotle disagreed with Plato
    c.  the nature of the good as it relates to the environment
    d.  the arguments for and against an afterlife
5.  The major philosophical theory that this excerpt treats is
    a.  natural rights theory
    b.  Aristotle's theory
    c.  Aquinas's theory
    d.  the new morality theory

---

**Sel. 4**   Sur                    1. _____

**Score** _____ %              2. _____

▶ 80%                              3. _____

**Score** = number correct × 20.    4. _____

5. _____

**Check answers with your**
**instructor.**

---

## B. Question

Having surveyed the excerpt, list here five questions you intend to answer when you study-read. Base them on the subheads and words and phrases in italics.

1. _____
2. _____
3. _____
4. _____
5. _____

Ask your instructor for sample questions.

## C. Read

With all these questions in mind, read the excerpt carefully. You may want to read it once through fairly quickly before you begin marking. Remember to underline only parts of sentences if possible and to write comments sparingly.

## D. Recite

Without looking back, write down in note-taking or paragraph form the important points made in the excerpt. After you have finished your summary, compare it with the excerpt. How accurate were you?

## E. Review

Now review all your material: underlinings, marginal comments, and recite notes. Yo may want to organize this material into one or more study maps.

## F. Study-Reading Questions

When you have carefully studied the information in this excerpt and in your notes, answer the following ten questions without looking back. Place all your answers in the answer box.

1. The excerpt suggests that certain types of human beings can be considered as natural resources to be used for the benefit of others.
   a. true
   b. false
2. Aristotle suggests that animals are
   a. equal to humans
   b. to be used by humans as they see fit
   c. better than humans
   d. part of God's plan
3. Aquinas notes that animals
   a. may be used by humans for their own needs
   b. are considered by God to be superior to humans
   c. are considered by God to be inferior to humans
   d. both a and c
4. Biblical scholars suggest that the Bible
   a. allows human beings to dominate and use natural resources
   b. requires that human beings respect their natural resources
   c. both a and b
   d. neither a nor b
5. Kant defines a person as
   a. being like a thing
   b. being unlike a thing
   c. being part of God
   d. with rights equal to an animal's
6. Kant believes that rocks have
   a. an equal status to human beings
   b. a superior status to human beings
   c. an inferior status to human beings
   d. a spirit within them
7. Kant defines a thing as an object that
   a. does not move
   b. thinks
   c. cannot make decisions for itself
   d. cannot grow
8. Michael Tooley defines self-consciousness as
   a. being aware of the concept of time
   b. liking oneself
   c. having a brain
   d. all of these

9. The excerpt suggests that animals do not have a sense of
   a. being alive
   b. being tortured
   c. being free
   d. duty

10. The excerpt argues that the wilderness has
    a. no moral sense
    b. a spiritual and moral sense
    c. the same consciousness as an animal
    d. the same consciousness as a human being

---

**Sel. 4   S-Read**

**Score** ____%

▶ 80%

**Score** = number correct × 10.

1. ____
2. ____
3. ____
4. ____
5. ____
6. ____
7. ____
8. ____
9. ____
10. ____

**Check answers with your instructor.**

---

 G. For Discussion and Writing

1. Reread Aristotle's and Aquinas's arguments in paragraphs 4–8. Summarize their arguments, then show where they differ.
2. Summarize the two biblical interpretations of the use of the earth.
3. In your own words, summarize Kant's argument. How does it differ from Aristotle's and Aquinas's?
4. In your own words, summarize Tooley's argument, then explain why he thinks newborns do not have the same rights as do adult humans.
5. In your own words, define *rights* and *duties*. Show how the concepts of rights and duties are both similar and different. Then discuss an animal (of your own choosing) that has rights but not duties.

## Self-Evaluation—Philosophy

Answer the following questions by circling yes or no. Your responses will help you assess your study-reading abilities in philosophy.

1. yes no  Was your score in Section F, Study-Reading Questions, below 80 percent?

2. yes no  Was it hard to remember most of the terms as you answered the study-reading questions?

3. yes no  Did you have a hard time remembering each philosopher's argument as you answered the study-reading questions?

4. yes no  Did you have difficulty understanding the primary-source excerpts taken from Aristotle, Aquinas, and Kant?

Scoring:  If you answered yes to two or more of these questions, you may need more practice in reading philosophy.

Follow-up:  To improve your skills in reading philosophy, consider these suggestions:

1. Read philosophy slowly and reread passages you do not understand at first.

2. When you come to a definition, underline or circle the main elements. To comprehend philosophy, you must understand the definitions.

3. Note how various terms and arguments in philosophy are interrelated. Make marginal comments suggesting how terms or arguments are similar.

4. Be sure that you can summarize a philosophical argument accurately, listing all the necessary steps, before you begin reading new material.

## Follow-Up

Now that you have read four study-reading selections on environmental studies, you may want to consider how your understanding of this issue has changed and how your abilities to read textbook material have improved. Individually, in small groups, or in large groups, you may want to consider the following questions.

### On Environmental Studies

1. What scientific evidence do you now have that helps you better understand the environmental problem?

2. How can industry help solve the pollution problem?

3. Do you think people have the right to control nature, or should nature control people?

4. After reading, discussing, and writing about these selections, has your attitude toward the environment changed? If so, how?

### On Study Reading

1. Of all the steps in the SQ3R—survey, question, read, recite, and review—which are still difficult for you to complete? Why?
2. Are your study notes effective study tools? If so, why? If not, why not?
3. If you created concept maps, were they helpful? If so, how?
4. What aspects of study reading do you still need to develop?

## Internet Activity

Use the Internet to find out more information about study reading and environmental studies. Break up into groups of four or five. To answer the following questions, use the Internet source and InfoTrac College Edition. Then return to your group with your information.

If you cannot access this source or InfoTrac College Edition, research the Internet to find information on textbook reading and the environment to answer these questions.

### On Study Reading

Go to the University of Texas, Austin, Learning Skills Center Study Tips web site to answer these questions:

1. What new information on reading textbooks did you find?
2. How does this information differ from what you learned about study reading in this chapter?
3. Describe how you located this information.

### On Environmental Studies

If you have access to InfoTrac College Edition, use this research tool to learn more about the environment to complete the following activities:

1. Locate and print an article of interest related to the environment.
2. Summarize this article.
3. Describe how you located this information.

# CHAPTER 6

# Critical Reading

*Y*ou may find this chapter challenging as you learn the important skills of reading longer sentences, understanding figurative language, analyzing the logic of particular statements, and drawing reasoned conclusions. Compared with your rate in rapid reading and overview skimming, your critical-reading rate will be slow.

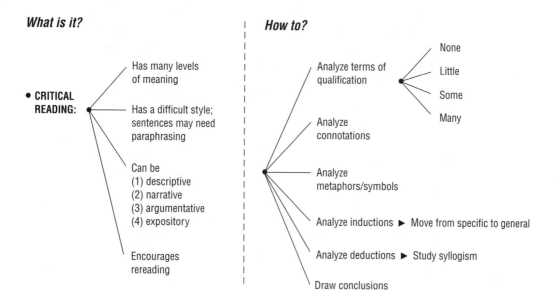

*What is it?*

● **CRITICAL READING:**
- Has many levels of meaning
- Has a difficult style; sentences may need paraphrasing
- Can be
  (1) descriptive
  (2) narrative
  (3) argumentative
  (4) expository
- Encourages rereading

*How to?*

- Analyze terms of qualification
  - None
  - Little
  - Some
  - Many
- Analyze connotations
- Analyze metaphors/symbols
- Analyze inductions ▶ Move from specific to general
- Analyze deductions ▶ Study syllogism
- Draw conclusions

# INTRODUCTION TO CRITICAL READING

. . . . . . . . . . . . . . . . . . . .

## CHECKLIST OF SYMPTOMS

Do you often

_____ 1. try to read difficult material only to give up halfway through?

_____ 2. have trouble getting through long and involved sentences?

_____ 3. feel defeated because you need your instructor or classmate to tell you what a particular work "means"?

_____ 4. put a story or a poem aside because you cannot understand the language or imagery?

_____ 5. have trouble expressing the thesis, or argument, of difficult material?

_____ 6. have difficulty drawing the correct conclusions or making the correct inferences from what you have read?

If you checked one or more of these symptoms, you should read this introduction carefully. Many of your reading questions will be answered, and you will learn ways to become a critical reader.

. . . . . . . . . . . . . . . . . . . .

## ONE-DIMENSIONAL VERSUS MULTIDIMENSIONAL MATERIAL

You have now reached the last stage in your development as an efficient college reader. You have likely established a comfortable rapid-reading rate of at least 400 wpm, and you should now be able to overview skim at rates of 800 wpm and above. In the earlier chapters, your purpose for reading (the Why) was mainly literal comprehension: to locate main ideas and supporting details as well as the structure of written material. Most of this material (the What) was *one-dimensional*—that is, you could effectively understand the selections in one reading.

In critical reading, however, your purpose goes beyond surface content. You need to do more: to analyze, critique, and understand deeply. More complex than most of your daily reading, this type of material is *multidimensional*. This means you may need to read a piece two or three times before you can effectively discuss and write about it.

These multidimensional works can be grouped into four types of writing: expository, argumentative, descriptive, and narrative. *Expository* writing explains a process or concept or gives convincing reasons for an opinion or idea. *Argumentative* writing presents a point of view. Though it often gives information, as does exposition, an argument also attempts to change the reader's mind regarding a particular issue. Examples of argumentative writing include editorials and

256

commentaries in newspapers and magazines. Often these two types of writing—expository and argumentative—overlap. For example, an article explaining the influence of the environment on criminal behavior is expository in that it is informative, but it is also argumentative because it attempts to show that environment makes a criminal behave antisocially. Because most of the critical selections that you will read in this chapter both inform and persuade, you will often see them labeled as *expository-argumentative*.

*Descriptive* writing differs from expository-argumentative material because it aims not to teach or persuade but, rather, to create or record an experience in sensory and psychological terms. Describing the activities of a fugitive as he attempts to hide from the law or recreating the smell of New York City at 8 A.M. on a summer workday are both examples of description. On the other hand, *narration* recounts a series of events, real or imagined. The incidents leading to the assassination of John Kennedy in 1963 (a nonfictional account) or the disintegration of a teenager's life as he takes, then sells, cocaine (a fictional account) are both examples of narration.

Just as exposition and argumentation overlap, so description almost always accompanies narration. For example, a novel or a biography will have sections of pure description (creating a setting or describing a character), though the overall intent of the work is to tell a story. As such, you will see in this chapter the term *description-narration* used to identify this sort of overlapping.

In other words, you can safely divide most critical reading into two types: exposition-argumentation and description-narration. Exposition-argumentation attempts to explain the world. Description-narration tries to recreate it or chronicle it.

## . . . . . . . . . . . . . . . . . . . . .
## *HOW TO PREVIEW SKIM MULTIDIMENSIONAL MATERIAL*

To read multidimensional material effectively, you must determine early on whether the material is expository-argumentative or descriptive-narrative, then choose and use appropriate critical practices. In both types of writing, you will need to preview skim, just as you did with one-dimensional material. Preview skimming critical material is a bit more thorough than that of rapid-reading material and a bit less thorough than an overview skim of one-dimensional material. When you preview skim critical material, you should read

1. the title
2. the first paragraph slowly and carefully
3. the first sentence of each of the following paragraphs
4. the final paragraph carefully and slowly

By following these steps, you will determine what the article is about and how difficult it is. After you have preview skimmed exposition-argumentation, you should be able to summarize the selection's thesis in a sentence or two; after a preview skim of fiction or nonfiction, you should be able to identify accurately the setting, the major characters, and the work's level of difficulty.

Having preview skimmed, you are ready to read the entire work. Unlike rapid reading, you should not critically read under time pressure. As you read a piece critically, even for the first time, you will need to reread a particularly difficult or interesting sentence or passage. In some cases, your reading rate of critical material can drop to 150 wpm. In reading poetry, your rate may even be lower.

· · · · · · · · · · · · · · · · · · · · ·

# HOW TO PARAPHRASE

Perhaps the most common problem that students face when they read multi-dimensional material is that they do not understand sentences that are very long or use difficult words. Instead of trying to understand such sentences before going on, students often continue reading, hoping that their confusion will go away. Instead, the confusion often increases.

When faced with difficult material, a critical reader knows how to *paraphrase:* to accurately restate a phrase, a sentence, or sentences in a simpler way. Though paraphrase is usually shorter than the original, it sometimes uses more words. Whether longer or shorter than the original, an effective paraphrase is worded in the reader's voice, with words and phrases familiar to the reader. If you copy parts of the difficult passage or merely use synonyms for difficult words, your paraphrases will not help you.

Look at the following passage on criminal behavior and the two paraphrases, one weak and the other acceptable. See how the weak paraphrase merely uses synonyms and omits a few words from the original. The helpful paraphrase attempts to make the sentence easier to understand without distorting the intent of the original passage.

> *EXCERPT:*
> *Mr. Stanton Samenow believes in a somewhat radical concept of criminal behavior; he contends that if a criminal chooses to engage in criminal activity, he has willfully elected a lifestyle which is antithetical to his society's mores.*

> *WEAK PARAPHRASE:*
> *Mr. Stanton Samenow believes in a rather controversial idea of criminal activity; he believes that if a criminal decides to get involved in criminal actions, he has chosen on his own to live a life that is opposite to the belief systems of society.*

> *ACCEPTABLE PARAPHRASE:*
> *Mr. Stanton Samenow's idea about criminals is very different from the one people normally have. He contends that a criminal consciously chooses a lifestyle that goes against everything that society believes in.*

In the weak paraphrase, note that rather than thinking through the passage's ideas, the reader has simply used synonyms for a few words and phrases: for *radical* (*controversial*), for *chooses to engage in* (*decides to get involved in*), and for *mores* (*belief systems*). In both the weak paraphrase and the original passage, the author's intent remains unclear. In the acceptable paraphrase, the vocabulary is simpler, and the point of the passage comes through more easily: Criminals are antisocial, and they choose to be so.

To paraphrase a difficult passage effectively, you should do the following:

1.  Read the difficult passage at least twice. To understand the context of the material, reread the sentences that come before and after the passage.
2.  If you remain confused after rereading, look up the meanings of any unfamiliar words. A difficult vocabulary often characterizes passages you need to paraphrase.
3.  If comprehending the vocabulary does not help you understand the passage, divide the passage into less complex phrases and clauses, which usually come before commas, dashes, semicolons, and colons.
4.  By dividing the passage into its structural parts, you should be able to determine the subject(s) and verb(s). Remember that subjects and verbs form the kernels of any sentence. Determine how subjects and verbs are connected.
5.  Try to put into your own words what the passage is saying. If you are concerned with copying parts of the passage as you paraphrase it, put the passage aside and write out the paraphrase without looking at the original.
6.  Finally, if the paraphrase expresses a key issue, write your paraphrase in the margin next to the original passage.

Try using these practices to paraphrase the previous excerpt on criminal behavior. As you read the passage, you should focus on the meanings of *radical concept, antithetical,* and *society's mores.* You may need to look up the terms *antithetical* and *mores,* so that you can determine early on that Samenow's position is out of the ordinary because he sees the criminal as choosing to be antisocial. Further, you need to see how the two main clauses relate. The first, up to the semicolon, is the more general statement, whereas the second is more specific. In the first clause, the author establishes that Samenow's position is unique. In the second, he explains this uniqueness. Such practices will help you arrive at an acceptable paraphrase.

You will find that paraphrasing difficult material can be very helpful. It often opens up the meaning of difficult material by encouraging you to reread, to consider new terminology, and to identify the key words in a passage. Further, paraphrasing often discloses sophisticated ideas that may be new to you. At other times, you may find that a complex style and difficult vocabulary merely mask a simple idea. In either case, paraphrasing can show you how clearly or unclearly a writer thinks.

Turn to Practices 6.1 and 6.2, beginning on page 270.

• • • • • • • • • • • • • • • • • • •

## HOW TO READ FOR INFERENCES

Along with paraphrasing difficult passages, a reader of multidimensional material can also interpret what is not stated directly. To *infer* is to "read between the lines." (This practice is much like the one you learned in Chapter 1 when you determined the implied main idea.) Reading for inferences is especially important with multidimensional material because the author expects the audience to go beyond the literal meaning.

In your critical reading of difficult material, you will learn to use the following practices to make correct inferences.

1.  Analyze the terms of qualification an author uses.
2.  Pay attention to the connotations of words as well as to metaphors, symbols, and allusions.
3.  Evaluate statements derived from inductive reasoning.
4.  Analyze the deductions made in critical material.
5.  Analyze the conclusions writers make by paying particular attention to the language and evidence they use.

We explore each in the sections that follow.

## Terms of Qualification

A *term of qualification* is a word or phrase that modifies the certainty of a writer's statement. Such terms suggest varying degrees of certainty toward a particular topic. A critical reader first identifies the qualifier then infers the author's attitude from it. Terms of qualification are divided into four categories, each expressing varying degrees of certainty: (1) words and phrases that express no doubt, (2) words and phrases that express little doubt, (3) words and phrases that express some doubt, (4) words and phrases that express much doubt.

Study the words and phrases in the following categories:

1.  Words and phrases that express no doubt: *all, surely, assuredly, there is no doubt, none, conclusively, undoubtedly, without reservation, never, clearly, absolutely, without hesitation, always, unequivocally, constantly, it is a proven fact, certainly, precisely, undeniably, it is undeniable, definitely, plainly, without a doubt, without question*
2.  Words and phrases that express little doubt: *most, seldom, there is little doubt, it is believed, mostly, rarely, with little reservation, almost never, usually, slightly, almost always, the consistent pattern, consistently, one can safely say*
3.  Words and phrases that express some doubt: *many, ostensibly, it seems, frequently, apparently, one can infer, often, somewhat, one can say with some reservation, may, might, likely, the hypothesis is, can, could, this may (might) mean, it is theorized that, one would assume, the results imply, it is possible that, the assumption is, possibly, it is probable that, one would infer, probably* (stronger than *possibly*), *the inference is, at times, it appears, seemingly*
4.  Words and phrases that express much doubt: *supposedly, it is guessed that, it is suspected that, it is conjectured that, it is rumored that*

In the following four statements, see whether you can determine how the qualifier in each alters its meaning. Then read the commentary that follows to see if you agree with our assessments.

*Statement 1:* This morning, the police department gave the press the following statement regarding the multiple murder case: "There is now no doubt that only one individual was responsible for all five killings."

*Statement 2:* On a recent news report, a criminologist noted that teenage criminals are only slightly influenced by their peers.

*Statement 3:* About his research on psychological therapy for criminals, the criminologist at State University stated, "It is now theorized that making criminals feel vulnerable and guilty for their actions is an effective deterrent for further criminal behavior."

*Statement 4:* Referring to the personal problems of Senator Good, a recent gossip columnist said, "It is now suspected that Senator Good was involved in the use and sale of heroin."

In statement 1, you should have identified the qualifier as *there is no doubt* and concluded that the police department must now have hard evidence in this case because *no doubt* adds certainty to the statement. With the word *slightly*, statement 2 suggests that teenagers involved in crime are barely influenced by their friends. You should have inferred, though, that friends influence these teenagers in some way, and you would want to look for further information regarding what those minor influences involve. In statement 3, you would have been wrong to infer that making criminals feel guilt stops their criminal behavior. The phrase *it is theorized* places this statement in the category of theory, not fact. Remember that *theories* are assumptions that have been studied carefully but have not been proven. Finally, you would have been correct in ignoring entirely the validity of statement 4. Conjecture and supposition can never be used as evidence to prove guilt or innocence.

As you can see, by identifying the qualifier in each statement, you can make worthwhile inferences. Remember that nowhere in these statements do the authors state these suggestions directly; you must read between the lines. Often, the inference you make is what helps you understand the significance of a statement. For example, you could not have used statement 4 to convict Senator Good, but with the inference that you made in statement 1, you would be correct in telling anyone that the murder case was either solved or close to being solved.

Because terms of qualification are so important in critical reading, you should study and become familiar with all of the phrases in these four categories.

Turn to Practice 6.3 on page 274.

## Connotations

Besides citing qualifiers, a critical reader can draw valid inferences by analyzing how an author uses words. Practically all the words in our language have not only literal meanings but also suggested ones. The *connotation* of a word is its suggested meaning. A critical reader can infer much about an author's unspoken attitude toward a topic by examining the connotations of his or her words. You will need to study connotations when you analyze advertisements, editorials, commentaries, and literature.

Many words in our language fall into one of three categories, each of which expresses an implied value: (1) a mildly positive or negative attitude, (2) a positive or negative attitude, or (3) a strongly positive or negative attitude. For example, depending on the extent of a burglary, the owner can feel *dismay* (a mildly negative emotion), *fright* (a negative emotion), or *terror* (a strongly negative emotion). Conversely, a person you know may be your *acquaintance* (a mildly positive term), your *friend* (a positive term), or your *confidant* (a strongly positive term).

Critical readers, therefore, pay attention to an author's word choice, or *diction*. By doing so, they can determine the writer's positive or negative feelings about a particular topic. Further, critical readers can identify and analyze peculiar uses of words. For example, if you read in a short story, "The nephew was perplexed upon hearing of the murder of his aunt and uncle," you should see the word *perplexed* as an unusual word choice. Sadness, grief, or shock, yes—but not perplexity! That is, *perplexed* is a mildly negative term used where a strongly negative term would be more appropriate. In seeing this word, the critical reader might ask, "Is the author suggesting that the nephew had bitter feelings toward his aunt and uncle or that he was unable to show appropriate feelings in times of grief?" Or "Am I reading satire? Humor?" As an analysis of this sentence suggests, the connotation of a single word can be so powerful that it forces you to rethink a character's motivation.

To see how one word reveals a character's feelings, consider the following sentence from a short story: "Mrs. Duncan was irate because the clerk had overcharged her by 25 cents." Clearly, being irate over such a small overcharge is strange behavior. A careful reader would analyze the connotations of *irate* and compare it with its context to see what they say about Mrs. Duncan's character.

Finally, consider the following sentence from a commentary in a newspaper: "These therapists are visionaries who have made many important breakthroughs regarding prisoner rehabilitation." A thoughtful reader knows that *visionaries* suggests farsightedness, imagination, and intelligence. By characterizing these therapists as visionaries, this writer reveals a strongly favorable attitude toward them.

Turn to Practice 6.4 on page 276.

## Metaphors and Symbols

Like connotations, metaphors encourage you to explore the suggestiveness of words. A *metaphor* is a direct comparison of two objects or ideas that do not at first seem related. A *symbol* is an object that represents a larger set of associations. Unlike a metaphor, a symbol does not explicitly relate the object to these associations.

Because metaphors are an integral part of the way humans use words, they play a role in the history of many words. Often, what we consider a synonym for a word was originally a metaphor for that word. Words and phrases such as *the blues* or *giant* have their origins in metaphor.

To understand how a metaphor works, you need to establish the equation that it suggests. In other words, you identify the two words that are being compared—*subject* and *image*. You then place the subject next to the image and list all the associations that these two words together suggest. Consider this sentence: "He is a raging bull." See how the following list helps explain the meaning of this metaphor:

| Subject | Image |
|---------|-------|
| he | raging bull |
| | associations: male, dangerous, violent, frightening, powerful, inhuman |

These associations suggest both the strength and the danger that this male individual may possess.

Advertisements widely use metaphors to make their products attractive and therefore more salable. The metaphors are often so out of the ordinary that you are made to think through the various aspects of the comparison. In one ad, for example, the advertisers describe a raincoat as "outdoor makeup." How can a coat be like makeup? Your answer would likely include some of the following associations:

| Subject | Image |
|---------|-------|
| coat | makeup |
| | associations: makes you pretty, makes you desired, is feminine, is nice to look at |

You can see that these associations suggest glamour and desirability. Clearly, the advertiser here wants you to consider the coat not only as a protective garment but also as an item that adds glamour and desirability to its user. But is this metaphor honest? Is this ad writer creating a false impression? These are the kinds of questions you need to ask as you analyze the metaphors advertisers use.

The area in which metaphors are most often used is literature—poems, plays, and fiction. To read literature critically, you need to identify metaphors and analyze their associations. If you read a metaphor without analyzing its suggestiveness, you will be ignoring one of the most powerful characteristics of literature. You can use the same practice for analyzing literary metaphors that you used with the previous two metaphors.

Consider the first line of Emily Dickinson's poem "My Life had stood—a Loaded Gun—." How is a person's life like a gun ready to go off? A list of associations would uncover the following:

| Subject | Image |
|---------|-------|
| speaker's life | loaded gun |
| | associations: violence, destruction, frustration, anger, volatility, hunting |

These associations suggest that the speaker in the poem has experienced a life of powerful emotions, danger, and adventure—a life that could end violently at any time. It is these inferences that a critical reader of literature brings to this work after reading the very first line.

Often, when you read a literary work, several metaphors work together. That is, several images, taken together, create a particular feeling in the reader, or what is known as a work's *mood*. When you have determined the mood, you can also infer the writer's attitude toward her or his subject, or the work's *tone*. As a critical reader, you can examine metaphors to determine both the mood and the tone of a piece, as well as other inferences.

Turn to Practice 6.5 on page 277.

Symbols are similar to metaphors in that the reader relies on the associations of the particular symbol to appreciate its impact. Unlike a metaphor, which connects the subject to its image, a symbol stands alone in a work. Further, though both metaphors and symbols are a part of the language of a work, symbols are also an integral part of the work's action, or story line. Symbols resemble metaphors in that they are omnipresent in our daily life—the golden arches of McDonald's or the stars and stripes of the U.S. flag. Both of these common U.S. symbols represent more than what they appear to be at first glance. The arches are like rainbows and golden like the sun; the stars on the flag suggest warmth and brightness.

As you read literature critically, consider both how the symbol facilitates the story's action and what its associations are, in a fashion similar to your analysis of metaphors. In the last exercise in the chapter, you will read a poem entitled "Sarajevo Bear." Consider how the bear as a poetic symbol both participates in the action of the poem and calls to mind numerous associations.

## Allusions

Allusions are often found in multidimensional material. As in the case of metaphors, their power resides in their suggestiveness. *Allusions* are references to people or occurrences in history, politics, or the arts. Unlike metaphors, which often do not require background reading to be understood, allusions test your knowledge of history, literature, art, and music. The more you read in those areas, the better your ability to appreciate allusions. If you come across a name from history or the arts that is new to you, look it up in the dictionary or an encyclopedia. You can also consult specialized references such as literary dictionaries and historical encyclopedias.

Consider the following allusion to the poet John Keats, made by a literary critic: "Many modern poets have the Keatsian love for the concrete." Keats was a British poet of the early nineteenth century whose poetry was known for its focus on objects in the world rather than on ideas. He considered these objects from several perspectives and through all the senses. Many critics consider him as great a poet as Shakespeare was a dramatist. To appreciate the point that this critic is making about modern poetry, you need all this information on Keats. In his allusion, this critic suggests that many modern poets also focus on the senses and on objects, rather than ideas, and may even be considered as great as Keats.

You will find allusions not only in literature and literary criticism but also in film, art, and theater reviews; in historical studies; in commentaries in newspapers and magazines; and even in some advertisements. By appreciating the allusions these writers use, you will derive a more critical understanding of their works.

# Inductions

Like metaphors, people use inductions in their everyday lives. An *induction* is a general statement derived from specific information. For example, you have had the flu once a year for the past five years. Each time you get sick, aspirin eliminates both the fever and the pain. From your several experiences with using aspirin, you conclude (or make the induction) that aspirin can reduce fever and pain. All inductions follow the same process: We gather data then make a general statement from them.

Inductions have several names, many of which you already know. They are most frequently called *generalizations.* Scientists often call their inductions *conclusions* or *hypotheses.* A hypothesis is a general statement derived from careful observation and analysis of data (often facts and figures). In expository writing, a general statement derived from an induction is called an *opinion, thesis,* or *argument.* The data used to support a thesis are referred to as *evidence, detail,* or *fact.* In analyzing inductions, you study the specifics to see if they are accurate and if they all relate to the thesis they have generated.

As a critical reader, you need to evaluate the soundness of an induction. A valid generalization must always have convincing details as its basis. Generalizations without sound evidence to support them are known as *sweeping generalizations* or *generalizations derived from insufficient evidence.* To determine whether a generalization is convincing, you must consider whether the details are both accurate and representative. For example, the results of a questionnaire from one U.S. high school would not warrant the generalization that many U.S. teenagers use drugs. The facts obtained from one high school do not represent schools across the nation.

All writers make generalizations of some sort, but you should most carefully scrutinize the generalizations made in editorials, commentaries, and advertisements. For example, you should question a statement such as the following: "Three out of four doctors recommend Aspirin X." Who are these doctors? Do they represent doctors throughout the country, or are they only doctors questioned in one hospital? If the latter is true, you would be correct to call this generalization unsound because of insufficient evidence. Similarly, a commentary about the military budget that states, "Military spending is highly wasteful" should include statistics from several branches of the military, showing where the waste is and how the various military branches compare. If you cannot find this evidence in the commentary, you should question the soundness of the generalization.

Critical readers constantly scrutinize a writer's inductions. They study the data to see if they are both accurate and representative. Only if the data are accurate and provide a representative sampling can the critical reader formulate a sound generalization.

# Deductions

Like inductions and metaphors, deductions are used by all of us to solve simple, everyday problems as well as complex, abstract ones. A *deduction* is a form of thinking beginning with a general statement, called a *major premise,* followed by a specific concern, called a *minor premise*, and ending with a statement combining both, called a *conclusion*. In a way, deductions are the opposite of inductions. Whereas inductions begin with a specific statement and end with a general conclusion, deductions begin generally and end with a detailed conclusion.

Here is how deductions work. Suppose that each time you shop at the mall you are afraid that you are going to be robbed. Your feelings about being robbed can be described by a deductive argument that works this way:

*Major Premise:* When I shop at the mall, I'm afraid I'm going to be robbed.

*Minor Premise:* I shopped at the mall this morning.

*Conclusion:* I was afraid I was going to be robbed.

A deduction is valid only if both the major and minor premises are correct. As a critical reader, you must analyze each premise to determine its validity, then determine from these premises whether the conclusion is *sound*, or true.

Analyzing deductions is difficult when the premises are not stated directly—that is, when you must deal with *hidden assumptions*. In such cases, you need to infer from the conclusion what the major and minor premises must have been. What is the hidden assumption in the following promotion for a gambling control center? "Our gambling center can cure your cravings." From this statement, you can infer the three parts of a deduction:

*Major Premise:* People who are sick with cravings should try to get cured.

*Minor Premise:* Gamblers are sick people.

*Conclusion:* Gamblers should try to cure their cravings to gamble.

You probably have no objection to the major premise—people sick with cravings should seek medical treatment. However, you would likely take issue with the minor premise. Are gamblers sick in the same way that heroin addicts are? Some gamblers do gamble to excess, but their desire to gamble is not a physical craving. Because the minor premise is not valid, the conclusion that gamblers should seek a cure does not necessarily follow. The writer of this ad purposely does not analyze this conclusion. She hopes that you will accept it without studying the premise she has based it on.

See how the following comment about lawbreakers also uses unstated assumptions: "These picketers and other lawbreakers who surrounded the federal building were mainly young adults." Equating picketing with lawbreaking is based on the following deduction:

*Major Premise:* Lawbreakers are people who disobey the law.

*Minor Premise:* Picketing is against the law.

*Conclusion:* The young adults who picketed are lawbreakers.

The major premise is valid; however, the minor premise is not. Picketing is legal as long as the picketers do not trespass. Whereas picketing is not a crime, the conclusion that picketers are lawbreakers is unsound.

Writers of commentaries and ads may use false implied assumptions to convince their readers of an unsound conclusion. As a critical reader, you need to analyze carefully the first two parts of the deduction to see if the conclusion follows logically. If one or both premises are invalid, the conclusion is unsound. Such an analysis is sometimes difficult and time-consuming, but it will often provide you with evidence for why an argument is unconvincing.

Turn to Practice 6.6 on page 280.

## Drawing Conclusions

All the practices you have learned so far—analyzing qualifiers, studying the connotations of words, examining metaphors, studying inductions, and so on—help you to draw sound conclusions from what you have read. By examining whether the writer's language is responsible or irresponsible, or whether the evidence presented is accurate, you can determine if the writer's conclusions are sound.

To assess the validity of conclusions, you need to ask some or all of the following questions concerning what you have read:

1. Is the evidence accurate? If not, in what ways is it inaccurate?
2. Are the deductions sound? Are there any invalid premises?
3. Is the language emotional? Is the language used to offend the reader rather than to accurately describe the person or topic?

Your ability to analyze conclusions plays its most important role when you read editorials and commentaries in newspapers and magazines. An *editorial piece* is a position that a newspaper or magazine takes on a particular issue: to endorse a particular local, state, or national candidate, for example. A *commentary* is an article written by a columnist (a syndicated or staff writer) who takes a position on a particular issue such as whether guns should be outlawed or whether murderers be given life in prison rather than executed. A columnist's position may not be the one that the publication takes. Each of these articles has a particular *slant*, or perspective, that is usually liberal, moderate, or conservative. In analyzing the piece's evidence and language, you can determine the writer's particular perspective.

Let's say you are reading a commentary about how to deal with teenage criminals, and the writer considers their chances for becoming productive citizens as "hopeless" and society as "pawns in their hands." You can conclude that this writer likely has negative feelings for young lawbreakers. Your job is to determine whether this language is too harsh and whether it inaccurately describes these young people. How, you could ask, does referring to a young person's behavior as "hopeless" accurately describe her or him? Or is it simply an easy way to dismiss teenage criminals as social outcasts? Further, are the citizens truly as helpless as "pawns" in these young people's hands? If you decide that the language is harsh and inaccurate, you can conclude that the assumption the writer makes concerning teenage criminals is not reasoned.

Similarly, if this commentary includes only vague statistics as proof, you are justified in questioning the writer's conclusions. For example, if the writer says that several elderly people in the country have been robbed by teenage boys, but he does not provide actual numbers, you can conclude that this evidence is vague and that the writer's conclusions should be questioned.

Finally, from the position he takes, you can determine this writer's perspective on crime. A conservative perspective would favor harsh punishment for teenage lawbreakers and would hold them, rather than society, responsible for their illegal actions. A liberal perspective, in contrast, would more likely favor leniency in punishing teenage offenders, particularly if it is their first offense, and would encourage more tax dollars to be spent for improving their environment and for counseling the teenagers. A moderate position would likely incorporate positions from both conservatives and liberals. As such, you might reasonably conclude that our writer has taken a conservative perspective on teenage crime. When reading any article with a particular slant, you should try to determine early on the perspective the writer is taking.

Drawing responsible conclusions is a central critical reading practice. Your own thoughtful conclusions are the ones you tend to remember once you have finished reading a piece of writing and continue to read in a particular topic. Such conclusions enable you to compare a given piece with others you examine. Moreover, the conclusions that you draw concerning a writer's strengths and weaknesses often determine whether you want to continue reading that particular writer.

Turn to Practices 6.7 and 6.8, beginning on page 282.

. . . . . . . . . . . . . . . . . . .

## *SUMMARY*

This introduction has provided you with many critical practices. In the exercises and reading selections that follow, you will be using all of these practices in various ways. As you read, you may want to go back to the introduction to review the practices we suggest you use in each case. For now, assume that critical reading is a multilevel activity that encourages you to reread and to rethink the purpose of what you are reading. As part of your rereading, you will be analyzing the suggested meanings of words, as well as the effectiveness of inductions and deductions. You will also draw conclusions about the nature and effectiveness of a given piece.

Your goal, then, is a challenging one—to become a proficient reader by going beyond the literal meaning of a work to its suggestions and its logical framework.

## Summary Box: Critical Reading

| What? | Why? | Acceptable Comprehension | Acceptable Rates |
|---|---|---|---|
| High-level science and applied science, literature, essays, commentaries, articles in all fields, ads | For inference, mood, and style; for thesis, support of thesis, evaluation of the argument and details | 80–90% | 150–300 wpm |

# PRACTICES:
# CRITICAL READING

Answers for these exercises are not provided in the answer key. Please check your answers with your instructor.

## 6.1   PARAPHRASING

Here is an excerpt on white-collar crime. Read it carefully and reread wherever necessary. Then, for each of the five sentences (from the passage) that follow, choose the best paraphrase from the list of four choices and place it in the blank. Remember that a weak paraphrase often uses synonyms and may sound more confusing than the original sentence. On the other hand, a helpful paraphrase keeps the intent of the original sentence but expresses it more clearly and uses simpler vocabulary. Before you choose the best paraphrase, you may want to re-read the sentences that come before and after the sentence you are paraphrasing—that is, to read it in context.

You may find the following term unfamiliar: *strain theory*, which refers to the frustration a person experiences in his or her particular social position.

## "WHITE-COLLAR" CRIME

### by Rodney Stark

1    Nothing is more embarrassing for strain theory than the frequency with which high-status people commit crimes. Merton's famous essay, "Social Structure and Anomie," essentially ignores the banker who embezzles or the physician who sells prescriptions to addicts, for only in this way could Merton sustain his thesis that crime and deviance are caused by the pains of poverty and want. While a graduate student, I asked a famous strain theorist how he explained upper-class criminals and was astonished when he said that was a job for psychotherapists because such people must be crazy. Eventually, however, social scientists accepted that many middle- and upper-class people commit crimes. And, from this recognition arose a new concept: white-collar crime.

2    **White-collar crime** is distinguished from other crime on the basis of the *social status of the offender*. The term *white-collar* indicates that a person wears a suit (with a white shirt or blouse) to work as opposed to blue-collar workers, who wear "work clothes" and do manual labor. Hence, white-collar crimes are those committed by "a person of respectability and high social status in the course of his occupation" (Sutherland, 1983).

3    This definition has caused no end of difficulties. Paramount is the necessity of classifying identical actions as different if done by persons of different status. For example, performing unnecessary automobile repairs is a white-collar crime only if it is initiated by an executive in an auto repair firm. When it is done by a gas station attendant, it is something else. Or, when a sales representative cheats on his income taxes by charging off automobile mileage from his holiday trips it is a white-collar offense, but when a janitor does likewise it is not. Thus, Susan Shapiro (1990) recently suggested that the status of offenders be dropped from the concept entirely and that a new concept of crimes involving violations of trust be substituted. She noted that upper-status persons are more often in positions of trust and thus social class can still be of importance in explaining these sorts of violations. However, the concept of trust liberates social scientists from being unable to deal with research that shows that it is not the rich, but rather the young, lower-income males who are most likely to cheat on their taxes (Mason and Calvin 1978).

4    For many social scientists, however, the problems inherent in the concept are outweighed by the capacity of the term *white-collar crime* to call attention to the fact that crime does not occur only among the lower classes—that when brokers dip into their clients' stock accounts they are doing something as fully criminal as when high school dropouts steal cars and sell their parts. All social classes have thieves. However, for other sociologists, white-collar crime serves as a conceptual device to protect strain theory from empirical falsification. That is, they argue that crime has different causes depending on the social class of the criminal. Hence, strain theory should be applied *only* to crimes committed by lower-class people. Crimes committed by middle- and upper-class people do not, therefore, challenge strain theory because the causes of their criminality must be sought elsewhere.

5    Indeed, there have been many efforts to formulate specific theories to explain white-collar crime (Sutherland, 1983; Coleman, 1987). In the end, however, each of these attempts is forced to argue that quite different motivations impel poor people and rich people to break the law. But is this true? Must we suppose that a gas station attendant stole from the cash register because he wanted more money but accountants have another motive when they embezzle? Is it useful to suggest that different causes lead doctors, on the one hand, and patients, on the other, to defraud Medicaid? Recently, Travis Hirschi and Michael Gottfredson (1987a) argued that it is not. White-collar crime, they argued, causes problems only for some theories. Other theories have no difficulty with the fact that princes as well as paupers can be overcome by greed and temptation. Let's examine such a theory.

Rodney Stark, *Sociology*, 4th ed., 184–187. © 1992 by Wadsworth, Inc. Reprinted by permission of the publisher.

• • • • • • • • • • • • • • • • • • • • • • • • • • • • • • • • • • •

1.    "**White-collar** crime is distinguished from other crime on the basis of the *social status of the offender*."
   a.  White-collar crime has status attached to it.
   b.  White-collar crime has several distinguishing characteristics.

    c. White-collar crime is separate from other sorts of deviance on the foundation of the individual's communal position.

    d. White-collar crime is unique because it depends entirely on one's place in society.

2.   "Thus, Susan Shapiro (1990) recently suggested that the status of offenders be dropped from the concept [of white-collar crime] entirely and that a new concept of crimes involving violations of trust be substituted."

    a. Susan Shapiro contends that it is trust, not status, that forms the basis of white-collar crime.

    b. So, Susan Shapiro has recently stated that a criminal's social position be completely eliminated from the definition and that a new notion of law-breaking focusing on the breach of faith be employed.

    c. For Susan Shapiro, trust plays a greater role in white-collar crimes.

    d. Susan Shapiro de-emphasizes the importance of status in the definition of white-collar crimes.

3.   "However, for other sociologists, white-collar crime serves as a conceptual device to protect strain theory from empirical falsification."

    a. Yet, other sociologists see that the concept of white-collar crime prevents one from carefully questioning strain theory.

    b. White-collar crime makes strain theory false.

    c. Yet, for several sociologists, white-collar crime provides a theoretical tool to defend strain theory from experiential distortion.

    d. Strain theory cannot be effectively defended by experimental studies.

4.   "Crimes committed by middle- and upper-class people do not, therefore, challenge strain theory because the causes of their criminality must be sought elsewhere."

    a. Crimes perpetrated by those in the middle and upper classes do not, therefore, call strain theory into question because the reasons for their criminal behavior must be found in other areas.

    b. One cannot call strain theory into question because the reasons for upper- and middle-class crime do not involve strain theory.

    c. Strain theory is challenged by the upper and middle classes.

    d. Strain theory involves criminal behavior of both the upper- and middle-classes.

5.   "Other theories have no difficulty with the fact that princes as well as paupers can be overcome by greed and temptation."

    a. Some theories can easily explain how money and other appeals can lead both the rich and the poor into crime.

    b. Princes and paupers are tempted into crime by different attractions.

    c. Greed and temptation are the principal causes of all crime.

    d. Various concepts do not have a problem with the notion that the aristocracy and the indigent succumb to avarice and enticements.

1. _____

2. _____

3. _____

4. _____

5. _____

Score _____ %

▶ 80%

Score = number correct × 20.

Check answers with your instructor.

## 6.2   MORE PARAPHRASING

The following excerpt is about control theory—one way to explain why people break the law. In this excerpt, you will find five italicized sentences. Read and, where necessary, reread the entire passage before you write paraphrases for these sentences in the spaces provided. Remember, try to make your paraphrase simpler than the original sentence without distorting the original meaning.

# CONTROL THEORY

*by Rodney Stark*

1    To formulate a more comprehensive sociological theory of deviance, the famous French sociologist Emile Durkheim (1858–1917) proposed, in effect, that we dismiss the question "Why do they do it?" and ask instead "Why *don't* they do it?" Since Durkheim's time, his advice has been heeded by many leading sociological and criminological theorists; this approach to deviance is known as **control theory.**

2    The initial assumption all control theories make is that life is a vast cafeteria of temptation. By themselves, [1] *deviant acts tend to be attractive, providing rewards to those who engage in them.* To some, theft produces desired goods, and alcohol and drugs supply enjoyment. Indeed, control theorists argue that norms arise to prohibit various kinds of behavior because without these norms such behavior would be frequent.

3    Put another way, when we consider what things people should not be allowed to do, we don't bother to prohibit behavior that people find unpleasant or unappealing. We assume that people won't do these things anyway. So we concern ourselves with things that people find rewarding and therefore might be tempted to do.

4    Thus, control theorists take deviance for granted and concentrate instead on explaining why people conform. Their answer is that people vary greatly in the degree of control their groups have over them. In any group, some people are rewarded more for conformity and punished more for deviance than other people are. Control theorists argue that conformity occurs only when people have more to gain by it than they have to gain by deviance.

5    In a classic paper, Jackson Toby (1957) described teenagers as differing in terms of their **"stake in conformity."** [2] *This phrase refers to what a person risks losing by being detected in deviant behavior.* Toby suggested that all of us are tempted but that we resist to the extent that we feel that we have much to lose by deviant behavior; for

instance, a boy with a low stake in conformity has little "incentive to resist the temptation to do what he wants when he wants to do it."

6    [3] *Therefore, like strain theorists, control theorists accept that access to desired rewards is unequal among members of any society.* Some people succeed, some get left out. [4] *But while strain theory argues that inequality pushes the have-nots to deviate, control theory stresses how the have-nots are free to deviate.* In the words of the song, "Freedom's just another word for nothing left to lose." Some people are free to deviate because they risk very little if their deviant behavior is detected. But for others the costs of detection far exceed the rewards of deviance.

7    For control theory, the causes of conformity are the **social bonds** between an indi-

vidual and the group. When these bonds are strong, the individual conforms. When these bonds are weak, the individual deviates. Because the strength of these bonds can fluctuate over time, control theory can explain shifts from deviance to conformity (and visa versa) over a person's lifetime. [5] *Because many bonds are not related to social class, control theory can explain both the conformity of the poor and the deviance of the wealthy.* But what are these bonds? There are four kinds between the individual and the group: attachments, investments, involvements, and beliefs (Hirschi 1969; Stark and Bainbridge 1987).

Rodney Stark, *Sociology*, 4th ed., 187. © 1992 by Wadsworth, Inc. Reprinted by permission of the publisher.

• • • • • • • • • • • • • • • • • • • • • • • • • • • • • • • •

1.  Paraphrase of sentence 1: _____
    _____

2.  Paraphrase of sentence 2: _____
    _____

3.  Paraphrase of sentence 3: _____
    _____

4.  Paraphrase of sentence 4: _____
    _____

5.  Paraphrase of sentence 5: _____
    _____

Score _____%

▶ 80%

Score = number correct × 20.

Check answers with your instructor.

## 6.3    UNDERSTANDING TERMS OF QUALIFICATION

Read each of the following ten sentences carefully. Then underline the terms of qualification. Finally, comment on how the qualifier alters the meaning of the statement, making it either stronger or weaker. Refer to page 260 for the lists of terms of qualification.

*Example:* The results of the experiment on the prisoner could mean that a cause for violent behavior can be identified.

*Explanation:* "Could mean" casts some doubt on the experimental results; that is, a cause of violent behavior may not be identified.

1. Without question, a burglar committed the seven robberies in the same city within a week.

   Explanation: _____
   _____

2. This state's prison system almost never grants pardons to those inmates who have been convicted of committing murder.

   Explanation: _____
   _____

3. The DNA results reveal unequivocally that Tom Barnes is not the murderer of his son.

   Explanation: _____
   _____

4. The popular governor stated in a press release that she may make it easier for several types of murderers to get the death penalty.

   Explanation: _____
   _____

5. The presidential candidate stated to reporters that violence to children is an issue that she will undoubtedly focus on in her campaign.

   Explanation: _____
   _____

6. It is theorized that genetics plays a role in the development of a criminal personality type.

   Explanation: _____
   _____

7. It is possible that all the prisoners in the county will be moved to a new facility by the end of the year.

   Explanation: _____
   _____

8. The robber apparently left no fingerprints.

   Explanation: _____
   _____

9. It is conjectured that the robber of the jewelry store wore gloves when he or she committed the crime.

   Explanation: _____
   _____

10. It is assumed that no more casualties will be pulled from the bombed building.

    Explanation: _____

    _____

Score _____ %

▶ 70%

Score = number correct × 10.

Check answers with your instructor.

## 6.4 ANALYZING CONNOTATIONS

Read the following ten sentences, each of which contains an italicized word or phrase having either a positive or a negative connotation. Determine if the word is (1) mildly positive or negative, (2) positive or negative, or (3) strongly positive or negative. Then substitute another word (just one) that belongs to one of the other two categories. You may refer to a dictionary or thesaurus for the exact meaning of the italicized word or for a synonym.

*Example:* I was outraged by your behavior.

*Explanation:* "Outraged" has a strongly negative connotation. "Upset" would have a mildly negative connotation.

1. Sometimes Joan is *unkind*.

   Explanation: _____

   _____

2. My wife was *ecstatic* after the jury read the verdict.

   Explanation: _____

   _____

3. The discussion ended in a *riot*.

   Explanation: _____

   _____

4. In his legal career, Sam was a *brilliant* criminal attorney.

   Explanation: _____

   _____

5. Unfortunately, the court proceedings were a *fiasco*.

   Explanation: _____

   _____

6. I could tell by the attorney's *devastated* expression that she had lost the court case.

Explanation: _____
_____

7. To our surprise, the prisoners completed a *gigantic* amount of work.

Explanation: _____
_____

8. The juvenile in custody shows nothing but *contempt* for the prison authorities.

Explanation: _____
_____

9. The judge referred to the defendants crimes as "those *abominable* actions."

Explanation: _____
_____

10. The mother referred to her daughter's crime as a mere *blunder.*

Explanation: _____
_____

Score _____ %
▶ 70%
Score = number correct × 10.
Check answers with your instructor.

## 6.5   ANALYZING METAPHORS

Read the following poem enough times to understand the basic story line. Then reread it to answer the questions after it. Half of them concern the metaphors Rodriguez uses, asking you to analyze subject and image. You may want to reread the section on metaphors in the introduction, pages 262–264.

Here is an example of how to analyze subject and image:

*Example:*    I noticed them sitting there
As orderly as frozen fish
In a package.
—From D. C. Berry, "On Reading Poems to a Senior Class at South High"

*Explanation:* By comparing students to frozen fish in a package, the poet is suggesting that they, though quiet and neat, are passive and unresponsive. Like fish in a package, they are cold and dead.

• • • • • • • • • • • • • • •

▬▬▬▬▬▬▬▬    *ALWAYS RUNNING*

• • • • • • • • • • • • • • •

▬▬▬▬▬▬▬▬    *by Luis J. Rodriguez*

All night vigil.
My two-and-half-year-old boy
and his 10-month-old sister
lay on the same bed,
facing opposite ends;                                                5
their feet touching.
They looked soft, peaceful,
bundled there in strands of blankets.
I brushed away roaches that meandered
across their faces,                                                 10
but not even that could wake them.
Outside, the dark cover of night tore
as daybreak bloomed like a rose
on a stem of thorns.
I sat down on the backsteps,                                        15
gazing across the yellowed yard.
A 1954 Chevy Bel-Air stared back.
It was my favorite possession.
I hated it just then.
It didn't start when I tried to get it going                        20
earlier that night. It had a bad solenoid.
I held a 12-gauge shotgun across my lap.
I expected trouble from the Paragons gang
of the west Lynwood *barrio*.
Somebody said I drove the car                                       25
that dudes from *Colonia Watts* used
to shoot up the Paragons' neighborhood.
But I got more than trouble that night.
My wife had left around 10 p.m.
to take a friend of mine home.                                      30
She didn't come back.
I wanted to kill somebody.
At moments, it had nothing to do
with the Paragons.
It had to do with a woman I loved.                                  35
But who to kill? Not her—
sweet allure wrapped in a black skirt.
I'd kill myself first.
Kill me first?
But she was the one who quit!                                       40

Kill her? No, think man! I was hurt, angry . . .
but to kill her? To kill a Paragon?
To kill anybody?
I went into the house
and put the gun away.                                               45

Later that morning, my wife came for her
things:
some clothes, the babies . . . their toys.
A radio, broken TV, and some dishes remained.
I didn't stop her.
There was nothing to say that my face                               50
didn't explain already.
Nothing to do . . . but run.

So I drove the long haul to Downey
and parked near an enclosed area
alongside the Los Angeles River.                                    55
I got out of the car,
climbed over the fence
and stumbled down the slopes.
A small line of water rippled in the middle.
On rainy days this place flooded and flowed,                        60
but most of the time it was dry
with dumped garbage and dismembered
furniture.
Since a child, the river and its veins of canals
were places for me to think. Places to heal.
Once on the river's bed, I began to cleanse.                        65
I ran.

I ran into the mist of morning,
carrying the heat of emotion
through sun's rays;
I ran past the factories                                            70
that lay smack in the middle
of somebody's backyard.
I ran past alleys with overturned trashcans
and mounds of tires.
Debris lay underfoot. Overgrown weeds                               75

scraped my leg as I streamed past;
recalling the song of bullets
that whirred in the wind.

I ran across bridges, beneath overhead passes,
and then back alongside the infested walls          80
of the concrete river;
splashing rainwater as I threaded,
my heels colliding against the pavement.
So much energy propelled my legs

and, just like the river,
it went on for miles.          85

When all was gone,
the concrete river
was always there
and me, always running.          90

Luis J. Rodriguez, *The Concrete River* (Willimantic, CT: Curbstone Press, 1991), 62–64. Used by permission of the publisher. Distributed by InBook.

• • • • • • • • • • • • • • • • • • • • • • • • • • • • •

1.  Reread the first eleven lines of the poem. In two or three sentences, retell the story there.

    _____

    _____

2.  Reread lines 25–27. What trouble is the speaker in?

    _____

3.  In line 32, the speaker states, "I wanted to kill somebody." Why is he angry?

    _____

4.  Reread lines 46–52. What does the wife do? Why do you think she does it?

    _____

5.  In lines 63–66, the speaker describes what the river meant to him when he was a child. Why does he return to the river whenever he has a problem?

    _____

    _____

6.  "as daybreak bloomed like a rose
    on a stem of thorns" (13–14)
    *Subject*       *Image*

    _____    _____
                 associations: _____
    Explanation: _____

    _____

7.  "Since a child, the river and its veins of canals
    were places for me to think. Places to heal." (63–64)
    *Subject*       *Image*

    _____    _____
                 associations: _____
    Explanation: _____

    _____

8. "I ran into the mist of morning,
   carrying the heat of emotion" (67–68)

   *Subject*      *Image*

   _____   _____

   associations: _____

   Explanation: _____

   _____

   _____

9. "recalling the song of bullets
   that whirred in the wind" (77–78)

   *Subject*      *Image*

   _____   _____

   associations: _____

   Explanation: _____

   _____

   _____

10. Reread the last four lines (87–90). The speaker compares himself to the concrete river. In what ways is the concrete river a metaphor for the speaker's life? In the poem, what associations does the speaker establish between himself and the concrete river that he continually returns to?

    Explanation: _____

    _____

    _____

Score _____ %

▶ 70%

Score = number correct ×10.

Check answers with your instructor.

6.6   DETERMINING HIDDEN PREMISES

Each of the following ten statements makes an assumption, based on deductive thinking, that is not stated directly. For each, write out this hidden premise as clearly as you can. First, read the statement carefully. Second, write down two parts of the deduction from the information that you have. Third, from the other two statements, infer the missing premise and write it down. After you have identified the hidden premise, you may want to discuss its validity with your instructor.

*Example:* I won't ask Mary if she stole the ring; after all, she's a woman.

*Deduction:* Major premise: (?)
Minor premise: Mary is a woman.
Conclusion: I won't ask her if she stole the ring.

*Hidden premise:* Women are incapable of committing robberies. (major premise)

1.  The reason I know so much about violence is that I was raised in Los Angeles.

    Major premise: _____
    Minor premise: _____
    Conclusion: _____
    Hidden premise: _____

2.  Jim, my five-year-old, is a destructive child. I don't worry, because he's only doing what's natural.

    Major premise: _____
    Minor premise: _____
    Conclusion: _____
    Hidden premise: _____

3.  A student of mine has been turning to crime lately. I'm sure he comes from an economically deprived environment.

    Major premise: _____
    Minor premise: _____
    Conclusion: _____
    Hidden premise: _____

4.  We will disrupt Mr. Jones's talk tomorrow. After all, freedom of speech guarantees us this right.

    Major premise: _____
    Minor premise: _____
    Conclusion: _____
    Hidden premise: _____

5.  A moral person does not lie. I'm sad to say that Jim lies constantly.

    Major premise: _____
    Minor premise: _____
    Conclusion: _____
    Hidden premise: _____

6.  John was seriously injured in a shooting incident outside his work. This is sad, but like everything in life, his injury was meant to happen.

    Major premise: _____
    Minor premise: _____
    Conclusion: _____
    Hidden premise: _____

7.  A God of love would not allow evil to exist. Unfortunately, there is much evil in the world.

    Major premise: _____
    Minor premise: _____

Conclusion: _____
Hidden premise: _____

8. Maria is college educated, so I'm sure she's not involved in the recent bank embezzlement.

Major premise: _____
Minor premise: _____
Conclusion: _____
Hidden premise: _____

9. Money is missing from my wallet. The first think I'll do is ask the five students who are bused from the poor side of town if they know anything about this missing money.

Major premise: _____
Minor premise: _____
Conclusion: _____
Hidden premise: _____

10. I found graffiti all over my wall this morning. It must have been done by gang members last night when I was sleeping.

Major premise: _____
Minor premise: _____
Conclusion: _____
Hidden premise: _____

Score _____ %

▶ 70%

Score = number correct ×10.

Check answers with your instructor.

## 6.7   Analyzing a Short Article

Carefully read the following article on animal abuse and violence. Then analyze various sections of the article for word connotations, details, hidden assumptions (premises), and conclusions you can reasonably draw. This exercise will test many of the critical practices you have been introduced to in this chapter.

# CROSS SPECIES ABUSE

*by Kathy Contino-Turner*

1    There was another disturbing report in the news this week. It happened in Monroe County in the village of Savona. According to the Associated Press, 13-year-old Eric Smith has been charged in the murder of four-year-old Derrick Robie. It is alleged that Smith beat Robie to death. A child accused of killing another child. Reports on Smith's background show the boy killed a friend's cat four years earlier, by choking it with a garden clamp. It's here that we see a connection, a way this boy might have been helped and a senseless death prevented.

2    Humane organizations in our community, state and across the nation have been leading the way by looking at the connection between violence against animals and violence against human beings. The Humane Society of the United States, the American Humane Association and others are continuing to expose educators, doctors, lawmakers and social workers to the link between animal cruelty and other forms of family violence, particularly child abuse.

3    There are several connections. First, as in the cases above, studies have shown that violence by children at a young age may mean the child, when older, will become violent against fellow human beings.

4    For example, the self-confessed Boston strangler, Albert DeSalvo, who in the early 1960s killed 13 women, admitted to having tortured and killed dogs and cats as a child. Carrol Edward Cole, executed in 1985, was one of the most prolific killers in modern history. His first act of violence as a child was to strangle a cat.

5    The list goes on to include such individuals as John Wayne Gacy, Brenda Spencer and most recently, Jeffrey Dahmer.

6    Most animal abusers won't commit sensational murders, but authorities believe they have already taken a giant step on the path of violence.

7    Groundbreaking studies by psychiatrist Alan Felthouse and others indicate that many criminals who have been violent toward people share a common history of brutal parental punishment and cruelty to animals. Anthropologist Margaret Mead said, "The most dangerous thing that can happen to a child is allow them to abuse an animal and get away with it."

8    A second area focused on by humane organizations is the connection between animal abuse and family violence. The pet is part of the cycle of family violence. A study conducted a few years ago in New Jersey looked at families being treated by the N.J. Division of Youth and Family Services for incidents of child abuse. In 88% of the cases, animal abuse had also occurred in the home. This study is consistent with a similar study conducted in England. It showed that in a group of families with a history of animal abuse, 83% were identified as *at risk* for abuse and neglect of children.

9    Finally, adults who abuse, many times use animals or family pets to buy the silence of their victims. There are many documented cases where animals were found at the center of abuse.

10    So what can we do? As parents, guardians, educators, members of society, we must affirm that any child who abuses an animal, needs immediate help. We must no longer stand for the old adage, *boys will be boys*. Further, we must recognize that if animal abuse is occurring in a home, other abuse may be occurring as well. Take seriously a child's reports of animal cruelty at home and urge your school district, judicial system and child welfare agencies to take acts of animal cruelty seriously.

11    This subject is not new. In fact, the National PTA Congress of 1933 reaffirmed this connection; here is a portion of that statement: "The cultivation of kindness to animals is but a

starting point toward that larger humanity that includes one's fellow of every race and clime. A generation of people trained in these principles will solve difficulties as neighbors, not as enemies."

*Kathy Contino-Turner is Director of Development for the Stevens-Swan Humane Society. For*

*more information, she recommends "Breaking the Cycle of Abuse," a pamphlet available for 50 cents from the National Humane Education Association, PO Box 362, E. Haddam, CT 06423-0362.*

Kathy Contino-Turner, "Cross Species Abuse," *Friends of Beaversprite News*, Little Falls, NY, December 1993, 3.

• • • • • • • • • • • • • • • • • • • • • • • • • • • • • •

1. What connection does the author suggest in the first paragraph? What argument, or thesis, does she infer here?

2. What effect does the term *disturbing* create in the first paragraph? That is, what are the word's connotations?

3. Reread paragraph 3. The author uses a term of qualification to establish the relationship between violence to animals and violence to humans. What is this qualifier? How does it affect your understanding of the relationship?

4. In paragraphs 4 and 5, the author lists the names of many criminals. Why?

5. In paragraph 6, the author refers to the "giant step on the path of violence" that criminals take when they abuse animals. What effect does the word *giant* have? What are its connotations?

6. In paragraph 7, the author refers to Alan Felthouse's studies as *groundbreaking*. What does this word suggest about Felthouse's work?

7. In paragraph 10, the author uses the adverb *seriously* twice. What is the effect of repeating this word?

8. Paraphrase the following statement from the PTA Congress, quoted in paragraph 11: "The cultivation of kindness for animals is but a starting point toward that larger humanity that includes one's fellow of every race and clime."

9. This article is based on a deduction that relates violence toward animals to violence toward human beings. "John" is an imaginary child who has committed violence toward an animal. Given the minor premise and the conclusion of this deduction, provide the major premise.

Major premise: _____
Minor premise: John has been violent toward his pets at home.
Conclusion: John may one day show violence toward human beings.

10. List the three strongest pieces of evidence the author uses to support her argument. How would you evaluate this evidence? Is it reputable? What do you conclude about the validity of the author's argument?

_____

Score ____ %

▶ 80%

Score = number correct ×10.

Check answers with your instructor.

## 6.8   ANALYZING A POEM

Here is a poem about the war in Bosnia between the Serbians, the Croatians, and the Muslims. Sarajevo, the city in Bosnia that hosted the 1984 Winter Olympics, was almost totally destroyed by this war. Though short, this poem says much about the suffering that war causes. To read and reread this poem, use all the critical practices you have learned. Then answer the questions that follow, referring to the poem as you answer.

## SARAJEVO BEAR

by Walter Pavlich

The last animal
            in the Sarajevo Zoo

a bear
            died of starvation

because the leaves                              5
                        had fallen

from the trees
            because

the air was
            getting colder                     10

so the snipers
                could more easily see

the few remaining people
                who were trying to

feed it.                                        15

Walter Pavlich, "Sarajevo Bear," *The Altantic*, March 1993,
55. Used by permission of the author.

• • • • • • • • • • • • • • • • • • • • • • • • • • • • •

1. Why did the bear die of starvation?
   _____

2. What do you think the fallen leaves (lines 5–6) and the cold air (lines 9–10)
   symbolize?
   _____

3. Who do you think the "few remaining people" were? How would you characterize them?
   _____

4. What were the snipers doing? How would you characterize them?
   _____

5. What are some of the associations that you bring to the word *bear?*
   _____

6. What do you think the bear in this poem symbolizes? Remember that a symbol can represent many moods and characteristics.
   _____

7. What is the overall mood of this poem?
   _____

8. How many sentences are in this poem? What do you think is the significance
   of this number of sentences?
   _____

9. Describe how the lines are positioned. What do you think is the effect of this
   positioning?
   _____

10. What do you think is the speaker's attitude toward war? That is, what is the
    poem's tone? How do you know this? Specifically, what evidence in the
    poem supports your answer?
    _____

Score _____ %
▶ 80%
Score = number correct × 10.
Check answers with your instructor.

In the following selections, you will practice your critical-reading skills to determine shades of meaning. As in previous parts, you will preview the material first. Then you will be given suggestions for reading this material carefully. Both the preview and critical-reading steps will be timed. Five preview-skimming questions and ten critical-reading questions follow each selection. The latter will include several inference questions (abbreviated *inf*) and one paraphrase question (abbreviated *P*). The questions for discussion and writing ask you to read and reread various sections of each selection. Answers for Selections 1 and 3 are listed on page 352; your instructor will provide answers for Selections 2 and 4.

As you did in Chapter 5, you will be able to evaluate yourself after each excerpt here so you can determine your strengths and weaknesses in reading various kinds of critical material and find ways to read the material more effectively.

You will note that all the selections in this part focus on crime, specifically what motivates lawbreakers and how to treat them. To prepare yourself for critically reading these selections, consider the following questions individually, in small groups, or in class discussion:

1. Do you think that lawbreakers are victims or victimizers of their surroundings?
2. How would you describe a gang member?
3. How should lawbreakers be treated once they are caught?
4. Is there more than one type of lawbreaker?

## TIMED SELECTIONS: CRITICAL-READING

• • • • • • • • • • • • • • • •

# *SELECTION 1*

**Vocabulary**
*mayhem:* the offense of seriously injuring a person; "The Coming Mayhem"
*predators:* destroyers; animals that feed on other animals; "the super-predators"
*accosted:* approached aggressively; "he was accosted on the sidewalk"
*preternaturally:* beyond what is natural; "a preternaturally youthful-looking 40-
    year-old"
*imposition:* the taking advantage of; "He is an imposition"

This commentary concerns the plight of U.S. youth as they face a violent society as either lawbreakers or victims of violence. Instead of supporting his argument with statistics and an analysis of these statistics, Richard Rodriguez essentially uses personal experience and anecdotes from others to get his point across. Like all effective commentaries, this one has a reasoned point of view; unlike most, the reader needs to infer Rodriguez's argument from the details that he presents.

**Reading Practices.**   To determine what Rodriguez thinks has caused violence among U.S. youth, use the following practices:

1.   Note the details that Rodriguez presents. What patterns emerge? What mood do these details evoke?
2.   Note how Rodriguez moves from a list of details and facts to a point of view regarding the causes of youth violence, presented in paragraph 14. From this paragraph, try to state this point of view in your own words.
3.   Underline or mark any details that strongly support Rodriguez's argument.
4.   Note how Rodriguez effectively uses questions throughout the commentary. Try to answer these questions from Rodriguez's point of view as you critically read.
5.   By the end of the commentary, see if you can list three major causes of violence among the young, as suggested by Rodriguez.

## A.  Preview Skimming

Preview skim the following commentary in 1:30 minutes (800 wpm). By the end of your preview, you should have some sense of the details that Rodriguez is using and of his general attitude toward violence among U.S. youth.

Remember, when you preview skim before you read critically, you should read

1.   the first paragraph (in this case, the first two, because they are short)
2.   the first sentence of each of the following paragraphs
3.   the entire last paragraph

When you have finished preview skimming, answer the five P-Skim questions without looking back at the article.

# THE COMING MAYHEM

*by Richard Rodriguez (1,200 words)*

**Pre-teens today are more violent than ever before. In their world—nothing matters. Where are all the adults?**

1 The monster has the face of a child. The nightmare figure outside our window is wearing Reeboks and is 7 years old.

2 In recent months, politicians and police chiefs have proudly reported a drop in the crime rate in major U.S. cities. Criminologists are warning, however, that youth crimes—particularly violent crimes by the young—are increasing and will continue to increase.

3 James Q. Wilson, for example, predicts that the growing population of teenage boys will mean an increase in murders, rapes and muggings. A new type of criminal is appearing. John J. Dilullo Jr. calls them "the superpredators." Remorseless, vacant-eyed, sullen—and very young.

4 A tough street kid (16 years old) says he thinks of himself as bad. But his younger brother, 9 years old, is crueler—"that mother scares even me."

5 We are entering a Stephen King novel: We are entering an America where adults are afraid of children. Where children rule the streets. Where adults cower at the approaching tiny figure on the sidewalk ahead.

6 A friend, a heavyweight amateur wrestler, warns me away from making a dinner reservation at a Venice Beach restaurant. "There are too many gang kids around after dark."

7 Adults put bars on their windows. Or move into fortified communities. Adults pay to send their children to safe, private schools. But sometimes now, the adult wonders if, perhaps, the monster is asleep in the bedroom down the hall.

8 It is the inner-city monster—the black kid in the Raiders' jacket—we imagine more quickly. But everyday in the paper, from rural America to the suburbs, come stories of young violence. A kid shoots up the chemistry classroom. A gang stomps a homeless man to death. Two boys in Beverly Hills murder their parents.

9 And it may not even be a case of "he" anymore. Youth counselors tell me that the toughest kids they meet now are girls. The girls are getting meaner than the boys. We adults are left feeling like children. We don't know if we are seeing the world for what it really is.

10 A father who lives in a suburb of Los Angeles says that his neighborhood appears safe—almost like the America he remembers from childhood. Kids play soccer in the park on Saturdays. Couples stroll the sidewalk on soft summer nights. "Why, then," he wonders, "did the local high school need to hire a full-time security cop this year?"

11 A 12-year-old tells me adults don't matter when you're in trouble. He avoids the parking lot of the mall, whether or not there are adults around. He avoids certain streets. The other day, he was accosted on the sidewalk, lost his jacket to a pair of young thieves while, all around him, adults passed oblivious.

12 Were we adults surprised last week to learn from a Louis Harris poll that teenagers live daily aware of danger? One in nine—more than one in three in high-crime neighborhoods—admit that they often cut class or stay away from school because of fear of crime. One in eight carry a weapon for protection.

13 A mortician in black Oakland says that kids often use his mortuary as a kind of hang-out. Kids come in to look at the corpses (most of the dead are young). The smallest ones will bring

their tiny brothers and sisters, tiptoe to peer inside the coffin. Death bears a familiar face.

14    We adults now name the young criminals super-predators. Perhaps we should think of them as the super-alones. There are children in America who have never been touched or told that they matter. Inner-city mama is on crack. Or suburban mama gives the nanny responsibility for raising the kids. Papa is in a rage this morning. Where are the aunts to protect the child? Where is there a neighbor who cares?

15    The child takes the role of the adult. A friend, now in prison for armed robbery, remembers his father's drunken rages—his father quoting the Bible with whiskey breath. My friend, one night, took a knife to his father's neck to protect a younger brother from being beaten to death.

16    "I don't know." The same, dull answer so many kids give you. The question may vary: What do you want to be? What is your happiest memory? Why did you murder the old lady for $20? The answer is always the same.

17    On the other hand, on Martin Luther King Jr.'s birthday, I was at my yuppie gym in front of a row of Stairmasters. The TV was blaring. On CNN, President Bill Clinton and Coretta Scott King were exchanging flatteries.

18    The buffed blond (a preternaturally youthful-looking 40-year-old) reached for the remote control. In an instant we were transported to MTV, where three black rapsters were talking about their music.

19    Question: Why is it that most of the people who buy black rap are white kids in the suburbs?

20    Answer: Because the rapster is glamorous for having a big, mean, thumping voice that extends beyond "I don't know."

21    There are adults who are preoccupied by guns. As though the means of violence were more important than the intent. Kids, after all, kill one another with baseball bats.

22    For the super-alone who have no one to touch or to love or the words to use, sex is a turn-on. But then, so is violence. On the suburban

computer screen, the terminator gets knocked down, but then pops right back up, over and over.

23    "Ever been in a real fight?" a cop asked me once, almost sneering. "For a kid who is a loser, it's the only time he comes out on top."

24    The loser becomes the winner. The kid whose life is out of control is suddenly in control with the thrust of a knife, a blow to the face, the snap of a trigger. *I am bigger than 5 feet tall. I am an adult.*

25    Billboards, high school teachers, strangers, cops, movie stars, department-store mannequins, employment counselors—America each day tells the child that he doesn't count. We don't need him. He is an imposition. There is no place for her.

26    Was there ever a generation of adults so ill-prepared to assume the central responsibility of adulthood—that of raising children?

27    Last week, Hillary Rodham Clinton was answering embarrassing questions about Whitewater even as she was selling her book on how to raise children. Newt Gingrich, meanwhile, was appearing on TV daily, ever more stout on the chicken-banquet circuit, urging a balanced budget "for our children and grandchildren."

28    The question remains: How shall we ever tell our children that they matter? Do we even believe it? The only institutions that are telling the young any such thing are religious institutions. Which perhaps explains why there is a religious revival in our prisons—a mass conversion to Islam and Christianity. And why the Million Man March last year was a truer milestone for America than anything said by politicians on Martin Luther King Jr.'s birthday last week.

29    "Perhaps we need the draft again," a youth counselor offered the other day. "We need boot camp to discipline the young and to prepare them for adult responsibility."

30    I wonder. Listening to the rapster at my yuppie gym on King's birthday, I wondered whether we need schools to teach adults how to be adults.

31    All around me, on treadmill and life cycles and Stairmaster, were Americans like myself—adults who do not intend to get old.

Richard Rodriguez, "The Coming Mayhem," *Los Angeles Times*, January 21, 1996, M1, M6. Copyright 1996, Los Angeles Times.

•  •  •  •  •  •  •  •  •  •  •  •  •  •  •  •  •  •  •  •  •  •  •  •  •  •  •

1.  Rodriguez emphasizes that though crime has generally declined,
    a.  it will increase again in the next five years
    b.  youth crimes are on the increase
    c.  cities are still facing an increase in crime
    d.  rural areas are facing an increase in crime
2.  The Harris poll that Rodriguez mentions says that
    a.  the elderly are frightened of the young
    b.  the middle class are fleeing the cities
    c.  teenagers are daily concerned about being in danger
    d.  teenagers are frequently not monitored by their parents
3.  A name that Rodriguez uses for violent youth is
    a.  super-predators
    b.  terminators
    c.  devourers
    d.  destroyers
4.  Rodriguez mentions black rapsters to show that
    a.  white youth buy their songs
    b.  they are glamorous
    c.  they are dangerous influences on black youth
    d.  both a and b
5.  Rodriguez ends his piece with a description of
    a.  a seven-year-old
    b.  the elderly sitting on park benches
    c.  teachers in violent high schools
    d.  adults working out in a gym

| | |
|---|---|
| **Sel. 1**  P-Skim | 1. _____ |
| **Time**  2:00 = 800 wpm | 2. _____ |
| **Score**  _____% | 3. _____ |
| ▶ 80% | 4. _____ |
| **Score** = number correct × 20. | 5. _____ |
| | **Check answers on p. 352.** |

# B. Critical Reading

You are now ready to read critically—to examine the details that Rodriguez uses, make inferences about what these details suggest about youth violence, and determine Rodriguez's understanding of the causes of youth violence.

In the answer box, record the time you start and the time you finish reading the commentary. After calculating the time, answer the questions without looking back at the selection.

1. *(Inf)* Rodriguez states that a mortician "says that kids often use his mortuary as a kind of hang-out" (paragraph 13). Why do you think this occurs in a crime-ridden area of Oakland?
   a. These children want to steal from the mortician.
   b. These young people want to get used to the deaths that are so common in their neighborhood.
   c. The mortuary is a safe place for them to play.
   d. all of these

2. Rodriguez believes that a major cause of youth crime is
   a. too much wealth in the United States
   b. young people being alone
   c. dangerous schools
   d. too many gangs

3. The most common response that young people give to why there is so much violence is
   a. "Life is rough."
   b. "The world is cruel."
   c. "Crime is fun."
   d. "I don't know."

4. *(P)* Choose the best paraphrase for the following statement: "There are adults who are preoccupied by guns. As though the means of violence were more important than the intent."
   a. Adults like guns because they want to do violence.
   b. Adults are obsessed with guns because the society is cruel.
   c. Adults are focused on guns because their interest centers on how to be violent rather than on the reasons for violence.
   d. There are older people who are obsessed with guns, as if the ways of violence were more significant than the desire to commit it.

5. *(Inf)* In considering one of the reasons for youth violence, Rodriguez says, "The loser becomes the winner." What is he suggesting?
   a. Young people always want to win.
   b. Young lawbreakers are basically losers.
   c. Successful citizens need to help youth involved in crime.
   d. In committing a crime, the young lawbreaker feels as if she or he has authority.

6. According to Rodriguez, what institution seems to give young lawbreakers a feeling of self-worth?
   a. the schools
   b. organized athletic organizations

   c. churches

   d. juvenile facilities

7. *(Inf)* Rodriguez states that "department store mannequins" tell the child "he doesn't count." Why?

   a. Mannequins have desirable bodies that one could never have.

   b. Mannequins look like dead bodies.

   c. Mannequins are almost always white.

   d. Mannequins are almost always in expensive stores.

8. Rodriguez ends with a description of adults exercising in the gym to show that

   a. The United States is a health-conscious country

   b. The United States is an affluent country

   c. U.S. adults want to look young

   d. U.S. adults are afraid of dying

9. Of the following people or institutions, which one does Rodriguez *not* mention as a cause of youth violence?

   a. uncaring adults

   b. the pleasure one feels in breaking the law

   c. lonely children

   d. adults obsessed with staying young

10. *(Inf)* Rodriguez seems to be saying that young people are

   a. to blame for violence in the United States

   b. as much to blame for U.S. violence as the schools and the jail system are

   c. victimized by an adult society that does not value them

   d. the most unruly sector of U.S. society

---

**Sel. 1   C-Read**

**Finish** ____:____

**Start** ____:____

**Time** ____:____

        min   sec

**Rate**____wpm

**Find rate on p. 343.**

**Score** ____%

   ▶ 80%

**Score** = number correct × 10.

1. ____

2. ____

3. ____

4. ____

5. ____

6. ____

7. ____

8. ____

9. ____

10. ____

Check answers on p. 352.

Record rate and score on p. 324.

## C. For Discussion and Writing

1. State in your own words the three most pressing causes of violence among youth, according to Rodriguez.
2. Select three details from the commentary and show how Rodriguez uses each to suggest one or several causes of youth violence.
3. Select three details concerning adults that Rodriguez presents in his commentary. Together, what image do these details create of the U.S. adult?
4. Consider Rodriguez's title—"The Coming Mayhem." Having critically read this commentary, what does this title suggest? Do you think it is an appropriate title?
5. Rodriguez places the bulk of the responsibility for youth violence on adults. Do you agree? Are there any other causes for violence among youth that are equally important and that Rodriguez has failed to mention?

## Self-Evaluation—Reading Commentary Pieces

Answer the following questions by circling yes or no. These responses will help you examine your ability to read commentaries critically.

1. yes   no   Was your score in Section B, Critical Reading, below 80 percent?

2. yes   no   Were two or more of your answers to the inference questions incorrect?

3. yes   no   Was your answer to the paraphrasing question incorrect?

4. yes   no   Did you have difficulty determining the writer's attitude toward violent youth?

5. yes   no   Was it hard to determine why the writer uses the anecdotes he does?

6. yes   no   Did you have a hard time inferring the writer's understanding of the causes of crime among youth?

Scoring:    If you answered yes to three or more of these questions, you probably need more practice in reading commentaries.

Follow-up:   To improve your critical skills in reading commentaries, consider the following suggestions:

1. Notice how opinions are presented in any commentary. For you to accept the writer's opinions, the writer must provide valid facts.

2. Be aware of language with strong positive or negative connotations. As you read, ask yourself how certain words or phrases suggest a particular point of view regarding the issue presented.

3. Realize that writers of commentary often make their points through implied assumptions. Become more familiar with

the three parts of a deductive argument. Apply this knowledge to the statements or conclusions that a commentary writer makes. Determine which assumptions the writer leaves out.

4. Commentaries usually present a liberal, moderate, or conservative point of view. Read more commentaries to determine for yourself what the accepted liberal, moderate, and conservative positions are regarding youth violence, gun control, capital punishment, and so on.

5. As you read more commentaries, you grow more adept at evaluating the responsible and irresponsible use of words, the validity of details, and the soundness of assumptions. With these skills, you can intelligently agree or disagree with a commentary writer. You will begin to see that even published commentaries may demonstrate errors in logic and documentation.

* * * * * * * * * * * * * * * * * *

# SELECTION 2

## Vocabulary

*proliferation:* to grow in quick succession; "such as a proliferation of highly efficient guns"

*intuitively:* in a manner not characterized by the conscious use of reason; "in many ways, intuitively satisfying"

*demographic:* related to the study of populations; "subtle demographic decreases"

*propensity:* tendency; "their propensity to commit crimes"

*mutually exclusive:* related so that each excludes the other; "as though they are mutually exclusive"

*posit:* assume; "to posit partial explanations"

Written by a history and policy studies professor, "The Violence Conundrum" is an essay examining the complexity involved in studying facts and statistics surrounding criminal behavior. This commentary article concerns the various reasons why crime seems to be declining in the late 1990s. Toward the end of this commentary, Monkkonen presents his thoughts on how criminology as a study should begin to interpret its research. Thus, Monkkonen both examines the current research in the decline in crime and assesses the present state of criminology as a research practice.

**Reading Practices.** To analyze this commentary more effectively, consider the following reading practices:

1. Read early on for the thesis or argument of the commentary.
2. Read the facts that Monkkonen presents to support this thesis, and consider what inferences he seems to be making by introducing these sometimes surprising facts about crime in the United States.

3. Consider the typical assumptions regarding criminal behavior—for example, poverty leads to crime, cities are more crime ridden than are rural areas. Then see whether Monkkonen's research supports, or challenges, these traditional assumptions about crime.

4. Finally, read the end of the commentary carefully to see how Monkkonen sees this field of criminology and how he believes criminologists should begin to conduct their research.

## A. Preview Skimming

Preview skim the following excerpt in 1:30 minutes (= 867 wpm). Determine this commentary's argument, skim for some of the facts Monkkonen presents, and see how he concludes his commentary. When you have finished your preview skim, answer the five P-Skim questions without looking back at the article.

### THE VIOLENCE CONUNDRUM
*by Eric H. Monkkonen (1,300 words)*

**Homicide rates across the country are falling dramatically. But no one really knows why.**

1    Violent crime, homicide in particular, has been declining for the past five years, both in large cities and across the country. Given that many of the underlying problems related to violence, such as a proliferation of highly efficient guns, have not gone away, this decline is nearly as surprising as it is welcome.

2    The national homicide rate has moved from a record high of 10.5 murders per 100,000 persons in 1993 to eight in 1995 (the most recent national data available from the FBI) and will probably be far lower for 1996 and 1997. In L.A. County, rates have been declining since 1992 and are now down to levels not seen since the mid-1970s. The exact timing and size of the downward shift differs from state to state and from city to city, making the phenomenon seem, on the one hand, to be local and, on the other, to be loosely national. But it can't be both. It is hard to see why Missouri, for example, should follow the pattern of New York or California.

3    This good news has caused various experts and policymakers to offer widely different explanations. They haven't yet debated the issue, perhaps because as long as rates decline, everyone is happy. But why do these experts disagree?

4    There are at least five reasonable explanations being offered for the decline. Each is, in many ways, intuitively satisfying. The explanations include recent changes in policing strategies emphasizing community policing; shifts in drug sales, especially crack, that make it less public and less likely to cause violence; subtle demographic decreases both in the numbers of young men and in their propensity to commit crimes; rising employment, which takes people into less risky lives, and increased imprisonment resulting from mandatory sentencing, such as California's "three strikes" law.

5    Yet, no one answer is definitive. There have been dramatic downturns before, ones that defy sensible explanation. In late-19th-century New York, for example, homicides declined at a time of corrupt and inefficient policing, terrible crowding and poverty, and when the likelihood

of a murderer getting caught and going to prison was very low. At the time, few social observers realized their good fortune. Today, we look at Jacob Riis' famous slum photographs of that era, unaware that he portrayed poverty and chaos from a peaceful world—the city's homicide rates were less than four per 100,000 through the 1890s. The still-unexplained low violence rates of that bursting city should caution anyone offering comprehensive theories today.

6    At the same time, the young were not nearly as violent as today. It is not that there were not young murderers then, for there were: boys of 13 and younger stabbing or stoning each other to death. But the rates per age group were low.

7    During the 20th century, the national homicide rate, as well as that of big cities like New York and Los Angeles, fell from the early years of the Depression through the early 1950s, when they flattened, then began the long increase that we hope has finally ended.

8    Only a blurry message may be discerned in the big picture. After each major war—the Civil War, World War I and II—homicide rates declined. So much for the notion that war gets men's blood boiling. Cities have grown steadily since the 19th century, while homicide rates have gone both up and down. So it is not pure urbanization at fault. Capital punishment steadily increased from the 19th century to the Depression, then dropped, only returning to popularity recently. These rates, too, marched to a different drummer, simply because relatively few murderers are executed.

9    This historical background leads one to be cautious about easy explanations. It also creates tolerance for our current ignorance. Understanding personal violence, its ebbs and flows, is a complex challenge. But it is an urgent challenge, and one that is particularly American, not only because individuals suffer but because it hurts our economy.

10    Politicians, including our president and many mayors, claim that community policing has led to the decline. The problem is, violent crimes have declined in cities without community policing. It is hard to argue that a change in policing in New York had reduced violence in Chicago.

11    New York had no uniformed police in the early 1840s; homicide rates decreased for two years after the city got its first police, then seesawed back to new highs. The same thing happened in the mid-1850s, when the police went through a dramatic breakup and recreation. Is it not possible that policing innovations came just as things had begun to change for other reasons?

12    Recent research by a group of social scientists associated with the National Consortium on Violence Research implies this might be the case. Working in several major cities, they discovered that the decrease in violence in these cities is for specific offenses, those related to crack. The drug now has a bad reputation; crack addicts are disdained by youth. At the same time, the crack markets have become less chaotic. Street-corner battles are no longer the cost of doing business. Just as with legal enterprises, the market shake-up has left a more orderly group of suppliers and buyers, who often work in less risky locations, using pagers and cell phones. Hence, the drop in drug-related crimes.

13    But there are other pretty good accounts for the decline in homicide, for example, a drop in the number of young males. Allan Abrahamse, at Rand Corp., has identified a group of young offenders in California who account for a high proportion of violent offenses. Small changes in the numbers and actions of these young men can dramatically affect homicide rates. Nationally, the proportion of young males aged 15–24 has declined slightly. However, the decline started at least two years before the drop in violence, and stopped two years ago. It is not purely demographics.

14    And, what about unemployment and high rates of imprisonment? For some reason, these two ideas have taken on ideological shading, as though they are mutually exclusive. Just getting 140 potential L.A. County shooters into prison or a job would reduce homicide rates by 10%. Has this happened? Maybe, but we can hardly find out if someone would have murdered if they

were not working, or were out of prison. So we cannot really test these hypotheses.

15     We have difficulty explaining homicides because they are relatively rare and because we have too many good explanations and too few actual tests of them. Careful research on homicide and personal violence is done by only a small number of people across the United States. It is characteristic of a field about which we don't know much to expect big solutions, big breakthroughs and for the experts to never say, "I don't know." For homicide, a national problem as well as a local problem, the first step toward knowledge is to allow experts to say how much they do not know, to allow them to posit partial explanations and then to be flexible in their policy applications.

16     Picking one explanation is not a good idea, yet. The systematic study of violence is young.

Accepting that understanding may come slowly and with enormous effort is an important step toward knowledge. Meanwhile, expect a diverse range of accounts for the decline in violence, but ask for some quality research to back them up.

17     If we wish to harken back to the "good old days," we must be careful in saying which ones. The mid-19th century would be a bad choice. We would be appalled at the level of violence then. The 1890s would be better, or maybe the early 1950s. Let us hope that the next decade will usher in continually falling rates, and that we will consider reducing violence as a serious public goal and not just at election time.

Eric H. Monkkonen, "The Violence Conundrum," *Los Angeles Times*, November 30, 1997, M1, M6. Copyright 1997, Los Angeles Times.

•  •  •  •  •  •  •  •  •  •  •  •  •  •  •  •  •  •  •  •  •  •  •  •  •  •

1.   Monkkonen's main argument is that
      a.  crime is on the decline
      b.  it is surprising that crime is on the decline
      c.  guns have recently become more efficient
      d.  only homicide has been declining recently

2.   Experts have come up with five possible explanations for this decline in crime.
      a.  true
      b.  false

3.   The explanations for this decline in crime
      a.  seem clear-cut
      b.  are few
      c.  are often not made by experts
      d.  are not easy to interpret

4.   One reason given for the drop in crime is
      a.  a wealthier United States
      b.  fewer people moving to the cities
      c.  less drug use
      d.  fewer young men

5.   The last paragraph suggests that, in the "good old days," there was
      a.  less crime
      b.  less law enforcement
      c.  not necessarily less crime
      d.  the same drug use as today

```
Sel. 2   P-Skim                    1. _____

Time   1:30 = 867 wpm              2. _____

Score   _____ %                    3. _____

    ▶ 80%                          4. _____

Score = number correct × 20.       5. _____

                                   Check answers with your
                                   instructor.
```

## B.  Critical Reading

Now read critically, paying particular attention to the facts that Monkkonen uses to support his argument and what he says about how he would like research in criminology to be conducted. In the answer box, record the time you start and the time you finish reading the commentary. After calculating the time, answer the questions without looking back at the selection.

1.  Which of the following has the author *not* given to explain the decline in crime?
    a.  fewer guns available
    b.  changes in police practices
    c.  changes in drug sales
    d.  more employment
2.  (*Inf*) Monkkonen describes the poverty in late-nineteenth-century New York to show that
    a.  poverty can lead to crime
    b.  poverty does not necessarily lead to crime
    c.  urban areas have traditionally had much crime
    d.  New York had poor policing even in the late nineteenth century
3.  The author presents which of the following as clear-cut fact?
    a.  The young are less violent today.
    b.  The young are more violent today.
    c.  Stabbings have been the main cause of youth homicides throughout history.
    d.  Drugs are the cause of increased violence among youth today.
4.  The author mentions that after various U.S. wars,
    a.  the young were more aggressive
    b.  the soldiers returned to more violent cities
    c.  drugs were easier to find
    d.  murder rates dropped

5. *(Inf)* In regard to community policing in urban areas, the author suggests that
   a. it almost always leads to a decline in crime
   b. it does not consistently lead to a decline in crime
   c. only New York has developed a successful community-policing system
   d. only Chicago has failed among big cities to use community policing effectively

6. *(P)* Paraphrase the following sentence from paragraph 11: "Is it not possible that policing innovations came just as things had begun to change for other reasons?"
   a. Didn't changes in policing happen for a reason?
   b. Could it be that police changes just happened to occur at the same time that other changes did?
   c. Is it not likely that new thinking in law enforcement occurred when the time was reasonable?
   d. Aren't there other reasons for changes in police behavior that we do not know about?

7. Which of the following is given as a reason for the decrease in crack-related crimes?
   a. Young people do not like the looks of crack addicts.
   b. Crack selling is now more organized.
   c. Crack selling has moved to safer locations.
   d. all of these

8. *(Inf)* The author infers that experts in the field of criminology
   a. have difficulty explaining homicides
   b. have difficulty admitting that they are uncertain about a particular issue in their field
   c. would prefer studying another field
   d. compare themselves to mathematicians in their precision

9. The author encourages experts in the field of criminology to
   a. present only conclusions they are sure of
   b. find a new way to calculate the number of homicides per decade
   c. be willing to present partial answers to crime questions
   d. all of these

10. *(Inf)* At the end of the commentary, what does the author suggest about how crime statistics and crime theories are used?
    a. They are used only among intellectuals.
    b. They are used to scare U.S. youth.
    c. They are brought out most often by politicians to get votes.
    d. They are discussed only with educators.

| | |
|---|---|
| **Sel. 2**   C-Read | 1. _____ |
| **Finish** _____:_____ | 2. _____ |
| **Start**   _____:_____ | 3. _____ |

| | |
|---|---|
| **Time** \_\_\_\_:\_\_\_\_ | **4.** \_\_\_\_ |
|         min   sec | **5.** \_\_\_\_ |
| **Rate**\_\_\_\_**wpm** | **6.** \_\_\_\_ |
| **Find rate on p. 343.** | **7.** \_\_\_\_ |
| **Score** \_\_\_\_% | **8.** \_\_\_\_ |
|      ▶ 80% | **9.** \_\_\_\_ |
| **Score** = number correct × 10. | **10.** \_\_\_\_ |

Check answers with your
instructor.

Record rate and score on p. 324.

 ## C. Questions for Discussion and Writing

1. Reread paragraph 4. What five explanations are given for a decrease in crime? For you, which of these seems the greatest deterrent to crime? Why do you think so?
2. What main point does Monkkonen argue for throughout this commentary? What evidence in paragraph 5 supports this point?
3. In paragraph 6, Monkkonen states that the youth today are more violent than they were in the past, but he provides no reasons for this fact. Why do you think today's youth are more violent than they once were?
4. In paragraph 9, Monkkonen mentions that crime "hurts our economy." In what ways do you think crime worsens a society's economy?
5. In paragraph 16, Monkkonen asks for criminologists to present "quality research" in the future. Reread paragraphs 15 and 16, then list those practices he thinks would help make future research in criminology more respected.

## Self-Evaluation—Reading Criminology

Answer the following questions by circling yes or no. These responses will help you understand your ability to read criminology critically.

1. yes  no  Was your score in Section B, Critical Reading, below 80 percent?
2. yes  no  Were answers to two or more of your inference questions incorrect?
3. yes  no  Did you answer the paraphrasing question incorrectly?
4. yes  no  Did you have difficulty remembering the major facts supporting the author's argument?

5.  yes   no   Did you find it hard to determine the author's attitude toward the discipline of criminology?

6.  yes   no   Did you have difficulty comparing the attitude toward crime expressed in this selection to that expressed in the previous one?

Scoring:      If you answered yes to three or more of these questions, you need more practice in reading criminology material.

Follow-up:    To improve your critical practices in reading criminology material, consider the following suggestions:

1.  Determine early on the author's attitude toward the causes of crime.

2.  Be sure you can easily recall the factors the author considers important in causing or halting crime.

3.  Compare the author's attitudes toward crime with those of other authors on the subject. Determine which author's point of view seems closest to your own.

4.  Begin to evaluate the author's evidence. Does it convincingly explain the causes of crime?

• • • • • • • • • • • • • • • • • • • •

# SELECTION 3

**Vocabulary**
*scoped:* looked over an area; "as they scoped out the young women"
*vatos:* dudes or guys; "A crew of mean-looking *vatos*"
*metamorphosed:* transformed; "some of the clubs metamorphosed into something more unpredictable"
*yesca:* slang for marijuana; "mostly downers and *yesca*"
*vatitos:* little dude or guy; "one of the *vatitos*"
*caló:* Chicano street slang—urban words and phrases that are neither Spanish nor English; "talked that *caló* slang"
*mescal:* Mexican liquor produced from the cactus plant; "drank mescal"

This is an excerpt from an autobiography by Luis Rodriguez entitled *Always Running*. Rodriguez is a Chicago-based poet and nonfiction writer who was a Los Angeles gang member in his youth. In this excerpt, Rodriguez recounts his junior-high years in San Gabriel, California, and recreates the environment that encouraged him to join a gang in the 1960s.

**Reading Practices.**   To determine what encouraged young Luis to join a gang, consider the following practices:

1.  Note the young Luis's personality and how gang membership satisfied many of his psychological needs.
2.  Consider why, according to Rodriguez, gangs existed in his neighborhood.

3.  Read carefully the sections on the school environment to determine why junior high was the turning point in Luis's decision to join a gang.
4.  After critically reading the excerpt, list several key factors that led to Luis's decision to join a gang.
5.  Do you think that Rodriguez sees his young self as a victim of society, a victimizer, or both?

## A. Preview Skimming

Preview skim the following excerpt in 2:30 minutes (= 1,000 wpm). By the end of your preview, you should have some idea of who Luis is, how he is treated and treats others, and the kind of environment he finds himself in. You should also have a general sense of how his parents respond to his unruly behavior.

Remember, in preview skimming critical material, you should

1.  read the entire first paragraph
2.  read the first sentence of most of the following paragraphs
3.  read the entire last paragraph

When you have finished preview skimming, answer the five P-Skim questions without looking back at the excerpt.

. . . . . . . . . . . . . . . . . . . .

## EXCERPT FROM ALWAYS RUNNING

. . . . . . . . . . . . . . . . . . . .

*by Luis J. Rodriguez (2,500 words)*

1   We didn't call ourselves gangs. We called ourselves clubs or *clicas*. In the back lot of the local elementary school, about a year after Tino's death, five of us gathered in the grass and created a club—"Thee Impersonations," the "Thee" being an old English usage that other clubs would adopt because it made everything sound classier, nobler, *badder*. It was something to belong to—something that was ours. We weren't in boy scouts, in sports teams or camping groups. Thee Impersonations is how we wove something out of the threads of nothing.

2   "We all taking a pledge," Miguel Robles said. "A pledge to be for each other. To stand up for the *clica*. Thee Impersonations will never let you down. Don't ever let Thee Impersonations down."

3   Miguel was 11 years old like the rest of us. Dark, curly-haired and good-looking, he was also sharp in running, baseball and schoolwork—and a leader. Miguel was not prone to loudness or needless talking, but we knew he was the best among us. We made him president of our club.

4   Thee Impersonations was born of necessity. It started one day at the school during lunch break. A few of us guys were standing around talking to some girls—girls we were beginning to see as women. They had makeup and short skirts. They had teased hair and menstruations. They grew breasts. They were no longer Yolanda, Guadalupe or María—they were Yoli, Lupe and Mari.

5   Some of the boys were still in grass-stained jeans with knee patches and had only begun

getting uncontrollable hard-ons. The girls flowered over the summer, and it looked near impossible for some of us to catch up.

6    Older dudes from junior high school, or even some who didn't go to school, would come to the school and give us chilled looks as they scoped out the young women.

7    That day, a caravan of low-scraping cars slow-dragged in front of the school. A crew of mean-looking *vatos* piled out, armed with chains, bats, metal pipes and zip guns.

8    "Thee Mystics rule," one of them yelled from the other side of the school fence.

9    Thee Mystics were a tough up-and-coming group. They fired their rigged .22s at the school and broke a couple of windows with stones. They rammed through the gate and front entrances. Several not-so-swift dudes who stood in their way got beat. Even teachers ran for cover. Terror filled everyone's eyes.

10    I froze as the head-stomping came dangerously my way. But I was also intrigued. I wanted this power. I wanted to be able to bring a whole school to its knees and even make teachers squirm. All my school life until then had been poised against me: telling me what to be, what to say, how to say it. I was a broken boy, shy and fearful. I wanted what Thee Mystics had; I wanted the power to hurt somebody.

11    Police sirens broke the spell. Dudes scattered in all directions. But Thee Mystics had done their damage. They had left their mark on the school—and on me.

12    Miguel and the rest of us started Thee Impersonations because we needed protection. There were other clubs popping up all over, many challenging anybody who wasn't into anything. All of a sudden every dude had to claim a clique.

13    Some of these clubs included Thee Ravens, The Superiors, Latin Legions, Thee Imitations, Los Santos and Chug-a-lug (a curious mix of Anglo and Mexican dudes). These were the "South-side" clubs (for South San Gabriel). The biggest on the Southside then were Thee Illusions and their allies: Thee Mystics.

14    Over in San Gabriel, other cliques were formed such as Thee Regents, The Chancellors, Little Gents, The Intruders and Little Jesters.

15    Most of the clubs began quite innocently. Maybe they were a team of guys for friendly football. Sometimes they were set up for trips to the beach or the mountains. But some became more organized. They obtained jackets, with their own colors, and identification cards. Later a few of the cliques became car clubs, who invested what little they had in bouncing low-riders, street-wise "shorts," splashed with colors, which cruised the main drags of local barrios or the main cruising spot we called the *boulevard*: Whittier Boulevard in East Los Angeles.

16    Then also some of the clubs metamorphosed into something more unpredictable, more encompassing. Something more deadly.

17    Junior high school became the turning point.

18    After grammar school, I ended up going to Richard Garvey Intermediate School. My father had gotten a job as a "laboratory technician" at a Los Angeles community college. So we moved into a larger, two-bedroom place in territory which stood between the two major barrios: *Las Lomas* and *Sangra*. This meant I had to go to Garvey.

19    In the mid-1960s, the students at Garvey had some of the worst academic scores in the state. There were no pencils or papers. Books were discards from other suburban schools where the well-off students turned up. The kids who lived in the Hills found their way into Garvey. And for half of them, the school was the end of the line: It had more than a 50-percent dropout rate among Mexicans before they even got to high school.

20    There were only a couple of Impersonations who made it there. Miguel Robles and the others ended up in another school. Garvey was Illusions and Mystics territory. I was on my own.

21    Again the first thing I noticed were some of the girls. The ones from the Hills weren't just blossoming women, though; they were already hardened, sophisticated. Some of them called

themselves *cholas*. They had long, teased hair, often peroxided black or red. They had heavy makeup, skirts which hugged their behinds, and they were all the time fighting, including with guys. The cholas laughed a lot and knew how to open up to every situation. They talked back, talked loud and talked tough. And they knew how to dance.

22     A few East L.A. people who moved into the Hills brought the East L.A. style with them. There were federally-subsidized housing projects not far from here called Maravilla. It was so named in the 1920s when Los Angeles city officials rebuilt the downtown area and got rid of the Mexicans in the inner core by offering land on the far outreaches of town for a dollar. When the Mexicans got wind of this they exclaimed *"¡Qué Maravilla!"*—what a marvel!—and the name took.

23     My first love at 12 years old was a girl from Maravilla named Elena, a chola, who came to Garvey all *prendida*. She didn't just know how to kiss, but how to take my hand through sections of her body and teach a preteen something of his own budding sexuality.

24     At Garvey, the dudes began to sport cholo attire: the baggy starched pants and suspenders over white T-shirts, the flannel shirts clipped only from the top button, the bandannas and small brim hats. It was hip. It was different. And it was what the cholas liked.

25     This is what I remember of junior high: Cholas who walked up the stairs in their tight skirts, revealing everything, and looked down at us, smiling at their power. Bloody Kotexes on the hallway floor. Gang graffiti on every available space of wall. Fires which flared from restroom trash bins. Fights every day, including after school on the alley off Jackson Avenue. Dudes who sold and took drugs, mostly downers and *yesca*, but sometimes heroin which a couple of dudes shot up in the boys' room while their "homeys" kept a lookout.

26     Yet most of the Mexican girls weren't cholas; their families still had strong reins on many of them. Mexicans were mostly traditional and Catholic. Fathers, mothers or older brothers would drop off these girls and come get them after school so no perceived harm would come their way.

27     One of them was Socorro, from Mexico, who was straight and proper, and tried to stop me from being a cholo. I asked her to become my girlfriend when word got around she liked me and Elena had left me for Ratón, a down dude from the Hills.

28     "They're trash," Socorro would often say in Spanish about the *cholillos*. "If you keep hanging out with them, you can say goodby to me forever."

29     I liked her, but we didn't last too long as a couple. I didn't want to be straight and proper. My next girlfriend was Marina, a girl from Lomas who had one of the highest, peroxided teases on her head with blonde streaks that accentuated her dark face.

30     It was at Marina's urging that I obtained my first tattoo. A dude named Angel charged $5 for an hour's work beneath the school's bleachers. They were crude, unadorned, hand-etchings. Angel used sewing needles, sterilized by placing them over a match flame. He then tied a tight wound of sewing thread on the end. Enough of the needle's point stuck out to penetrate below the skin. Angel dipped the needle into a bottle of black India ink, allowing the thread to soak it up. Then he punctured the skin with quick up and down motions, filling the tiny holes with ink from the thread.

31     I got the tattoo on my upper right arm. It was an outline of a cross beneath the words *"Mi Vida Loca."*

32     We drove teachers nuts at Garvey. A number of them were sent home with nervous breakdowns. We went through three teachers and five substitutes in my home room my first year at the school.

33     One of my teachers was a Cuban refugee named Mr. Enríquez. We made him wish he never left the island. He could hardly speak English. And when he spoke Spanish, it was a sure sign we were in trouble.

34    Every morning Mr. Enríquez entered the class and got bombarded with spit balls and jelly beans. Sometimes he'd turn around to write something on the chalk board and everyone would drop their books all at once.

35    Often you could find Mr. Enríquez with his head on his desk, cursing into folded arms.

36    Then there was the science teacher, Mrs. Krieger. She must have been 80 years old or more. It took her half the class period to walk up the stairs and down the hall to her classroom. By that time most of the class was gone. Once, as she creaked around to write something on the chalk-board, we threw her rain-stained, beat-up ency-clopedias, which were as ancient as she was, out the windows. Then we threw out the desks and chairs. Before long, most of Mrs. Krieger's class-room was scattered across the front lawn—and she didn't realize it until a school official ran puffing up the stairs to investigate what the hell was going on.

37    The school's teachers were made up of misfits, those that other schools didn't want or who for some reason couldn't cut it. The gym teacher looked like a refugee from the Marines who shouted commands even in normal conver-sation, was always dressed in shorts and never failed to have a stainless steel whistle hanging from his bull-neck. The shop teacher was Mr. Stone, who acted exactly as if he were carved out of a thick piece of gray granite. He dealt with us harshly, always on his guard. But one day we broke through his defenses.

38    The shop class was inside an old bungalow at the back of the school. The front door had "Las Lomas" spray-painted on the outside fol-lowed by the words *Con Safos*, the cholo term that signified nobody should mess with this—if they valued their life. Mr. Stone was inside show-ing our class how to cut a piece of wood on a ro-tary saw.

39    Then Elías, one of the *vatitos*, started a racket from the back of the room. Mr. Stone turned around to discipline him. But he forgot to turn off the saw. It sliced away at the board . . . then his finger. Man, what a mess! Mr. Stone

turned a sickening pale color as soon as he real-ized what had happened.

40    "God damn it!" he yelled, "God damn it!" as his face wrinkled with every throb of pain.

41    An ambulance came and rushed Mr. Stone away. School officials shoved everyone else into another classroom until they could hold meet-ings to determine who to blame. But Elías and I sneaked out and returned to the wood shop bungalow. The door was still open. We foraged through the piles of sawdust and wood pieces and found Mr. Stone's finger. It looked pur-plish with dried blood and bone chips on one end. Elías carefully placed it inside an empty cigar box.

42    For weeks we kept the finger in Elías' locker. He'd bring it out to scare some of the girls and to show it off to incoming students un-til it shriveled away, like a dried sliver of old fruit.

*   *   *

43    "You can't be in a fire and not get burned."

44    This was my father's response when he heard of the trouble I was getting into at school. He was a philosopher. He didn't get angry or hit me. That he left to my mother. He had these lines, these cuts of wisdom, phrases and syllables, which swept through me, sometimes even mak-ing sense. I had to deal with him at that level, with my brains. I had to justify in words, with ideas, all my actions—no matter how insane. Most of the time I couldn't.

45    Mama was heat. Mama was turned-around leather belts and wailing choruses of Mary-Mother-of-Jesus. She was the penetrating emo-tion that came at you through her eyes, the mother-guilt, the one who birthed me, who suf-fered through the contractions and diaper changes and all my small hurts and fears. For her, dealing with school trouble or risking my life was nothing for discourse, nothing to debate. She went through all this hell and more to have me— I'd better do what she said!

46    Mama hated the cholos. They reminded her of the rowdies on the border, I suppose our relatives, who fought all the time, talked that *caló* slang, drank mescal, smoked marijuana and left

scores of women with babies bursting out of their bodies.

47    They were her uncles. Her father's friends. Her brothers. To see me become like them made her sick, made her cringe and cry and curse. Mama reminded us how she'd seen so much alcoholism, so much weed-madness, and she prohibited anything with alcohol in the house, even beer. I later learned this rage came from how Mama's father treated her siblings and her mother, how in drunken rages he'd hit her mom and drag her through the house by the hair.

48    The school informed my parents I had been wreaking havoc with a number of other young boys. I was to be part of a special class of troublemakers. We would be isolated from the rest of the school population and forced to pick up trash and clean graffiti during the rest of the school year.

49    "Mrs. Rodríguez, your son is too smart for this," the vice-principal told Mama. "We think

he's got a lot of potential. But his behavior is atrocious. There's no excuse. We're sad to inform you of our decision."

50    They also told her the next time I cut class or even made a feint toward trouble, I'd be expelled. After the phone call, my mom lay on her bed, shaking her head while sobbing in-between bursts of how God had cursed her for some sin, how I was the devil incarnate, a plague, testing her in this brief tenure on earth.

51    My dad's solution was to keep me home after school. Grounded. Yeah, sure. I was 13 years old already. Already tattooed. Already sexually involved. Already into drugs. In the middle of the night I snuck out through the window and worked my way to the Hills.

Luis J. Rodriguez, *Always Running: La Vida Loca: Gang Days in L.A.* (Willimantic, CT: Curbstone Press, 1993), 41–48. Used by permission of the publisher. Distributed by In-Book.

• • • • • • • • • • • • • • • • • • • • • • • • • • •

1.  Luis says he and his friends originally became part of the Thee Impersonations because
    a.  they could sell drugs more easily
    b.  it was a group they could call their own
    c.  they could meet girls more easily
    d.  all of these
2.  The intermediate school that Luis attends
    a.  has a good academic reputation
    b.  does not have any gangs on its campus
    c.  has a poor academic reputation
    d.  both b and c
3.  Rodriguez refers to "cholo attire" that included
    a.  bandannas and small brim hats
    b.  tight-fitting jeans
    c.  baseball caps
    d.  all of these
4.  Rodriguez refers to the teachers at his intermediate school as
    a.  well meaning
    b.  intelligent
    c.  too strict
    d.  misfits

5.  At the end of the excerpt, it seems that Luis
    a.  gets beaten by his father
    b.  sneaks out of his house in defiance of his father's orders
    c.  is expelled from the gang he belongs to
    d.  is sent to juvenile hall

| | |
|---|---|
| **Sel. 3**   P-Skim | 1. _____ |
| **Time**   2:30 = 1,000 wpm | 2. _____ |
| **Score** _____ % | 3. _____ |
| ▶ 80% | 4. _____ |
| **Score** = number correct × 20. | 5. _____ |
| | **Check answers on p. 352.** |

## B. Critical Reading

You are now ready to read critically and carefully to understand why Luis joined a gang and to evaluate his home and school environment. You should also be able to determine whether Luis is more a victimizer or a victim of society.

In the answer box, record the time you start and the time you finish reading the article. After computing the time, answer the questions without looking back at the selection.

1.  *(Inf)* Early in the excerpt, Rodriguez notes, "Thee Impersonations is how we wove something out of the threads of nothing." This suggests that the club
    a.  provided a solid foundation for him
    b.  gave him meaning in an otherwise meaningless life
    c.  was as meaningless as his life
    d.  provided him with ways to make money
2.  Thee Impersonations' first leader is Miguel. Rodriguez describes him as
    a.  very defiant
    b.  intelligent and strong
    c.  unfit for the position of leader
    d.  much older than the rest of the club
3.  In considering the strength of Thee Mystics, Luis realizes that he
    a.  wants to scare an entire school, just like Thee Mystics
    b.  is angry toward a school system that has so often put him down
    c.  is basically shy and scared
    d.  all of these
4.  *(Inf)* Rodriguez notes that "Junior high school became the turning point." What do you think he means?
    a.  He would probably drop out of school during his junior-high years.
    b.  He would probably straighten out his life in junior high.

      c. Junior high provided all the reasons for his becoming a gang member.

      d. Junior high was the most difficult time in his life.

5. Rodriguez describes his junior high school as having

    a. no pencils or paper

    b. discarded books from the richer schools in the district

    c. a 50 percent drop-out rate for the Mexican students

    d. all of these

6. In describing why the boys dressed as cholos, Rodriguez provides all the following reasons *except*

    a. it was different

    b. it was stylish

    c. it was not allowed in school

    d. many of the girls liked it

7. *(Inf)* Why do you think Elías and Luis save Mr. Stone's severed finger?

    a. To impress their peers by showing how defiant they could be.

    b. To make money by charging people to see it.

    c. To remind themselves how unruly their shop class was.

    d. To satisfy their obsession with death.

8. Select the best paraphrase for Rodriguez's description of Mama: "She was the penetrating emotion that came at you through her eyes."

    a. She had powerful emotions that hurt you.

    b. She had eyes that hurt you.

    c. She had strong feelings that she sent out when she stared at you.

    d. She was the deep sentiment that manifested itself in her vision.

9. *(Inf)* In what ways do Luis's parents discipline differently?

    a. Mother is logical; Father is physical.

    b. Father is logical; Mother is physical.

    c. Father is loud; Mother is silent.

    d. Father is hateful; Mother is kind.

10. *(Inf)* This excerpt ends with the suggestion that Luis will

    a. run away from home

    b. obey his mother

    c. continue to live a gang lifestyle

    d. become a writer

---

**Sel. 3**   C-Read

**Finish** \_\_\_\_:\_\_\_\_

**Start** \_\_\_\_:\_\_\_\_

**Time** \_\_\_\_:\_\_\_\_

        min   sec

**Rate**\_\_\_\_**wpm**

**Find rate on p. 343.**

1. \_\_\_\_\_

2. \_\_\_\_\_

3. \_\_\_\_\_

4. \_\_\_\_\_

5. \_\_\_\_\_

6. \_\_\_\_\_

7. \_\_\_\_\_

**Score** ____%                    8. ____

▶ 80%                               9. ____

**Score** = number correct × 10.   10. ____

Check answers on p. 352.

Record rate and score on p. 324.

 C. For Discussion and Writing

1.  Rodriguez says that "Thee Impersonations was born of necessity" (paragraph 4). What evidence can you find in this excerpt that Luis needed to be in a gang?

2.  Rodriguez speaks of his fascination with the gang called Thee Mystics, noting, "I froze as the head-stomping came dangerously my way. But I was also intrigued. I wanted this power" (paragraph 10). What does gang membership have to do with power? Specifically, what power does Luis derive by being a member of Thee Impersonations?

3.  In paragraphs 21–29, Rodriguez talks about the girls who influenced him in junior high. Reread these paragraphs to determine what roles these young women played in Luis's decision to be a gang member.

4.  The excerpt ends with an analysis of Rodriguez's parents. How do their responses to Luis's gang activities differ? Who do you think is the more effective parent? Why?

5.  A strong argument can be made that Luis is a victim of society; there is also evidence in this excerpt that Luis victimizes society as a gang member. Locate evidence that Luis is both victim and victimizer. Then decide where you stand on this issue: Is society to blame for Luis's behavior, or is Luis responsible for his own behavior?

## Self-Evaluation—Reading Nonfictional Narratives

Answer the following questions by circling yes or no. These responses will help you assess your ability to read nonfictional narratives, such as autobiography and biography, critically.

1.  yes   no   Was your score in Section B, Critical Reading, below 80 percent?

2.  yes   no   Were two or more of your answers to the inference questions incorrect?

3.  yes   no   Was your answer to the paraphrasing question incorrect?

4.  yes   no   Did you have a hard time understanding Luis's motivations in choosing a gang life?

5.  yes   no   Was it hard to visualize the characters that Rodriguez portrays?

6.  yes    no    Did you have a hard time finding evidence in the excerpt that Luis was both a victim and a victimizer of society?

Scoring:    If you answered yes to three or more of these questions, you probably need to improve your critical practices in reading nonfictional narratives.

Follow-up:    To improve your critical reading of nonfiction, consider the following suggestions:

1.  Try to visualize the characters and analyze their motivations.

2.  Examine the writer's word choice carefully to see how particular words or phrases shape your understanding of the characters and actions in the story.

3.  An adept biographer or autobiographer selects significant moments in a subject's life. Analyze these moments to determine the ways they are important. Ask questions like "How does this event change the subject's life?" "Why does a particular event recur in the subject's life?"

4.  Biographers and autobiographers often bring a political or ideological perspective to the interpretation of their own or another's character. Early on in your reading, determine what this perspective is, so you can better understand the character being portrayed. For example, assuming that society victimizes a minority is an ideological perspective that you can use to understand the Luis of *Always Running*.

5.  As you continue to read biography and autobiography, you will improve your ability to evaluate nonfictional narratives. Some will seem "truer" than others; that is, they will have intelligently and sensitively captured the life moments of their subjects. You will realize that language, character, and story line all contribute to the power and merit of successful autobiographies and biographies.

•  •  •  •  •  •  •  •  •  •  •  •  •  •  •  •  •  •  •  •

# SELECTION 4

### Vocabulary

*macrohistorical:* pertaining to the more general aspects of history; "This chapter will outline the macrohistorical"

*macrostructural:* pertaining to more general structures; "macrostructural events"

*repatriation:* sending one back to one's country of birth; "the repatriation and deportation of Mexicans"

*cohort:* a group of persons sharing a particular statistical or demographic characteristic; "male cohorting tradition"

*longitudinal study:* a study taken over a relatively long time; "in a longitudinal study of two barrios"

*nested:* an environment favoring growth and development; "partially nested levels of subcultures"

*syncretization:* the combination of differing beliefs; "The Syncretization of a Street Subculture"

*paucity:* scarcity; "the paucity of employment opportunities"

This selection is from an anthology of essays on gangs entitled *Gangs in America.* James Diego Vigil, one of the contributors, is an anthropologist who presents a scholarly view of gang life in Los Angeles, describing gang behavior from a sociological and an anthropological perspective. This selection complements Selection 3 because Vigil introduces concepts that help explain Luis's adolescent gang behavior.

**Reading Practices.**    To appreciate the points Vigil makes, consider the following practices:

1.  Underline the central anthropological terms that Vigil uses; make sure you understand his explanation and use of terms such as *cholo, assimilation, acculturation,* and *socialization.*
2.  Trace carefully cause-effect relationships that Vigil establishes, particularly the historical causes of choloization, the effects of assimilation and acculturation on the Mexican immigrant family, and the social causes of gang activity.
3.  Determine the ideological perspective that Vigil brings to his study: Does society create the cholo, or is the cholo also responsible for his social position?
4.  Paraphrase especially difficult sentences after you have critically read the selection once and are considering some of the questions for discussion and writing.

## A.  Preview Skimming

Preview skim the Vigil selection in 3 minutes (= 933 wpm). In your preview, determine generally what the term *cholo* means, identify the key historical moments that made the cholo a social class in Los Angeles, and determine society's role in developing the cholo lifestyle.

When you have finished your preview, answer the five P-Skim questions without looking back at the selection.

# CHOLOS AND GANGS: CULTURE CHANGE

# AND STREET YOUTH IN LOS ANGELES

*by James Diego Vigil (2,800 words)*

[1] In a 1905 photograph of a Mexican immigrant settlement near downtown Los Angeles, the subtitle prominently displayed is "Cholo Court." The arrangement of a clump of small shanties and haphazard lean-tos set off by a mound of rubbish in the foreground is not the inspiration for the name of this "apartment" complex. Instead, the name is derived from the people. *Cholo* is what the American and established Mexican-American residents called these poorest of the poor, marginalized immigrants. The term itself is several hundred years old and used in various (and mostly Indian) areas of Latin America to describe an indigenous person who is halfway acculturated to the Spanish ways; in short, a person marginal to both the original and the more recent European culture.

[2] Culture change includes modernization, urbanization, and acculturation, and the latter process broadly describes what takes place when two cultures meet (especially when there is an imbalance of power between them), with change taking place in one or both cultures. *Cholo* is a term that, from early times to the present, has been associated with culture change, symbolizing a people caught between two cultures (Vigil, 1988a).

[3] During the Spanish colonial period, *cholo* also meant a "marginalized" person's ethnic background and social status (Vigil, 1984). This chapter will show how the cholo process has continued and persisted in the United States; indeed, Chicano street populations who have undergone intense culture change embrace and use this label with pride to denote their speech, dress, and other customs and habits, as well as themselves. Because of these culture contacts, conflicts, and changes, the "choloization" (i.e., marginalization) of the Mexican population has made some youth more at risk to become gang members. This chapter will outline the macrohistorical and macrostructural events that shaped the cholo subset of the Mexican population, clarify distinctions between the concepts of cholos and gangs, and examine how U.S. choloization affects gang formation. In previous work on gangs (Vigil, 1988a), I have utilized a "multiple marginality" conceptual framework that integrates several interrelated variables, but here I would like to devote attention to the macrohistorical, culture change, and subcultural themes.

## IMMIGRATION

[4] Continual Mexican immigration in this century has added new elements to the cholo historical phenomenon. Many immigrants, already considered cholos in their native country, underwent further—if different—marginal experiences in the United States to add a binational dimension to the word and process of cholo (Chavez, 1988). Others who were less marginally adapted in Mexico became cholos in the United States, through a secondary process of choloization and in response to conditions in the United States. What this means is that a steady stream of cholos arrive and/or are produced in each generation, and because of their backgrounds they are at risk of becoming gang members. In earlier decades, cholos struggled to keep afloat on the environmental fringes and economic margins, and as the American social and economic system underwent transformations, so did they.

[5] Los Angeles, for example, underwent a major industrialization and urbanization boom in the early twentieth century that required tens of thousands of workers. Mexicans constituted a

primary source of labor for such enterprises, and immigrated by the hundreds of thousands in the 1920s (Gamio, 1969). After the late 1920s, economic restructuring with the Depression, the repatriation and deportation of Mexicans to Mexico, and World War II combined to forge something radically new out of the Mexican, and especially the cholo, population. In that period, what Bogardus (1926), a sociologist at the University of Southern California, once referred to as a "boy gang" was now transformed into a gang. The gang membership came from the ranks of cholos; the earlier boy gang was actually a barely changed manifestation of the Mexican *palomilla* (literally, covey of doves) male cohorting tradition.

6    What factors led to this transformation and acceleration of boy gang to gang? Combined with earlier racist practices in schools, public facilities, and the like, the events of the repatriation added insult to injury; the Mexican people learned anew that they were not welcome. Repatriation involved returning Mexican workers and families, now unwanted, to Mexico (Hoffman, 1974). When the Depression created hardships for the U.S. population in general—especially sharp competition for jobs—it affected the low-income, and especially cholo, Mexican population even more adversely. One can imagine the thoughts that ran through the minds of these people as they lost jobs, household and family stability, and their already tenuous hold on America, and simultaneously learned that they had lost their purpose here and were to be sent home.

7    One reaction to such racist treatment involved an increase by some Mexicans in challenging and somewhat antisocial behavior, especially among the second-generation youth, who liked to consider themselves American but (as historical events dictated) realized they were being rejected. Indeed, families with what previously had appeared to be successful cultural adaptation strategies were being thwarted. The response of such individuals often was aimed at proving that they were American, by frequenting

restricted movie theaters, swimming pools, and restaurants, with the understanding and expectation that they might be turned away. Approximating a mild form of antisocial behavior, such incidents became even more inflamed during World War II, when the Zoot Suit Riots erupted. Preceded by a steady increase in Anglo-Mexican friction, these 1943 riots culminated with servicemen and Anglo citizens hunting down and beating up Mexican youth dressed in "zoot suits" (Mazon, 1985; McWilliams, 1968).

8    The Zoot Suit Riots, and especially the increase in anti-Mexican sentiment among the Anglo-American population, have been underscored as the turning point in the development of a serious gang problem. Previously, the public and police attitude toward the street youth had produced many forms of harassment, but with the hysteria of the war and the surge of Mexican civil-rights strivings, there was a sharp increase in media and police activities that focused on the youth population, cholos and noncholos alike. Newspapers especially took aim at the dress of the *pachucos*, the label for Mexican-Americans who wore zoot suits and affected a "hip" street style. This, however, was a veiled disguise for a more generalized anti-Mexican media campaign. Police, announcing that street "punks" were breaking laws and threatening the fabric of society, launched roadblocks and roundups to drive the youths into jail or into orderly behavior (McWilliams, 1968). According to Alfredo Gonzales (1981), the events of this period mark the beginning of the "labeling" of the youth as gang members; the labeling in turn led to an intensification of gang participation rather than diminishing the phenomena.

9    As these events unfolded, World War II took many positive Mexican male role models away from the *barrios* (neighborhoods) to fight the war; ironically, this occurred soon after segments of the population had been repatriated. The males that were left in the community for the younger cohort to look up to were those rejected from service, with criminal records, and usually the poorest of the poor cholos. Thus

"model absence" was a major turning point in transforming the boy gang into a gang.

10    In a longitudinal study of two barrios in East Los Angeles, Joan Moore (1978) and her colleagues at the Chicano Pinto Research Project (CPRP) have documented how the war and its aftermath changed the nature and trajectory of youth groups, and in concert with choloization generated negative gang and drug activities, with the latter, in time, acting as a force of change. During the first decades in the barrios of El Hoyo Maravilla and White Fence, the youth groups followed more a palomilla cohorting pattern of mischief rather than mayhem, gradually coalescing into the "boy gangs" that Bogardus noted. In the CPRP investigations, it is remarkable that one of the barrios used the group name of the local parish they attended, Purisima, and only after the war did the name White Fence become common; the name change marks the shift from palomilla/boy gang to gang.

11    With the Depression over, repatriation complete, and World War II under way, there were other changes, especially more immigration. The war made the United States short of labor, and the government was prodded by agribusiness interests—now in need of field and other laborers—to enact laws to bring "guest workers" to work sites. Thus the *bracero* (field hand; from *brazos*, arms) program was initiated; when the war ended, this program continued. With the boom in the American economy in the aftermath of World War II, there was need for even more such laborers, even though there were repetitions of repatriation efforts (such as Operation Wetback in 1954) to complicate and exacerbate choloization further. Mexican immigration burgeoned with both documented and undocumented workers entering the United States, a pattern that ebbed and flowed into subsequent decades (Moore & Pachon, 1985).

12    Meanwhile, many of the original barrios found another type of migration taking place. Improvements in the work and earning powers of many families resulted in social mobility. Moving up also included moving out of the barrio.

Barrios became for Mexicans a stepping-stone to the American dream of a better home and neighborhood. Returning GIs were a part of this process. The nation, appreciative of their war record, created many federal programs to aid their readjustment, and Mexican-American GIs—like others—took advantage of these opportunities. Housing loans made it easier to move out of the barrio. A side effect of this process was that the barrio would have even fewer positive role models, thus robbing barrio youths of such influences at both ends of the war.

## ACCULTURATIONAL AND GENERATIONAL CHANGE

13    Through all these transformations there were some families who were unable to become socially mobile, instead suffering one setback after another and thus experiencing long-term poverty. Although most immigrant families were subjected to economic shifts and culture change, some of the families were burdened even more. When generational and status change is throttled, choloization is intensified. In time this tended to change the conditions in the barrios, with the less successful families left behind and with less hope and inspiration shaping the future of the new generations of youth. A budding, incipient underclass began to form.

14    With the passage of time choloization began to take new twists and turns. Specific time and place revisions affected how the immigrant population would recreate a new culture in the United States. None contributed more to the creation of a cholo subculture than the dynamic events listed above. A general cultural orientation began to evolve in all barrios that became a part of this experience.

15    At first, immigrants arrived just to work and survive, but soon after, some of the families began to adapt to U.S. culture. With the first generation, it was relatively simple to retain their native lifeways as workplace, home, and social and recreational activities kept most of the population together. Throughout the 1920s and 1930s this connection with their primary ethnicity

remained; this is when the palomilla pattern prevailed (Bogardus, 1934). With the second generation, there was a sharp departure from the past. These "Americans" earnestly sought to capture the "dream." Practicing a type of secondary ethnicity, they learned the English language and Anglo-American ways while, in varying degrees and intensities, retaining their association and familiarity with Mexican customs. Assimilation was the answer to some, those who wished to forget their past and look only to the future, especially if rapid social and residential mobility was desired. Acculturation, however, was the more common route for most of those from the second generation. In the Mexican case, as in most immigrant communities, it was more often unidirectional acculturation because of the asymmetrical power relationships dictated by the dominant Anglo-American group.

16    For a significant group of Mexicans, both immigrant and native cholos, the environmental and socioeconomic obstacles (as well as the historical dynamics noted above) operated to strain cultural adaptation strategies, whether of assimilation or acculturation. As a result, a large segment of the community experienced personal and group alienation from both cultures—the depth and degree, of course, mediated by other circumstances. To reiterate, this is a throttling of generational and status change, and thus an intensification of choloization; it can result in "erring acculturation," where movement to an established conventional life-style is stymied and thus a propensity arises to create a new subculture and/or accept the cholo one.

17    It is this cultural transitional process that creates the confusion and ambiguity that affect youths' sense of cultural identity and loyalty. When ethnic boundaries are weakened by culture change, as happens in the cultural transition process between the first and second generations, there is a change in the ethnic group's ability to command and retain the involvement, attention, and identity of its members. In such circumstances, a subculture based on new boundaries evolves and becomes a cohesive cultural system. The subculture of cholos can be defined broadly in this manner, but with the understanding that even this subculture can be divided further into smaller subcultures. In short, subcultures and smaller subcultures evolve over several generations (Molohon, Paton, & Lambert, 1979).

18    The U.S. experiences of Mexicans over several generations have given rise to various subcultural strata within that group. The subcultural strata have been shaped by the dynamics and variations of change reflected in each generation. One must think of partially nested levels of subcultures to appreciate the complexity and diversity of the Mexican-American community. The first generation is the broadest subculture, for it represents the initial phase of adaptation to living and working conditions, racial disparagement, and institutional neglect and is a commonly shared phenomenon. With the second generation as cultural transitionals, another subculture evolves—namely, that of the cholo—and it involves more extensive culture conflict. Most individuals work their way through this phase without knowing they are cholos, as I have defined the term broadly, and opt for assimilation or a mixed acculturation strategy that incorporates elements of Mexican and Anglo-American culture, including in some cases bilingual fluency (Buriel, 1984).

19    A considerable number of individuals of this group, however, are unable to devise a smooth, consistent strategy of adaptation. For them, often, the effects of racism, the persistent cycle of poverty with little chance of social mobility, and the general malaise engendered by problems with school and employment have dominated their lives and impeded acculturation, as well as overall cultural adaptation. These are the individuals who are the end product of the choloization process, for they become identified with the label *cholo*. Cholo identification is reflective of their plight—no way out, locked in—or what has been referred to as the underclass (Moore, 1985; Wilson, 1987), members of which suffer from "persistent and concentrated

poverty"; in short, a cholo is a type of institutionalization of marginalization. This cholo lifestyle is an American experience set in the strains and stresses of prolonged immobility, of missed opportunities and social setbacks, that affects how Mexican culture is relinquished and American culture acquired, an adjustment process that spawns a mixed culture. An individual's status as a cholo may be of relatively short duration or it may be lifelong in nature. Similarly, gang members drawn from the ranks of cholos may remain in the gang briefly or for prolonged careers; the latter tend to be the individuals who reflect the most intense multiple pressures and conflicts of choloization.

## THE SYNCRETIZATION OF A STREET SUBCULTURE

20    The rise and formation of the gang subculture revolves around the broader backdrop of culture conflict and choloization of the second-generation Mexican-American population. The process becomes more intensified in the third generation, within which a subculture of the streets has become institutionalized. This gang subculture is nested within and part of the broader cholo and Mexican-American subcultures.

21    Participants in the gang subculture are drawn largely from youths who, in middle childhood, have relied increasingly on street peers for socialization. Youths with particularly problematic, traumatic family and personal experiences—mostly unsupervised and lacking adult guidance, coming from the most choloized segments of the population—are forced to the streets because it is a convenient open space for play and socializing and a relief from their drab backgrounds. In doing so, these youths—as young as 8 years old—must learn how to survive fear-inspiring situations, particularly encounters with strangers (mostly other youths like themselves) who approach them as fair game. Street peers, some slightly older and a few in their early teens, become the major agents of socialization to help in their adjustment. The friends one makes on the streets and the activities that are learned there often carry over into the school setting, where friendship bonds and street lessons are reinforced as indifference or hostility to school and authority grows.

22    During adolescence, problems with age and sex role identification exacerbate structural and environmental stresses. Street youths at this point typically become school dropouts, thus providing themselves with more time for street affairs. Lacking training of any sort, too young to fill most jobs, and facing the paucity of employment opportunities for low-income minority youth populations generally, such youths are clearly at risk for joining in and following gang patterns.

23    Most of the time spent with gang street peers is devoted to having a good time—drinking beer or wine, smoking marijuana, or participating in recreational events such as parties and sports. At times, however, gang activities take on a more deviant character, as members strive to live up to street-induced notions of "manly" behavior or to demonstrate their loyalty to the gang: gang fights, for example, and sometimes criminal activity directed outside the gang arena. It is the latter, less widely accepted activities that have gained the public's attention. Part of this gang pattern derives from tradition (i.e., gang lore and mythology, intergenerational influences) and part stems from technology (i.e., movie and television images of violence, availability of guns, and mind-altering chemical substances). Such socially destructive habits lend a pervasive aura of death to drug use and abuse and barrio gang rivalries. Although participation in such habits enhances one's status and recognition—for doing these "gang" things shows courage and *huevos* ("balls")—it is clear that conditions conducive to street socialization and its processes have altered adolescent "storm and stress" dynamics (Vigil, 1988b).

24    As Moore (1978) has argued convincingly, the introduction of heroin use, and especially heroin and other drug dealing, in the late 1940s and early 1950s was a major factor in changing

the gang into a more formalized unit and furthering its evolutionary path of palomilla to boy gang to gang subculture. It was also in the 1940s in some barrios, and greatly intensified by the 1960s, when third-generation, street-socialized gangs became more extensive, with each new generation of barrio youth growing up in the presence of the institutionalized street gangs. Within each generation are youths with problematic backgrounds who increasingly are pushed into the streets and drawn into the gangs.

25   This gang subculture has changed realities such that new immigrant children have to adapt and contend with it; one Latino youth even told me that gang-banging (fighting) is like "showing you are American," or assimilated. As Plant (1937) remarked, commenting on "white ethnic" youth in the 1930s, "If it is true that the triumphs and tragedies of the street flow into and become a part of the child, then all programs of personality change must manage somehow to change the street." There is a clear interplay between street socialization and the evolution of a gang subculture. Macrohistorical forces and structural conditions have altered social control institutions in such a way that children are forced to deal with the streets as a social arena.

C. Ronald Huff, ed., *Gangs in America* (Newbury Park, CA: Sage, 1990), 116–126. © 1990 Sage Publications, Inc. Reprinted by permission of the publishers.

• • • • • • • • • • • • • • • • • • • • • • • • • • • • • • • •

1. For Vigil, the term *cholo* originally referred to
   a. any Mexican immigrant
   b. the poorest and most disconnected Mexican immigrant
   c. the successful Mexican immigrant
   d. a juvenile delinquent

2. Vigil notes that Mexicans often immigrated to Los Angeles when
   a. natural disasters occurred in Mexico
   b. the Mexican government expelled its poorest citizens
   c. the city needed labor for its expanding industries
   d. they became wealthy in Mexico

3. Vigil notes that the Mexican gang problem in Los Angeles worsened after
   a. the Spanish-American War
   b. the Civil War
   c. the Zoot Suit Riots
   d. none of these

4. Vigil believes that Mexican gang members learn most about gangs from their
   a. fathers
   b. friends on the street
   c. relatives in Mexico
   d. viewing of television

5. Vigil concludes by noting that
   a. gang violence is on the decrease
   b. more Mexicans are being assimilated into U.S. culture
   c. younger children are joining gangs
   d. street socialization plays a major role in the development of gang behavior

**Sel. 4**   P-Skim                1. \_\_\_\_\_

**Time**   3:00 = 933 wpm          2. \_\_\_\_\_

**Score**   \_\_\_\_ %               3. \_\_\_\_\_

   ▶ 80%                           4. \_\_\_\_\_

**Score** = number correct × 20.   5. \_\_\_\_\_

**Check answers with your instructor.**

## B.  Critical Reading

Now go back to read the selection critically, filling in the details you missed in your preview. Carefully consider the terms that Vigil introduces and determine clearly the cause-effect relationships that influence the cholo lifestyle.

1.  Which statement does *not* describe a cholo?
    a.  He is very poor.
    b.  He has a strong Spanish identity.
    c.  He feels that he does not belong to any culture.
    d.  He uses the term *cholo* with pride.
2.  (*Inf*) Choloization seems most closely related to
    a.  social change
    b.  skin color
    c.  dress
    d.  the Catholic religion
3.  (*Inf*) Vigil suggests that a major cause of Mexican gang activity is
    a.  U.S. racist practices
    b.  the dissolution of the Mexican-American family
    c.  the loss of strong ties to the Catholic Church
    d.  the rise of the Mexican-American middle class
4.  Vigil notes that when Mexican-American youth were labeled "gang members" by the police and other authority figures,
    a.  gang participation increased
    b.  gang participation decreased
    c.  gang members developed greater pride
    d.  gang members began cooperating with the police
5.  During World War II, what one event helped increase gang activity in Los Angeles?
    a.  fewer positive Mexican male role models
    b.  the ease with which firearms could be purchased
    c.  poorer economic conditions in the barrio
    d.  less state support for schools

6. *(P)* Choose the most effective paraphrase for the following sentence: "In the Mexican case, as in most immigrant communities, it [acculturation] was more often unidirectional acculturation because of the asymmetrical power relationships dictated by the dominant Anglo-American group" (paragraph 15).
   a. For Mexicans, becoming part of the United States meant adopting the ways of the white American.
   b. Power relationships among Mexicans and U.S. citizens are never equal.
   c. With Mexicans, as with other foreign societies, acculturation often happened in one direction due to the unequal power forced on the Mexicans by the more powerful British-Americans.
   d. With Mexicans, as with most first-generation groups, changing cultural behavior often meant taking on the white U.S. culture because this culture had more power.

7. Vigil contends that when the Mexican youth begin to fall away from their traditional cultural practices,
   a. the parents also fall away from their cultural practices
   b. the culture loses its authority to shape the youth's behavior
   c. cholos lose their control over the youth
   d. the youth take on the values of the Anglo Americans

8. The cholo who tends to stay in a gang for a long time often
   a. wields great power in the Mexican-American community
   b. makes much money illegally
   c. has the most social and cultural conflicts of any Mexican-American social group
   d. no longer feels marginalized

9. For Vigil, Mexican-American gang activity is influenced by all of these factors *except*
   a. Mexican tradition
   b. movie and television viewing
   c. ties to family in Mexico
   d. availability of drugs

10. *(Inf)* Why does one Latino youth say that gang-banging or fighting is like "showing you are American"?
    a. Fighting has become accepted street behavior in the barrios of the United States.
    b. Anglo-American youth tend to fight more than do Mexican-American youth.
    c. All immigrant youth originally began their life in the United States by fighting in the streets.
    d. all of these

| **Sel. 4**  C-Read | 1. _____ |
| **Finish** _____:_____ | 2. _____ |
| **Start** _____:_____ | 3. _____ |

Time _____:_____

       min   sec

Rate_____wpm

**Find rate on p. 343.**

Score _____%

    ▶ 80%

**Score** = number correct × 10.

4. _____

5. _____

6. _____

7. _____

8. _____

9. _____

**10.** _____

**Check answers with your instructor.**

**Record rate and score on p. 324.**

 ## C. For Discussion and Writing

1. Read this selection over to define as completely as you can the terms *cholo* and *choloization*.
2. Define the anthropological terms *acculturation* and *assimilation* as used by Vigil. Then discuss how these terms help you understand the behavior of the cholo in Los Angeles.
3. In paragraphs 6–10, Vigil describes how Mexican-American boy gangs became modern gangs. Reread this section and discuss the factors that led to this transformation.
4. In paragraph 19, Vigil provides a thorough character profile of the cholo in Los Angeles. Reread this paragraph and summarize the key aspects of the profile. Based on your reading of the entire excerpt, do you think any other characteristics should be included in this profile?
5. Review the Selection 3. Describe Luis Rodriguez in a short paragraph. Then, to determine if Luis fits Vigil's profile of the cholo, summarize Vigil's profile and apply it to your description of Luis.

## Self-Evaluation—Reading Academic Material in the Social Sciences

Answer the following questions by circling yes or no. These responses will help you understand your ability to critically read academic material in the social sciences.

1. yes  no  Was your score in Section B, Critical Reading, below 80 percent?
2. yes  no  Were two or more of your answers to the inference questions incorrect?

3.  yes   no    Was your answer to the paraphrasing question incorrect?

4.  yes   no    Did you have a hard time understanding the various cause-effect relationships that the author established?

5.  yes   no    Was it hard to understand and remember the various terms the author introduced?

6.  yes   no    Did you have difficulty understanding the author's sometimes complicated writing style?

Scoring:    If you answered yes to three or more of these questions, you most likely need more practice in reading academic material in the social sciences.

Follow-up:  To improve your critical skills in reading this academic material, consider the following suggestions:

1.  Academic material in the social sciences often presents several technical definitions that are usually interrelated. As you read, be sure that you understand each term and its relationship to the other terms before you continue reading.

2.  The sentence structure of academic material is often complex. Use your paraphrasing abilities whenever you need to put an important sentence in your own words.

3.  Academic material in sociology and anthropology establishes several cause-effect relationships, which you should look for. Be sure to separate causes from effects. Note that multiple causes often lead to a single effect.

4.  Authors of sociological and anthropological material write from specific ideological perspectives. Early on in your reading, try to determine the writer's attitude toward society, government, and culture. As you read, determine whether this perspective clarifies or distorts the social issue under discussion.

## Follow-Up

Now that you have read four critical-reading selections, you may have changed some of your ideas regarding crime and criminal behavior and improved some of your critical-reading practices. You may want to answer the following questions singly or in small or large groups.

### On Breaking the Law

1.  What factors do you now think help create a criminal: society, the individual, or a combination of factors?

2.  Why do you think the formal study of crime is so complicated?

3.  How do you think criminals should be rehabilitated? Or do you think that criminals can never be rehabilitated?

4.  What do you think are the root causes of gang activity? How do you think gang members can change or be changed for the better?

**On Critical Reading**

1.  Has your ability to read for inferences improved? If not, what part of this reading practice do you still need to work on?
2.  Can you draw reasoned conclusions? If not, what about drawing conclusions still confuses you?
3.  What type of critical reading is the easiest for you to understand: commentaries, narratives, or academic material? Why do you think this is so?
4.  What aspects of critical reading do you still need to work on?

## Internet Activity

Use the Internet to do more research on critical reading and criminology. Break up into groups of four or five. To answer the following questions, use the Internet source and InfoTrac College Edition. Then return to your group with your information.

If you cannot access this source or InfoTrac College Edition, research the Internet to find information on critical reading and criminology to answer these questions.

**On Critical Reading**

To answer the following questions, see if you can access San Jose State's Interactive Critical Thinking Tutorial web site.

1.  What new information on critical reading did you find?
2.  Does any of this information differ from what you learned in the introduction to this chapter?
3.  Describe how you accessed this information.

**On Criminology**

If you have access to InfoTrac College Edition, use this research tool to learn more about criminology to complete the following activities:

1.  Locate and print an article of interest related to the topic of breaking the law.
2.  Summarize this article.
3.  Describe how you located this information.

## How to Record Your Scores on the Progress Chart

After you have finished a timed selection and have entered your time and score in the score box:

1.  Find the correct selection number on the top row of the chart. Transfer your rate (wpm) to the chart, under the selection number. Make a dot, X, bar, or other mark. (If you know your time only, not your rate, you must first look up your wpm in Appendix B. Then mark that number on the chart.) Note

that the acceptable or "target" rates for the featured skill are shaded. Do your rates fall within the target areas?

2. Transfer your critical reading (C-Read) comprehension score to the top blank on the chart. Note that the acceptable or "target" percentage for that selection is printed underneath the blank. Does your score meet—or surpass—the target percentage?

3. Connect the rate marks with a line to see your progress clearly. Remember, though, that your scores will not necessarily rise steadily. The different selections contain too many variables—difficulty, your interest in or familiarity with the topic, and so forth.

. . . . . . . . . . . . . . . . . . . . . . . .

# *PROGRESS CHART: CRITICAL READING*

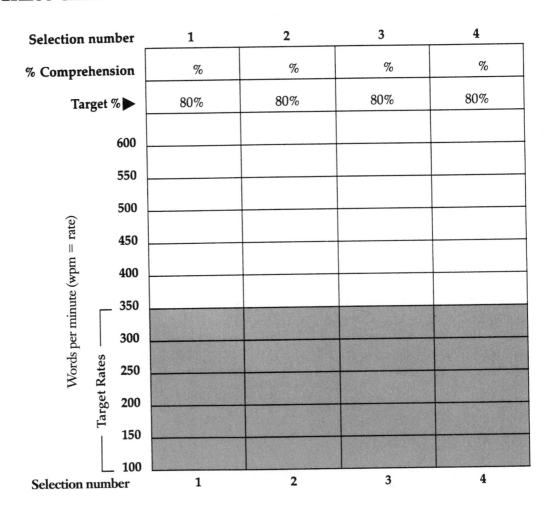

| Selection number | 1 | 2 | 3 | 4 |
|---|---|---|---|---|
| % Comprehension | % | % | % | % |
| Target % ▶ | 80% | 80% | 80% | 80% |

Words per minute (wpm = rate)

| | 1 | 2 | 3 | 4 |
|---|---|---|---|---|
| 600 | | | | |
| 550 | | | | |
| 500 | | | | |
| 450 | | | | |
| 400 | | | | |
| 350 | | | | |
| 300 | | | | |
| 250 | | | | |
| 200 | | | | |
| 150 | | | | |
| 100 | | | | |

Target Rates

**Selection number**     1          2          3          4

# *Scanning*

*T*his chapter will help you become more self-aware when you scan for information, and thus more accurate and efficient. Neither reading nor skimming, scanning is a semireading skill we use every day as we search through print for answers to specific questions. These questions can range from simple to quite difficult and sophisticated.

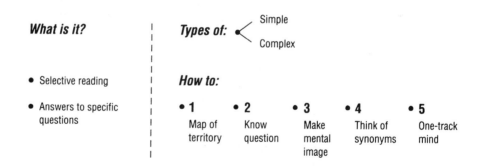

**What is it?**

- Selective reading
- Answers to specific questions

**Types of:** Simple / Complex

**How to:**

- **1** Map of territory
- **2** Know question
- **3** Make mental image
- **4** Think of synonyms
- **5** One-track mind

# INTRODUCTION TO SCANNING

· · · · · · · · · · · · · · · · · · · ·

## CHECKLIST OF SYMPTOMS

Do you often

_____ 1. avoid looking things up in reference books because it takes too long?

_____ 2. fail to find the answer to a question, only to have others find it for you?

_____ 3. waste time looking for an answer in the wrong places?

_____ 4. find an answer much more slowly than others do?

_____ 5. get distracted from your search and end up reading irrelevant things?

If you checked one or more of these symptoms, this chapter can help you. You may very likely be a good, careful reader, one who likes to "read it all and not miss anything" regardless of time. But if these traits become problems, this chapter can help.

· · · · · · · · · · · · · · · · · · · ·

## WHAT IS SCANNING?

Reading experts consider scanning a form of selective reading ("skip-reading"), such as you studied in Chapters 2 and 5. However, scanning differs greatly from both preview and overview skimming, as well as from skimming in general.

When you *preview* skim a work, you prepare for a full reading and comprehension of the material by getting the "big picture." When you *overview skim* a work (after a short preview), you read only the key parts of the material to understand the main ideas. In both situations, the material is new; you start with no preconceptions, ready to learn some new ideas.

In contrast, *when you scan print, you begin with a specific question that has a specific answer.* Since you seek very limited information, you read even less of the material than in previewing or overviewing. Scanning is the fastest way you will ever process print. Let's say you want to find in your daily paper the answer to the question, "Who won the Plush-Green Open yesterday?" You look, or scan, through the print for the answer. You ignore or mentally discard material that does not pertain to your question. When you find the part that probably contains the answer, you slow down and read carefully. "So, Joe Tschopper won!" You then respond with a small "Aha!"

Technically a sort of scanning occurs in our normal, continuous reading. Some regressions are a "scanning backward" to check or correct a specific word. Such regressions take place so rapidly—in hundredths of a second—that we are not aware of them. But they provide valuable feedback to the brain, clearing up ambiguous messages and inaccuracies.

However, we are more interested here in the conscious scanning we must do in connection with our reading. This type may *precede, follow,* or *substitute for* complete reading:

1.  *Scanning that precedes reading:* You might first scan through a news story about food poisoning to see which cities were involved. If your city was mentioned, you would return to the beginning of the story and read very carefully.
2.  *Scanning that follows reading:* Your sociology professor makes a statement in class that seems to contradict the textbook. You scan back over the chapter to find the exact point in question before you raise your hand.
3.  *Scanning that substitutes for reading:* You might scan a magazine to see if it contains an article on that talk-show host you love to hate. Seeing none, you toss the magazine back on the shelf. In each of these examples, you began with a specific question, then read selectively—only enough to answer your question.

As you might have guessed, scanning skills are constantly used in all office work—at desk or computer—and in reference, research, and business tasks. We also use these skills in ordinary living—whenever we look up a phone number, check directions in a manual, look for a particular road sign. We scan our computer screens with the "scroll," "page up," "page down" keys. Scanning tasks vary tremendously, from simple recognition ("Where's the word *dilemma* in my dictionary?") to demanding and complex questions ("How can I support my term-paper thesis that Hemingway was kind to animals?").

Whatever the situation, scanning does little good unless it is both *accurate* and *fast.* A person who finds the wrong answers, or finds the right ones slowly, is at a disadvantage. Luckily, all scanning improves markedly with practice, as you might discover after taking a clerical job or writing umpteen research papers. In this chapter, you will find two kinds of scanning practices—simple and complex. If you need basic perceptual (speed-of-recognition) drills, please ask your instructor for help.

. . . . . . . . . . . . . . . . . .

## *HOW TO SCAN—IN GENERAL*

1.  Always start with a "map of the territory"—preview it first. Know how your library, telephone directory, and newspaper are arranged. Familiarize yourself with the table of contents and index of your book or manual. This way, you will not waste time looking blindly in unlikely places.
2.  Know the specific question, whether yours or posed by someone else. Understand clearly what it is you are scanning for.
3.  Next, make a mental image of the item or fact you are looking for. Cue your eyes and brain consciously for that one image and nothing else.
4.  If that item or fact does not appear, be ready to paraphrase—that is, think of synonyms or "translations" for your question. If the word *gym* does not work, look for *spa, health club, recreational facilities,* and so on.

5.  Keep a one-track mind; be alert; be aggressive. Sometimes it helps to stand up as you scan, especially if you are easily seduced into reading irrelevant material.

    You may want to complete Practices 7.1–7.4, starting on page 330.

6.  For more complex scanning, do all the above plus the following. You will need a thorough prior knowledge of the material you are working on, as well as a familiarity with patterns of organization, stylistic devices (placement, diction—all the writer's choices), rhetoric and logic and rules of evidence. In fact, complex scanning is a part of *interpretation* or *critical reading*, requiring intelligence and patience. It is a skill you need in order to avoid a common error: uncritical acceptance of the printed word.

    You may want to complete Practices 7.5–7.10, starting on page 334.

. . . . . . . . . . . . . . . . . . . .

# SUMMARY

Scanning is a highly directed way of searching print for answers to questions. When we scan, we process print faster than any other kind of reading or skimming, at speeds well over 1,000 wpm, because we read only the part that contains our answer. Scanning tasks range from the very simple, such as the perception and recognition of identical elements; to the less simple, such as "translating" the question into various terms, to the very complex, such as collecting evidence or tracing an idea.

All scanning improves greatly with practice. For the best performance, review the six scanning tips occasionally.

*Note:* If you set out to scan the classifieds in the evening newspaper and soon find yourself reading the latest discoveries about Mars, you have violated all our rules. But all is not lost. A lot of good reading gets done that way.

## SUMMARY BOX: SCANNING

| What? | Why? | Acceptable Comprehension | Acceptable Rates |
|---|---|---|---|
| *Simple:* lists, perception drills, dictionary, White Pages, tables, signs, classified ads | To find particular facts, words, names, numbers, and specific information | 100% | 1,000 wpm and up |
| *Less simple:* Yellow Pages, reference works, tables of content, indexes, card catalogs | To find services, data, resources, when exact wording not available | 100% | |
| *Complex:* continuous prose—documents, articles, books, long descriptions | To follow an argument, style, reasons, motifs, patterns, support for inference, evidence of sound reasoning vs. propaganda and bias | 100% | |

# PRACTICES: SCANNING

The answer key for the odd-numbered practices is provided in Appendix C. Please see your instructor for answers to the even-numbered practices. Use time pressure to improve your efficiency, but remember that scanning accuracy, or your score, should be 100 percent. Where wording is flexible, count your answer correct if it is substantially like the answer key.

If you cannot find an answer after a reasonable search, move on to the next question.

**Simple Scanning**

7.1 LOCATING SPECIFIC ITEMS IN A TEXTBOOK
7.2 REPHRASING THE QUESTION
7.3 SPOTTING CLUES: TRANSITIONS AND SIGNALS
7.4 SCANNING THROUGH CONTINUOUS PROSE

**Complex Scanning**

7.5 SCANNING BIOLOGY TEXTS
7.6 SCANNING PHILOSOPHY TEXTS
7.7 SCANNING COMMENTARY (OPINION)
7.8 SCANNING CRIMINOLOGY TEXTS
7.9 SCANNING NONFICTIONAL NARRATIVES
7.10 SCANNING SOCIOLOGY TEXTS

. . . . . . . . . . . . . . . . . .

# SIMPLE SCANNING

### 7.1  LOCATING SPECIFIC ITEMS IN A TEXTBOOK

As fast and as accurately as possible, scan this textbook to answer the following questions.

1. What is the copyright date for this book?
   _____

2. Scan the introductory section "To the Student." How many areas of reading proficiency do the authors contend there are? _____

3. Scan the introductory section "About the Authors." From what university did Anne G. Phillips earn her master's degree? _____

4. Which chapter has the fewest pages? _____

5. How many chapters begin with a "Checklist of Symptoms"? _____

6. What is the third point in the Overview Skimming introduction under "How to Overview Skim—In Detail"? _____

7. Of all the reprinted selections, which is the only one about retirement? Selection _____ in Chapter _____.

8. Of all the reprinted selections, which one seems to discuss the discomfort men feel? Selection _____ in Chapter _____.

9. If you want to review tips for owning a franchise business, which selection might you wish to reread? Selection _____ in Chapter _____.

10. In the introduction to Chapter 7, some of our regressions are said to be "a scanning _____."

Time _____:_____

min    sec

Score _____%

Score = number correct × 10.

Check answers on p. 353.

## 7.2 REPHRASING THE QUESTION

When you use reference works, directories, almanacs, or similar sources to answer a question, you must usually keep your mind flexible. That is, you must think of synonyms to rephrase your question or topic. Read the following topic. Then scan through the list and check any likely synonyms. Leave the others blank. Remember to time yourself.

*Example:* motels in town

a. _____ Hotels
b. _____ Best Western
c. _____ Motor hotels
d. _____ Restaurants
e. _____ Resorts
f. _____ Accommodations
g. _____ Lodging

Did you identify "d. Restaurants" as your misfit? How many seconds did you take to spot the category that does not fit? Now do the next five the same way. See if you can finish all five in 45 seconds or less.

1. My congressional representative
   a. _____ Federal offices
   b. _____ County government
   c. _____ Government, city
   d. _____ Voter registration
   e. _____ Elections, board of

2. U.S. population, twentieth century
   a. _____ American colonies, 1630–1780
   b. _____ Demographics, American
   c. _____ Census, statistics
   d. _____ U.S. census figures
   e. _____ Population by states, 1900–1990

3. City trash pickup
   a. _____ City services
   b. _____ Waste removal, local
   c. _____ Municipal garbage department
   d. _____ Government offices, city
   e. _____ Information, City Hall
4. Family problems
   a. _____ Counseling, family
   b. _____ Therapists—children, family, marital
   c. _____ Referral service, psychological
   d. _____ Family fun parks
   e. _____ Agencies, city and county
5. Fix the dent in my Toyota Camry!
   a. _____ Body repair
   b. _____ Import autos
   c. _____ Foreign cars
   d. _____ Automotive repair
   e. _____ Domestic car care

Time _____:_____

min     sec

Score _____%

Score = number correct × 10.

Check answers with your instructor.

## 7.3 Spotting Clues: Transitions and Signals

Scan the list of signals for the ones that point to the content you want. Place the letter next to the appropriate number, as we have done for 1.

| If you're scanning for: | | Look for words like: |
|---|---|---|
| 1. spatial relationship | _k_ | a. to start, first, next, later, last |
| 2. a contrast | _____ | b. again, i.e., in other words |
| 3. what a person looks like | _____ | c. similar, as, resembling, like |
| 4. additional points | _____ | d. descriptive details |
| 5. a comparison | _____ | e. for example, an instance, to illustrate |
| 6. categories/classifications | _____ | f. group, type, class, sort |
| 7. a repetition | _____ | g. finally, to sum up |
| 8. a specific case | _____ | h. and, also, plus, besides |
| 9. steps, or time line | _____ | i. but, however, on the other hand, counter to |

10. cause and effect          _____      j.  leading to, the result, because of, since

11. the conclusion            _____      k.  here, there, in the northeast, above, on the left

Time _____ : _____
　　　min　sec

Score _____ %

Score = number correct × 10.

Check answers on p. 353.

## 7.4  SCANNING THROUGH CONTINUOUS PROSE

Here you will scan through previous pages in this book. Since you have already worked these chapters, you do not need to start with a preview. Remember to paraphrase or think of synonyms for the specifics in the question. If you cannot find an item after a reasonable search, go on to the next item.

*Note:* Questions 1 through 5 require you to scan within Chapter 1.

1. Practice 1.2: How many of the five paragraphs are about music? _____
2. Practice 1.5: How many of the five paragraphs concern political issues? _____

3. Practice 1.8: Locate the paragraph that considers Greek roots. Which Greek root refers to love in a giving, generous sense? _____
4. Practice 1.9: Which paragraph supports the statement that women are more nervous than men? _____
5. Practice 1.9: Two reasons are given for why women live longer than men. What are these two reasons? _____  _____
6. Chapter 3, Selection 2: Locate the paragraph number in which the title of a play is mentioned. _____
7. Chapter 3, Selection 6: How many paragraphs are devoted to poor reasons for getting married? _____ How many to good reasons? _____
8. Chapter 3, Selection 10: What is the name of Gary Bauer's research group? _____

9. Chapter 4, Selection 10: What were the three advantages Jeff and Jo Sprawls had when they started their Pak Mail store? (*Hint:* look for a synonym for *advantages* in a subhead.)
    a. _____
    b. _____
    c. _____
10. Same selection: What are the two ways that student workers tend to cast the Sprawls in parental roles? (*Hint:* Look for a synonym for *parent* in a subhead.)
    a. _____
    b. _____

Time \_\_\_\_\_ : \_\_\_\_\_
      min   sec

Score \_\_\_\_\_ %

Score = number correct × 10.

Check answers with your instructor.

. . . . . . . . . . . . . . . . . . . . . . .

# COMPLEX SCANNING

The following six exercises will challenge your complex-scanning abilities. These questions send you back to selections in Chapters 5 and 6. You will scan for things like organizational patterns, general and specific information, word choices, and style.

### 7.5   SCANNING BIOLOGY TEXTS

Find Selection 2 in Chapter 5. If you have read it previously, skim it now to refresh your memory. If the selection is new to you, study-read it before you do the following:

1. Scan through the subsection "Deforestation" for the phrase that shifting cultivation was once called. _____
2. Scan for the name of the ship that was involved in the disaster off the coast of Alaska. _____
3. In the subsection "Fossil Fuels," find the number of the paragraph describing the dangers of strip mining. _____
4. Scan through the subsection "Nuclear Reactors" to find the answer to this question: What facility produces more radioactivity and carbon dioxide than a nuclear reactor? _____
5. Scan the subsection "Nuclear Waste Disposal" to identify the material that must be isolated for 250,000 years. _____

Time \_\_\_\_\_ : \_\_\_\_\_
      min   sec

Score \_\_\_\_\_ %

Score = number correct × 20.

Check answers on p. 353.

### 7.6   SCANNING PHILOSOPHY TEXTS

Find Selection 4 in Chapter 5. Skim it to review, if you have already read it. Otherwise, study-read it before you do the following:

1. Find the subsection "Natural Law Morality and Judeo-Christian Morality." Write out the phrase that describes how Thomas Aquinas interpreted Aristotle. _____

2. In this same subsection, scan for the word *stewardship*. How do the authors define it? _____

_____

3. In paragraph 10, scan quickly through to determine its organizational pattern. _____

4. In paragraph 15, scan quickly for the three humans that Tooley claims do not possess "self-consciousness."

   a. _____
   b. _____
   c. _____

5. In the subsection "Rights and Duties," scan for the three organisms or objects that cannot perform duties.

   a. _____
   b. _____
   c. _____

Time _____:_____

min    sec

Score _____%

Score = number correct × 20.

Check answers with your instructor.

## 7.7   SCANNING COMMENTARY (OPINION)

Find Selection 1 in Chapter 6. Skim it if you have already read it, or read it critically before you answer the following:

1. What conclusion did the Louis Harris poll arrive at? _____

_____

2. What synonym does Rodriguez give for his term *super-predators*? (*Hint:* You can find this synonym in the same paragraph in which he mentions super-predators.) _____

3. What question does Rodriguez ask concerning rap music? _____

_____

4. Scan paragraphs 27–31. Which institution tells children they still have worth? _____

5. Scan paragraphs 20–31. Who are the three political and historical figures Rodriguez mentions?

   a. _____
   b. _____
   c. _____

Time _____:_____

min    sec

Score _____%

Score = number correct × 20.

Check answers on p. 353.

## 7.8 SCANNING CRIMINOLOGY TEXTS

Find Selection 2 in Chapter 6. Skim it for review if you have already read it. If you have not, read it critically before you do the following:

1. Scan paragraphs 1–5 to determine how many years crime has been on the decline. _____

2. Scan paragraphs 3–6. What apparently was Jacob Riis's profession? _____

3. Scan paragraph 12. What verb does Monkkonen use to describe how young people feel about crack addicts? _____

4. Scan paragraph 14. Monkkonen refers to "these two ideas." What are they?
   a. _____
   b. _____

5. In paragraph 16, find the adjective Monkkonen uses to describe the level of development of the discipline of criminology. _____

Time _____:_____

min     sec

Score _____%

Score = number correct × 20.

Check answers with your instructor.

## 7.9 SCANNING NONFICTIONAL NARRATIVES

Find Selection 3 in Chapter 6. If you have read it critically, skim it for review. If you have not, read it critically before scanning for the answers to the following questions:

1. What is the name of the "straight and proper girl" Luis knew in junior high? _____

2. What instrument was used to give Luis a tattoo? _____

3. Which of Luis's junior-high teachers looked as if "he were carved out of a thick piece of gray granite"? _____

4. What sentence does Luis's father use to describe his response to his son's difficulties at school? _____

5. In the section on Luis's mother, what is the one prohibition she imposes on the house? _____

Time _____:_____

min     sec

Score _____%

Score = number correct × 20.

Check answers on p. 353.

## 7.10    SCANNING SOCIOLOGY TEXTS

Find Selection 4 in Chapter 6. If you have already read it, overview skim it for review. If you have not, read it critically before you do the following:

1.  Scan through the first three paragraphs. Which one introduces the thesis of this selection? Paragraph number: _____
2.  Scan the subsection "Immigration." List the two major turning points in the development of the Mexican gang in Southern California.
    a. _____
    b. _____
3.  Scan the subsection "Acculturational and Generational Change." Define *erring acculturation.* _____
4.  Scan paragraph 18. What categories are "subcultural strata" divided into?
    _____
5.  Scan the subsection "The Syncretization of a Street Culture." What "major factor" makes the Mexican-American gang "a more formalized unit"?
    _____

Time _____:_____

      min   sec

Score _____%

Score = number correct × 20.

Check answers with your instructor.

# Follow-Up

Now that you have completed these ten scanning practices, you may want to consider how your scanning abilities have improved. Individually, in small groups, or in large groups, you may want to consider the following questions.

1.  Which scanning activity do you find easiest?
2.  Which scanning activity do you still find difficult?
3.  Do you now see scanning as quite different from the other reading skills you have learned in this textbook? If not, which reading skills do you think are similar to scanning?
4.  Which of your current courses best lends itself to the scanning practices you have learned? How could you apply your scanning abilities to this course?

# Internet Activity

Use the Internet to find out more information about scanning. Break up into groups of four or five. To answer the following questions, go to the online

Writing Center at Marist College and find the section concerning study-skills habits. Then return to your group with your information.

1.  What new information on scanning did you find?
2.  How does this information differ from what you learned about scanning in this chapter?
3.  Describe how you located this information.

# *Common Reading Terms*

*CLOSURE:* making complete meaning from incomplete stimuli. For example, in simple materials, we can comprehend close to 100 percent of the meaning of a page even if our eyes perceive only 80 percent of the print.

*COMPREHENSION:* understanding the meaning of a word, phrase, sentence, or passage. Many factors, possibly dozens or more, combine to make it possible for us to grasp the meaning of written language—that is, to "read."

*EXPOSITION:* writing that expounds—that is, explains, sets forth, or interprets an idea or other subject. Expository writing uses all the common writing patterns.

*EYE SPAN:* the distance, around a point of fixation, in which the eyes can recognize letters and words. For most readers, maximum eye span is a radius of two inches of print left, right, above, and below the point of fixation. This is about 29 letter spaces, 17 of which can be seen clearly.

*FIXATION:* concentrated, clear focus by the eyes on one spot. Fixation is possible only when the eyes are not moving.

*FIXATION POINT:* the point along a line of print where the eyes pause to focus sharply. Perception grows blurry away from the fixation point.

*MAPPING:* putting written material into a visual format. Mapping often helps us remember how main ideas and minor details are related.

*OVERVIEW SKIM (OVERVIEW):* to read only the key parts of written material to understand its main ideas, skipping over most details. "Reading" rates of over 800 wpm are actually skimming rates, since the eyes cannot see all the print at those rates. This term can also be used as a noun.

*PARAPHRASE:*   to restate the meaning of a passage in different wording to make it clearer while being true to the intent of the original. A paraphrase will include main points and most details. It may be as long as the original or longer. Ideally, none of the exact wording of the original will be retained (quoted).

*PERCEPTION:*   an eye/brain activity in which the eyes see and recognize—and the brain comprehends—symbols such as familiar letters and words. Fast recognition of words and patterns is of course useful in better reading, and the speed and accuracy of perception can be increased through practice. But true comprehension of the meaning of a passage is a complex process that takes place in the brain, not in the eyes or through perception alone.

*PERIPHERAL VISION:*   the ability of the eyes to see around a fixation point. Good peripheral vision aids in faster reading.

*PREVIEW (PREVIEW SKIM):*   to pass through written material quickly to prepare for complete comprehension, critical reading, or overview skimming. A preview focuses on major features—length, graphics, style, subheads, beginnings, and endings. "Preview It First" is a useful habit for all assigned reading. In study reading, the preview is carefully directed and is often called a *survey*.

*RATE:*   the speed at which we read, usually expressed in words per minute (wpm). Rate means little by itself, without some measure of our comprehension. Also, our eyes cannot perceive all the words on a printed page at rates higher than 800 to 900 wpm. At these high rates, we are skimming, or reading selectively.

*RECITE:*   to reproduce, without referring to the material and preferably in our own words, the meaning of a passage we have read. Reciting is a way of self-testing to see if we have really comprehended the material.

*REGRESSION:*   eye movement backward to a previous section of print. It is like a fixation in reverse. Regressions often are necessary for full comprehension of difficult material, but they are merely a poor reading habit in lighter material, slowing the reader down unnecessarily and garbling the writer's message.

*RETURN SWEEP:*   the movement of the eyes from the end of a line back to the beginning of the next line. Skipping or repeating a line is common in beginning readers.

*SCAN:*   to process print at a high speed, looking for answers to specific questions. Only passages relevant to the question are actually read. Scanning searches range from simple—"Who wrote this book?"—to complex—"Is this writer presenting all or only some of the evidence?"

*SKIM:*   to read selectively, slowing for main ideas and speeding up for or skipping many of the details. This variable rate yields an overall rate of 700 to 800 wpm and up. The skimmer does not start out with a specific question, as in scanning, but aims for the overall structure and content. See *PREVIEW SKIM* and *OVERVIEW SKIM* for two common types of skimming.

*SUBVOCALIZE:* to hear "the words," or "inner speech," when one is reading silently. This is common, even among fast readers with good comprehension. It especially occurs when one reads slowly, writes a composition, tries to comprehend difficult material, or reads literature (for example, poetry). During subvocalization, the throat muscles are tensed as if for speech, but at very rapid reading or skimming rates, the subvocalizing tends to drop out. Reading can then take place between eyes and brain only—one "reads the ideas" on the page rather than the individual, sounded words. *Subvocalizing* literally means forming the words "under" an audible level.

*SUMMARIZE:* to present the content of written material in a more concise form than the original. A summary includes main points, conclusions, and possibly some major details. Little (if any) of the original's exact wording will be retained (quoted).

*VOCALIZE:* literally, to give "voice" or sound to the words while one is supposedly reading silently. It can range from an inaudible moving of the lips, to whispering the words or mumbling. See *SUBVOCALIZE.*

# *Rate Table*

## How to Figure Your Rate (Words per Minute) Using the Rate Table

For timed readings, record your time to the nearest 15 seconds: 0:30, 2:45, and so forth. (For 8 minutes or more, record it to the nearest 30 seconds.) Some wpm rates for timed selections are given with the selection, in the text. If your rate is not given, you can find it quickly by using the table on the next four pages.

The table is easy to use:

1.  *Find the length* (NO. OF WORDS) *of your selection in the left-hand column of the table.* The length is printed in the text just after the title. Lengths range from about 800 to 4,000 words.
2.  *Find your reading time at the top of the table.* Run a finger down that column until you come to the line that *intersects* with the NO. OF WORDS line. This figure will be your rate—words per minute. For example, if you read a 3,000-word article in 4 minutes, your rate was 750 wpm.
3.  *Record this rate on your Progress Chart:* Rapid Reading, page 117; Overview Skimming, page 192; or Critical Reading, page 324.

# RATE TABLE FOR FIGURING WORDS PER MINUTE (WPM)

| NO. OF WORDS | TIME (min:sec) | | | | | | | | | |
|---|---|---|---|---|---|---|---|---|---|---|
| | 0:30 | 0:45 | 1:00 | 1:15 | 1:30 | 1:45 | 2:00 | 2:15 | 2:30 | 2:45 |
| 4000 | 8000 | 5333 | 4000 | 3200 | 2667 | 2286 | 2000 | 1778 | 1600 | 1455 |
| 3500 | 7000 | 4667 | 3500 | 2800 | 2333 | 2000 | 1750 | 1556 | 1400 | 1273 |
| 3400 | 6800 | 4533 | 3400 | 2720 | 2267 | 1943 | 1700 | 1511 | 1360 | 1236 |
| 3300 | 6600 | 4400 | 3300 | 2640 | 2200 | 1886 | 1650 | 1467 | 1320 | 1200 |
| 3200 | 6400 | 4267 | 3200 | 2560 | 2133 | 1829 | 1600 | 1422 | 1280 | 1164 |
| 3100 | 6200 | 4133 | 3100 | 2480 | 2067 | 1771 | 1550 | 1378 | 1240 | 1127 |
| 3000 | 6000 | 4000 | 3000 | 2400 | 2000 | 1714 | 1500 | 1333 | 1200 | 1091 |
| 2900 | 5800 | 3867 | 2900 | 2320 | 1933 | 1657 | 1450 | 1289 | 1160 | 1055 |
| 2800 | 5600 | 3733 | 2800 | 2240 | 1867 | 1600 | 1400 | 1244 | 1120 | 1018 |
| 2700 | 5400 | 3600 | 2700 | 2160 | 1800 | 1543 | 1350 | 1200 | 1080 | 982 |
| 2600 | 5200 | 3467 | 2600 | 2080 | 1733 | 1486 | 1300 | 1156 | 1040 | 945 |
| 2500 | 5000 | 3333 | 2500 | 2000 | 1667 | 1429 | 1250 | 1111 | 1000 | 909 |
| 2400 | 4800 | 3200 | 2400 | 1920 | 1600 | 1371 | 1200 | 1067 | 960 | 873 |
| 2300 | 4600 | 3067 | 2300 | 1840 | 1533 | 1314 | 1150 | 1022 | 920 | 836 |
| 2200 | 4400 | 2933 | 2200 | 1760 | 1467 | 1257 | 1100 | 978 | 880 | 800 |
| 2100 | 4200 | 2800 | 2100 | 1680 | 1400 | 1200 | 1050 | 933 | 840 | 764 |
| 2000 | 4000 | 2667 | 2000 | 1600 | 1333 | 1143 | 1000 | 889 | 800 | 727 |
| 1900 | 3800 | 2533 | 1900 | 1520 | 1267 | 1086 | 950 | 844 | 760 | 691 |
| 1800 | 3600 | 2400 | 1800 | 1440 | 1200 | 1029 | 900 | 800 | 720 | 655 |
| 1700 | 3400 | 2267 | 1700 | 1360 | 1133 | 971 | 850 | 756 | 680 | 618 |
| 1600 | 3200 | 2133 | 1600 | 1280 | 1067 | 914 | 800 | 711 | 640 | 582 |
| 1500 | 3000 | 2000 | 1500 | 1200 | 1000 | 857 | 750 | 667 | 600 | 545 |
| 1400 | 2800 | 1867 | 1400 | 1120 | 933 | 800 | 700 | 622 | 560 | 509 |
| 1300 | 2600 | 1733 | 1300 | 1040 | 867 | 743 | 650 | 578 | 520 | 473 |
| 1200 | 2400 | 1600 | 1200 | 960 | 800 | 686 | 600 | 533 | 480 | 436 |
| 1100 | 2200 | 1467 | 1100 | 880 | 733 | 629 | 550 | 489 | 440 | 400 |
| 1000 | 2000 | 1333 | 1000 | 800 | 667 | 571 | 500 | 444 | 400 | 364 |
| 900 | 1800 | 1200 | 900 | 720 | 600 | 514 | 450 | 400 | 360 | 327 |
| 800 | 1600 | 1067 | 800 | 640 | 533 | 457 | 400 | 356 | 320 | 291 |

| NO. OF WORDS | TIME (min:sec) | | | | | | | | | |
|---|---|---|---|---|---|---|---|---|---|---|
| | 3:00 | 3:15 | 3:30 | 3:45 | 4:00 | 4:15 | 4:30 | 4:45 | 5:00 | 5:15 |
| 4000 | 1333 | 1231 | 1143 | 1067 | 1000 | 941 | 889 | 842 | 800 | 762 |
| 3500 | 1167 | 1077 | 1000 | 933 | 875 | 824 | 778 | 737 | 700 | 667 |
| 3400 | 1133 | 1046 | 971 | 907 | 850 | 800 | 756 | 716 | 680 | 648 |
| 3300 | 1100 | 1015 | 943 | 880 | 825 | 776 | 733 | 695 | 660 | 629 |
| 3200 | 1067 | 985 | 914 | 853 | 800 | 753 | 711 | 674 | 640 | 610 |
| 3100 | 1033 | 954 | 886 | 827 | 775 | 729 | 689 | 653 | 620 | 590 |
| 3000 | 1000 | 923 | 857 | 800 | 750 | 706 | 667 | 632 | 600 | 571 |
| 2900 | 967 | 892 | 829 | 773 | 725 | 682 | 644 | 611 | 580 | 552 |
| 2800 | 933 | 862 | 800 | 747 | 700 | 659 | 622 | 589 | 560 | 533 |
| 2700 | 900 | 831 | 771 | 720 | 675 | 635 | 600 | 568 | 540 | 514 |
| 2600 | 867 | 800 | 743 | 693 | 650 | 612 | 578 | 547 | 520 | 495 |
| 2500 | 833 | 769 | 714 | 667 | 625 | 588 | 556 | 526 | 500 | 476 |
| 2400 | 800 | 738 | 686 | 640 | 600 | 565 | 533 | 505 | 480 | 457 |
| 2300 | 767 | 708 | 657 | 613 | 575 | 541 | 511 | 484 | 460 | 438 |
| 2200 | 733 | 677 | 629 | 587 | 550 | 518 | 489 | 463 | 440 | 419 |
| 2100 | 700 | 646 | 600 | 560 | 525 | 494 | 467 | 442 | 420 | 400 |
| 2000 | 667 | 615 | 571 | 533 | 500 | 471 | 444 | 421 | 400 | 381 |
| 1900 | 633 | 585 | 543 | 507 | 475 | 447 | 422 | 400 | 380 | 362 |
| 1800 | 600 | 554 | 514 | 480 | 450 | 424 | 400 | 379 | 360 | 343 |
| 1700 | 567 | 523 | 486 | 453 | 425 | 400 | 378 | 358 | 340 | 324 |
| 1600 | 533 | 492 | 457 | 427 | 400 | 376 | 356 | 337 | 320 | 305 |
| 1500 | 500 | 462 | 429 | 400 | 375 | 353 | 333 | 316 | 300 | 286 |
| 1400 | 467 | 431 | 400 | 373 | 350 | 329 | 311 | 295 | 280 | 267 |
| 1300 | 433 | 400 | 371 | 347 | 325 | 306 | 289 | 274 | 260 | 248 |
| 1200 | 400 | 369 | 343 | 320 | 300 | 282 | 267 | 253 | 240 | 229 |
| 1100 | 367 | 338 | 314 | 293 | 275 | 259 | 244 | 232 | 220 | 210 |
| 1000 | 333 | 308 | 286 | 267 | 250 | 235 | 222 | 211 | 200 | 190 |
| 900 | 300 | 277 | 257 | 240 | 225 | 212 | 200 | 189 | 180 | 171 |
| 800 | 267 | 246 | 229 | 213 | 200 | 188 | 178 | 168 | 160 | 152 |

| NO. OF WORDS | TIME (min:sec) | | | | | | | | | |
|---|---|---|---|---|---|---|---|---|---|---|
| | 5:30 | 5:45 | 6:00 | 6:15 | 6:30 | 6:45 | 7:00 | 7:15 | 7:30 | 7:45 |
| 4000 | 727 | 696 | 667 | 640 | 615 | 593 | 571 | 552 | 533 | 516 |
| 3500 | 636 | 609 | 583 | 560 | 538 | 519 | 500 | 483 | 467 | 452 |
| 3400 | 618 | 591 | 567 | 544 | 523 | 504 | 486 | 469 | 453 | 439 |
| 3300 | 600 | 574 | 550 | 528 | 508 | 489 | 471 | 455 | 440 | 426 |
| 3200 | 582 | 557 | 533 | 512 | 492 | 474 | 457 | 441 | 427 | 413 |
| 3100 | 564 | 539 | 517 | 496 | 477 | 459 | 443 | 428 | 413 | 400 |
| 3000 | 545 | 522 | 500 | 480 | 462 | 444 | 429 | 414 | 400 | 387 |
| 2900 | 527 | 504 | 483 | 464 | 446 | 430 | 414 | 400 | 387 | 374 |
| 2800 | 509 | 487 | 467 | 448 | 431 | 415 | 400 | 386 | 373 | 361 |
| 2700 | 491 | 470 | 450 | 432 | 415 | 400 | 386 | 372 | 360 | 348 |
| 2600 | 473 | 452 | 433 | 416 | 400 | 385 | 371 | 359 | 347 | 335 |
| 2500 | 455 | 435 | 417 | 400 | 385 | 370 | 357 | 345 | 333 | 323 |
| 2400 | 436 | 417 | 400 | 384 | 369 | 356 | 343 | 331 | 320 | 310 |
| 2300 | 418 | 400 | 383 | 368 | 354 | 341 | 329 | 317 | 307 | 297 |
| 2200 | 400 | 383 | 367 | 352 | 338 | 326 | 314 | 303 | 293 | 284 |
| 2100 | 382 | 365 | 350 | 336 | 323 | 311 | 300 | 290 | 280 | 271 |
| 2000 | 364 | 348 | 333 | 320 | 308 | 296 | 286 | 276 | 267 | 258 |
| 1900 | 345 | 330 | 317 | 304 | 292 | 281 | 271 | 262 | 253 | 245 |
| 1800 | 327 | 313 | 300 | 288 | 277 | 267 | 257 | 248 | 240 | 232 |
| 1700 | 309 | 296 | 283 | 272 | 262 | 252 | 243 | 234 | 227 | 219 |
| 1600 | 291 | 278 | 267 | 256 | 246 | 237 | 229 | 221 | 213 | 206 |
| 1500 | 273 | 261 | 250 | 240 | 231 | 222 | 214 | 207 | 200 | 194 |
| 1400 | 255 | 243 | 233 | 224 | 215 | 207 | 200 | 193 | 187 | 181 |
| 1300 | 236 | 226 | 217 | 208 | 200 | 193 | 186 | 179 | 173 | 168 |
| 1200 | 218 | 209 | 200 | 192 | 185 | 178 | 171 | 166 | 160 | 155 |
| 1100 | 200 | 191 | 183 | 176 | 169 | 163 | 157 | 152 | 147 | 142 |
| 1000 | 182 | 174 | 167 | 160 | 154 | 148 | 143 | 138 | 133 | 129 |
| 900 | 164 | 157 | 150 | 144 | 138 | 133 | 129 | 124 | 120 | 116 |
| 800 | 145 | 139 | 133 | 128 | 123 | 119 | 114 | 110 | 107 | 103 |

| NO. OF WORDS | TIME (min:sec) | | | | | | | | | |
|---|---|---|---|---|---|---|---|---|---|---|
| | 8:00 | 8:30 | 9:00 | 9:30 | 10:00 | 10:30 | 11:00 | 11:30 | 12:00 | 12:30 |
| 4000 | 500 | 471 | 444 | 421 | 400 | 381 | 364 | 348 | 333 | 320 |
| 3500 | 438 | 412 | 389 | 368 | 350 | 333 | 318 | 304 | 292 | 280 |
| 3400 | 425 | 400 | 378 | 358 | 340 | 324 | 309 | 296 | 283 | 272 |
| 3300 | 413 | 388 | 367 | 347 | 330 | 314 | 300 | 287 | 275 | 264 |
| 3200 | 400 | 376 | 356 | 337 | 320 | 305 | 291 | 278 | 267 | 256 |
| 3100 | 388 | 365 | 344 | 326 | 310 | 295 | 282 | 270 | 258 | 248 |
| 3000 | 375 | 353 | 333 | 316 | 300 | 286 | 273 | 261 | 250 | 240 |
| 2900 | 363 | 341 | 322 | 305 | 290 | 276 | 264 | 252 | 242 | 232 |
| 2800 | 350 | 329 | 311 | 295 | 280 | 267 | 255 | 243 | 233 | 224 |
| 2700 | 338 | 318 | 300 | 284 | 270 | 257 | 245 | 235 | 225 | 216 |
| 2600 | 325 | 306 | 289 | 274 | 260 | 248 | 236 | 226 | 217 | 208 |
| 2500 | 313 | 294 | 278 | 263 | 250 | 238 | 227 | 217 | 208 | 200 |
| 2400 | 300 | 282 | 267 | 253 | 240 | 229 | 218 | 209 | 200 | 192 |
| 2300 | 288 | 271 | 256 | 242 | 230 | 219 | 209 | 200 | 192 | 184 |
| 2200 | 275 | 259 | 244 | 232 | 220 | 210 | 200 | 191 | 183 | 176 |
| 2100 | 263 | 247 | 233 | 221 | 210 | 200 | 191 | 183 | 175 | 168 |
| 2000 | 250 | 235 | 222 | 211 | 200 | 190 | 182 | 174 | 167 | 160 |
| 1900 | 238 | 224 | 211 | 200 | 190 | 181 | 173 | 165 | 158 | 152 |
| 1800 | 225 | 212 | 200 | 189 | 180 | 171 | 164 | 157 | 150 | 144 |
| 1700 | 213 | 200 | 189 | 179 | 170 | 162 | 155 | 148 | 142 | 136 |
| 1600 | 200 | 188 | 178 | 168 | 160 | 152 | 145 | 139 | 133 | 128 |
| 1500 | 188 | 176 | 167 | 158 | 150 | 143 | 136 | 130 | 125 | 120 |
| 1400 | 175 | 165 | 156 | 147 | 140 | 133 | 127 | 122 | 117 | 112 |
| 1300 | 163 | 153 | 144 | 137 | 130 | 124 | 118 | 113 | 108 | 104 |
| 1200 | 150 | 141 | 133 | 126 | 120 | 114 | 109 | 104 | 100 | 96 |
| 1100 | 138 | 129 | 122 | 116 | 110 | 105 | 100 | 96 | 92 | 88 |
| 1000 | 125 | 118 | 111 | 105 | 100 | 95 | 91 | 87 | 83 | 80 |
| 900 | 113 | 106 | 100 | 95 | 90 | 86 | 82 | 78 | 75 | 72 |
| 800 | 100 | 94 | 89 | 84 | 80 | 76 | 73 | 70 | 67 | 64 |

# Answer Key

Answers are given here only for odd-numbered practices in Chapters 1 and 7 and odd-numbered selections in Chapters 3, 4, 5, and 6. Your instructor can provide answers for the even-numbered practices in Chapters 1 and 7; for the even-numbered selections in Chapters 3, 4, 5, and 6; and for all "For Discussion and Writing" questions.

Some leeway is allowed in certain types of questions: for example, those calling for restating (paraphrasing), summarizing, and secondary writing patterns. If your answer differs significantly from the key in such cases, discuss the possibilities with other students and your instructor.

# CHAPTER 1, ESSENTIAL READING SKILLS: ODD-NUMBERED PRACTICES

## Practice 1.1

1. T
2. T
3. MI
4. MI
5. T
6. MI
7. T
8. MI
9. MI
10. T

## Practice 1.3

(You may want to argue for other main-idea sentences than those listed below.)
1. 1
2. 1
3. 2
4. 4
5. 2

## Practice 1.5

1. Supporting Detail Sentences: 2, 3, 4, 5
   Transitions: 2—for example
2. Supporting Detail Sentences: 2, 3, 4, 5
   Transitions: 3—first, 4—then, 5—ultimately
3. Supporting Detail Sentences: 2, 3, 4, 5, 6
   Transitions: 2—for one, 4—secondly,
   6—finally

4. Supporting Detail Sentences: 2, 3, 4, 5, 6, 7, 8
   Transitions: 2—for example, 5—another
   example, 7—third
5. Supporting Detail Sentences: 2, 3, 4, 5, 6, 7
   Transitions: 4—and, 5—in contrast, 7—and

## Practice 1.7

(You may want to argue for other organizational patterns.)
1. chronological
2. compare-contrast
3. description
4. example
5. definition

## Practice 1.9

Answers may vary, but responses should be essentially the same as those given.

Topic of entire passage: reasons why women live longer

Main idea: Women's longer life expectancy results from genetic, behavioral, and psychological reasons.

Dominant pattern: reasons why

Summary: Researchers keep looking for reasons why women live longer than men. They think it may be because of different lifestyles, genes, and hormones.

# CHAPTER 3, RAPID READING: ODD-NUMBERED SELECTIONS

## Selection 1

### A. Preview Skimming
1. a
2. b
3. a

### B. Rapid Reading
1. c
2. b
3. b
4. c

## Selection 3

### A. Preview Skimming
1. c
2. a
3. b

### B. Rapid Reading
1. a
2. c
3. e
4. b

## Selection 5

### A. Preview Skimming
1. a
2. b
3. a

### B. Rapid Reading
1. b
2. d
3. c
4. a

## Selection 7

**A. Preview Skimming**
1. b
2. b, d
3. a

**B. Rapid Reading**
1. a
2. a
3. a
4. b
5. b

## Selection 9

**A. Preview Skimming**
1. b
2. c
3. b

**B. Rapid Reading**
1. b
2. a
3. b
4. b
5. a

# CHAPTER 4, OVERVIEW SKIMMING: ODD-NUMBERED SELECTIONS

## Selection 1

**A. Preview Skimming**
1. b
2. a
3. c

**B. Overview Skimming**
1. a
2. a
3. a
4. b

## Selection 3

**A. Preview Skimming**
1. b
2. a
3. 1993

**B. Overview Skimming**
1. b
2. a
3. a
4. b

## Selection 5

**A. Preview Skimming**
1. b
2. a
3. c

**B. Overview Skimming**
1. c
2. b
3. b
4. d

## Selection 7

**A. Preview Skimming**
1. b
2. c
3. b

**B. Overview Skimming**
1. b
2. c
3. a
4. b

## Selection 9

**A. Preview Skimming**
1. a
2. a
3. c

**B. Overview Skimming**
1. a
2. d
3. a
4. e

# CHAPTER 5, STUDY READING: ODD-NUMBERED SELECTIONS

## Selection 1

### A.  Survey
1. d
2. a
3. a
4. d
5. b

### B.  Question
(Questions will vary.)
1. What is ecology?
2. What is biodiversity?
3. Why is biodiversity so important?
4. What are the living members of an ecosystem?
5. What are the nonliving members of an ecosystem?

### F.  Study-Reading Questions
1. b
2. d
3. d
4. a
5. d
6. c
7. b
8. b
9. b
10. b

## Selection 3

### A.  Survey
1. c
2. c
3. c
4. d
5. d

### B.  Question
(Questions will vary.)
1. What are hazardous wastes?
2. What is recycling?
3. How have companies attempted to conserve energy?
4. What is consumerism?
5. What areas related to consumer rights does consumer protection deal with?

### F.  Study-Reading Questions
1. a
2. b
3. c
4. a
5. a
6. b
7. d
8. a
9. b
10. d

# CHAPTER 6, CRITICAL READING: ODD-NUMBERED SELECTIONS

## Selection 1

### A.  Preview Skimming
1. b
2. c
3. a
4. d
5. d

### B.  Critical Reading
1. b
2. b
3. d
4. c
5. d
6. c
7. a
8. c
9. b
10. c

## Selection 3

### A.  Preview Skimming
1. b
2. c
3. a
4. d
5. b

### B.  Critical Reading
1. c
2. b
3. d
4. c
5. d
6. c
7. a
8. c
9. b
10. c

# CHAPTER 7, SCANNING: ODD-NUMBERED PRACTICES

## Practice 7.1

1. 2000
2. 7
3. University of Chicago
4. Chapter 2
5. 6
6. "Time Yourself Rigorously"
7. Selection 9, Chapter 4
8. Selection 2, Chapter 3
9. Selection 10, Chapter 4
10. "backward"

## Practice 7.3

2. i
3. d
4. h
5. c
6. f
7. b
8. e
9. a
10. j
11. g

## Practice 7.5

1. slash-and-burn
2. *Valdez*
3. 16
4. coal-burning plants
5. plutonium isotope ($239^{Pu}$)

## Practice 7.7

1. "teenagers live daily aware of danger"
2. super-alones
3. "Why is it that most of the people who buy black rap are white kids in the suburbs?"
4. religious
5. Hillary Rodham Clinton, Newt Gingrich, Martin Luther King, Jr.

## Practice 7.9

1. Socorro
2. sewing needles
3. Mr. Stone
4. "You can't be in a fire and not get burned."
5. no alcohol

# INDEX

· · · · · · · · · · · · · · · · ·
*NOTES*

• • • • • • • • • • • • • • • • • •

*NOTES*

. . . . . . . . . . . . . . . . . .
*NOTES*

## NOTES

*NOTES*

. . . . . . . . . . . . . . . . . .

*NOTES*

*NOTES*